THE POLITICAL CONSEQUENCES
OF THE REFORMATION

THE
POLITICAL CONSEQUENCES
OF THE REFORMATION

*STUDIES IN SIXTEENTH-
CENTURY POLITICAL THOUGHT*

By the Rev. R. H. MURRAY, M.A., Litt.D.
Author of "Erasmus and Luther: Their Attitude to Toleration"

New York
RUSSELL & RUSSELL
1960

Published, 1960, by Russell & Russell, Inc.,
by arrangement with Ernest Benn, Ltd., London
Library of Congress Catalog Card No: 60–6040

PRINTED IN THE UNITED STATES OF AMERICA

PREFACE

FOR over twenty years I have been reading the authors whose writings are analysed in this book. I approached them in the first instance without much criticism and with a receptive mind in order to allow their way of thinking to permeate my intellect until they became part of the mental furniture of my mode of thought. Naturally I recognised that till I had done so my criticism would not be adequate. It would of course be wanting in sympathy, and it would rather tend to defend me against their spirit than enable me to appreciate it. In the passing of the years I have submitted to such seminal thinkers as those dealt with in this book, and have learned to live in the atmosphere of their ideas to such an extent that I could almost anticipate the turn of their thoughts on a given subject. Then I changed my method, and stood, as it were, at a considerable distance from my authors in order to be able to attempt calmly to estimate what their influence on the Reformation really had been. To be in contact with great men and their writings has been the keenest of pleasures, and it will be a matter of satisfaction to me if I can in any wise convey to the reader some of my own joy.

The following publishers generously allowed me to use extracts from books published by them, and I desire to thank them most cordially : Macmillan & Co. (*Anglican Essays*) and the S.P.C.K. (the Rev. R. H. Murray, *Erasmus and Luther : Their Attitude to Toleration*).

Mr Laski read my manuscript with the care and attention that men seldom bestow upon their own labour. My wife gave me the benefit of her searching criticism. I thank both of them most warmly for their criticism no less than for their counsel.

ROBERT H. MURRAY.

BROUGHTON RECTORY,
    HUNTINGDON.
        December 1925.

INTRODUCTION

THE BACKGROUND OF THE REFORMATION

SHAKESPEARE takes occasion to remind us that England used to be "that utmost corner of the West." Before the Columbian discovery she was at the end of the world, and was regarded as almost out of the world. So her position appeared to the Greek geographers and to the mediæval monks: the maps of the one and the charts of the other attest this. She had been the outpost of European civilisation, and now she became the very heart of it. Her Western situation had been a barrier to her progress, and this barrier was at a stroke transformed into the surest and quickest road to progress. Her limited island area, her tremendous change from pasturage to tillage during the sixteenth century, and her unexploited resources of mineral wealth obliged her to turn to the sea. Conditions at home synchronised with the altered conditions abroad, and her maritime development commenced.

What the Mediterranean had been in the past the Atlantic was to be in the future. The Papacy had been a Mediterranean Power. The Crusades had been Mediterranean wars. Athens, Rome, Constantinople, Venice and Genoa had been notable centres in the Middle Sea. The shores of Western Spain, Portugal, England and Germany were not lapped by its blue waves. The estuaries of the Mersey, the Clyde and the Lagan resounded to the solitary cry of the bittern and the ripple of the stray fishing-boat. Within a generation after 1492 the change from the shores of the Mediterranean to those of the Atlantic had begun, and the change forms one of the outstanding factors in the background of the Reformation.

Before the appearance of Sir Charles Lyell's *Principles of Geology*, in 1830, science contemplated changes as catastrophic. Earthquakes, volcanoes, eruptions and floods were the phenomena ordinarily shaping the world. For these Lyell substituted glacial action, the slow denudation by rivers, subsidence and elevation and the like. In the history of mankind the point of view in, say, Calvin's day is similar. The attention of the observer was arrested by such a dramatic scene as the Völker-wanderung, or the irruption of the Turks into Europe in 1453. As in geology, the mightiest forces are not the vast ones, but the steady, almost imperceptible action of small powers. Nature never makes a leap. Calvin could scarcely see that the horizontal divisions of the mediæval world were to be replaced by the vertical ones of the modern world. There was a contracted world for him. There is a world conterminous with nothing less than the boundaries of the globe for the generations after him.

The labours of Colet and Calvin were in no small degree aided by the geographical, astronomical and economic revolution which was in process in their time. The opening up of a new continent, the discovery of new planets and the export to Europe of the new silver created a ferment which left the minds of men ready to receive new impressions. The arrival of the silver raised prices in a fashion similar to our war prices, making labour dear, and thereby changing the tillage system to pasturage. In the agricultural world men are upset and not a few homeless, and as the cake of custom is irretrievably smashed they are not so unwilling to hear new doctrine as their fathers would have been. It may well be, as the late Dr J. Gairdner contended, that there were no general hungering and thirsting after truth in the shape of Reformation doctrine; but when are there ever such a hungering and thirsting? Still, there is no doubt that the cake of custom was hopelessly broken, and therefore men like Colet obtained a hearing which, under fifteenth-century circumstances, would have been denied them. The old world which men knew was disappearing, and with its disappearance the old paths were disused. The new world which men knew not was appearing, and with its appearance new paths were used.

The invention of printing gave a guarantee that the work of the men of the Renaissance would remain, that the new paths could be trodden now by all, and not, as in mediæval days, by the select few. True, these paths were still considered to require supervision. For the *Index Librorum Prohibitorum* in England was established in 1526, thus preceding the first *Index* on the Continent by twenty-five years, and that of Rome by thirty-three. Men like Dr Putnam assume that the censorship of books is primarily ecclesiastical—Papal, in fact—in origin. Such an assumption, however, is totally unwarranted. As a matter of fact, up to recent times the right of censorship of printed books was inherent in the State simply because the right to print was a prerogative of the monarch, be he king, viceroy, archbishop or pope. When Charles I. proclaimed that "the print is the king's in all countries" he proclaimed the precise truth.

The soil had been ploughed in many directions, and was ready for any seed that might fall. Some seed fell by the way-side, in the shape of the *Epistolæ Obscurorum Virorum*, that stern survey of the state of the clergy. How much satire undermined the prestige of Rome is plain to all who turn over the flying sheets of the time. These satirists realised the sagacity of this expedient. Their pamphlets circulated on all sides, creating and moulding public opinion. They assumed that the corruption of the clergy in general, and the friars in particular, was a matter known to all. The *Ship of Fools*, for instance, is in reality what Erasmus's *Praise of Folly* is only on the surface. It is a skit on the follies of mankind, whereas the work of Erasmus is, in fact, an exposure of the follies and frauds of those who professed to serve the Church. For this very reason it must be counted among the forces preparing for the Reformation.

The urgent need for true religion was so apparent that Erasmus wrote the *Enchiridion Militis Christiani*, 1503, proving that he realised as keenly as his friend Colet the purge of the Church from formalism. Rites, he argued, and ceremonies possess in themselves no value. Indeed he was careful to let Colet know that " I wrote [it] to display neither genius nor eloquence, but simply for this—to counteract the error which makes religion depend on ceremonies, and in more than Jewish observances, while strangely neglecting all that pertains to true piety. I tried to teach, moreover, the art of piety after the manner of those who have composed the rules of [military] discipline."

INTRODUCTION

In 1511 appeared the *Encomium Moriæ* (*Praise of Folly*). At a time in which printing was yet in its infancy, the first edition appeared with no less than eighteen hundred copies —an enormous issue for those days—yet less than a month after the appearance of the book for sale there were no more than six hundred with the bookseller. It was printed more than seven times in the course of a few months. To the friars his satire was as the sword of Gideon, and to all his wit was as the spear of Ithuriel. Fortunate it was for Erasmus that Folly wore such a mask. The lash of Juvenal or Swift is forgotten in the mocking smile of Lucian or Voltaire.

Erasmus satirised follies of all kinds: the student for his sickly look, the grammarian for his self-satisfaction, the philosopher for his quibbling, the sportsman for his love of butchery, the superstitious for his belief in the virtues of images and shrines, the sailor for his folly in praying to the Virgin, and the sinner for his foolishness in believing in the efficacy of pardons and indulgences. The king no less than his subjects, the cardinal no less than his clergy, winced at the scourge of this merry-andrew.

The main object of Erasmus in writing the book which dissolved all Europe in laughter was the reform of religion. He was, however, wise enough to know that the more subjects he embraced in his popular writing the more chance there was of its being read. This is evident in the fierceness underlying his ideas. The credulity of the time moves him to indignation which is not quite in keeping with the light tone Folly deigned to assume. She might laugh at those who calculated with mathematical precision the number of years, months and hours of purgatory, and at those who fondly believed that they could wipe off a whole life of sin by a small coin. Folly, all unconscious of her high mission, was lowering the prestige of the orthodox, thereby preparing the way in no small degree for the reformer. Kings and nobles, cardinals and bishops read the *Praise of Folly* with a degree of delight which would have been much diminished had they grasped its inner significance.

One outcome of its perusal was that mediæval masterpieces were taken down from the shelves to which they were chained.

INTRODUCTION

Among these mediæval masterpieces were the writings of
John Wyclif. Professor A. F. Pollard emphasies the extraordinary parallelism between the ideas of this fourteenth-
century reformer and those of the Reformation about to be
ushered in. Wyclif exalted the royal power to a height which
would have satisfied fully Machiavelli and Bodin. Wyclif
called upon the State to reform the corrupt Church. He
repeatedly regards the Papacy in the form he knew it as the
most signal manifestation of the spirit of Antichrist—an
attitude assumed by Luther and Cranmer. Like the last, too,
Wyclif disliked that abuse of excommunication and its powers
which practically turned it into a sort of County Court notice.
He unsparingly criticised the whole principle of monasticism
which Henry VIII. was to sweep away. Wyclif no less unsparingly criticised the ideas which might lead to a social
revolution, showing himself at one with the underlying
conservatism of the sixteenth century. Though he seemed to
regard celibacy as the higher ideal for the clergy, Wyclif
pleaded for the permission of clerical marriages, and this is,
of course, the tone of the 1549 Act of Parliament. In accordance with the spirit of the sixteenth century, he also pleaded
for the place of the preacher, he deliberately used the vernacular, he resolutely appealed to the Bible, and he insisted on
popular support for his claims. Time after time he dwelt upon
the supreme importance of spiritual religion and the supreme
unimportance of mere ceremonies; and here we find him in
agreement with Luther and Calvin. Wyclif and Erasmus are
are of one mind on this point. Wyclif reduced the real presence
in Holy Communion to a spiritual presence.

A German traces the growth of his Church to Martin
Luther, a Swiss to John Calvin. Herein lies the strength and
the weakness of the Lutheran and the Calvinist. On the other
hand, the Anglican cannot trace the growth of his Church to
any one individual in the same sense that the Lutheran or the
Calvinist can. John Wyclif is a great man in the firmament of
Anglicanism—that is all. In him the spirit of Puritanism is as
incarnate as in John Knox. There is in Wyclif that narrowness
of sympathy we sometimes associate with the Puritan of the

past. We also note the same uncompromising rejection of mediævalism as a whole, the same pronounced individualism, the same preference for sweeping change, the same desire for a breach with the past as complete as possible, and the same dislike of tradition that remind us of Thomas Cartwright. We sorely miss in the morning star of the Reformation that width of sympathy which turned the Church of England into that broad-minded body which constituted one of her greatest glories. She could be the mother of children so different as Thomas Cartwright and Richard Hooker.

The Wyclif of the past and the Erasmus of the present stirred up the feeling that there was something wrong, perhaps fundamentally wrong, with the Church. There had been such a feeling in the fourteenth century, but it had come to nothing. Now there was such a vague feeling again. Now combined with this feeling in the sixteenth century there was added the fact that the universe seemed to be dissolving. Columbus and Copernicus upset or seemed to upset the teaching of the Church. The Church had been proved to be inaccurate where she could be tested. Perhaps she was also inaccurate where she could not be so readily tested. Why was the world so full of unrest? Why was it so difficult to win one's daily bread? Why were wages decreasing and prices increasing? Why were labourers deserting the land and flocking to the town? The situation was not unlike that of our own day. Something, men realised, was radically at fault, and there sprang up the idea that something must be done. The last cry has probably given rise to as many evils as cures. At the same time, when men utter this cry, there is, as a rule, something gravely at issue. People usually know when they are ill, though their diagnosis of their complaint leaves something to be desired. Was not Rome a centre of evil to the Church? Popes like Alexander VI. or Leo X. were much more the head of an Italian State than the head of the Church. Why should an Englishman, a Frenchman or a German be at the mercy of such foreigners, such mercenary foreigners?

Omnia Romæ venalia was as true in Henry VIII.'s time as it was in Jugurtha's. Did anything help the reformer of

England, France or Germany in his early days so much as
the knowledge that many patriots believed in him? The
condition of the Papacy strengthened this feeling enormously.
The Popes, from Sixtus IV. to Leo X., aimed at the creation of
Papal States; and they were right, from their point of view,
to pursue such an aim. For on the possession of such States
depended the permanence of the Papacy. It gave, however, a
fatal advantage to the reformer, for he could—and did—argue
that contributions taken from his native land, be it England,
France or Germany, were supporting Italian dreams of con-
quest. The College of Cardinals, the Curia, the Popes—were
they not all essentially Italian in their outlook? Since Julius II.,
with the single exception of Adrian VI., all the Popes have
been Italians. The possession of States placed the Popedom
in a contradictory position. They were apostles of peace who
were constantly forced to go to war in order to defend their
property. They were men of the other world, and yet were
they not daily forced to interfere in the affairs of this?

The Conciliar Movement had failed in the past to effect
reform and was destined to fail in the future. The growing force
of nationality proved too much for any hope of its success. A
General Council had been held on the very eve of the Reformation; it was a failure, as all its predecessors had been. When
Julius II. convoked it in 1512, men understood that this was
a shrewd move in the game of controlling his opponents. It
sat from 1512 to 1517, and what had it accomplished? Was
Pico della Mirandola wrong in telling the Pope that if there
was any real desire for reform the old laws of the Church
would suffice without enacting new ones? Had he not begged
the Pope and the assembled Fathers to reform morals? Had
there been any result of this speech, which was every whit
as remarkable as John Colet's Convocation sermon of 1512?
Yes; there had been results, but they were not pleasing to
any who had the interests of the Church at heart. For the Fifth
Lateran Council, 1512-1517, had achieved the abolition of the
Pragmatic Sanction of Bourges, the charter of liberties of the
Gallican Church. It had confirmed the Bull *Unam Sanctam*,
in which Boniface VIII. declared the salvation of men to

depend on their submission to the Papal See. It had forbidden, under pain of excommunication and heavy fines, the printing of any books without the approval of the Bishop and the Inquisitor, and in Rome of the Cardinal-Vicar and the Master of the Palace.

Men like Bishop Creighton used to speak of the Reformation as " a great national revolution which found expression in the resolute assertion on the part of England of its national independence." This is only true in part, and is not at all true to the extent that this historian thought. There was some assertion of our national independence, but it was just as much implicit as explicit. There was at the same time the feeling that England should not be at the beck and call of any State, Italian or other. Combined with this feeling there was also the sense of dissatisfaction expressed with the working of the Church by such men as Colet, Dean of St Paul's. The truth is that the sixteenth-century movement constitutes a testimony to the danger of putting off reform. There might have been a preserving revolution in the thirteenth century instead of the destroying one of the sixteenth.

Men vaguely perceived that the old order had come to an end in the State. For after 1492 the nationalities of such lands as England, France and Spain were unconsciously forming themselves. Subconsciously much more than consciously, this formation was at work. The catastrophe of the Fifth Lateran Council, as it was the catastrophe of the Council of Constance, lay in the fact that national sentiment was waxing while the desire for joint European action was waning. Who, then, understood this vital fact? Ecclesiastical authority was breaking down, and as there must be authority, secular was taking the place of ecclesiastical. The national State steps proudly on the stage. Bodin stands forth as the first to proclaim the existence of the nationality of the sovereign.

Bossuet was not wrong in indicating the new domination of the State. What the people gained, said he, in rejecting the Pope was to give themselves a lay Pope, and to place in the hand of the magistrates the authority of the Apostles. That the Reformation aided the cause of despotism is an undoubted fact. Can it be held responsible for the success of that cause? This is as much to be found in Roman Catholic countries as in Protestant. Was Philip II. of Spain a less absolute ruler than Henry VIII.? In Spain the Church was scarcely less subservient than in Saxony. Indeed, did not Spain owe her success in crushing the movement against absolutism to the close union between the spiritual and the secular arms? The French Church was every whit as obsequious as the German. It is significant that only two bishoprics, Cambrai and Utrecht, vanish from the map before the Treaty of Westphalia, 1648, and both vanish through the action of Charles V.

The State stands before us, and we meet its subjects as individuals. The danger of the new individualism is obvious. It is as clear in Thomas Murner as it is in Thomas Cartwright. What alleviated the danger was the fresh importance attached to conscience. The most wonderful of all the mediæval centuries was the thirteenth, and it was late in that century, as Lord Acton used to point out, that the psychology of conscience was closely studied for the first time, and that men began to speak of it as the audible voice of God, which never fails or misleads, and that ought to be obeyed, whether enlightened or darkened, whether right or wrong. Bishop Creighton insisted that conscience had a larger hold of the Teuton than of the Latin or the Slav, and that this formed the strength of the Reformation. " Conscience," he wrote, " was appealed to as the supreme judge, and the intellectual controversy was only an expression of this in the region of theology. I admit that this setting of morality in the foremost place narrowed the scope of religion, and put Christian truth in a secondary place. I admit that it set up a standard of morality which was mainly dictated by social needs rather than spiritual truth. But I think that conscience created the form of religion, not that the theology of the sixteenth century formed a morality."

Clearly if conscience possessed rights, when consciences differed there must be room for toleration. Such were the sentiments of the Politiques and of Sir Thomas More. Toleration certainly was the ideal, but, while it possessed advantages, did it not possess disadvantages? Did it not threaten destruction

INTRODUCTION

to that new body, the national State? For how could the State endure if there were different bodies within it? There must be unity of aim, and how could toleration secure this unity of aim?

The Renaissance scholars eagerly sought the manuscripts of the past. With the exception of Lorenzo Valla, however, it had not occurred to the Italian humanists to employ the new learning to clear the source of Christian theology. In the north, though not in the south, Greece rose from the dead with the New Testament in her hand. Erasmus published his edition of it under the title of the *Novum Instrumentum*, and indeed it proved to be a new instrument of thought. Though it was printed at Bâle, it was the result of his stay in Cambridge. He may be reckoned the first of the great scholars of that university to whom the students of the Apostolic writings owe so weighty a debt. In a beautiful old cloister of Queens' College his study was situated. To the observer of the slow growth of toleration these rooms in the old tower are sacred. Doubtless his editing does not reach the level of Joseph Scaliger, Isaac Casaubon or Richard Bentley, but it merits the supreme distinction of being probably the first Greek edition that had ever appeared. " A shock thus was given," writes Mark Pattison, " to the credit of the clergy in the province of literature equal to that given in the province of science by the astronomical discoveries of the seventeenth century." Truth was no longer a treasure to be discreetly hidden in a napkin. The *Novum Instrumentum*, like the *Novum Organum* of Bacon, appealed to facts, not to authority. Erasmus fought " absolutely the opinion of those who refuse to the common people the right to read the divine letters in the popular language, as if Christ had taught unintelligent mysteries understood only by some theologians. . . . I long that the husbandman should sing portions of them to himself as he follows the plough, that the weaver should hum them to the tune of his shuttle, that the traveller should beguile with their stories the tedium of his journey."

Erasmus wrote a series of Latin paraphrases of all the books of the New Testament except the Revelation of St John the

xx

Divine. These were meant to bring home to the reader the substance and thought of the several books in a form making a ready appeal to his mind. These paraphrases diffused the opinions of the author of the *Praise of Folly* on such matters as fasts and feasts, the monastic life, the worship of relics, and the like. Authority received rude blows from comments like these on Matthew xvi. 18 : " Upon this rock I will build my church." The author expresses his surprise that these words should be applied exclusively to the Roman Pontiff, " to whom they undoubtedly apply first of all, seeing that he is the head of the Christian Church ; but they apply, not to him only, but to all Christians." It was not a little difficult for the husbandman, the weaver, the traveller to distinguish between text and paraphrase, between St Matthew and St Erasmus. The blending of the two renders intelligible the belief in Europe that the Bible was composed as a pamphlet on the reforming side. It was, in fact, directed from its origin—the only origin at least the ordinary man knew—against the Pope and the Roman Church.

The appeal to the Bible was the soul of the Reformation. The Renaissance left the people untouched. The Reformation touched them deeply, and it touched them through the Sacred Record. Between Rome and the people there stands not only the might of the Sovereign but also the might of the Bible. The place of the infallible Church was taken by an infallible Book. The change was gain, but not all pure gain. The Bible belongs to a past age and records many types of civilisation. It records principles : it refuses to record maxims for the indolent or for those who prefer authoritative rules to guide every action in life. Therefore the reader must interpret it anew in the light of the present. Its truths are unchanged : its aspects are continually changing. That is, its interpretation must vary from age to age. The reformer asserted the priesthood of the believer, and this assertion carried with it the right to examine for oneself, regardless of any *Ita scriptum est*. Thus was provoked that habit of inquiry that lies at the very base of individualism. The interpretation of the Bible was left to the ever-varying necessities of the individual. Men were convinced that the salvation of each soul was dear in the sight of God, and they were convinced that nothing, and no one, must stand between the soul and its Creator. As the national State emerges, so does the individual, with all the advantages as well as all the drawbacks of his newly found liberty.

R. H. M.

December 1925.

CONTENTS

PAGE

PREFACE ix

INTRODUCTION xi

CHAPTER

I. THE WORLD OF MACHIAVELLI 1

II. LUTHER AND THE STATE CHURCH 40

III. JOHN CALVIN AND HIS *INSTITUTES* 80

IV. BODIN AND THE THEORY OF SOVEREIGNTY 129

V. CALVIN'S DISCIPLES 169

VI. LEAGUERS AND JESUITS 212

VII. BRITISH SPECULATORS 238

GENERAL WORKS OF REFERENCE 283

CHRONOLOGY OF WRITINGS 285

INDEX 287

CHAPTER I

THE WORLD OF MACHIAVELLI

AT first sight it seems a strange phenomenon that before the Renaissance no independent work in political theory had appeared for nearly fifteen hundred years—none since the time of Cicero if we except such writings as the *De Civitate Dei* of St Augustine, the *De Monarchia* of Dante, and the *Defensor Pacis* of Marsiglio of Padua; in the first two treatises Platonic influence is easily discerned: the Monarcha of Dante's work is Plato's heaven-born statesman. The reason is that until after the Renaissance there was no conscious desire for moral or political speculation. Under the world-empire of Rome the absence of independent political life combined with the vast development of municipal law and administration left little room for the dreams of the philosophers. The world-emperor ruled over the world-empire: that was enough for the Roman lawyers. Imaginary—and impossible—States had for them not a vestige of interest. Speculation as to the form or the end of government was scarcely possible—was certainly unpractical—so long as men deemed the Holy Roman Emperor the successor of the Cæsars. All were content to accept unquestioningly the theory of the Holy Roman Empire. Loyalty to king or feudal lord was habitual or natural, unless the rule was very oppressive or unless their immediate lord rebelled.

Travellers tell us that in Arctic regions a vessel sometimes lies for a long time firmly bound in a vast field of ice. The sailor who week after week surveys from the mast-head the monotonous expanse of whiteness sees an apparently solid surface, motionless and immovable, yet all the time the ice is steadily drifting to the south, carrying with it the embedded ship. At last, when warmer climes are reached, that which in the night seemed a rigid mass is in the light of dawn a tossing mass of ice-blocks, through which the vessel finds her homeward path. So it was throughout the Middle Ages. Beyond question these ages were largely unpolitical; even so the human mind was not content to do without a living and active political theory. Speculation was not so energetic as in modern times; yet a few, like Marsiglio of Padua, had been pondering over the conditions of membership of the national States arising at the conclusion of the fifteenth century. In the *Defensor Pacis*, published in 1324, he asserts the complete authority of the civil power and the purely voluntary nature of religious organisation. He therefore repudiates every kind of political claim put forward on behalf of the ecclesiastical organisation, and with this repudiation he exposes the iniquity of persecution. "The rights of the citizen," concludes Marsiglio, "are independent of the faith they profess; and no man may be punished for his religion." Neither St Athanasius nor St Ambrose protested more powerfully on behalf of liberty of conscience.

The voice of Marsiglio of Padua awoke no responsive echo. In mediæval times the alliance between Christianity and the Empire became so firmly welded that the Church was not *a* State; it was *the* State. The State as such was merely the secular side of the universal ecclesiastical corporation. The Church took over from the Roman Empire her theory of the absolute jurisdiction of the sovereign authority. It developed this doctrine into the *plenitudo potestatis* of her head, who was the ultimate dispenser of law, the sole legitimate source of all earthly power. There were struggles between the Pope and the Emperor, but the contest lay between two officials, never between two separate and distinct bodies. There was no quarrel between Church and State in our sense of the term. This statement is as true of Dante and Marsiglio as it is of Boniface and Augustinus. The vice of the mediæval State, like that of the classical State, was that it united Church and State in one. The fundamental idea of the mediæval mind was that of a uniform single empire—it never contemplated the absurdity of several empires—resting entirely upon a Christian basis. The mediæval basis of unity was undoubtedly religious. No heretic, no schismatic, no excommunicate could possibly enjoy the rights of citizenship. This principle, founded upon the Code of Justinian, formed the ground of the claim of the Pope to bind and unloose the allegiance of the subject to the Holy Roman Empire, a claim that brought all his woes upon the head of the unfortunate Roman Catholic. Herbert Spencer teaches us that evolution lies largely in the change from the homogenous to the heterogeneous. No mediæval mind could grasp such a conception. To such a mind politics and theology are practically synonymous terms.

In the fifteenth and sixteenth centuries that new birth of the human spirit which we call the Renaissance took place. Man conceived a passionate desire for extending the limits of human knowledge and for employing his powers to newer and better advantage. The general ferment and the shaking of men's traditional beliefs extended to all departments of human thought, even to the fundamental questions of society itself. It was towards the close of the Middle Ages that the enormously seminal influence of Greek art and literature began to remould the world. Admiration for antiquity became the hall-mark of the Renaissance. Art and literature threw off to a very large extent the forms of mediævalism and looked for all their inspiration to the models of the classical world. The dominant intellectual note of the age was freedom—freedom from the restraints which had been imposed upon men's thoughts and actions by the methods and dogmas of the schoolmen, and freedom to revel in every species of activity which the untrammelled spirit of the ancients had suggested. The free critical methods of the new movement are readily discernible in the doctrines of the time. While, however, each man of letters asserted his freedom to his own opinions, he had but little interest that others should enjoy the same measure of toleration; this forms a marked characteristic of the scholars of the New Learning.

While men's minds were thus speculating, the grand geographical discoveries of the age assisted in upsetting the mediæval preconceived notions as to world-empire. Men indeed, to use M. Taine's picturesque phrase, opened their eyes and saw. They saw the physical bounds of the universe suddenly and enormously enlarged; for the discoveries of Nicholas de Cusa and of Nicholas Copernicus shadowed forth the secret of the universe. The New World, in a sense not

3

far different from Canning's, did undoubtedly redress the balance of the Old. The New World—or rather the New Worlds—was added to the Old, and the conception of an apparently limitless continent destroyed that of a limited one. Men for the first time conceived a more correct idea of the globe they were inhabiting. Hitherto they had not even professed to have any knowledge of geography; there is no mention of it in the Trivium and Quadrivium, which were then supposed to form a cycle of things known, if not of things knowable. Dante had made the conception of the nearness of hell very vivid, and it constituted a serious obstacle to the work of the navigator. The mediæval mind placed the happy Isles of the Blessed in the mysterious West, and, illogically enough, located the openings into hell in the same region. Naturally sailors did not care to adventure too far from land when such a belief was prevalent. In a mediæval text-book occurs the question: "Why is the sun so red in the evening?" The answer is: "Because he looketh down upon hell and reflecteth the flames thereof."

If the thirteenth century be the most wonderful the world has seen, surely the year 1492 is the most wonderful year Anno Domini. For then Columbus discovered America, and the mind of Copernicus was seething with ideas destined to overthrow the Ptolemaic system. Three national monarchs were reigning in England, France and Spain respectively. Bacon's *tres magi*, Henry VII.; Louis XI. and Ferdinand the Catholic, ruled over consolidated kingdoms, the latter in this very year conquering Granada. Then Lorenzo de' Medici died, and with his death France entered upon her part in the creation of international European relations. Thus she came into intimate contact with Spain and Germany, feeling powerfully the influence of Italy. Because of her relations with the last country, France in this fateful year began a career which in the end compelled her to cast in her lot with Latin nations, not with Teutonic, when the Reformation pressed for settlement. With her England concluded the Treaty of Étaples, marking the rise of modern commerce. In Germany the peasants of Kempten still continued their revolt against feudal oppression. On the other hand, by the influence of Torquemada, the Jews were expelled from Spain, and one hundred and fifty thousand had to abandon their homes. The Moors also could this year read their doom of expulsion. The world of 1492 was then composed of mediæval and comparatively modern elements. A young man of twenty-two, one Nicholas Machiavelli (1469-1527), surveyed this medley with precocious eyes, and his whole after-life was coloured by the mixture of new and old, in which the new predominated.

It is not unusual to perceive in the year 1492 the end of the Middle Ages, and yet we wonder if Machiavelli so regarded this year. His interest in the problem of the State is that of a man who studies it scientifically with the passionless motive of simply ascertaining the methods to sustain its ends. Behind this seeming passionlessness of brain there beats a heart passionately feeling the ills of his country. The tradition of the Middle Ages weaves no spells over him, largely, we suspect, because for him they had ended with the Black Death of 1348. Giovanni Boccaccio's *Decameron* is remarkable as marking the beginning of great Italian prose. It is no less remarkable as testifying to the complete demoralisation due to the Plague. More than half the population of Asia and Europe were swept away by this appalling epidemic, and the *Decameron* shows impressively—because it does so unconsciously—the collapse of the moral fabric of society. Machiavelli was not a native of Florence for nothing, and his passionless scientific interest in problems of statesmanship betrays that he can come to the study of the present utterly untrammelled by any Christian conceptions of the past. Classical history exercised a fascination he could not resist. He is, however, so absorbed with his labours that two of the greatest forces of the new age leave him wholly unmoved. The invention of gunpowder and the rise of the Reformation stand outside his ken. Just as Aristotle was blind to the destruction of the City-State that his pupil was to accomplish, so Machiavelli could set himself the task of estimating the functions of the Prince without in the least perceiving how fundamentally these functions were to be changed by the energy gunpowder

5

put into his hands and by the rise of that spirit of nationalism that was to leave its lasting impression on all the Prince undertook. Because politics had been synonymous with theology and because Machiavelli was determined to sever the tie between them, he was blinded to the power exerted by such an overwhelming current as the Reformation. He was so disgusted with such arguments as to whether the Pope should be compared to the Sun and the Emperor to the Moon, whether the fact of Samuel deposing Saul and the offerings of the Magi to the infant Saviour could show the dependence of the Empire on the Church, that he could not grasp the fact that theology, new as well as old, still counted. He snapped his fetters in one direction only to reimpose them in another. To him there was nothing great or noble in Savonarola, a mere " weaponless prophet."

Machiavelli was a man immersed in the affairs of his native city, being elected in 1498 Secretary to the Ten, and holding that important position until the downfall of the Republican Government in 1512. Four times he went on a mission to the King of France and once to the Emperor Maximilian I. at Innsbrück. He was with Cæsar Borgia, Duke of Valentinois (1476-1507), in the campaign of 1502, and on behalf of his republic he transacted business with Julius II. at Rome. In daily contact with men guiding the diplomatic destiny of their country, the young Secretary watched with observant eyes their methods. In matters of the mind he was superior to a man like Cæsar Borgia, but was he not inferior to him in matters of action? The Duke well knew how to turn to his own advantage the warring passions of his rivals and the realities of a momentarily changing situation. The Duke was not a great statesman, not a great soldier, yet what was Machiavelli to think of a man who could create a State out of nothing, could intimidate all men, even his own father, Alexander VI.? What some statesmen and some soldiers could not accomplish, Cæsar Borgia had accomplished. True, he enjoyed the support of France, and of course of the Vatican. Nevertheless, in spite of the existence of powerful enemies he had more than held his own. How had he done so? Machiavelli experienced no difficulty in noting that such a triumph had been mainly won by magnificent audacity and by no less magnificent—so it seemed to the Secretary—craft. As an anatomist dissected the body, so he dissected the diplomatic body, earnestly seeking for the germs of success in his endeavours. He was no lettered recluse, seeking in books the experience which life denied him. Before his eyes there unrolled a tangle of infamy. He spent his days among men steeped in crime, ready to sell themselves to the highest bidder, devoid of all ethical considerations. The truth is that Machiavellianism was already old when Machiavelli invented it.

Circumstances mould men more plainly than men mould circumstances. So Bismarck confessed on a memorable occasion. At the beginning of the nineteenth century the age of machinery reaches another stage in its career. Men compete with men as they had scarcely competed before. David Ricardo perceives this, and he invents the economic man, the being who is engrossed with his own self-interest. Just as Ricardo conceived this economic man, so Machiavelli conceived a political one. The beginning of the sixteenth century afforded an unexampled opportunity for such a political negotiator, and much that Machiavelli did was simply to analyse his functions. Given the circumstances of his epoch, what considerations ought to actuate him? As the economic man divested himself of all ethical considerations, the political one did exactly the same. Cæsar Borgia had pursued a line of policy. Supposing he had gone a step farther with it, what would have happened? What might have happened? Ricardo devised his ideal capitalist. Machiavelli devised his ideal diplomatist. He was Cæsar Borgia with something superadded. He was to be a statesman somewhat abler and more acute, more audacious and more unrestrained, a Cæsar Borgia, or a Louis XI.—as Commines regarded him—if you like, raised to the nth degree of power. Machiavelli's three books, the *Discorsi*, the *Principe*, and the slight *Vita di Castruccio Castricani*, all mingle the ideal with the real. Men of a smaller breed employed petty trickery and tergiversation that failed to secure their ends. Men of the ideal Valentinois employed trickery and tergiversation on a wholesale scale, and almost invariably secured their ends. Why, thought the Secretary, employ means of circumvention if not on a large scale, or at least on a scale large enough to ensure success?

Americans are apt sometimes to argue that they seldom in the course of their negotiations employ force. For example, they send dispatches to Mexico; they do not send troops. But the Mexicans, as well as everyone else, are well aware of the fact that behind the dispatches—discreetly in the background—lie the officers trained at West Point. When Cornet Joyce came to seize Charles I. on a June morning in 1647, the King turned inquiringly to Joyce, asking the question: " What commission have you to secure my person? " The Cornet turned to the soldiers who had fought at Naseby, and, pointing to them, he said: " It is behind me." " It is as fair a commission and as well written as I have seen a commission written in my life: a company of handsome, proper gentlemen as I have seen a great while."

Machiavelli realised as clearly as Charles I. the urgent need for his republic to possess such handsome, proper gentlemen in its own service. The *condottieri* had all fought for their captains and for themselves, ultimately ruining the States that had enlisted their services. Cæsar Borgia had raised a levy of one man from each household throughout his possessions and had formed the nucleus of his own army. The new national States like France and Spain were pursuing a similar policy, and the Swiss had their own soldiers. Surely what the Swiss had accomplished, the Florentines could accomplish. Machiavelli turned the forces of his mind ardently to the creation of a national militia. His *L'Arte della Guerra* betrays at every turn that he was not a soldier. Take, for instance, his rooted disbelief in the efficacy of fire-arms. His book betrays, however, the patriotic soul of the man whose energies are absorbed by distributing arms, enrolling infantry, and generally stirring up the enthusiasm of his fellow-citizens.

In his new rôle as soldier he preserves his old rôle of statesman and of the methods the statesman ought to employ. The members of the militia must be honest and well-conducted men. Their captains must be born to instruct and born to command. Their moral character is not at all in question. Indeed goodness of heart might prove a hindrance in actual warfare. For such a captain might not exercise those acts of ruthless warfare which he — as well as the statesman — is obliged to execute. Now we must not misunderstand Machiavelli's meaning. In private life he genuinely admired virtue, and his own life was not altogether out of keeping with this frank admiration. But for him, as indeed for the men of the Renaissance, virtue was a matter entirely for the individual. To such men there was no connection of any kind whatsoever between the private conscience of the man and the public conscience of the State to which he belonged. Such a connection implies the conception of social personality, that the State is a self-governing unit, and that its members realise themselves in its unity. Not one of these ideas ever entered the mind of Machiavelli, or indeed of his contemporaries.

During the Middle Ages Providence—so men thought— had occasionally transformed social conditions. The Black Death of 1348 constituted to the intelligence of the Secretary a complete break with tradition. For the future the old had gone, to be replaced by the new, and the new consisted exclusively in the observance of the laws by which transformations were wrought. How were they wrought during the sixteenth century? From his point of vantage as a Secretary, Machiavelli was quite certain that these new laws were to be found in the will of the Prince or the General. Given such a presupposition, how could he entertain the conception of public morality? Many a time Machiavelli had gazed at the cathedral of his native city. Brunelleschi's dome crowns it, and in it he unites the diversity of Gothic and Oriental elements harmoniously. The work of the statesman was the exact opposite of Brunelleschi. For Machiavelli was to divide the hitherto united styles of theology and politics. Michelangelo won his colossal figure of David from the shapeless marble. Wholly nude, this youth presents himself as energy and simplicity personified. Nicholas Machiavelli's State was as nude ethically as Michelangelo's *David*. As this statue inaugurated a real revolution in art, so *Il Principe* inaugurated a real revolution in the science of politics. Both destroyed every mediæval tradition and both destroyed every conventional form. As the gigantic figure of David led the way for the sculptor, so the no less gigantic figure of the Prince led the way for the politician. Neither Machiavelli nor Michelangelo dreaded any obstacle in the way of their political or artistic designs; for all ideas issued spontaneously from an imagination trained to obey the laws of political or artistic craft. No doubt each day brought them face to face with fresh difficulties; but they were invariably ready to attack them with victorious vigour. Machiavelli's faith in his statesmanlike conceptions was as unshakable as Michelangelo's faith in his æsthetic conceptions.

A commanding grasp of a general position was more suited to Machiavelli's intellect than the knowledge of details. The Venetian Ambassadors and his fellow-citizen, Guicciardini (1523-1589), far surpassed him in that backstairs' knowledge on which Lord Acton used to lay so much stress. The fleeting favour of the Prince, the intrigue of to-day and the possible move of to-morrow—all these were as familiar to Guicciardini as they were unfamiliar to Machiavelli. Nor was he ever an envoy of more than secondary rank. At the same time he stood far above his contemporaries in his discernment of the signs of the times. Cross-currents baffled him: main currents never did. The tendency of the policy of a prince or of his people, the elements of the political strength of Pope or King—these were matters wholly within his competent grasp.

Favouring the popular party in Florence, Machiavelli lost his Secretaryship in 1512 when the Medici returned. Thrown into prison, he was put to the question with ropes and pulleys. In his evil days his thoughts turn for a confidant not to his wife or his children but to the Ambassador, Francesco Vittori. In happy days he had known Vittori, and this recollection bound the two men together. What, however, Vittori really valued in his friend was the keen intellect of the man able to summon all his powers to the discussion of the political issues in which both felt so lively an interest. Machiavelli turns increasingly, now that he has left office—or rather now that office has left him—to authorship. He busied himself with the *Discorsi* and with the *Principe*. By the beginning of 1515 his correspondence with Vittori ceases, for he is entirely absorbed with his writings.

The only method of perceiving the originality of an author is to note what other contemporary authors were capable of writing, and from this angle we briefly survey what Savonarola and Pontano were meditating. Savonarola, in his *Del Reggimento del Governo della Citta di Firenze*, describes the ideal Prince in language that marks no break with the world that came to an end in 1348. In true scholastic fashion we meet with a ruler who exercises his sway for the good of his people. True, there are bad princes, and for a description of them he falls back on the pages of St Thomas Aquinas. A tyrant in Florence is plainly deplorable, and yet, as Savonarola knew to his cost, Florence was the seat of power of the Medici. Is a Republic with Gonfalonier and Signory with a Council of Eighty more advisable? Is it more advisable with a Great Council as in Venice? The test for the monk, as we are astonished to ascertain, is purely one of expediency. Pontano was humanist as well as politician. He has the knowledge of the past as well as the experience of the present on which to draw. What has he to tell us in his *De Principe*? We learn such platitudes as that the Prince should love justice and respect the gods; that he should be clement and prudent, faithful to his word; that above all, he should be the friend and patron of men of letters. Does Pontano not relate that when Jacopo Piccini threatened Calixtus III., the Pope exclaimed that he had nothing to fear, since Rome contained three thousand *literati*, whose counsels and wisdom would enable him to repel any army, however formidable? We can well imagine the curl of the lip of Machiavelli as he read a production that emanated from a man who was one of the chief ministers of the Court of Ferdinand of Aragon. The ex-Secretary, for his part, would prefer his stout Florentine militia to even three thousand *literati*.

The two main writings of Machiavelli are the *Principe* and the *Discorsi*, and each strikingly supplements the other. The first treats of principalities and the second of republics. By December 1513 he had finished the first, but the second remained unfinished. In form the *Discorsi* professes to be a commentary on the history of Livy, but in substance it discusses principalities, together with reflections on the course of history that are eminently suggestive. The laboratory of such an experimental scientist as this statesman is the efforts of statesmen in the past. Therefore the searching study of history is vital. To Machiavelli as to Guicciardini the cyclical theory of events was one that commended itself warmly. They both held that the past shed light on the present in general and that the past of Rome shed light on it in particular. The Renaissance exerted its influence resoundingly when it persuaded these two thinkers that republics like Sparta, Athens and, above all, Rome are preferable to any monarchy. The classical State, whether of Greece or Rome, exalted country at the expense of the citizen, who could realise his life only in the corporate life. Naturally what applied to the Prince applied no less strongly to the principality.

Men like Savonarola and Pontano devised their conceptions, and with them the last of the idealistic States had almost disappeared. With Machiavelli the first of the realistic States appeared in his *Discorsi* quite as much as in his *Principe*. The men of the older school asked: "What is the best form of government?" Machiavelli had travelled long past a stage like this. He did not even ask: "What is the best form of government adapted to Florence?" Pragmatist to the core, he was simply concerned with the durability and the prosperity of his own State. For him, if not for others, the day of the general problem had gone, for he was too keen-sighted not to perceive that the authority of the Holy Roman Empire had vanished. Instead of the wide issues of a world-empire, he was forced to consider the narrower issues of a City-State like Florence. Unlike Bodin, he does not survey general European history, contenting himself with that of Rome.

The old order had been the Empire or the Church, the commune, the guild, the scholastic system: the individual is always part of some group, and has no existence apart from it. The new order was the State, the national Church, the merchant, the individual. The old order had been authority and asceticism; the new was reason and joy in the whole of life. For a thousand years there had been as much authority in social life as in intellectual. Unknown men had been content to build the cathedrals of the Middle Ages, whereas the men of the New Age asserted themselves to the utmost. The thirst for glory became unquenchable. Genius prevents man finding an equal, pride prevents him from lowering himself to an inferior. The statues used to be within the cathedral, for they were erected to the glory of God. Now they stood in the market-place to be seen of men. Man used to be bound to a bishop, a lord, a municipality, to a school, or a body. Now he proudly steps on the stage as himself, eager to develop his capacities for his own benefit, with boundless confidence in his will, his superiority and his infinite variety. The body dissolves into the units which compose it. There is no longer the Papacy: there is the Pope, who is a lord like other lords. There is no longer the Holy Roman Empire: there is the Emperor, who is also a lord no more than other lords. There is no longer the city: there is the Prince. There is no longer the university: there is the spirit of humanism. The painter ceases to depict the group: the portrait is his masterpiece. He used to describe on the walls of cemeteries the triumph of death: now he describes on the walls of houses the triumph of life. The quest is no more the One in the Many: it is the Many in the One.

Mandeville's *Fable of the Bees* is popularly supposed to teach that private vices are sometimes public benefits. More clear-sighted than Bernard Mandeville, Machiavelli perceived the individuality of the Italian—*il suo particolare*—threatened the ruin of the State. His egotism combined with his lack of morality left but poor stuff for the Prince to erect the foundations of his polity. At the very time when Martin Luther was feeling the bitterness of the truth that man's nature owns a deep tinge of original sin, Machiavelli was making a similar discovery in the world of politics. Of the connection between these two aspects of man's nature, Machiavelli, with his deep

13

disdain of theology, entertained not the remotest conception. On the one hand he noted the egotism of the individual, issuing in forms of wickedness; on the other hand he also noted public good, issuing in little. Was not the remedy perfectly plain? There must be force to coerce egotism and wrong, and this force must be exercised by the Sovereign. Pagan to the core, Machiavelli exalted the spirit of antiquity above that of Christianity. He hated the Papacy with a passion that would do discredit even to a bitter Protestant. Virtue never has to him the Christian sense of goodness; it always means courage and energy for evil as much as for good.[1] Such virtue issued in glory. Did not men value glory more than aught else in the world? Did not glory, and glory only, render them immortal and like unto the gods? Men, he stoutly maintained, preferred infamy to oblivion, for at least infamy served to transmit their names to posterity. He used to repeat with keen enthusiasm the encomium of Gino Capponi upon " those who loved their country better than the safety of their souls." " Let us be Venetians first," said Father Paul, " and Christians after," and the sentiment is sufficiently akin to the mind of Machiavelli.

The Greekless ex-Secretary had barely read Aristotle's *Politics* even in a Latin dress, and it is therefore vain to seek for an imitation of the *Politics* in the *Prince*. There is, however, a curious resemblance between the attitude of the two men towards their chosen studies. Just as Aristotle divorced ethics from politics, so Machiavelli's impassive intelligence divorced them. Just as Aristotle founded his theory on researches into more than one hundred and fifty Greek constitutions, so Machiavelli plunged into the past and into the present. His observant mind noted what applied to the present in the history of Greece and Rome, especially Rome, and it also noted what he saw in the course of his negotiations with many courts. Aristotle and Machiavelli did not entertain the idea that a great State is a large one, for they thought that it was essentially one that exercised its functions vigorously. Nor

[1] *Cf.* E. W. Mayers, *Machiavellis Geschichtsauffassung und sein Begriff virtù*; *cf.* Meinecke, *Die Idee der Staatsräson*, p. 40.

did they believe that all the inhabitants of the State ought to be citizens. In Florence, as in Athens, the citizens formed but a small proportion of the total number of the inhabitants. The idea that mere birth or residence ought to confer citizenship is an outcome of the French Revolution of 1789. It is neither a part of the Athenian nor of the Florentine conception. Machiavelli would cordially have endorsed the great proposition that Aristotle laid down when he held that man is born to be a citizen.

The central feature of the *Discorsi* no less than of *Il Principe* is the foundation and the formation of the State. In the Middle Ages there had been liberties, but no liberty—that is, there were class liberties of the lords, the squires, the citizens and the clergy, but there was no liberty common to these four classes. From this angle there were estates, but there was no State, no body uniting all living on the same soil. True, John proclaimed himself Rex Angliæ, not Rex Anglorum. He was, however, a fortunate exception, for all other kings throughout the sixteenth century called themselves kings of their people, not of their country. It is significant that Mary is always known as Mary Queen of Scots, not Queen of Scotland. Henry IV. was the first Frenchman to call himself King of France. Nor is this a distinction without a difference. To take a case in our own day, it was a matter of no little moment that William II. was the German Emperor, not Emperor of Germany.

Machiavelli was determined that, so far as one thinker could, he would put an end to the conception of estates and replace it by that of the State, and his *Discorsi* and his *Principe* are two of the most influential of all the writings of his generation.[1] The *Discourses* are divided into three books. The first treats of the methods by which States are founded and of their internal organisation; the second of the methods of aggrandising them and of conquests; and the third is devoted to the exposition of what amounts to a philosophy of history. Behind all three books the question of the unity of the State

---

[1] *Cf.* Benoist, "L'État italien avant Machiavelli," *Revue des deux Mondes*, May 1907.

perpetually appears; if it disappears, it is only for a moment. What is the essence of this unity in a republican State? What is the relation between this State and its dependencies? The answer to this second question, it is obvious, goes some way towards a solution of the first. Machiavelli notes keenly that the heaviest servitude is that imposed under a republic, inasmuch as it is more lasting. Moreover, the aim of the republic is to enervate and weaken all others in order to increase its own stability. No prince accordingly will attempt this enervation unless he is some barbarous destroyer of countries and devastator of all human civilisation, similar to the princes of the East. "For if he have some humanity and rectitude, he will bear equal affection towards every city beneath his sway."[1]

Machiavelli never contents himself with sonorous commonplaces. He analyses the method pursued by the mediæval republics and finds it dangerous to the last degree. "Republics, he coolly holds, "have three modes of aggrandising their States: First, by confederation among themselves on the Etruscan or Swiss plan; secondly, by placing the conquered on the same footing with themselves, although in such wise as to retain the supreme command, the seat of empire and the glory of their common enterprises, which was the plan pursued by the Romans; thirdly, by creating subjects and not associates, as did the Spartans and the Athenians. This third method is the worst, since to undertake to hold and govern cities by violence, especially those which have been used to freedom, is a difficult and wearisome matter. To carry it out with success it is necessary to be very strongly armed, and to enlarge cities by adding many strangers to the population. Sparta and Athens failed to do this and therefore were destroyed. It was instead done by the Romans, who at the same time also followed the second method and grew powerful. First of all they made the peoples of Italy their colleagues, binding all to themselves by common laws, but invariably retaining rule and empire in their own grasp. Afterwards, with the aid of these colleagues, they subjugated foreign peoples, who, having been under the dominion of monarchs, were not accustomed to liberty. And

---

[1] *Discorsi*, Bk. II., ch. ii., p. 191.

therefore, when the Italians tried to rebel, the Romans were already very strong and could reduce them by submission, having first known how to increase their own cities by means of foreigners, inasmuch as they understood the need of imitating nature, and that no slender stem can ever sustain a stalwart tree. Then, as regards the first method, that of a confederation, it was that which was observed by the Etruscans, who, by means of the union of twelve cities, governed by a league, were very mighty both in warfare and commerce, and held in respect from the Tiber to the Alps." [1]

For Machiavelli the prime test of statesmanship is success, and, tried by this test, the Romans emerge from it triumphantly. They aimed at creating comrades, not subjects, when they conquered a people, and "it was the more praiseworthy in them, inasmuch as they were the first to adopt it; they had had no predecessors on that road, nor was their example afterwards copied by others." [1] Much as this appreciator of Roman polity had broken away from the past, he was never able to effect a complete severance. Who indeed is? Machiavelli belonged to the class of political philosopher who destroys more than he creates. He destroys the mediæval notion without quite creating one in its place. Who can be both destroyer and creator? Not Machiavelli and not anyone else. Such considerations will enable us to understand that he is more anxious to study the methods of the preservation of the State than to set out a theory of State. Under his circumstances nothing else was open to him, and it is nothing short of amazing that he accomplished his task so unmistakably. The generations come and the generations go, and Machiavellianism remains a permanent factor, not waning but, if anything, waxing.

The Florentine is in few respects a follower of Aristotle, yet in curious ways he reminds us of the father of political philosophy.[2] He has certainly no intention of wasting his time in considering what is the ideal polity. Still, like Aristotle, he is conscious that the State, in some fashion, has laws of its

---

[1] *Discorsi*, Bk. II., chap. iv.
[2] Ellinger, "Antike Quellen der Staatslehre Machiavellis," *Zeitschr. f. d. ges. Staatswissenschaften*, Band xliv.

growth and health discoverable by the political physician who ponders over the past. At the beginning of the third book of the *Discorsi* he informs us that governments and institutions require long life for their development, and in order to possess this long life they must be organised in such a way as to be often able to recur to their fundamental principles. He inevitably falls back on Roman history for the illustration of this far-reaching idea. Nor does he turn aside from examples more pertinent in his own day. His mediæval world ended in 1348, and he recognises that during the thirteenth century the Christian religion stood a chance of extinction through corruption. Fortunately St Francis of Assisi and St Dominic rescued it by restoring it to its original principles. What these original principles were Machiavelli does not attempt to define, for he was intuitive enough to realise that there are principles that are as much perceived in feeling as in anything else. As many motives evade the economic calculus, so many also evade the political calculus. There is neither clearness nor precision in much that we read in the *Discorsi*, but is the State a body about which it is entirely possible to be either precise or clear even in our own day? It possesses first principles, and these first principles must tend to its unity. With unity there must be the Prince to preserve it, to develop it. When Abbé Sièyes was asked what he accomplished during the days of the Reign of Terror, his answer was: " I lived." Machiavelli flourished in an age when States as august as the Holy Roman Empire were falling into stages of decay, and he bent all his efforts to the task of the preservation of the institution on which, in his judgment, everything else depended. The prime consideration was that the State must live. With Michelet he holds, *le nouveau Messie est le roi*.[1]

Many chapters of the second book of the *Discorsi* and a few of the third are devoted to the art of war, an art so important that the author wrote a special treatise on it. He still retains his boundless belief in a national militia and his equally boundless disbelief in the *condottieri*.[2] Long sight in the art of war

---

[1] *Histoire de France*, ix., p. 301.
[2] *Discorsi*, Bk. II., chap. xxiv.; cf. *Il Principe*, chap. xxi.

was not his, for he expressed his lack of faith in fortresses and his greater lack of faith in fire-arms. After all, the latter mistake was not unpardonable in the second decade of the sixteenth century. In 1896 Lord Kelvin denied the possibility of the aeroplane.

Progress was a thought that did not enter into the mind of this amateur writer on warfare. As Bacon, to use the caustic phrase of Harvey (1578-1657), wrote on science like a Lord Chancellor, so Machiavelli wrote on strategy and tactics like a Lloyd George. Progress was, however, a thought not unknown to the mind of his day. Guillaume Postel (1510-1581), professor of mathematics and languages in the Collège de France, wrote *De orbis terrarum concordia libri quatuor*. In it we meet with a crowd of ideas and facts invoked to-day by the defenders of the theory of indefinite progress. For instance, Postel teaches that wars and the calamities which follow in their train are the providential means destined to push nations into the path of progress. The conquests of the Mohammedans seem to him to be the exception to this rule, and he hoped his book would be instrumental in leading them to the light and unity of the Christian faith.[1] In a chapter devoted to the development of the dogma of the Trinity, Postel writes the following passage, in which we have no trouble in recognising the fundamental idea of the work of Lessing : " Lex Mosaica fuit velut *rudimentum* quoddam legis divinæ. . . . In ea lege, ut in summa Dicam, Deus fecit cum Israële, quod optimus *præceptor* cum adolescente admodum *discipulo*, cui cum radicibus disciplinæ ob ætatis teneritudinem et ignorantiam etiam ludos solitos permittit. . . . In tradendis disciplinis autoritas est ratione prior. Unde merito scriptum est : Nisi credideritis non intelligetis. Quod non solum in sacris, sed in humanioribus literis locum habet. Quis enim posset puerum formare statim ab ipsius elementis refractarium ? Debebat itaque præcedere religio, sequi ratio." [2]

As we turn over the folio of Postel we catch a glimpse of

---

[1] *De orbis terrarum*, ii., præf., p. 126. On Postel, *cf.* Sir G. Butler's interesting account in *Studies in Statecraft*, pp. 38-64.

[2] *De orbis terrarum*, iii., pp. 23-24. The italics in the quotation are mine.

the true spirit of the Renaissance writer. Do we remember sufficiently how long it was before this spirit of the belief in progress was destined to prevail? In political circles, as well as in literary and scientific, it was not rare to meet with the ancient notion of the circular theory of the movement of peoples and civilisations. If on the one hand there are the names of Rabelais, Campanella and Francis Bacon, on the other hand there are the no less renowned names of Machiavelli, Bodin and Montaigne.

Machiavelli estimated the level of human character as low as either Montaigne or Luther. The world is neither better nor worse than it was a thousand years ago; such was Machiavelli's sober conclusion. As the amount of matter on earth is exactly what it was in the time of Plato, so is the amount of badness and goodness. Power, in accordance with Bishop Berkeley's law, used to be in Assyria, then in Media, then in Persia, until at last it came to Italy and Rome. Badness and goodness are therefore simply migrating westward—that is all. There is no progress: the world is always the same.[1] Are there not revolutions? Yes, but they only alter the distribution of power. Some institutions improve and others fail to do so: the level is the same after a revolution as before it. Still, if there is no progress, there is at least no decadence. Machiavelli contents himself with reproducing the despairing doctrine of the Stoics on the cyclical movements of men and institutions. In his opinion every form of society and government bears within it a germ of corruption, an element of dissolution and ruin.[2] In a circle ceaselessly turn all the imaginable social forms.

That history repeats itself is a fundamental assumption with this philosopher.[3] That it repeats itself with just the tiny shade of alteration that makes all the difference is an assumption not quite so familiar to him. The character of men remains: accidents alter. The far-seeing man can note accidents in the past like those in the present, and given the sameness of man he can divine what under the circumstances he will do—nay,

---

[1] *Discorsi*, Bk. II.
[2] *Ibid.*, Bk. III., chap. ii.; Bk. III., chaps. i. and xliii.
[3] *Ibid.*, Bk. I., chap. xxxix.; *cf.* Bk. III., chap. xliii.

what he *must* do. For there is a species of historic fatalism in all that Machiavelli writes. In the *Discourses* and in *The Prince*, in his poems [1] and comedies, in fact in every line he writes, we always hark back to the notion that men are essentially the same in all ages. A thousand times we learn that as it was in the beginning with the character of man, so it is now, and ever shall be, world without end. We are too apt to take for granted that man continually changes under the influence of laws and institutions, the customs and manners of society. There is an innate conservatism in us that Machiavelli is quick to recognise, and of the truth of this conservatism no one can doubt. There is a unity in human nature, as Burke in imperishable language was to point out. Of course Machiavelli, unlike Burke, does not entertain for a moment the idea that the State is a divine institution.

His attitude towards religion is Gibbonian. We learn, with no surprise, that " the sagacious politician will always respect religion, even if he have no belief in it, since there have been frequent proofs that through inculcating it, even by craft, much valour has been roused for the defence of the country. . . . And the Romans, either in good faith or by calculation, always enforced respect for religion, and found their profit therein." [2] In a word, for the people all religions were equally true, for the philosopher equally false, and for the ruler equally necessary. Faith, hope and charity formed the trinity of the Christian. *Virtù, fortuna* and *necessità* formed the trinity of this pagan philosopher. Virtue, whether for good or for evil, is the most important quality for the State. " Infamous and detestable are the destroyers of religions, of monarchies, of republics; the enemies of virtue, of letters, and all that is useful to mankind." [3] The guilds of the Middle Ages his pagan genius ignores as if they had never existed. Feudalism and the Papacy he wishes to extirpate, for either of them forms an *imperium in imperio*, standing in the way of the State.

" Liberty," thinks Machiavelli, " always implies equality,

---

[1] Prologue of *Clizia ; Asino d'Oro*, chap. v.
[2] *Discorsi*, Bk. I., chap. xiv.
[3] *Ibid.*, Bk. III., chap. xli.

and sovereignty, inequality. How, for instance, could liberty
be established in Milan or Naples, where there is no sort of
equality among the citizens; or who might hope easily to
change by law a similar state of things? To effect a gradual
alteration in all this would demand a wise man, able to discern
things from a great distance; but such men are always few,
and hardly ever find favour with the multitude." [1] Feudalism,
with its system of liberties, and the Papacy, with its claim to
sovereignty within the State, form obstacles to the growth
of liberty which presupposes civic equality. The influence of
Roman thought, everywhere perceptible, is quite plain here.
With little belief in the law of nature, Machiavelli had some
belief in a form of it, the *jus gentium*. Under the force of these
two aspects of the law of nature the Romans came to hold
that *omnes homines natura æquales sunt*. This idea lies behind
the growth of the French, the Italian, and the other communes of the Middle Ages. To a man of the people who,
during the revolt of the Ciompi in 1378, tried to arouse the
people against the nobility, Machiavelli attributes these words:
" Nor must you let yourselves be cowed by that nobility of
blood of which they make boast to us; for all men, having
had the same beginning, are of equally ancient birth, and nature
has made them all in the same fashion. Were we all stripped
naked you would find us alike; dress us in their clothes and
they in ours, without doubt we should seem noble and they
mean, forasmuch as it is only poverty and riches that make
us inequal." [2]

Between the unmorality of the *Discorsi* and of *Il Principe*
there is not a point of difference. More men have read the
latter than the former—that is really all there is to say. The
word morality for their author possesses no meaning when
men come to apply it to public affairs. Nor do we wonder
greatly when we remember the inchoate nature of the State.
We might produce many passages on the identity of the
unmorality of Machiavelli's two important books. Here is one.
" When, however, the State is once founded," he drily remarks,

---

[1] *Discorsi*, Bk. I., chap. xviii.
[2] Machiavelli, " Storie," in the *Opere*, i., p. 166.

" it should be entrusted to the care and guardianship of many, to ensure its duration; inasmuch as although one man only is needed for its foundation, the interests and the wills of many joined together are required for its preservation. And thus did Romulus, who, in confiding the State to the care of the Senate, proved by his deeds that he had not been incited by any greed of power. If, however, he had not been alone in the beginning, it would have happened with him as with Ægidius, who, wishing to rule the Spartans once more in accordance with the laws of Lycurgus, was killed by the Ephors. Greater acumen had Cleomenes, who, comprehending the necessity of standing alone and taking advantage of the first opportunity, had all the Ephors put to death, after which he was able to re-establish the laws of Lycurgus, and would have succeeded in maintaining them, but for the power of the Macedonians and the weakness of the other Republics of Greece." [1]

Before the day of the Jesuits Machiavelli preached—and practised—the doctrine that the end justifies the means. Guicciardini might think that such a maxim was only to be discussed in a whisper among friends. Machiavelli bluntly wrote down that " where it is an absolute question of the welfare of our country, we must admit of no considerations of justice or injustice, of mercy or cruelty, of praise or ignominy; but putting all else aside, must adopt whatever course will serve its existence and preserve its liberty." [2] Half-measures he utterly abhorred. Men of his time occasionally hesitated between an adoption of the precepts of Christianity and those of political expediency. He never hesitated even for a single second. Christian morality, in his opinion, was absolutely out of the question. He was as earnest in his policy of Thorough as Strafford or Richelieu himself. " Good men," the Secretary instinctively felt, are unsuited for political crises, because they will not, as Sir Robert Walpole put it, " go the necessary lengths." The policy must never be undertaken half-heartedly. " The Romans avoided such measures, deeming them most pernicious; since government consists in nothing more than

---

[1] *Discorsi*, Bk. I., chap. ix.
[2] *Ibid.*, Bk. III., chap. xli.

in restraining subjects in such wise that they may not harm you, and hence you should either benefit them so as to win their liking, or curb them so that it may be impossible for them to work you harm."[1] Obviously there are three methods of ruling a subject and divided city: by murdering the party leaders, by removing them, or by winning them to peace. The last is the most unsafe method, the first the most safe. Since similar deeds are of their nature grand and generous, a feeble republic cannot perform them, and is so incapable of them that it can barely be led to adopt the second remedy. It is into such errors that the princes of his day always fell, owing to the weakness of that generation, caused by the slender education of its members, and their scanty knowledge of history, which made them deem ancient methods as partly inhuman and partly impossible.

In the judgment of Machiavelli the men of his generation entertained certain modern notions far removed from the truth, like that judgment of the wise men of his own city who said that it was advisable to hold Pistoia by means of factions, and Pisa by fortresses. They failed to perceive that fortresses were useless, and government by means of faction always a danger. In fact, when a Prince governs by such means, he has always one party against him; this party will seek aid from without, and thus at the first occasion he will have foes both within and without the walls. If, too, the government be a republic, it can find no better means of dividing itself—as happened to the Florentines, who, by seeking to reunite Pistoia by means of parties, only succeeded in creating division among themselves.[2]

Machiavelli proceeds to show the necessity of Thorough. Why did not Giovanni Paolo Baglioni seize Julius II., his cardinals, and their riches when he had the opportunity? Machiavelli answers his question by dilating on the stupidity of half-measures. " It could neither be goodness nor conscience that restrained him, since no pious respect could have a place in the bosom of a guilt-stained man who had seduced his own

---

[1] *Discorsi*, Bk. II., chap. xxiii.
[2] *Ibid.*, Bk. III., chap. xxvii.

sister and murdered his cousins and nephews in order to reign; but they arrived at the conclusion that men do not know how to be honourably bad, or perfectly good; and a completely wicked act has some greatness or some element of generosity, so that they cannot perform it. Thus Giovanni Paolo, who had not shrunk from incest and public parricide, could not, or rather dared not, even on a just occasion, accomplish an enterprise for which everyone would have admired his courage, and which would have procured him eternal remembrance as the first man to show prelates of how little account are those who live and rule after their fashion, and who would thereby have done a deed whose greatness would have surpassed every infamy and every danger that might have ensued from it." [1]

There are limits to the possibilities of force and fraud, as there are limits to everything else. Men, when they are actually rising in the world, are not prudent in relying on them. When they have definitely risen in rank, then they may. "Frequently," we read, "fraud and stratagem are also required; indeed, fraud alone may sometimes suffice, but never force alone. Xenophon, in his *Life of Cyrus*, teaches us the necessity of deceit; since the latter's first expedition against the King of Armenia was full of fraud, and succeeded by stratagem, not by violence. And the observance of this method is necessary not only to princes but likewise to republics, at least until their power be consolidated, as is proved by the example of the Romans." [2] Fraud is a hard necessity, it seems, in a practical world. Fraud is no necessity, it also seems, in an ideal world. Is there any connection between the ideal world and the practical world in which Machiavelli lives, moves, and has his being? None whatever. Therefore he calmly writes: "Although of its nature fraud is always detestable, yet its use may sometimes be necessary, and even, as in warfare, for instance, glorious. In fact, he who overcomes his enemies by fraud is no less extolled than he who overcomes them by force. Of which we may read so many examples that I need not quote any. . . . I

---

[1] *Discorsi*, Bk. I., chap. xxvii.
[2] *Ibid.*, Bk. II., chap. xiii.

will only say this, that I discern no glory in fraud that makes you break your pledged word and settled terms, for such fraud, even if it may sometimes win you states and kingdoms, as we have treated of above, will never win you glory. But I speak of the fraud that is directed against the enemy who does not trust you, and which really consists in your management of the war." [1]

Machiavelli was no mere Mephistopheles, for a twinge of conscience now and then came to him, as it came to Cavour when he remarked: " What a precious set of rascals we should be if we did for ourselves what we are doing for our State ! " When such a pang visited Machiavelli, he consoled himself with the thought of Richelieu: that he had no enemies save those of the State, and that the State at all costs—even the cost of morality—must be preserved. During the World War President Murray Butler declared he was a peace-at-any-price man. Astonished by this declaration the audience breathlessly waited, when Murray Butler completed his declaration: " The present price is war, and I am prepared to pay it." Machiavelli felt instinctively that he had no *locus standi* if there was not a State, and if there was not the means of its preservation, and he was prepared to pay any price for this preservation. The theory of the State mattered nothing to him: the fact of the State and its durability mattered everything. When the great *condottieri*, Giovanni dalle Bande Nere, lay dying, he bade a monk shrive him. " Father," he said, " you are a monk; you have lived as a monk; you have done well. I am a soldier; I have lived as a soldier; I have done well. Give me absolution." In some such spirit the author of *The Prince* stands before us, as Hobbes stands before us. Whatever men may say, they reserve their heart's contempt for the pedant and the hypocrite; their ready forgiveness for the man who refuses to deceive himself and yet in the dim light of a difficult world acts according to the light that is in him.

Suppose we ask such questions as the following: Is fraud ever honourable? Is intrigue ever the salvation of one's country? Is it right to be cruel in war in order to bring it to a more speedy

---

[1] *Discorsi*, Bk. III., chap. xi.

conclusion? It is safe to say that the average thoughtful man will return an indignant negative to all three questions. Suppose that instead of making them abstract we turn them into concrete queries—Is it right to delude our enemies during the course of war? Is it proper to employ spies? Is it permissible to employ the blockade in order to starve out the foe? To the three present queries we feel reasonably confident that the average thoughtful man will return a prompt affirmative, yet we have done but little more than to alter the abstract into the concrete. We delude our enemies when we possibly can, we employ spies during peace as well as during war, and we certainly employed the blockade, and the vast majority of our citizens approved—and still approves—of all three methods. We all cry out when we read in the cold print of Machiavelli's *Discorsi* or of his *Principe* that it is infamous that the statesman should play the fox as well as the lion. We cry out that we shall not, we must not, debase the moral coinage in any such manner, and we go on deluding our enemies in every way we can contrive. "Where there is no vision the people perish," so spoke an inspired prophet of old. The future lies with him and men like him, not with Machiavelli. For he who builds entirely on what is will never see what is to be. Machiavelli paid the penalty in a lifelong narrowness of vision. He gave up to party what was meant for mankind. Parties come and go, and he who makes Bibles of their fading script rarely sees far. At the same time, while we try to lift up our hearts to the level of the prophet, we must not forget the fact that the *sursum corda* is a matter not of to-day or to-morrow, but of many a to-morrow. The teaching of Machiavelli does debase the moral coinage, for it leaves us content with what is actually happening, and no idealist can ever be in such a position. The Italian thinker disbelieved in progress, and the State had not yet attained such a moral life as that which greets us to-day. For in the days of this publicist the State was simply emerging, and if it had neither a reality of being nor a sense of responsibility on the part of more than a handful of its citizens, the case against him does not altogether go by default.

During the year 1513 Machiavelli wrote the whole of *Il Principe* with a severely practical object. Its first conception runs back to the notion of forming a new State in Parma and Modena, or elsewhere, for Giuliano de' Medici. What he should do for the formation is of course what Cæsar Borgia had already done. On the death of Giuliano in 1516 the dedicatory epistle was addressed to Lorenzo de' Medici. Like so many other sixteenth-century books, it circulated in manuscript before it was published in 1532.

In the letter of dedication addressed to Lorenzo, Machiavelli says that, in the hope of winning his princely favour, he begs to offer him his most precious possession—namely, the knowledge of the deeds of great men, acquired by lengthened experience of modern and continued experience of ancient affairs. He therefore proposes to teach in a short time that which he (the author) had acquired only with infinite pains and trouble. Nor should he be charged with presumption, since exactly as mountains are best seen and delineated from the plain, and plains from mountains, so, to understand completely the people, it is necessary to be a prince, and to understand completely princes it is necessary to be one of the people.

Il Principe is far different from the loose texture of the *Discorsi*. It is short and compact, leaving no doubt on the mind of the reader as to what the author means. His plan may be right or it may be wrong, but of its wisdom he does not entertain the smallest doubt. Roman history falls into the background, to be largely replaced by the history of contemporary events. Julius Cæsar no longer struts across the pages; it is another Cæsar, the infamous Borgia. Alexander Borgia and Francesco Sforza, Ferdinand the Catholic and Louis XII.: these are the men who engross our attention. The pith of the book is to be found in the vision of a redeemed and united Italy, for a realist like Machiavelli has his dreams. If anyone denies his power of seeing visions, let him read the final exhortation to the tyrant transformed into the princely deliverer of his beloved Italy. The thinker desired office for no base reason, but for the altogether worthy one that he ached to take his share in the reconstruction of his own country. The master of the prudences and the imprudences of the political philosopher of the *Discorsi* reveals all the eagerness of a young man who is simply anxious to serve L'Italia.

In his *Discorsi* he has analysed republics, and now he turns his attention to principalities. There are the hereditary and the new principalities, and each receives treatment from a physician skilled in diagnosis and no less skilled in remedy. The sixth chapter leads us to an examination of the conduct of the new Prince of a new State, and we are bidden admire the rule of Cæsar Borgia. There is a detachment in the interpretation of the character of this ruffian in the pages of Bishop Creighton that provoked Lord Acton to righteous indignation. The historian must of course be fair-minded, but there is a fair-mindedness that betrays him into the slurring over of foul deeds. In spite of the advocacy of Creighton, we are entirely on the side of Acton in this controversy. Machiavelli himself shows none of that detachment of the Anglican of our day, and he sees the actions of the Duke as they actually were. Condemn Machiavellianism as loudly as we please, can we altogether resist the conviction that as our world is constituted there are sound constituents in it? Nevertheless " it seems good to me to propose him as an example to be imitated by all those who, through fortune and the arms of others, have attained to supreme command. For with his great mind and lofty ambitions it was not possible for him to govern otherwise." [1]

Let us imitate Cæsar Borgia, and let us also imitate such men as Agathocles and Oliverotto da Fermo. Agathocles, " having by his military excellence become Prætor of Syracuse, and having first sought the friendship of the Carthaginians, then assembled the people and the Senate, and caused all the Senators and popular leaders to be slaughtered by the soldiery. Thus his security was established, and he succeeded in everything by his own deeds. It certainly cannot be said that it is a virtue to murder citizens, betray friends, and be without faith; but if we were to consider the courage of Agathocles in affronting and escaping from danger, in enduring and overcoming

---

[1] *Il Principe*, chap. vii.

adversity, we can see no reason for judging him inferior to any most excellent captain. Nevertheless, his atrocious cruelty and inhumanity, together with his innumerable wickednesses, prevent us from ranking him among the most excellent of men; nor can we attribute to fortune or virtue that which he accomplished without either the one or the other." [1] Why, asks Machiavelli, did Agathocles remain in security when so many tyrants do not? The answer is quite simple: " All depends as to whether cruelties are well done or ill. Those may be said to be well done, if it may be permitted thus to speak of evil deeds, which are done suddenly for the sake of establishing a safe position, and not continued afterwards. Ill done are those which are also carried on afterwards. It is requisite from the first to calculate what cruelties are necessary, execute them at one stroke, and then reassure men's minds, otherwise you are forced to be always sword in hand. Injuries which are suddenly inflicted are less felt, and therefore give less offence, while nevertheless producing all the desired effect; benefits, on the contrary, should be conferred gradually, so that they be better relished." [1]

Oliverotto da Fermo was brought up by his uncle, Giovanni Fogliani. " He dedicated himself to arms, and becoming a very skilful commander, determined to seize Fermo. He therefore wrote to his uncle that he wished to enter the city with a hundred knights in order to exhibit his splendour, and his uncle gave him an honourable reception, and lodged him in his own palace. Oliverotto, having arranged the plot with his confidants, invited his uncle and all the first men of Fermo to a banquet, and then had them all murdered at the same moment. After which he rode through the city that was now his own, and would later have become a very formidable man had not the Duke of Valentinois caused him to be strangled." [1]

The main strength of the Prince lies in his army,[2] not in his people. The soldiery can repel the enemy abroad and the enemy at home. The nobles are not to be trusted,[3] for they

---

[1] *Il Principe*, chap. viii.
[2] *Ibid.*, chap. x. *Cf.* chap. xii. on the sources of strength of Cæsar Borgia.
[3] *Ibid.*, chap. ix.

desire to be the masters of the Sovereign. The consent of the people is far more vital to the Prince than that of the nobles. Without general good will the State cannot stand. *Inter arma silent leges* is not a maxim that commended itself to him, for he was accustomed to think that there was an intimate connection between good armies and good laws. Both, in his curious judgment, were simultaneously present or simultaneously absent. Thinkers of the calibre of Savonarola and Pontano had put a halo round the character of the Prince as well as of his office. Machiavelli rudely removes this halo. His Prince could dispense with religion and justice, with modesty and generosity. If he will preserve his power, he must set to work " to learn how to be dishonest, and to make use or not of this knowledge according to circumstances." [1] The Prince stands for the safety of the State, and everything must yield to its preservation. " Let him be heedless of the risks of infamy for such vices, without which it is hardly possible for him to save the State; for if all things be well considered, something that seems virtue will be found among them, to follow which would entail his ruin, and something that seems vice, to follow which will ensure his safety and prosperity." [1] " Might is right, right is might "—this is the first and last word of Machiavelli and, indeed, of Spinoza. The infallibility of the State—for to Machiavelli there is no distinction between Society and State —means that there is no law, moral or otherwise, above that of the State.

The Prince is all the time surveyed in a public capacity, and his prosperity is taken as synonymous with that of his principality. Should he be liberal or parsimonious? He should not be liberal, save with the spoils of war, for what he spends is not his own. Should he be cruel or clement, loved or feared? The answer is: " In general terms, it is certainly far better to be considered merciful; nevertheless, mercy must not be badly employed. Cæsar Borgia was esteemed a cruel man; nevertheless, that cruelty of his had set Romagna to rights, united it and brought it to a state of peace and good faith. And, in fact, he was more merciful than the Florentines, who, in order to

---

[1] *Il Principe*, chap. xv.

avoid cruelty, allowed Pistoia to be destroyed by factions. It would be better, were it possible, to be loved and feared at the same time; but as that is not possible, it is better to be feared, when you have to choose the alternative. Love is maintained by a bond of obligation, which, owing to the wickedness of human nature, is always broken whenever it clashes with private interest; but fear is maintained by a dread of punishment that never abandons you. Men love at their own pleasure, but fear at the pleasure of the Prince, who should therefore depend upon that which is his own, not upon that which is of others. Yet he may be feared without being hated if," he cynically adds, " he refrain from touching the property and womankind of his subjects, and if he avoid bloodshed excepting when there is good cause and manifest justification for it; inasmuch as men more easily forget the loss of their father than of their property. Besides which, when you begin to live by other's property there is no end to it, whereas occasions for bloodshed may seldom arise."[1]

Chapter eighteen is the notorious chapter on the question of keeping one's word or breaking it. A mind in which there was no disguise, he proceeded to unpack it on paper with a realism akin to Swift's. Of course it is, we learn, right to keep faith. Having paid this perfunctory tribute to virtue, he comes to business: "Nevertheless experience has proved in our own times that the princes who have achieved great deeds are those who have held good faith of small account, and have known how to bewilder men's brains by cunning, and in the end have succeeded better than those whose actions have been ruled by honour." In this chapter, in a spirit of sheer brutal empiricism, he proceeds to tell us that " there are two modes of fighting, one by law, the other by force: the first is proper to man, the second to brute beasts; and as the first is not always efficacious, so it is frequently necessary to recur to the second. Therefore a prince should know how to play both the beast and the man, as indeed the ancients tried to signify by the fable of Achilles educated by Chiron the centaur. A prince, then, should know how to assume the beast nature of both the

---

[1] *Il Principe*, chap. xvii.

fox and the lion, for the lion cannot defend himself against snares, nor the fox against wolves. . . . Those that merely play the lion do not understand the matter. Therefore a prudent lord neither could nor should observe faith, when such observance might be to his injury, and when the motives that caused him to promise it are at an end. Were all men good this precept would not be good; but since men are bad and would not keep faith with you, you are not bound to keep faith with them." Machiavelli dots the "i's" and strokes the "t's" of the eighteenth chapter by referring to examples within the ken of everyone. We condemn this chapter, and yet, as we condemn it, is there not the uneasy feeling that, things being what they are, the "good" man cannot always keep faith with the "bad"? "It is necessary to give a good colouring to your nature, and be a great dissembler and dissimulator, because men then readily allow themselves to be deceived. Alexander VI. did nothing but deceive, and thought of nothing else during the whole of his life, nor did any other man ever vow with stronger oaths to observe promises which he afterwards broke; nevertheless, he succeeded in everything, for he was well acquainted with this part of his work." What the Pope practised Hobbes preached when he wrote that at all times and in all circumstances the "cardinal virtue" of statesmen is "force and fraud." The relation between State and State, in the opinion of the philosopher of Malmesbury, was "the posture of gladiators."

On his return from Egypt, Napoleon was most careful to attend lectures, for the characteristic reason that Parisians must not suspect that he was merely a soldier. Similarly, the Prince cannot possess the virtues in public life, for what he wants is simply virtue, in the Italian sense. At the same time his subjects must not be aware of this aspect of his character. They ought to believe that he is as ideal in private life as Machiavelli wants him to be in public life. Put bluntly, such sentiments revolt us. Yet at bottom what he means, to some extent, is that a statesman—or indeed any public man—cannot always speak out. His utterance must be guarded, knowing full well at home that the opposition and the ambassadors are listening to every word he says, and, for the matter of that, to every word he does not choose to say. For the silences of a statesman are every whit as serious as the speech. Speech, to use Talleyrand's words, is given to conceal thought, but so too is silence. From another angle, respect must be officially given where there is no concurrence on the part of the individual paying this respect. An English judge shows deference to the temple of an Indian god, and he will even determine whether property has or has not been left to the god Vishnu. Napoleon paid deference to the Mohammedan creed, and rightly did so. Did he not overstep the line when he allowed the Mohammedan doctors to believe that he himself was seriously willing to consider his conversion to their faith? At the same time we feel bound to admit that it is quite likely that Machiavelli himself, in this instance, would have commended the worldly wisdom of the greatest genius in war the earth has ever seen.

Towards the conclusion of *The Prince* the people momentarily emerge. The Sovereign should encourage his citizens quietly to devote themselves to their own occupations and businesses. Trade is important, and so too is agriculture. There must be bread for the folk, and circuses are also desirable. In fact, industry and commerce, agriculture and festivities stand all pretty much on a level, for they all tend to reconcile the inhabitants to the rule exercised over them.[1] The attitude, in fact, is not unlike that of Quesnay, who argued: "Pauvres paysans, pauvre royaume; pauvre royaume, pauvre roi."

We have come to the conclusion of this slender volume. The world has not yet finished with a book written in 1513. The problems it raises are in their sphere as alive as those raised by Butler's *Analogy* are in theirs. A Philip II. and an Elizabeth in the sixteenth century, a Louis XIV. and a William III. in the seventeenth, a Marlborough and a Luxemburg in the eighteenth, a Napoleon and a Wellington in the nineteenth, a Ludendorff and a Lenin in the twentieth—all are occupied with the question of private and public morality, and we may conjecture that to the crack of doom *The Prince* will be a living issue. Men so anxious as Lord Morley and

---

[1] *Il Principe*, chap. xxi.

Lord Acton were to blend public and private morality, regret-
fully admit that Machiavelli is still, in spite of four centuries
since his death, with us. Lord Acton holds that " he is not a
vanishing type, but a constant and contemporary influence."
Lord Morley also maintains that he " represents certain living
forces in our actual world ; that Science, with its survival of the
fittest, unconsciously lends him illegitimate aid."

We all know that St Augustine stoutly held that, apart
from justice, great States were simply great robber-States. Some
have held that the waning of the Middle Ages is not to be
taken in any such year as, say, either 1348 or 1492, but simply
when the influence of the African Father reached vanishing-
point. From this attitude the *Discorsi* just as much as *Il
Principe* testify to the eclipse of St Augustine. The spirit of
Machiavelli, from this standpoint, marks therefore the conclusion of the Middle Ages. The law of God and the law of
Nature, the Bible and the tradition of the Church—all alike
are ignored. It is somewhat noteworthy that his contemporaries
were in no wise scandalised by his sentiments. Guicciardini
read both his important works, commenting on them, but he
is not in the least shocked. Neither Leo X. nor Clement VII.
felt that the teaching to which they listened was in the least
immoral. Curiously enough, Agostino Nifo di Sessa brought out
in 1523 a poor plagiarism of *The Prince*, and he suppressed
the last chapter, but not the eighteenth. Contemporaries saw
that Machiavelli was unscrupulous enough, but they also saw
that he aimed at one end—national greatness. To reach it
every means seemed fair in his eyes, but when his policy gained
it, it was not for himself. He never saw things as they might
be : he saw them as they were—as less than they were—and
hence, missing possibilities, he missed statesmanship. In truth,
he committed the fundamental blunder of a low-strung mind—
he mistook prudence for policy in the large sense of the term.

Charles V., his son and his courtiers all perused *The Prince*.
Catherine de' Medici brought it to France as Thomas
Cromwell brought it to England.[1] When murdered, both

---

[1] *Cf.* J. W. Horrocks, *Machiavelli in Tudor Political Opinion and Discussion*. Thesis of London University: unpublished, but in the Library of the University.

Henry III. and Henry IV. had it on their persons. Richelieu thought so warmly of it that he ordered Louis Machon, Archdeacon of Toul, to write a vigorous *apologia*. Like Leo X. and Clement VII., Sixtus V. pondered over its maxims, making a summary of them in his own handwriting. In truth, *The Prince* became the handbook of princes.[1] In spite of the attacks of Bodin and Campanella, the book made its way with statesmen, and a reader like Christina of Sweden was forced to admit that "there are certain ills only to be cured by blood and fire," a sentiment strikingly like Bismarck's blood and iron. For Harrington, Machiavelli is "the only politician of later ages." Frederick the Great wrote in his youth a *Réfutation du Prince de Machiavel*, and spent the rest of his life in adhering practically to its teaching. "The acts of the statesman," declared Napoleon, "which considered individually are so often blamed by the world, form an integral part of a great work, afterwards to be admired, and by which alone they are to be judged. Elevate your imagination, look farther before you, and you will see that the personages you deem violent, cruel, and what not, are only politicians knowing how to master their passions, and expert in calculating the effect of their actions. I have shed blood, and it was my duty; I may perhaps shed more, but without anger, and merely because blood-letting is one of the prescriptions of political surgery. I am the man of the State, I am the Revolution."[2] Nor is it to be forgotten that when Machiavelli penned his last chapter, in which he dreamed of the future of the land he loved, he wrote in his exhortation a tolerably precise description of that which, after the lapse of more than three and a half centuries, our fathers witnessed. His method was to found his views on experience combined with history. Cavour and Victor Emmanuel, Mazzini and Garibaldi proved that experience and history could execute the prophecy made by Machiavelli.

The invasion of Belgium by the Germans and Dr von Bethmann-Hollweg's palliation of that lawless deed have

---

[1] *Cf.* W. Alison Phillips, "The Influence of Machiavelli on Reformation in England," *The Nineteenth Century*, December 1896.

[2] *Mémoires de Madame de Rémusat*, i., p. 335.

raised anew the problem of the conduct of the Prince or of the people, for the people are as likely as any Prince to indulge in the view that necessity knows no law, and that they must hack their way through to some social reform.[1] They forgot Napoleon fell because he trusted in bayonets as Bismarck fell because he trusted in a false ideal of German greatness. Both lead to the " force and fraud " contemplated by Hobbes. In 1897 that singularly candid thinker, Henry Sidgwick, discussed the question in two penetrating essays. He concludes that so far as the past conduct of any foreign State shows that reciprocal fulfilment of international duty cannot reasonably be expected from it, then any other State that may have to deal with it must be allowed a corresponding extension of the right of self-protection, in the interest of humanity no less than in its own interest. " It must," he believes, " be allowed to anticipate attack which it has reasonable grounds for regarding as imminent, to meet wiles with wiles as well as force with force, and to be circumspect in the fulfilment of any compact it may make with such a State. But I do not regard this as constituting a fundamental difference between public and private morality; similar rights may have to be exceptionally claimed and exercised between man and man in the most orderly society that we have experience of; the difference is mainly in the degree of exceptionality of the claim." [2] Making allowance for the fact that Machiavelli wrote in 1513 and that Sidgwick wrote in 1897, is the gulf between them wholly unbridgeable? There is the Machiavelli of chapter eighteen of *The Prince*, but there is the Machiavelli who implored the sovereigns of his day to meditate on the days of Nerva and Marcus Aurelius. In those days of benevolent despots you perceive "a prince secure amidst a secure people. You will behold the Senate established in authority and magistrates in honour. The rich there will enjoy their own riches; virtue and nobility are exalted; peace and goodness

[1] *Cf.* A. Schmidt, *N. Machiavelli und die allgemeine Staatslehre der Gegenwart.*
[2] I quote from *National and International Right and Wrong*, p. 46, a reprint from Sidgwick's *Practical Ethics.*

prevail; rancour, licence, corruption and ambition are extinguished. Those were the golden times in which each one could hold and defend his own opinion. Then did the world triumph, for the Prince was full of reverence and glory, the people of love and confidence. Glance, then, at the state of things under the other emperors, and you shall see terrible wars, discords and seditions; cruelty in peace and in war; princes slain by the sword, civil dissensions, foreign wars; a sorrowful Italy torn by misfortune, with her cities ravaged and ruined. You shall see Rome burnt, the Capitol destroyed by the citizens, the ancient temples desolate, their ceremonies neglected, the town filled with adulterers, the sea covered with exiles, her rocks stained with blood. . . . You shall see informers rewarded, slaves seduced against their masters, servants against their patron; while those that have no enemies are persecuted by their friends. Then you will know what Rome, Italy and the world owed to Cæsar. . . . Indeed, if a prince seek worldly glory, he should desire to rule a corrupt city: not to spoil it like Cæsar, but to re-order it like Romulus." [1]

REFERENCES

BIBLIOGRAPHIES

Burd, L. A., *Cambridge Modern History*, vol. i., pp. 719-726, Cambridge, 1902.

Mohl, R. von, *Geschichte und Literatur der Staatswissenschaften*, iii., p. 521 (for the most complete survey of Machiavellian literature up to 1858), Erlangen, 1855-1858.

BOOKS

Acton, Lord, *History of Freedom and Other Essays*, London, 1907.

Burd, L. A., *Il Principe di N. Machiavelli*, edited by L. A. Burd, with an Introduction by Lord Acton, Oxford, 1891.

Couzinet, L., *" Le Prince" de Machiavel et la Théorie de l'Absolutisme*, Paris, 1910.

Ferrari, G., *Machiavel, Juge des Révolutions de Notre Temps*, Paris, 1849.

Ferrari, J., *Histoire de la Raison d'État*, Paris, 1860.

---

[1] *Discorsi*, I., chap. x.

REFERENCES

Knies, C. G. A., *Niccolò Machiavelli als volkswirthschaftlicher Schrift-steller*. *Zeitschrift für die gesammte Staatswissenschaft*, Tübingen, 1852.

Lavollée, R., *La Morale dans l'Histoire*, Paris, 1852.

Leo, H., *Studien und Skizzen zu einer Naturlehre des Staates*, Halle, 1833.

Macaulay, Lord, " Essay on Machiavelli," *Edinburgh Review*, March 1827.

Mackintosh, Sir J., " On the Writings of Machiavel," *Miscellaneous Works*, London, 1846.

Maulde la Clavière, M. A. R. de, *La Diplomatie au Temps de Machiavel*, Paris, 1892.

Meinecke, F., *Die Idee der Staatsräson*. München and Berlin, 1924.

Morley, Lord, *Machiavelli*, London, 1897.

Mundt, T., *Machiavelli und der Gang der Europäischen Politik*, Leipzig, 1853.

Nourrisson, J. F., *Machiavel*, Paris, 1883.

Owen, J., *The Skeptics of the Italian Renaissance*, London, 1893.

Quinet, E., *Les Révolutions d'Italie*, Paris, 1843.

Sclopis, F., " Montesquieu et Machiavel," *Révue historique du Droit français et étranger*, vol. ii., Paris, 1856.

Sidgwick, H., *Practical Ethics*, London, 1897.

Symonds, J. A., *The Age of the Despots*, London, 1875.

Toffanin, G., *Machiavelli il " Tacitismo,"* Padova, 1922.

Tommasini, O., *La Vita e gli Scritti di Niccolò Machiavelli nella loro relazione col Machiavellismo*, Torino, 1883. (There is a bibliography.)

Venedy, J., *Machiavel, Montesquieu, und Rousseau*, Berlin, 1850.

Villari, P., *Niccolò Machiavelli e i suoi Tempi illustrati con nuovi documenti*, Milano, 1895-1897.

Waille, V., *Machiavel en France*, Paris, 1884.

CHAPTER II

LUTHER AND THE STATE CHURCH

ONE of the astonishing matters in the world of thought is to note the different routes by which men travel to the same conclusions. To Machiavelli the State is a purely human institution, whereas to Martin Luther (1483-1546) it is a divine institution. Differing so fundamentally in their main idea, it is difficult to think of any agreement between them. At bottom the amazing matter is that the outcome of the labours of both was the supremacy of the Sovereign. Machiavelli never dreams of resorting to Holy Writ or the Fathers for proof of his conceptions, and Luther constantly resorts to both sources. The methods and the illustrations of the two differ by worlds, and the singular result is the unanimity with which they exalt the State. They essayed the same task, each in accord with his own talent.

To the classics Luther thought that he owed little, confessing more than once, " I am only a barbarian." [1] He is no intellectual Melchizedek. His debt, however, was greater than he imagined.[2] Undergraduates imbued with the spirit of humanism had been in his circle, and he could not escape their influence. He knew well the Latin poets and orators, placing Virgil first in his regard. Greek he did not study till he commenced it with Philip Melanchthon in 1518, and he was never familiar with it. Melanchthon has been called the Preceptor of Germany : he was also the Preceptor of Luther. He failed to give his friend that love of Greek which meant so much to him, for Luther to the last day he lived preferred the Vulgate to the Greek New Testament. He possessed a bowing acquaintance with the *Phædo* of Plato : the *Ethics* and the *Physics* of Aristotle he knew, though he knew both in a Latin dress. In fact the only book he was familiar with in the original was

---

[1] Oergel, *Vom jungen Luther*, 105-113, 131.

[2] Luther's *Briefe* (W. and S.), 1, 22, 49, 54f., 61ff., 94, 98, 134f., 138, 140, 426 ; his *Briefwechsel* (Burkhardt), 3ff. ; *Colloquia*, (B.), 1, 262 ; *Werke*, Erl. ed., xxv. 338f.

the *Iliad*. The Promethean philosophy of rebellion was not in his thoughts. Sympathy with the past is as little in his nature as it is in Machiavelli's. To some of us the Stoics are feeling after God if haply they may find Him : to Luther they are guilty of a supreme " piece of foolishness." It is more intelligible that even in 1511 he regards Aristotle as a " relater of fables."

Slightly changing the Voltairean remark, we may place it in the mouth of St Augustine, " L'Église, c'est moi," for these words represent the vast and permanent influence of the African thinker. Since the twelfth century his work had occasionally been eclipsed till Luther gave it fresh life. St Augustine, like Bishop Lightfoot, made his knowledge definite, giving it rigid form. Shades of meaning were as abhorrent to him as they were to Luther. Neither man could see that a thing is not the less real because its limits cannot be accurately defined. A hill is a hill and a plain is a plain though one cannot fix the point where the hill merges into the plain. George Eliot thought the highest lot was to possess definite beliefs, and such a lot was Luther's. Legality characterised the Augustinian theology just as it came to characterise the Lutheran and the Calvinist. John Austin allowed that the earthly sovereign might commit iniquity but not injustice. To St Augustine, God was an irresponsible sovereign. To Luther this conception was a revelation he embraced with enthusiasm. His theology is more life than learning, more creed than comprehension, more narrow light than broad liberty.

In 1511 Luther went on a mission to Rome, and he saw the sights of the capital of Christendom with rapture. A change had passed over it of which he was unaware, though it was a change pregnant with far-reaching consequences on the work of his life. In 1492 Columbus had pierced the veil which concealed another continent from the eyes of men, and at once the process of transformation began. The centre of Europe had been all-important, whereas now the circumference of the continent assumed this pride of place. As sixteen centuries before Corinth and Athens had yielded their position to Rome and Ostia, so now Venice and Genoa fell before the increasing sway of Cadiz and Lagos. It was the same in the north. The Atlantic immediately dominated the new situation, leaving the Baltic and the Mediterranean no more than inland lakes. Men had looked ecclesiastically and commercially to the south, whereas now they were to look to the north and the west. Westward ran the course of commerce from Lubeck and Stralsund to Amsterdam and Bristol. The direction of the expansion has, on the whole, been constantly westward, as Berkeley indicates in his famous poem. The fall of Constantinople in 1453 was felt only forty years afterwards in the then remote continent of North America, east and west thus beginning to realise the future intimacy of the union between them. Every great movement, widening the geographical outlook of a people, at the same time widens their intellectual and political outlook. The Crusades effected this important service for the Middle Ages, and the colonisation of America effected it for the seventeenth and succeeding centuries. It is, indeed, difficult not to speak of such an event as the discovery of America almost exclusively in terms of geography. Yet the moment men completely realised there was another continent where the eagle of the Holy Roman Empire had never flown, that moment the whole structure of mediævalism was undermined. Columbus discovered a new world beyond, and Copernicus announced new worlds above. Scarcely any discovery of the nineteenth century, not even Darwin's, had such far-reaching effects as these two which made the Reformation inevitable.

After the year 1492 the leadership of Europe shifted decisively from the south to the north. As Hegel put it, the crossing of the Alps by Julius Cæsar was an event of the same magnitude as the crossing of the Atlantic by Columbus. By both events new spheres were opened out for peoples ready to unfold capacities which were pressing for development. The shores of the Ægean and the Adriatic became what the Breton coast had long been. Cadiz, Lisbon, Cherbourg, Antwerp, Rotterdam, Hamburg, Plymouth and Bristol were the gates through which the busy traffic poured. The tie of Germany, from the tenth to the fifteenth century, had been with Italy—that is, with the south. Henceforth the tie was with the north, and with this transfer the rise of Prussia became possible. The cities of Germany soon became aware how closely their fortunes were to be bound up with the success of the Reformation. The boll that has sent forth so many twigs and branches was once a twig itself.

Momentous as the revolution in the world of nature, there was a revolution in the world of mind no less momentous. For Luther, horrified by the indulgences Tetzel was selling, was reaching conclusions painfully at variance with accepted opinion.[1] As the place of the Church recedes from his mental horizon, that of the Council emerges. Hegel brings the manuscript of his *Phaenomenology* to Jena the very day of the battle between the French and the Prussians, and is surprised to hear that there is a war in progress. The investigation of his thought may presumably be studied *in vacuo*. The thought of Luther differs by worlds. It is largely conditioned by circumstance, for he was as wonderful an opportunist as Cromwell. No one, held the English Puritan, goes so far as he who does not know whither he is going. Luther goes far for precisely this reason; he never asks to see the distant scene as one step is enough for him. From St Augustine he had learned that the centre of dogma is a proper conception of sin. The African theologian had described as penetratingly the City of the Devil as the City of God, and here Luther followed him. The centre of the pupil's dogmatic position was the irremediable corruption of man. Logically the matter was clear to his mind. Sin, justification and faith were all intimately bound together. The fulfilment of God's commands is beyond the evil nature of man. Is Christianity then a doctrine of despair? This despair is to Luther the very condition of our salvation. Our powerlessness proves the necessity of our redemption. There is nothing good in us: we possess no merits of our own. Christianity, however, has accomplished all, has won all for us. The Son of Man died that the sons of men might become the Sons of God. Faith in God

---

[1] In *Luther's Staatsauffassung* (1917), H. Jordan has gathered the political utterances of the reformer in handy form. *Cf.* F. Meinecke, *Luther über christlichen Geminwesen und christlichen Staat, Historische Zeitschrift*, Band 121, p. 1ff. (1920).

is " a simple obedience of the Spirit." [1] This faith does not proceed from us, and works apart from us our salvation. Man is nothing, God is everything. He held with all his might that it is faith and faith alone which saves us.[2] Faith in its turn produces works, just as the tree bears fruit, though these works do not and cannot justify or save a man, simply proving " our inward justice." In a word, faith is in our souls a living law through which God thinks, acts, works in us, substituting His justice for ours, His life for ours, and revealing to us, in the depths of our misery, our healing. In truth Luther is no longer a humanist in 1516, he is no longer a mystic : he is a theologian with a system, which as effectually shook Europe one way as Columbus and Copernicus shook it another way.

Scholars—*e.g.* Denifle—have analysed the diverse and heterogeneous elements in the doctrines of Luther. They justly deny his originality, showing where he borrowed from St Paul and St Augustine, from Ockham or Hus, from Carlstadt or Erasmus. They sometimes forget that when he made these borrowings his own, he re-created them, welding them in the flame of his fiery zeal. The ideas of Rousseau are to be read substantially in Montaigne and in Locke. Nevertheless, Rousseau invested them with the shirt of Nessus, rendering them a burning force. Originality is of the highest importance : so too are the energy and the initiative which oblige men to recognise the leadership of the man of action, who is sometimes a thinker. " La cœur a ses raisons," wrote Pascal in a pregnant saying, " que la raison ne connoît point," [3] and the saying is eminently true of Luther. " Credo in Newmannum " was once a watchword which inspired a movement. " Credo in Lutherum " was once a watchword which inspired a movement in another age. For the German reformer had a genius for action. He united two qualities, and these were religious enthusiasm and that power for action which imposed his views on those with whom he came into contact. His ardent and inflexible soul,

---

[1] *Ficker,* ii., p. 275 ; cf. *ibid.,* ii., p. 332.
[2] *Ibid.,* i., pp. 114, 324 ; cf. *ibid.,* ii., p. 124.
[3] *Pensées* (1829 ed.), p. 32.

inspired by enthusiastic mysticism, gave him an incomparable driving force, whose relentlessness crushed all opposition.

At the great crises of her history Germany has never lacked able men : she has sorely lacked statesmen. In 1520 neither Luther nor Melanchthon was fitted to control the forces they had called into existence. Luther was a leader of opposition *against* Rome : he was not a statesman *for* a new order. To whom was he to turn? The thoughtful Jakob Wimpheling was old and out of sympathy with the new school of reform. There were scholars like Mutianus and such members of his circle as Georg Spalatin, Eoban of Hesse and Crotus Rubianus. There were humanists like Johann Reuchlin and Ulrich von Hutten ; there were antiquarians like Conrad Peutinger ; there were satirists like Sebastian Brandt and Thomas Murner ; there were artists like Albrecht Dürer ; there were citizens like Wilibald Pirkheimer ; there were revolutionaries like Andreas Bodenstein von Carlstadt ; and there were rulers like Frederick the Wise. Was there a statesman in their ranks? The annals of the Diet attest the fact that some of its members possessed as little experience as the makers of the French Revolution. The truth is, the Reformation drifted without statesmanlike guidance from its leading spirit. Feeling within Luther was red-hot, and words gushed forth like an impetuous current, but the brain did not work as if packed in ice. As Erasmus indicated, the judgment of the reformer was not restrained. Gustavus Adolphus, Richelieu and Bismarck perceived the limits within which their tasks were to be completed. It is a rare sense, one of the rarest, and it was denied Luther. It is possible that Philip of Hesse might in 1520 have grasped this sense, had he been old enough ; but then he was only fifteen years of age.

The three most important pamphlets which, next to his translation of the Bible, Luther ever wrote were composed during the last half of the memorable year 1520. These are *To the Christian Nobility of the German Nation on the Improvement of the Christian Estate*,[1] *A Prelude on the*

---

[1] *Werke* (Weimar ed.), vi., pp. 381-469 ; Erl. ed., xxxi., pp. 277-360. *An den christlichen Adel deutschen Nation vom des christlichen Standes Besserung* (ed. K. Benrath, Halle, 1884).

Babylonian Captivity of the Church, and *On the Freedom of a Christian Man*. These little quarto pamphlets are now brown and worm-eaten, each with its engraved and allegorical title page. Then they came fresh from that new invention, the printing press, voicing plainly in town and country, in farm and workshop, the dimly felt religious aspirations, and the no less deeply felt political discontents. Luther wrote rapidly, with little care for style and with no ambition for literary renown. The first pamphlet appeared about the middle of August, and by the eighteenth no less than four thousand copies were already in circulation. The warning of Staupitz not to publish it arrived too late.

The author's friends, the Knights, were loud in their demand for its appearance. Luther gave a detailed description of the Roman exactions, setting forth, as Machiavelli had done, the argument that Germany—and indeed other countries—was being exploited on the pretext that contributions were required for the administration of the Church. As Savonarola assailed the political interests of the Papacy, so Luther assailed the economic. The religious attacks of either would have been ignored : their practical attacks could not be. When Pompanazzi attacked the conception of the immortality of the soul, he did so purely as an academic argument. He was careful to point out that all he wrote he submitted to the judgment of the Apostolic See. As his belief did not affect the purse of the Pope, it was allowed freedom of expression.

At Rome everything was for sale : livings, dignities, cardinalates, the Papacy itself, changing hands for money. When these are not sold, it is possible to sell pardon for sins. There is a regular scale. The fine for adultery is one hundred and fifty ducats, for the murder of two daughters eight hundred ducats, and so on. " The Lord," remarked an official at the Court of Innocent VIII., who had bought his tiara, " does not will the death of a sinner ; he wills that he shall live and shall pay." Nicolas V., a Mæcenas if ever there was one, wore diamonds and pearls over the crown and thorns of the Redeemer. His sixteenth-century successor was a far different type. When Michelangelo was finishing the statue of Julius II.

he represented the Pontiff with one of his hands raised either for blessing or cursing. The sculptor inquired what he was to put in the other hand. Was he to carve a book ? "Place a sword there," answered Julius II., "I do not know letters." The popes of the first half of the sixteenth century, with the honourable exception of Adrian VI., have the sword in their hand on behalf of their Italian States and of the interests of their children. They are chiefs of principalities, not heads of the Church, requiring incessant supplies of money for the furtherance of their secular interests. Men spoke of the avarice of the Church, the sensuality of the Church, the ambition of the Church, because these were the matters they either saw or heard. Leo X. abdicated the government of souls in favour of letters and learned men, who pay in homage what others pay in money.

Erasmus wrote for princes and learned men, and he scarcely moved the people. They saw that simony was rampant in the Church, though humanistic disputes never crossed their horizon. They neither read nor wrote. They sowed their corn, they planted their vine, they manufactured their goods—and they resented the exaction of the ecclesiastical tax-gatherer.[1] It was indeed as an orthodox member of the Church that Luther had attacked Tetzel, who was acquiring riches by the dissemination of heretical doctrine. Such devoted supporters of the Church as Eck, Wimpheling, Karl von Bodmann, Archbishop Henneberg of Mayence and Duke George of Saxony felt that Rome

---

[1] On the financial burden born by Germany *cf.* Aschenberg, *Niderrheinische Blatter* (Dortmund, 1801), i., pp. 295-301 ; Bezold, p. 88ff. ; Dieckhoff, pp. 242-256 ; Eichmann, *Recursus ab abusu* (Berlin, 1903), p. 76ff. ; Evers, *Martin Luther*, ii., p. 447ff. ; Finke, 5ff. ; Förstemann, i., pp. 62-64 ; Gebhardt, *Die Gravamina*, pp. 95ff., 112ff. ; Gemeiner, iv., p. 132 : Hefele-Hergenröther, viii., p. 792 ; ix., pp. 89-93 ; Hutten, *Oratio dissuasoria* (in *Hutteni Opera*, ed. Böcking), v., p. 168ff. and *Onus ecclesia* (*ibid.*, c. 23) ; Janssen, *Frankfurts Reichskorrespondenz*, ii., pp. 978ff., 983 ; *Janssen-Pastor*, i., pp. 18, 741ff. ; ii., pp. 18, 170ff. ; Kalkoff, *Alexander*, pp. 218-219 ; May, *Albrecht II.*, i., p. 159 ; A. O. Meyer, p. 70ff. ; Paulus, *Tetzel*, 149 ; Riffel, i. pp. 123-134 ; Sanuto, xxiv., pp. 105, 448 ; Sinnacher, vii., p. 263 ; Theiner, *Mon. Pol.*, p. 390ff. ; Ulmann, ii., p. 711 ; Varrentrap, p. 48 ; Werner, p. 29ff. ; Canon Xanten, *Codex Trier Sachen und Briefschaften*, fol. 27-39.

was too covetous. The Emperor Maximilian had sorrowfully confessed that the Roman curia drew from Germany a revenue a hundredfold greater than his own. " Omnia Romæ Venalia " was as true in Luther's time as in Jugurtha's. In Ulrich von Hutten's *Vadiscus, seu Trias Romana*, this line of argument is fiercely wrought out. In Saxony, as in France on the eve of the Revolution, the taxes were light, and this lightness made the peasant resent the Roman exactions all the more. Luther cleverly took advantage of this resentment, and interlaced political and religious motives in the fashion which made Ranke regard this interlacing as the most striking feature of the sixteenth century. Just as Innocent III. failed because he found himself opposed to the rising forces of nationality, so Leo failed, and for precisely the same reason. The fact that he appealed to the Christian nobility of the German nation showed how conscious Luther was that he could reckon on the support of the natural leaders of his fellow-countrymen. It is sometimes remarked that few states or dynasties have accomplished more for themselves than Prussia and the Hohenzollerns ; and few have been more conspicuously the heirs of time and the beneficiaries of circumstance. What is true of Prussia and the Hohenzollerns is also true of Luther and the Reformation. The time was ripe, the circumstance was propitious, and his genius gave power to both time and circumstance.

As Machiavelli freed the State from considerations of moral law, Luther likewise freed it from the control of the Church. Is it not the duty of the State, he argued, to check and control all forms of combination injuring the welfare of the people? Thus he won the sympathy of the multitude by his stern attitude to capitalism, luxury and immorality.

The claims of the Papacy rested in no small degree on the Old Testament, and in his appeal " To the Christian Nobility of the German Nation "[1] Luther resorts to the New Testament

---

[1] Schmoller, *Geschichte der nationalökon, Ansichten in Deutschland während der Reformations-periode* (1861), pp. 36, 39, 102ff., 228f. ; Kolde, *Luther*, i., p. 256 ; A. E. Berger, *Luther*, i., p. 325 ; F. v. Bezold, *Geschichte der deutschen Reformation*, p. 369 ; Evers, iii., pp. 497-521.

in order to prove the priesthood of all believers.[1] He uses the Old Testament, just as Dante used it in his *De Monarchia*, to attack the claim of the Church that, because the Pope crowns the Holy Roman Emperor, therefore the head of the State is subject to the head of the Church. Just as the Israelites were delivered from the Egyptians, just as they were delivered from the might of Babylon, so all the reformers would be delivered from the power of Rome. The Romanists had, in effect, shut themselves within three walls. First, they said the temporal power had no rights over them; second, the Scriptures could be expounded only by the Pope; and third, no one but the Pope could summon a Council. Even if Hus had been wrong in his beliefs, " heretics must be conquered with the pen and not with fire. If to conquer with fire were an art, the executioners would be the most learned doctors on earth." He proceeds to level the three walls of the foundations, praising the Greeks and all who had separated themselves from this Babylon. The element of negation is then prominent in his pamphlet. It is an element not only in the Reformation, but also in every revolution ever made. Did not the constitutionalists of 1789 begin by demolishing feudalism before they could raise the building of fraternity and equality?

The patriot and the prophet are impossible to dissociate in the composition of the work. There is rage against the offences committed by the Papacy, and there is rage against the offences committed by the same authority against his beloved land. In his desire to secure a foundation for his evangel he appeals to the rulers who had listened to it. As the early Fathers asserted the rights of the State, so he followed in their train. The theory of sovereignty that Innocent IV. invented on behalf of the papal monarchy he turns to the interests of the German Prince.

The attitude of Luther towards the authority of the State is more intelligible if we consider the position the Fathers adopted towards it. Their point of view was influenced by Seneca, who regarded coercive government as due to the

---

[1] A. Harnack, *Dogmengesch.*, III. iv., p. 830; Maurenbrecher, *Studien und Skizzen*, pp. 342-347.

increase of vice.[1] Persecuted as the Christians were in the
first century, Clement of Rome directs the Corinthians to submit themselves to their " rulers and governors upon earth." [2]
Polycarp meets Ignatius on his way to martyrdom, still the
latter asks his followers to " pray also for kings and powers
and princes and for them that persecute you and hate you." [3]
The early liturgies attest how faithfully these directions were
obeyed.[4] The apologists naturally employed arguments drawn
from this obedience in their defence.[5] Irenæus follows, perhaps
unconsciously, Seneca, and anticipates the Fathers of the sixth
and seventh centuries in looking on government as the consequence of man's corruption and as a remedy for this corruption. " They [*i.e.* men] might attain to some degree of justice,
and exercise mutual forbearance, through dread of the sword
plainly set before them." [6] Government to man in a state of
innocence is dispensable: to man in a fallen state it is indispensable. He refers to the verse in Proverbs: " By me
kings reign, and princes administer justice," [7] and the views
of St Paul in the Epistle to the Romans: " Let every soul be
subject unto the higher powers. For there is no power but of
God: the powers that be are ordained of God." [8] Passages like
these satisfy him that authority ultimately comes from God,
that He subjected men to the rule of their fellow-men in order
to compel them to some measure of righteousness and just
dealing. How far this is removed from the mediæval conception is obvious in the pages of St Thomas Aquinas, who,
in regarding government as the necessary instrument of perfection for mankind, approximates to the classical ideal.[9] At
the end of the second century Irenæus plainly considers civil
authority binding on all. If the ruler is unjust, God will punish
him: resistance is unlawful.

---

[1] Cf. *Epist.*, 90, § 38ff., § 46.

[2] Clem., lx., lxi.

[3] Polyc., *Ad Phil.*, xii.   [4] Const., *Ap.*, viii. 12.

[5] Just. Mart., *Apologia*, i. 17; Tertullian, *Apologia*, 30, 39; *Ad Scap.*, 2;
Arnob., iv. 36; Athenagoras, *De Leg.*, xxvii.; Dion. Alex., *Ap. Eus.*, H. E.,
vii., xi.; Theophilus, i. 11.

[6] *Adv. Hær.*, v. 24.   [7] Prov. viii. 15.

[8] Rom. xiii. 1.   [9] Cf. *De Regimine Principum*, passim.

Though Theophilus of Antioch refuses to worship the king, still he is to be " reverenced with lawful honour, for he is not a god but a man appointed by God, not to be worshipped but to be judged justly." For in some respect his stewardship is committed to him by God.[1] It may well be that he was as suspicious of the lawlessness of the Christian community— or at least a section of it—as Luther was of the anarchical tendencies of the Anabaptists. Justin Martyr, another second-century writer, insists that Christ ordered His followers to pay their taxes, and quotes His words on the duty of rendering to Cæsar the things which are Cæsar's. For while they can only worship God, in all other ways they gladly serve their rulers.[2]

There is much in common between the thought of Theophilus of Antioch and Clement of Alexandria, who considers that the Sovereign ought to rule according to the laws.[3] To the same school of thought belong the ideas of Origen, who thinks that the Church is more divine and more necessary than the State, justifying the refusal of some Christians to serve in the army or in public offices.[4] The old conception, however, prevails in St Optatus of Milevis, who has to face the results of the Donatist schism in North Africa. The Church is torn in twain. What is more natural or more obvious than to confront the schismatics with the authority of the Empire? Of course the Donatists protested that the Emperor stood outside matters ecclesiastical. Against this protest Optatus set the conception that the ruler is the representative of God on earth. Did not St Paul command Christian men to offer up prayers for kings and those set in authority? It is quite true that the Empire is not in the Church, nevertheless to Optatus as to Ambrose the Church is in the Empire. There is no one over the Emperor save God only, who made him Emperor.[5] The day when Constantine was to be the patron and protector of the Church was in sight, and the protests of Donatus were unavailing.

---

[1] *Ad Autolycum*, i. 11.　　　　　　　　　　　　[2] *First Apology*, 17.
[3] *Strom.*, i. 24. *Cf.* St Thomas Aquinas, *Summa Prima Secunda*, qu. xc.
[4] *Contra Celsum*, viii. 73-75.
[5] *De Schisma Donatistarum*, iii. 3 ; Ambrose, *Epist.*, xxi. 36 ; Enarr. in Ps. xxvii. 43.

The fall of Adam dominated the thought of St Ambrose, who conceives that the task of government is divine, for it is the sovereign remedy for sin. According to him the authority of rulers is imposed on the foolish in order that they, no matter how unwillingly, may obey the wise.[1] The Emperor is the son of the Church.[2] It is an easy transition to St Augustine, who entertains the same conception of the functions of the State.[3] Like St Optatus, he firmly holds that the ruler is the representative of God. True, there are emperors as evil as Nero, but even such as he receive their power through the providence of God, when He judges that any nation may stand in need of such governors.[4] The State may be a *grande latrocinium*. It may also, when Christian, merge itself in the Church.[5] The civil power thereby becomes the servant of the Church, and its officers obey her behests. Indeed the ecclesiastical society takes the place of the *civitas superna*,[6] and becomes the only earthly *civitas*.[7]

The conception that the ruler represents God grows. To Ambrosiaster the King is reverenced on earth as the " Vicar of God." He has " the image of God as the bishop has that of Christ."[8] Clearly to this writer the Sovereign receives his authority directly from God himself, a standpoint familiar to Luther. From the time of Constantine, the Emperor was regarded as invested with a certain spiritual character and authority.[9] He was acknowledged, at least by those who considered him orthodox, to possess the right of taking a prominent part in ecclesiastical affairs, of summoning councils, issuing edicts, proscribing heresy, and imposing the true faith on his subjects by his sovereign word. His person, acts, letters were

---

[1] *Epist.*, xxxvii. 8.
[2] *Ibid.*, xxi. 36; Enarr. in Ps. xxxvii. 43.
[3] *Quar. Prop. ex Ep. ad Rom.*, 72; *De Civi. Dei*, xix. 5.
[4] *De Civi. Dei*, v. 19, 21.
[5] *Epist.*, cv. 5, 6.
[6] *Serm.*, ccxiv. 11.
[7] *Epist.*, cxxxvi. 16, 17; cf. *De Civi. Dei*, xix. and xxi.
[8] Ambrosiaster (Pseudo-Aug.), *Quæstiones Veteris et Novi Testamenti*, xci. 35.
[9] Euseb., *De Vita Constant.*, i. 44; iii. 10; Mansi, xi. 6; xii. 976.

characterised as " sacred "; his office was a Divine creation. Did not his authority spring directly from the Deity?

No one was more impressed by the feeling of reverence for the Emperor than Gregory the Great was. In the spirit of Cicero,[1] he holds that men are equal, but they are different in condition as a result of sin. As all men do not live equally well, one man must be ruled by another; there is a brutal tendency in mankind that can only be repressed by fear.[2] In the same fashion as both St Augustine and St Isidore of Seville he wrestles with the problem of the bad ruler.[3] To Gregory the sovereign was the Lord's anointed, God's earthly representative. What, however, was the duty of the subject if the Emperor did not live in conformity to his high calling? To him the path of duty was plain. The ruler, good or evil, must be reverenced as the minister of God, who bore His sword. Is any proof of this standpoint required? In that case the Old Testament furnishes clear guidance. Was not Saul an evil king? Was not David a good subject? And yet did not David refuse to lay his hand on the Lord's anointed? Did he not even repent that he cut off the hem of Saul's garment? Good subjects therefore will not even criticise rashly or violently the conduct of bad rulers; for to resist or offend against a ruler is to offend against God, who has set him over men.[4] That this is no casual *obiter dictum* is evident from his treatise on the Book of Job, where he urges the same attitude on the part of the subject. At the same time Gregory was clear that the Bishop of Rome, as the successor of St Peter, was the supremely constituted authority in the Church. The two conceptions are irreconcilable, but this no more distressed him than it did Cyprian. There are few Carlstadts in the world, and perhaps it is as well for the happiness of mankind.

Gregory the Great saw no opposition between Ecclesia and Republica, though he plainly perceived the opposition between

---

[1] *De Leg.*, I. x, 28; xii, 33.
[2] *Exp. Mor.* in Job xxi. 15.
[3] *Libri Moralium* in Job xxv. 16.
[4] *Regulæ Pastoris*, iii. 4; *Mor.*, xxii. 56; xxv. 34ff. *Cf.* Gregory of Tours, *Hist. Fran.*, v. 19.

Ecclesia and Sæculum, or the world. Cæsar was to confine himself to the things which were Cæsar's. His only concern with the things of God was when the law and order of the Church were exposed to danger.[1] Was action to be taken against the pagans, the heretics or even against ecclesiastics?[2] The Emperor hastened to the assistance of Gregory when his assistance was invoked.[3] There was—there always is—a delicate border-line. The Church plainly had a duty towards the poor, the weak and the oppressed.[4] If an imperial officer was guilty of grave crime, she no less plainly felt bound to interfere. Still, Gregory considered that bishops ought not to meddle with matters belonging to the jurisdiction of Cæsar.[5] The character of Gregory forms a curious contradiction. At times he was as independent in spirit as Luther himself, addressing the Emperor in terms the reformer scarcely exceeded in addressing Leo X. In life, if not in his study, Gregory was as subservient as any Lutheran pastor was to his Prince. In this sense it is not too much to say that Gregory the Great and Luther were *servi servorum* of man, not of God.

The secular estates, already covetous of increased power, were invited in the fiery pages of *The Christian Nobility* to take their stand against the Papacy and the hierarchy, just as they would against a destroyer of Christendom,[6] and " to punish them severely " for different disorders, fiscal and others, and " for the abuse of excommunication and their shocking blasphemies against the name of God." [7] In short, could they not " put an end to the whole affair "? The State has also a moral or ethical nature. This comes out plainly in *A Prelude on the Babylonian Captivity of the Church*. There the political philosopher claims that " no laws can be imposed upon Christians by any authority whatsoever, neither by man nor by angels,

---

[1] *Epist.*, xi. 29.

[2] *Epp.* i. 72 ; ii. 29 ; iii. 59 ; iv. 7, 26, 32 ; v. 7, 32 ; vi. 61 ; viii. 4, 19 ; xi. 12, 37 ; xiii. 36.

[3] Cf. *Mor.*, xxxi. 8.

[4] *Epp.* i. 39a, 47, 59 ; v. 38 ; ix. 4, 55, 182 ; xi. 4.

[5] *Ibid.*, ix. 76. *Cf.* ix. 47, 53.

[6] *Werke*, Weim. ed., vi., p. 428 ; Erl. ed., xxi., p. 307.

[7] *Werke*, Weim. ed., vi., p. 429 ; Erl. ed., v., p. 70.

except with their own consent, for we are free of all things." [1]
" What is done otherwise is gross tyranny. . . . We may
not become the servants of men. . . . But few there are who
know the joy of Christian liberty." [2]

Luther shows the Emperor, the princes, and the whole
German nobility the method by which Germany may break
away from Rome, and undertake its own reformation. He sets
to work to remove the distinction between the clerical and
the lay estate. The law of the land covers everyone within the
bounds of the kingdom, clergy as well as laity. The ecclesiastical authority of Rome therefore ceases, a view warmly attacked
by Prierias in his able reply.[3] His view of all ecclesiastical
authority, anticipating Bodin's opinion, excludes every extension of that authority to the sphere of political or civil life.
Everyone living within the boundaries of any given State is
subject to its laws, and is not subject to the laws of any outside
body. In fact, mediæval unity was essentially false : it was a
principle of domination destroying the liberty of the individual
and thereby that of the State. By breaking this unity Luther
made possible the era of modern nations.

All men are priests, Luther concludes. His teaching is in
no wise new : the Fathers emphasise the priesthood of the laity
just as much as he. Ignatius and Polycarp make no mention of
a sacrificial priesthood. Justin Martyr, for example, points out
that all Christians " are the true high-priestly race of God." [4]
According to Irenæus, " all the righteous possess the sacerdotal
rank " [5] and " all the disciples of the Lord are Levites and
priests." Tertullian, when a Montanist, asks : " Are not even
we laics priests ? " [6] He uses the terms presbyter and sacerdos
interchangeably. In the same strain Origen inquires if the

---

[1] *De Captiv. Babyl.*, *Werke*, Weim. ed., vi., p. 537 ; Erl. ed., v., p. 70.

[2] *Ibid.*, Weim. ed., vi., p. 356 ; Erl. ed., v., pp. 68, 70.

[3] *Errata et argumenta Martini Luteris recitata, detecta, repulsa et copiosis-
sime trita ; per Fratrem Silvestrum Prieratem, Magistri sacri palatii, Romæ,*
1520—*Werke*, Weim. ed., vi., pp. 328-329 ; Erl. ed., ii., pp. 79-80 ;
Kampschulte, Univ. Erfurt, ii. 77.

[4] *Dial.*, 116ff. Cf. *Tryp.*, 117.

[5] *Hær*, IV. viii. 3 ; V. xxiv. 3.

[6] *De Exhort. Cast.*, vii.

layman knows his privileges. "Dost thou not know," he demands, "that the priesthood is given to thee also, that is, to all the Church of God and the people of believers?"[1] He constantly speaks of the true Christian as a priest.[2] According to Jerome the priesthood of the layman is his baptism.[3] St Augustine maintains that "He gives the name priesthood to the very people whose priest is the mediator of God and man, the man Christ Jesus."[4] Nor did this conception disappear in the Middle Ages. Marsiglio of Padua holds that all priests, be they popes, cardinals or bishops, are alike in their essential power of absolution of sin and the consecration of the elements in Holy Communion. It is a pregnant fact that Philip Melanchthon and John Calvin, the two most influential of the Reformation theologians, were laymen.

John Hus believed that the essence of the Church lay in her being the assembly of believers, acknowledging Christ alone as her head. There is in her only one class, and all the spiritual belong to it. This view Luther always held. It is as clear in his *Exposition of the Psalms* in 1539 as it is in 1520. Under this conviction he sets the hierarchy aside, and the secular powers have authority to do so. When they are on the side of the Gospel, they may exercise their great power unhindered, "even against the Pope, bishop, priest, monk, or nun, or whatsoever else there be."[5] "St Paul says to all Christians, Let every soul—hence I suppose, even the Pope himself—be subject to the higher powers, for they bear not the sword in vain. . . . St Peter too foretold that men would arise who would despise the temporal rulers, which has indeed come to pass through the rights of the clergy." The rulers ought to appear before the ordinary courts of the land. Indeed "the secular power has become a member of the ghostly body, and, though its office is temporal, yet it has been raised to a spiritual dignity: its work may now be done with absolute freedom and unhindered

---

[1] *In Lev. Hom.*, ix. § 1.
[2] *Ibid.*, iv. 6; vi. 5; ix. 1, 8; xiii. 5.
[3] *C. Lucif.*, iv.
[4] *De Civi. Dei.*, XVII. v. 5.
[5] *Werke*, Weim. ed., vi., p. 409; Erl. ed., xxi., p. 284.

among all the members of the whole body, punishing and compelling where guilt deserves it or necessity demands it, regardless of Pope, bishop, priest, let them threaten and ban as much as they please." [1]

With Machiavelli Luther boldly substitutes secular [2] for ecclesiastical authority. What Henry VIII. did in England and Philip II. in Spain, Luther did in Germany. The English substitution was fundamentally altered by the Puritans, but Louis XIV. and Joseph II. can trace their descent from their German parent. To Luther as to Althusius, to German thinkers as to Anglican divines, the civil power is indeed a spiritual body. To the reformer the State is no mere police State, no body whose chief duty is to ensure the keeping of contracts. His mind contains in germ the wonderful conception of Edmund Burke that the State is a divine institution. For, according to the Irish thinker, "without society man could not by any possibility arrive at that perfection of which his nature is capable, nor even make a remote and faint approach to it. He, the Divine Author, gave us our nature to be perfected by our virtue. He must therefore have willed the means of its perfection. He must therefore have willed the State, and He willed its connection with Himself, the source of all perfection." It is in truth a conception as old as Cicero, and as recent as Hegel and the powerful school founded by Fichte and himself. Society is a partnership, an association for the greater purposes

---

[1] *Werke*, Weim. ed., vi., p. 410; Erl. ed., xxi., p. 285.
[2] On Luther's attitude to the State, *cf.* F. v. Bezold, *Kultur der Gegenwart*, ii., pp. 5, 66, 85; K. Holl, *Luther u. das landesherrliche Kirchenregiment*, pp. 1ff., 19-22, 54; K. Müller, *Kirche, Gemeinde u. Obrigkeit nach Luther*, pp. 54, 61, 67, 74ff., 79, 81ff.; P. Drews, pp. 74, 81, 90, 95ff., 98-99, 100-104, 301; P. Wernle, *Die Renaissance des Christentums im 16. Jahrhundert*, p. 36; K. Sell, *Der Zusammenhang von Reformation u. politischer Freiheit*, pp. 44-79; Köstlin, *Luther's Theologie*, i[2], p. 274; ii[2], p. 321; W. Friedensburg, *Schriften des Vereins für Reformationsgesch.*, No. 100, p. 90; G. Krüger, *Philipp Melanchthon*, p. 14ff.; Ellinger, *Philipp Melanchthon*, p. 588; G. Rietschel, *Lehrb. der Liturgik*, p. 278; Köstlin-Kawerau, ii., p. 10; F. G. Ward, *Darstellung u. Würdigung*, p. 21; E. Brandenburg, *Luther's Anschauung vom Staate*, p. 13ff.; N. Paulus, *Protestantismus u. Toleranz*, pp. 7ff., 14; Böhmer, pp. 135, 164, 166; Kolde, *Friederich der Weise*, pp. 38, 69ff.

of our being, for the promotion of science, art, virtue. " It is," Burke holds with passion, " not a partnership in things sub-servient only to the gross animal existence of a temporary and perishable nature. It is a partnership in all science ; a partnership in all art ; a partnership in every virtue and in all perfection. As the ends of such a partnership cannot be obtained in many generations, it becomes a partnership not only between those who are living, but between those who are living, those who are dead, and those who are to be born."

By the end of August 1520 another new book was in the press. The title of the new Latin publication, which was immediately translated into German, was *A Prelude on the Babylonian Captivity of the Church*.[1] In the second book, as in the first and third, there is the same exaltation of private judgment. " Neither Pope, nor bishop, nor any man has a right to dictate even a syllable to the Christian without his own consent ; any other course is pure tyranny." [2] If you have grasped the Word in faith, then, according to *The Freedom of a Christian Man*, " you have fulfilled all the commandments, and must be free of all things " : the believer becomes " spiritually lord of all," and by virtue of his transcendent dignity " he has power over all things." [3] With this reliance on individual reason is combined the mystical feeling. There exists, he thinks, in the assembly of the faithful, and through the illumin-ation of the Divine Spirit, a certain " inward sense of judging concerning doctrine, a sense which, though it cannot be proved,

---

[1] *Werke*, Weim. ed., vi., p. 584ff. ; Erl. ed., v., p. 13ff. ; Evers, iii. pp. 533-561.

[2] *De Captiv. Babyl.*: *Werke*, Weim. ed., vi., pp. 484(497)-573 ; *Opp. lat. var.*, v., pp. 16-118 : " Dico itaque : Neque papa neque episcopus neque ullus hominum habet ius unius syllabæ constituendæ super christianum hominem, nisi id fiat eiusdem consensu ; quidquid aliter fit, tyrannico spiritu fit." On the super-fluousness of laws cf. *Werke*, Weim. ed., vi., p. 354 ; Erl. ed., v., p. 94 : " Hoc scio, nullam rempublicam legibus feliciter administrari. . . . Quod adsit eruditio divina cum prudentia naturali, plane superfluum noxium et scriptas leges habere ; super omnia autem caritas nullis prorsus legibus indiget." *Cf.* also *Werke*, Weim. ed., vi., p. 555 ; Erl. ed., v., p. 94 : "Christianis per Christum libertas donata est super leges hominum."

[3] *Von der Freyheyt eynes Christen Menschen*: *Werke*, Weim. ed., vii., pp. 23, 27ff. ; Erl. ed., xxvii., pp. 179, 185ff.

is nevertheless absolutely certain." [1] He proceeds to show that the Sacraments had been perverted, and in fact led into a Babylonian Captivity. The withholding of the Cup in the Eucharist he calls the first captivity, the belief in Transubstantiation the second captivity, and the third was the perversion of the meaning and uses of the rite Jesus had instituted.

The last great tract of 1520, *On the Freedom of a Christian Man*, [2] breathed the very spirit of individualism to an even greater extent than the tract Calvin wrote on this subject in 1539. Like the *Decretum* of Gratian, it is one of the most important political pamphlets ever published. The doctrine of the sovereignty of the individual was fraught with weighty consequences in the sixteenth century, and with almost weightier consequences in its influence on Rousseau, and thereby on the French Revolution, in the eighteenth. Man emerged from his position as a mere member of the Church or the State, and acquired an individuality of his own. In his emergence Luther occupies no mean place. Alongside him stands the inventor of printing, thereby permitting free circulation to ideas which for the first time entered the minds of more than a select few. Gutenberg rendered the work of Luther possible : the reformer was among the first to use the printing press for popular effect. Alongside the inventor of printing stands that notable man the inventor of gunpowder, thereby putting into the hands of all an argument against authority more potent than that of all the philosophers from Marsiglio of Padua to Luther. As Leonardo da Vinci held, Truth is the daughter of Time.

Into the ferment of the early sixteenth century Luther's *Freedom of a Christian Man* was the electric spark which exploded the gunpowder.[3] The time and the place of the appearance of a doctrine are no less important than the doctrine itself.

---

[1] *Werke*, Weim. ed., vi., p. 561 ; Erl. ed., v., p. 102 ; Köstlin, *Luther's Theologie*, ii², pp. 175, 180-181, 206-207, 249-253 ; Loofs, *Leitfaden der Dogmengesch.*, iv., pp. 711, 721ff., 737.

[2] *Werke*, Weim. ed., vii., pp. 12(20)-38 ; Erl. ed., xxvii., pp. 175-199. It is printed in Latin in *Werke*, Weim. ed., vii., p. 39ff.; Erl. ed., iv., p. 206ff. It is printed in German in *Werke*, Weim. ed., vii., p. 12ff. ; Erl. ed., xxvii., p. 175ff.

[3] Döllinger, *Luther, eine Skizze* (in Weltzer and Welte, *Kirchenlexikon*).

In America stress was laid on the equality of man, but it was an equality to be sought within the existing political order. The war between North and South for the liberation of the slave is no doubt an exception, yet that war was as much fought over the right of a State to secede as over any other matter. The French, more logical than the Americans, made the equality of man a vital issue, and with them its propaganda was as intense as if it had been a question of faith. How different was the destiny which awaited the theory of the equality of all in France, and in the United States! Peter Lombard believed as fervently as Luther in justification by faith. With the one it was a mere dogma, with the other it was the most living of all issues, and hence its different influence on the fortunes of the human race.

The little pamphlet of thirty pages opens with the paradox that "A Christian man is the dutiful servant of all, subject to everyone." It is characteristic of the author that he appeals for the proof of the truth of this paradox not to Jesus, Who taught it, but to St Paul. The eloquence of the moving language employed brought home to the heart of the people that it was enough to have experienced the power of faith in tribulation, temptations, anxieties and struggles to understand that in it lay the true freedom of a Christian man. The spirit of the priesthood of all believers breathes in every word of the booklet as it breathed in the teaching of John Hus. The believer, incorporated with Jesus by faith, receives from Him his priesthood. All are priests, like the Saviour, with Whom all are one. The peasant tills the ground, the priest celebrates Holy Communion—that is all. There is no difference between them save of office. In a word, Orders are not a sacrament; they are a matter of Church organisation. There was no monopoly of the priesthood: it was the privilege of all faithful Christians. Inevitably it suggested that a national Church could come into being without being in any wise cut off from the communion of saints or fellowship with the Divine Head of one great body.

The writer insisted, with all the eloquence at his command, upon the dignity which faith and a state of grace could impart to every calling, even the humblest.[1] A thought had escaped from the soul that was common to all and made an immediate appeal to every humble heart. *The Freedom of a Christian Man* is a book for every century, though it bears the distinguishing marks of its own. Luther's vivid writing impressed on all that life in this world, and the most insignificant employment, when illumined by religion, has in it something of the infinite. The German people had outgrown the conception of the duality of life, and found the new conception of its essential unity. One outstanding effect was the emphasis laid on vocation in relation to daily occupation. The " Saint's Rest " was in the world to come : in this he was to labour at his calling. Business henceforth became a sacred office in which it was a man's bounden duty to do his utmost *ad majorem Dei gloriam*. Luther was fortunate in the moment in which he launched forth this idea, for Europe was about to change from the agricultural to the capitalistic system. The Reformation occurred in the midst of the beginning of modern capitalism. This new industrial form gave rise to an enormously potential revolutionary force. The sanctity of the monastic life was transferred to the common round, the trivial task. Man no longer was made for a function : a function was made for man.[2] The "religious" were no longer men and women in a monastery : life and religion were now fundamentally one.[3]

Priestly ideas no more dominated men, and a new lay attitude to the world replaced the ecclesiastical attitude of the Middle Ages. In mediæval cathedrals there were two distinct churches : that of the clergy, which has its centre in the choir,

---

[1] On Luther's attitude to the modern world *cf.* Denifle, *Luther und Luthertum*, i., p. 689; i², p. 723; W. Hermann, *Zeitschrift für Theol. und Kirsche* (18,1908), pp. 74ff., 147ff.; G. Kawerau, *Theolog. Literaturztng.* (1884), p. 37ff.; P. M. Rade, *Christliche Welt* (1904, No. 26) ; and above all, Troetsch, *Die Bedeutung des Protestantismus für die Entstehung der modernen Welt* (*Histor. Zeitschrift*, 97), p. 1ff.; and his *Kultur der Gegenwart*, i., pp. 4, 397; K. Rieker, *Staat und Kirche nach lutherischer, reformierter, moderner Anschauung*, in *Hist. Vierteljahrschrift*, i., p. 370ff. (1898).

[2] *Cf.* Maurenbrecher, *Studien und Skizzen*, pp. 342-347.

[3] Hagen, ii., pp. 223-224.

and that of the parish. The two churches, as it were, now became one. In the first tract of Luther, the life of the State was to be one. In the second, the life of man was to be one. In the third, the life of the State and that of the individual were to be one: they were to be joined in harmonious union, a union in which neither was to attain mastery over the other. Formerly it was *orare est laborare* : now it was *laborare est orare*, with the result that justification was at once given to social service, the worth of which the world is only beginning to realise.

Christian ethics till now had a divided ideal. It taught some men devotion to others, and self-sacrifice on their behalf. It taught holiness and righteousness as the ideal of the monk and the nun. The two ideals were parallel and independent. Luther joined them in the one end of human service. The mediævalist had taught that what was natural was wrong. Luther taught that what was natural was right. Human life, in its innermost being, is in harmony with the eternal law of morality. No doubt a heavy price had to be paid for this change. For example, the denial of the honour accorded throughout the Middle Ages to virginity had the effect of making the social position of woman wholly dependent on her marriage. The state of poverty was once the sign of a saint: now it was the mark of a failure. Other-worldliness was no longer the motive. A good citizen of this earth was thus preparing for his citizenship in the New Jerusalem. He is a saved man, and his life on earth is as sacred as in heaven.[1] Other-worldliness had rendered men indifferent to the secrets of the universe, of the ground beneath them and the heavens above them. They had been so preoccupied with the Word of God that they omitted to consider the works of God. The globe acquired a fascination for mankind hitherto unknown.

There are phrases in other writings of Luther which seem far removed from the spirit of this tract. In them he manifests

---

[1] M. Weber points out that the Calvinist had a calling not merely in religion but also in business. *Cf.* his *Die Protestantische Ethik und der Geist des Kapitalismus* in *Archiv. für Socialwissenschaft und Socialpolitik*, xx. For the effect of Beruf (calling), *cf.* p. 38 ff. and Part II., pp. 1-100.

as real a dislike as Machiavelli of "Master Omnes"—"the many-headed monster." Nevertheless, we must sharply distinguish between the relations the writer is contemplating. When he speaks of the attitude of man to God, he works himself up into a dislike of the mob. When he discusses the attitude of man to man this dislike is absent. He is, however, clear that " we must not hearken too much to the mob, for they are fond of raging. . . . They have no idea of self-restraint or how to exercise it." [1] In 1525 he contemplated marriages between nobles and the daughters of burghers, of the rising merchant class.[2] Serfdom, however, did not strike him as contrary to Christ.[3] " When the mother carefully looks after her family, provides for her children, feeds them, washes them and rocks them in the cradle," her calling is " a happy and a holy one." [4]

It is easy to make a catena from writers who preach the doctrine of the freedom of a Christian man before Luther. Men like Andreas Proles,[5] Vicar-General of the Saxon Augustinian Congregation, before 1503; like Gottschalk Hollen, the Westphalian preacher, in 1517; manuals like the *Wybegertlin* [6] and the *Ermahnung* [7] are just as emphatic and as plain-spoken on the worth of work. Luther, however, spoke with that power over men which they lack. It is significant that in the pre-Lutheran Bible—*e.g.* that which came from Augsburg in 1487—the translation of Eccles. xi. 22 is: "Trust God, and stay in thy place," whereas Luther rendered it: " Trust God and abide by thy calling." Luther indeed restored to the heart the freedom that had long been denied it. We might say of him what Voltaire said of Montesquieu, that humanity had lost its title-deeds and Luther had recovered them.

In the last resort Luther exalts the lay authority at the expense of the ecclesiastical. What else could he do? To whom

---

[1] *Werke*, Weim. ed., xix., p. 635; Erl. ed., xxii., p. 259. Cf. *Kriegsleutte auch ynn seligen Stande seyn künden* (1526).

[2] *Werke*, Weim. ed., x. 2, p. 157; Erl. ed., xxviii., p. 200.

[3] *Werke*, Weim. ed., xvi., p. 244; xxxvi., p. 359; Erl. ed., xxxv., p. 233; xlviii., p. 385.

[4] *Opp. lat. exeg.*, iv., pp. 202-204.

[5] Sermon on Marriage in his *Sermones dominicales*, Leipzig, 1530.

[6] Mayence, 1509.   [7] Mayence, 1513.

could he appeal save the ruling classes of his own land? To whom did the French and English reformers appeal? Calvin had behind him the free, vigorous communities of Swiss peasants, trained to independence by their contest with Austria. Of course Luther had behind him the strength and the intelligence of the larger German cities, but the bulk of his followers were oppressed farmers who had become savage since the peasant wars. The natural result was the immense increase in the power, not of the German State, but of the territorial States. The Prince waxed as great as the mind of Machiavelli desired, and the Holy Roman Empire waxed correspondingly less. Luther aimed at saving Germany, yet by his actions he left no more than the shell of an empire, which crumbled to pieces at the touch of a Napoleon. In his first pamphlet he attacked abuses in relation to the State; in his second he attacked abuses in relation to the Church, and in his third he discovered the individual, whom these abuses had concealed. With the Church and the State reformed there was room for a man to live the good life. This principle of moral individualism comes from the German prophet, and proved one of the greatest factors in the success of his movement. Theologically it formed the essence of his message, for it was the doctrine of justification by faith alone. Tauler and the *Theologica Germanica* had begun the work which another disciple of mysticism had so ably continued. This disciple could not believe that a man became just by doing just acts. On the contrary, he came to believe that a man must first be just, and then he will do just actions. The heart must be changed: the rest will then follow. It was with a shock of surprise that he learned that repentance meant not, as in the Vulgate translation, to do penance, but, as in the Greek Testament, to change one's mind.[1] Righteousness is from within, not from without—a God-inspired life of faith, not a formal life of works. It springs directly out of the relationship of the soul to Christ, its Saviour, not out of any outward mortification. Then, like Christian in *The*

---

[1] Luther's *Briefe* (*De Wette*), i., pp. 34, 46, 253; *Werke*, Erl. ed., xxvii., p. 344; lxiii., p. 238f.; *Op. varii arg.*, i., p. 213; ii., p. 180; *Op. exeg.*, xiv., p. 243.

Pilgrim's Progress, the bondage of sin falls from man when he sees the cross. It was this moral freedom which Luther made men realise, and it was this realisation which gave the Reformation its moving impulses. No masses or indulgences were required. No priest was to stand between the soul and God. That Luther believed in individual liberty *The Freedom of a Christian Man* proves. That he promoted princely absolutism all the after-history of Europe proves. As Harnack put it, " Kant and Fichte were both of them hidden behind Luther." [1] That he promoted freedom of inquiry is similarly attested, for Ewald, Darwin and Kelvin trace their descent from him.

The law of nature occupies an important though subordinate place in the theology of Luther. [2] At one time he gives it the Roman meaning of " natural equity," [3] and the kindred one that it is the ordinance " which also heathen, Turks and Jews must keep." [4] The imperial jurisconsults found in it the origin of international law, and Luther found in it the source of all written law. He develops its importance when he sees it as a law of reason which " issuing from free reason overleaps all books," [5] and is in truth the Christian law of love which also the Lord declares in Luke vi. 31 and Matt. vii. 12 : " Whatsoever ye would that men should do to you, do ye even so to them." [6] It is easy to make the deduction that there is in existence apart from the sacred record a natural law which binds the conscience of all, and it is no less easy to see that one

---

[1] *Preussische Jahrbücher*, 1909, *Hft.* i., p. 35.

[2] *Cf.* W. Diethey, "Auffassung und Analyse des Menschen in xv. u. xvi. Jahrhundert " (*Archiv für Geschichte der Philosophie*, iv., 1891, pp. 604-651), and part ii., v., 1892, and "Das naturrliche System der Geistswissenschaften in xvii. Jahrhundert," v., 1892, pp. 480-502 ; an article by E. Troeltsch on the work of Seeberg, *Lehrbuch der Dogmengeschichte* in the *Göttingesche gelehrte Anzeigen*, 1901, No. 1, pp. 15-30 ; H. Summermaine, *L'Ancien Droit*, 1874 ; R. Stammler, *Wirtschaft und Recht*, 1896.

[3] *Ermahnung zum Frieden auf die* 12. *Artikel der Bauern*, Erl. ed., xxiv[2], p. 290 ; Tischreden, ed. Förstemann and Rindseil, iii. p. 320 ; iv., p. 486 ; *Warnung an siene lieben Deutschen*, Erl. ed., xxv[2], p. 15.

[4] *Ermahnung*, pp. 279, 282.

[5] *Von weltlicher Obrigkeit*, Erl. ed., xxii., p. 105.

[6] *Grosser Sermon vom Wucher*, Weim. ed., vi., p. 49.

day such a law depends solely for its efficacy on the inward monitor. Kant can wonder at the moral law within, but utterances like the preceding paved the way for its efficacy. The teaching of Romans ii. 15 influenced Luther to some extent.[1] Melanchthon knew how Socrates, Plato and Aristotle valued this idea. For Luther it is more satisfactory to detect the law of nature in the Decalogue than in the classics.[2] He finds it among the pagans as well as among the Turks and Jews.[3] If the law of nature as well as the written law fails, we must fall back on the Wundermann, who is in effect the Prince of Machiavelli.[4]

The conception of natural law influenced the fertile mind of Lorenzo Valla. In his three Ciceronian dialogues on "Lust," written in 1431, he compares the claims of Epicurean, Stoic and Christian morality on mankind.[5] Though Christian morality wins, it is obvious that Valla entertains a lively admiration for the Epicurean school. The claims of nature are urged, for are they not good and laudable? Wine is the father of all pleasures, a sentiment Valla cannot reconcile with Christianity. Celibacy is a crime, for nature is against it, and Platonic influence is evident in the author's defence of the community of wives. Natural law was apt to impress the eighteenth century marvellously: we are apt to forget how much it changed the sixteenth. Philip Melanchthon,[6] Huldreich Zwingli,[7] John Calvin,[8] John Knox,[9] George Buchanan, Richard Hooker [10] Philippe de Duplessis-Mornay,[11] François Hotman,[12] Juan Mariana,[13] Lambert Daneau and

---

[1] Köstlin-Kawerau, ii., p. 457; Loofs, *Leitfaden zum Stud. der Dogmengesch*, pp. 721-722, 770-775, 778; E. Ehrhardt, *La Notion du Droit Naturel chez Luther*, passim.

[2] *Werke*, Erl. ed., xlvi., p. 84.   [3] *Ibid.* xxiv., p. 263.

[4] *Werke*, Weim ed., vi., p. 554; Erl. ed., xxxix., pp. 288, 289.

[5] Voigt, *Wiederbelebung des classischen Alterthums*, i., p. 469.

[6] *Opera*, xxi., pp. 116-120, 391-392.

[7] O. Dreske, *Zwingli und das Naturrecht*, pp. 24, 26.

[8] *Cf.* my chapter on "Calvin."

[9] *Works*, iv., pp. 496ff., 539ff.

[10] Cf. *The Laws of Ecclesiastical Polity*, i., pp. 178-181.

[11] *Cf.* his *Vindinac contra Tyrannos.*

[12] *Cf.* his *Franco-Gallia.*   [13] *Cf.* his *De rege et regis institutione.*

Johannes Althusius [1] were all believers in natural law. The Old Testament justified resistance to tyranny, and when this justification was combined with the natural law doctrine of the sovereignty of the people, democracy was beginning to find a basis for its position. Hooker, like Aquinas, can discern the origin of the State in a social contract made under the régime of the law of nature.[2] A king, he asserts, who does not base his doctrines upon the general consent is a tyrant.[3] It is not for nothing that men note in sixteenth-century theology a federal character, a feature that is specially marked in Calvinistic thought. In the doctrine of the law of nature we perceive that there are natural rights, imprescriptible and inalienable. These rights are the right to justice, the right to liberty, and the right to freedom in religion. These rights have been recognised, it is held, by a pact, a contract. The party violating the promises of the pact, *ipso facto* breaks it, and at once releases the other party from all obligations to keep it. There is the right of resistance when anyone violates the natural rights guaranteed by the contract.

The destinies of theories are strange. In the sixteenth century the conception of natural right is a friend to freedom, and in the seventeenth century a friend to absolutism. In his *De Jure Belli et Pacis* Grotius analyses with penetrating power the new conception ; Hobbes employs it to defend the Stuart policy ; Milton and Roger Williams to set forth the advantages of toleration. The law of nature succeeded in preserving that toleration which was at last the fruits of the revolution of 1688, and this forms its most notable services. It has an after-history, apart from Rousseau, in the eighteenth century,

---

[1] *Cf.* his *Politics* ; *cf.* also Gierke, *J. Althusius*, p. 144f. There is an elaborate account on pp. 76-122.

[2] Cf. *The Laws of Ecclesiastical Polity*, i., p. 186ff. Engelbert von Volkersdorf seems to have spoken of *pactum subjectionis* for the first time during the quarrel of the Investitures. *Cf.* H. Rehm, *Geschichte der Staatsrechtwissenschaft*, p. 180. *Cf.* above all, Gierke, *Althusius*, pp. 142-144, 146, 151-153. Gierke finds the beginnings of the Original Contract in the *pactum* of Manegold of Lautenbach, as developed through the *pactum* of Engelbert and others.

[3] *The Laws of Ecclesiastical Polity*, i., p. 191ff.

for the Deists in England and the supporters of the Aufklärung
in Germany adhered to this conception.

While in the background of the mind of Luther there is the
idea of natural law, in the foreground there is the necessity of
working out the relations of his party to the State. The position
he arrived at was at once the strength and the weakness of
his movement. His work, *On the Secular Power: How far
Obedience is due to it*, appeared in March 1523. In the
appeal *To the Christian Nobility of the German Nation on
the Improvement of the Christian Estate* he had certainly
elevated the civil power to ecclesiastical rank. The new book
flatly contradicts this standpoint. The task of the State is
conceived to be secular: it has no duty to make men pious, for
laissez-faire is its proper attitude in these high matters. It is
a position strikingly like the Gallican one. The Gallican doctors
admit that the Church has coercive power, even in the external
forum; but this constraint is moral and supernatural.[2] Can
there be such a thing as a Christian State? asks Luther. No,
for God calls such a body into existence on account of the
wicked.[3] The world through sin was estranged from God.
The Prince therefore simply had to maintain order by force
when peace was disturbed or men suffered injustice. The
State is in itself a moral organism outside and apart from the
Church, a view which was one day to effect weighty results.

Real Christians require no secular rulers. To Stoics like
Posidonius and Seneca, to Fathers like St Augustine and
Gregory the Great, it was possible to conceive the State without coercive power. Though William of Ockham conferred
such power on the State, yet in his *Dialogus*, Marsiglio of

---

[1] *Von welltlicher Ueberkeytt wie weytt man yhr Gehorsam schuldig sey*:
Werke, Weim. ed., xi., pp. 229 (245-248); Erl. ed., xxii. pp. 60-105. Cited
by Castellion in his *De hæreticis* (Magdeburg, 1554), pp. 29-45. *Cf.* also
E. Brandenburg, *Luther's Anschauung von Staate u. der Gesellschaft*, p. 25;
H. Hermelink, *Zeitschrift für Kirchengeschichte* (29, 1908), pp. 267ff., 479ff;
Luthardt, *Luther's Ethik*, ii., p. 81ff; Paulsen, *Geschichte des gelehrten
Unterrichts*, i², p. 209; Luther's *Brief* (*De Wette*), ii., pp. 23f., 249, 254,
262, 281f., 299; *Werke*, Erl. ed., xxii., pp. 59ff., 68, 82, 85, 89-90, 93;
Corp. Reform., i., pp. 600ff., 604.
[2] Almain, *Expositio*, iii., c. 18, p. 1113. [3] *Werke*, Erl. ed., xxi., p. 285.

Padua in his *Defensor Pacis* and Jacques Almain in his *Expositio . . . super potestate summi pontificies*, 1512, grant that "He who has supreme control in temporal matters must govern only in the temporal: he who holds it in spiritual must not meddle with public matters."[1] Such a theory, working in practice, would have excluded the Massacre of St Bartholomew, the devilries of Alva, and those wrought in France after the Revocation of the Edict of Nantes.

Luther's *Von weltlicher Obrigkeit* speaks most plainly in favour of toleration; it reaches a loftiness of thought as penetrating as that of *The Freedom of a Christian Man*, and this loftiness was not approached till the days of Milton's *Areopagitica*, one hundred and twenty-one years later. The great revolutionary believes that "no one can command or ought to command the soul, except God, Who only can show it the way to heaven." He puts forth the plea that "the thoughts and mind of man are discerned only by God," and hence it is useless and impossible to command or by force to compel any man's belief. The conclusion is inevitable. "Faith is a voluntary matter which cannot be forced: indeed it is a Divine work in the spirit. Hence it is a common saying which is also found in Augustine: 'Faith cannot and ought not to be forced on anyone.'"

Some, however, adduce the argument that the aid of the State ought to be invoked, especially to prevent heretics from leading the people astray. They quote passages like Romans xiii. 1: "Let every soul be subject unto the higher powers. For there is no power but of God: the powers that be are ordained of God." It is also material to their point of view that St Peter says: "Submit yourselves to every ordinance of man for the Lord's sake: whether it be to the king as supreme; or unto governors, as unto them that are sent by him for the punishment of evildoers, and for the praise of them that do well."[2] In spite of his leaning to St Paul, Luther boldly places the last quotation alongside the sayings of Jesus Christ, applying Matthew xx. 21: "Render therefore unto Cæsar the things which are Cæsar's; and unto God the things that are God's."

---

[1] Almain, *Expositio*, i., c. 7.   [1] 1 Peter ii. 13-14.

It " is the duty of the bishops, not of princes. For heresy can never be kept off by force; another argument is required for that; this is another quarrel than that of the sword. If this fails, the worldly power avails naught, though it fill the world with blood. Heresy is a spiritual matter that cannot be hewn down by iron, nor burned by fire, nor drowned by water. But God's Word meets it, as Paul says, ' Our weapons are not carnal, but mighty in God ' (2 Cor. x. 4-5)."

In the same year as the publication of the *Von weltlicher Obrigkeit* Luther sent forth his exposition of the First Epistle to St Peter.[1] On the exhortation to fear God and honour the King he remarks : " If the civil magistrate interferes with spiritual matters of conscience in which God only must rule, we ought not to obey at all, but rather lose our head. Civil government is confined to external and temporal affairs." He powerfully urges : " If an emperor or prince asked me about my faith, I would reply, not because of his command, but because of my duty to confess my faith before men. But if he should go further, and command me to believe this or that, I would answer, ' Dear Sir, mind your secular business : you have no right to interfere with God's reign, and therefore I shall not obey you at all.' "

There is a similar standpoint advanced by Hooper in 1548, in his *Declaration of the Ten Holy Commandments of Almighty God*. He points out : " As touching the superior powers of the earth, it is not unknown unto all them that hath readen and marked the scripture, that it appertaineth nothing unto their office to make any law to govern the conscience of their subjects in religion, but to reign over them in this case as the word of God commandeth. Deut. xvii. 1 ; 1 Sam. xii. ; 2 Chron. viii. ; Wisd. vi." [2] Robert Browne, in his famous short *Treatise*

---

[1] *Werke*, Weim. ed., xiv. 1(13)-9 ; Erl. ed., lii., pp. 213-287.

[2] *Early Writings of Bishop Hooper*, Parker Society, p. 280. *Cf.* his *Epistola ad Episcopos, Decanos, Archidiaconos, et ceteros Cleri Ordinis, in Synodo Londinensi congregatos*, in 1559; *Later Writings of Bishop Hooper*, p. 386: " Profecto Christus non ignem, non gladium, non carceres, non vincula, non violentiam, non confiscationem bonorum, non reginæ majestatis terrorem, media organa constituit quibus veritas sui verbi mundi promulgaretur ; sed miti ac diligenti prædictione evangelii sui mundum ab errore et idololatria converti præcepit."

of Reform, published in 1582, enunciated the same views on the relations between the secular power and the Church. He also wrote a far-reaching short pamphlet, entitled: *Of Reformation without tarrying for any; and of the Wickedness of those Preachers who will not reform themselves and their charge, because they will tarry till the Magistrate command and compel them*. His individualism called upon him to leave the Church of England. Its forms and its organisations stood between the soul and God: they prevented, in his view, a renewal of man's unending yearning for communion with God. The new spirit had to express itself in new forms, or rather in the absence of forms. In his book, *On the Secular Power*, Luther substantially adopts the Augustinian view that the State possessed no coercive jurisdiction. The Christianity of the State was to him a doubtful proposition. Indeed the body politic exists for the sake of the wicked: the fall of man is its *raison d'être*—that is, this body resembles W. von Humboldt's *Ideen*, of which the essence is the denial that the State enjoys the right to be anything more than chief policeman: it is, in Huxley's phrase, anarchy plus the policeman. It is removed by a world from the Hobbeian conception of the State: "*non est super terram potestas quæ comparetur ei.*"

The German State was changing in character. Its members had been agriculturists, and under the rise of capitalism some of them were turning to business. The agricultural régime was one that Luther understood: the business one was remote from him. In his *Von Kauffshandlung und Wucher* he spoke strongly on the action of the trading companies. He cared nothing for the foreign trade that brought wares from Calcutta, Calicut, and other places. Were not these spices and costly fabrics of silk and cloth-of-gold only for purposes of luxury and display? What use did they serve? Did they not remove money from the people and their rulers? Here he anticipated a favourite argument of the mercantile school of the seventeenth century. True, patriarchs like Abraham bought and sold, but if they did they bought and sold cattle, wool, grain, butter and milk. These are God's gifts, which He raises from the earth and distributes among men. The new trade simply means the

" throwing away of our gold and silver into foreign countries." [1]
As he anticipated the mercantile theory, so he also obviously
anticipated the Physiocratic theory. Nature worked along with
man on the soil, and there was no such co-operation in business.
The profit from trade is indeed unnatural.[2] Moreover, a
merchant can " in a short time become so rich as to be able
to buy up emperors and kings." [3] This attitude is no new one.
In the *An den christlichen Adel* Luther denounces the trading
companies and the usury they exacted. He disavows acquaintance with figures and cannot understand how a hundred florins
can gain twenty annually. Here appears the mediæval notion
that money was barren metal. It is far more important to till
the soil than to trade. " It is, indeed," he is persuaded, " high
time that a bit were put in the mouths of the Fuggers and
other companies." [4]

The reformer's humanistic training appears in his statement that " we despise the arts and languages, but refuse to
do without the foreign wares which are neither necessary nor
profitable to us. ... Is not this a proof that we are true Germans
—*i.e.* fools and beasts? " He insists that God " has bestowed
upon us, as He has bestowed upon other nations, sufficient
wool, hair, flax, and everything else for becoming clothing,
but now men squander fortunes on silk, satin, cloth-of-gold
and absurd foreign goods." [5] He anticipates the doctrines of
Lassalle when he holds that wages tend to the cost of the
maintenance of the worker. It seemed to him that the price
of an article depended on the cost of labour involved in making
it, and in the state of society in which he lived such a crude
criterion was not so unfair as it looks. The scholastic notion of
a just price was a leading idea in his mind, and he thought
that it was possible to fix this price. Profit might be made,
but not such " as might cause loss to another." [6] He opposed

---

[1] *Werke*, Weim. ed., xv., p. 294ff.; Erl. ed., xxii., p. 201ff.
[2] *Werke*, Weim. ed., vi., p. 466; Erl. ed., xxi., p. 357. *Cf.* Ward,
Darstellung, pp. 73, 83; Krause, *Eoban Hessus*, ii., p. 107.
[3] *Werke*, Weim. ed., xv., p. 312ff.; Erl. ed., xxii., p. 223.
[4] *Werke*, Weim. ed., vi., p. 466; Erl. ed., xxi., p. 357.
[5] *Werke*, Weim. ed., vi., p. 465ff.; Erl. ed., xxi., p. 356.
[6] *Werke*, Weim. ed., xv., p. 296; Erl. ed., xxii., p. 204.

the idea of buying cheaply and selling dearly : such a practice was " to open the door and window to hell." [1] He also opposed the artificial scarcity which merchants like the Fuggers aimed at creating.

There was a new world around him : the effects of the discovery of Columbus could not be undone. Men were sending their goods no longer to Venice and the Mediterranean but to the north—that is, to the Atlantic Ocean. Money might be as barren as Luther thought it; the merchant class, however, stood in urgent need of it, and they offered high rates. Luther was unaware of the possibilities that lay hidden behind the discovery of America, still he did see that usury was growing, though he did not diagnose the cause with sufficient accuracy. It is hard to say whether he hated the devil or the Pope the more. It gave him peculiar pleasure to attack them simultaneously. In his *An den christlichen Adel* he exclaimed that "the greatest misfortune of the German nation is easily the traffic in interest. . . . The devil invented it, and the Pope, by giving his sanction to it, has done untold evil throughout the world." [2] He felt as strongly on this matter in 1539 when he published his *An die Pfarhernn wider den Wucher zu predigen* as he felt in 1520. He held the same opinion in 1542. [3] He would refuse usurers the Sacrament, absolution and Christian burial. [4] He quotes such texts as Exodus xxii. 25; Leviticus xxv. 36; Deut. xxiii. 19; St Matt. v. 42 and, above all, St Luke vi. 35. Some say that the New Testament verses are counsels, not commands : Luther maintains strongly that they are commands which bind men to obey them. Still, he allows some exceptions to his rigid rule. As the Emperor Justinian allowed mitigated usury to men in urgent need of money, Luther is willing to permit it where the loan is a work of mercy to the needy. Here is a case in point. In 1532 the widow of Wolfgang Jörger offered him five hundred florins for the use of poor students of divinity in Wittenberg, asking him in what form she ought

---

[1] *Werke*, Weim. ed., xv., p. 295 ; Erl. ed., xxii., p. 202.
[2] *Werke*, Weim. ed., vi., p. 466 ; Erl. ed., xvi., p. 356.
[3] *Cf.* the *Tischreden* (Mathesius), p. 259 ; *Werke*, Erl. ed., lvii., p. 360.
[4] *Werke*, Erl. ed., p. 285.

to give her bequest. He advised her to lend it at interest, and in this advice Melanchthon concurred.[1]

In the midst of speculations like these came the explosion of the Peasants' Revolt. Its primary motive was economic. The lords' tyranny, the tithes and the taxes had long pressed severely on the mass of the people. The message of Luther made them feel these burdens more acutely than they had ever felt them before. His gospel of Christian liberty proved a mighty solvent. For the spiritual freedom which he taught, multitudes substituted freedom from political oppression, from social injustice and from economic burdens. Roman Law was widening its far-reaching influence.[2] Like heady wine, the reading of the Bible intoxicated and exalted them, leading not to revolution but to absolute anarchy. Its influence was as much indirect as direct.[3] For some Anabaptists, like other men from the Gnostics to Schleiermacher, denied the necessity of reading it. There was as much connection between Luther and the outbreak as there was between Hus and the extreme fanatics of his party, or between Wyclif and Wat Tyler.

Luther wrote a single-sheet entitled *Against the Murderous, Thieving Hordes of Peasants*, or more shortly, *Against the Insurgent Peasants*. It was composed before the complete defeat in the decisive days of May 1525. In it Luther, like the Tudors, sacrificed liberty to order. In the *Exhortation to Peace* the pamphleteer seeks to put the truth before the peasants and their lords, and he addresses each side in turn. The peasants are right in their demand to choose their own pastors and in their repudiation of the heriot. They are wrong

---

[1] *Cf.* his letter to Dorothy Jörger, 7th March 1532, Erl. ed., liv., p. 277; *Briefwechsel*, ix., p. 160. *Cf.* Evers, iii., pp. 210-227; *Werke*, Erl. ed., xvi., pp. 82-93, 97-98.

[2] Egelhaaf, *Deutsche Geschichte*, i., p. 544ff.; Lamprecht, *Deutsche Geschichte*, v., p. 99ff.; Janssen, *Geschichte des deutschen Volkes*, passim; Brunner, *Grundzüge der deutschen Rechtsgeschichte*, p. 216.

[3] On the effects of sermons and pamphlets on the revolt *cf.* Hagen, ii., pp. 155-277; Arx, *Gesch. des Cantons von St Gallen*, ii., p. 492; Baumann, *Quellen*, p. 377; Jörg, pp. 191-200, 251, 292; Riggenbach, p. 198; Schade, *Satiren u. Pasquille*, ii., pp. 1-41, 277-288; Friedrich, *Astrologie und Reformation*, pp. 63-78, 156-158; Baur, pp. 131-144, 217-219, 512-514.

in their desire to divide the tithes between the priest and the poor : it is simply robbery, for the tithes belong to the Government. They are also wrong in craving the abolition of serfdom on the ground that Christ has freed all : this makes Christian freedom a carnal thing, and is therefore unjustifiable. The Gospel is concerned with spiritual, not temporal, affairs. Earthly society cannot exist without inequalities ; the true Christian finds his Christian liberty and his opportunity for Christian service in the midst of them and in spite of them.[1] Some say that the rebellion has been caused by the doctrine of the prophet, but he avers that he has always taught obedience to the powers that be. Those who take the sword shall perish by the sword, and every soul should be subject to the authorities in fear and honour.

He lives in the moment and takes no thought for the morrow. Sufficient unto the day is the change in the view thereof. As Carlyle held that the skins of the French aristocracy bound the new edition of Rousseau's works, so the skins of the German peasants bound the new version of Luther's ideas. Is it not the prerogative of genius to be fertile in contradiction, to nourish its development on inconsistencies? He knew not whither he was going—he did not wish to know. Forces, incalculable forces, were driving him. God would provide the opportunity : God would reveal how it ought to be sued. Had the man who executed Louis XVI. been content with the Tennis Court oath, the House of Bourbon might still be reigning in Paris.

The fates of theories are strange, and if the father of one of them could see the developments of some of his children he would stand aghast. There is a statement of the theory of the Social Pact in the *De Regimine Principum* of St Thomas Aquinas. To him, as to Hooker in his *Of the Laws of Ecclesiastical Polity*, it furnishes a cogent argument on behalf of absolute monarchy. To Locke it affords a convincing statement on the right of the individual to set a limit to the power of the State. To Rousseau it yields a clear account in favour of an extreme form of democracy. These doctrines are divergent : the Anabaptist application of Luther's was simply more thorough. The revolutionary drew back in horror.

---

[1] *Werke*, Weim. ed., xviii., p. 293ff. ; Erl. ed., xxiv. 2, p. 273ff.

When episcopal authority was abolished, the Elector of Saxony assumed jurisdiction as a sort of bishop. As Melanchthon put it, he was the principal member of the Church.[1] This jurisdiction dealt above all with matrimonial cases—which, according to Luther, belonged entirely to the secular courts—matters of tithe, certain offences against ecclesiastical or secular law, and points of Church discipline affecting public order. This was all in accordance with Luther's statement that the Church possessed no power to govern, that the only object for which she existed was to make men pious by means of the Word, that the secular authority was the only one able to make laws and formally to claim obedience "whether it does right or wrong." [2] It follows that the State in assuming such jurisdiction was doing nobody any injustice; it was merely exercising its right. The authority it employed was not ecclesiastical, but only the common law exercised for the purpose of preserving sound doctrine and the true Church.

Next came the appointment of ecclesiastical superintendents by the Sovereign, the nomination or removal of pastors and unqualified teachers, the carrying out of visitations, the drawing up of Church regulations, and the convening of synods or consultations. To the assumption of all these powers by the State, Luther raises no objection, partly because the power of the keys, according to him, included no coercive authority, and partly because the idea of the leading member of the Church was great enough to carry such functions with it. The introduction of the Consistories of 1539 was the outcome of the conviction that if the Church possessed no legal power of coercion for the maintenance of order she is doomed to perish. After some hesitation Luther gave his consent to the new institution. He consoled himself with thinking that though it was appointed by the Sovereign it was a spiritual tribunal of the Church. After his death in 1546 the Consistories retained the name of the Ecclesiastical Courts, though as a matter of fact they became a department of the civil judicature. The

[1] *Cf.* Melanchthon's tract, *De potestate papæ*, added to the Schmalkaldic Articles in *Die symbolischen Bücher*, 1907, ed. Müller-Kolde, p. 339.
[2] Luther, *Von guten Werken*, 1520, *Werke*, Weim. ed., vi., p. 259ff.

policy Machiavelli had proposed in secular fashion for the aggrandisement of the Prince, Luther in ecclesiastical fashion had executed. The *Civitas Dei* of St Augustine is the *Landeskirche* of Luther.

As More felt in his day, as Burke felt long after, Luther felt that when a separation was effected between security— the security of society—and liberty, neither was safe. Sir Thomas More pleaded for toleration till toleration endangered the commonwealth. Edmund Burke argued for liberty in America : he refused to argue for licence in France. So, too, Martin Luther wrote on behalf of the freedom of a Christian man till revolt threatened that and much else besides. More was a conservative, Luther was a conservative, and Burke was a conservative. They were three of the great conservatives of history. The practice of all three seemed to depart widely from their creed. Coleridge, however, insists that in Burke's writings at the beginning of the American Revolution and in those at the beginning of the French Revolution, the principles are the same and the deductions are the same. The evidence is not nearly so strong in the case of Luther, yet it might be urged in his defence, as in More's and Burke's, that had his knowledge of the facts been ample, and above all, had not his experience been cast in such a whirlpool as the Peasants' Revolt, he might have arrived at conclusions far different from those of his pamphlets of 1524-1525. Luther regarded Thomas Münzer's policy of revolution just as More regarded Thomas Cromwell's policy of reformation. Like Joseph II., the German reformer was tempted to take the second step before he had taken the first, but the moment he foresaw the consequences of raising his foot to take the second step he replaced his foot on the first step. He was not going to witness the devastation of Saxony by a spirit which, in the words of Burke, " breaks the locality of public affections."

A clear parallel exists between the monk of Erfurt and the squire of Schönhausen. With Luther man exists for God, with Bismarck man exists for the State, but this State is theocratic. If progress is synonymous with democracy, then both were reactionaries. As Luther created a new form of ecclesiastical organisation, so Bismarck created a new form of Empire. Bismarck as little foresaw what form his unity—federal, monarchical or republican—would assume as Luther foresaw the creation of his State-Church. Making allowance for the different ages in which the lot of each was cast, both were essentially feudal in their conceptions, believing in the dependence of class on class by a graduated scale. Status, not contract, was their ideal : the authority of the expert was to settle questions in dispute. What concern had οἱ πολλοι with them? Judged, however, by the standard of the centuries in which they lived, there is much to choose between them. Could they have changed the age in which they lived, Luther would have been far more tolerant than Bismarck, and Bismarck would have fallen below the standard Luther attained. For Luther was the prophet of a Revolution, Bismarck the statesman of a counter-Revolution. They were opportunists of the first order, akin to Cæsar, Cromwell or Napoleon. Though Luther was as opportunist as Bismarck, he lacked the Prince's power in seizing opportunities fully when they occurred, and, above all, in creating them at the exact time required. The two men conceived vast purposes, they knew how to carry them out, and they allowed events to shape and even control their course to its destined goal.

REFERENCES

Baur, A., *Deutschland in die Jahren* 1517-1525, Ulm, 1872.

Berger, A. E., *Martin Luther in kulturgeschichte Darstellung*, Berlin, 1894-1898.

Bluntschli, J. K., *Geschichte der neueren Staatswissenschaften*, München, 1881.

Burkhardt, C. A., *Geschichte der sächsischen Kirchen-und Schulvisitationen von* 1524-1525, Leipzig, 1879.

Cardauns, L., *Die Lehre vom Widerstandsrecht des Volkes gegen die rechtmässige Obrigkeit im Luthertum und im Calvinismus des sechzehnten Jahrhunderts*, Bonn, 1903.

Carrière, M., *Die philosophische Weltanschauung der Reformationszeit in ihren Beziehungen zur Gegenwart*, Leipzig, 1887.

Ehrhardt, E., *La Notion du Droit Naturel chez Luther*, Montauban, 1901.

Geiger, L., *Die Satiriker des 16. Jahrhunderts*, Berlin, 1876.

Grisar, H., *Luther*, Freiburg im Breisgau, 1911-1913.

REFERENCES

Hagen, C., *Deutschlands literarische und religiöse Verhältnisse im Reformationszeitalter*, Frankfurt, 1868.

Monnier, M., *La Renaissance de Dante à Luther*, Paris, 1884.

Murray, R. H., *Erasmus and Luther : their Attitude to Toleration*, London, 1920.

Poincenot, E., *Les Idées de Luther sur la Répression de l'Hérésie*, Montauban, 1901.

Richter, A. L., *Die evangel. Kirchenordnungen des 16. Jahr.*, Weimar, 1846.

Rieker, K., *Die rechtliche Stellung der evangelischen Kirche in Deutschlands*, Leipzig, 1893.

Schade, O., *Satiren und Pasquille aus der Reformationszeit*, Hanover, 1856-1858.

Schrechenbach, P. F., *Luther und der Bauernkrieg*, Oldenburg, 1895.

Schulthess-Rechberg, G. von, *Luther, Zwingli und Calvin in ihren Ansichten über das Verhältniss von Staat und Kirche*, in *Beiträge zur Rechtswissenschaft* (Zurich), xxiv., 1909.

Sell, K., *Luther's Einfluss auf der politische Geschichte Deutschlands*, Leipzig, 1899.

Seton-Watson, R. W., *Tudor Studies*, London, 1924.

Stahl, J. F., *Der Protestantismus als politisches Prinzip*, Berlin, 1853.

Stolze, W., *Der deutsche Bauernkrieg*, Halle, 1908.

Treitschke, H., *Luther und die deutsche Nation*, in *Preussische Jahrbücher*, November 1883.

Troeltsch, E., *Die Soziallehren der christlichen Kirchen (Archiv. für Staatswissenschaft*, xxvi.-xxx.), 1913.

Ward, F. G., *Darstellung der Ansichten Luther's vom Staat*, Jena, 1898.

Waring, L. H., *The Political Theories of Martin Luther*, London, 1910.

Weber, M., *Die protestantische Ethik und der Geist des Kapitalismus (Archiv. für Socialwissenschaft*, xx. and xxi.).

CHAPTER III

JOHN CALVIN AND HIS *INSTITUTES*

GOETHE wished that the Reformation had been conducted by a man like Erasmus rather than by a man like Luther. His wish was a vain one. It is true that Nature does not normally take a leap; it is no less true that she has her earthquakes—to say nothing of her atoms—as well as her still slow processes, her Etnas as well as her Jungfraus. In times when vast forces are called into being, the eruption of a volcano may accomplish in a week what the silent processes of nature may not accomplish in an age. Erasmus could never have left the impression on the world which Luther left. The arguments of the scholar were cogent: the arguments of the reformer were compelling. Could the Renaissance, as Goethe implies, ever have become the *via media* between reaction and reform? For an answer to such a question we simply mention the circumstance that in 1528 it is probable that three men were in Paris together—Loyola, Rabelais and Calvin. Is there any common denominator to cover the ideas of these three?

John Calvin (1509-1564), a Picard of Noyon, attended lectures at the Sorbonne, as was fitting for a young Frenchman.[1] A learned man, he was skilled in Latin, Greek and Hebrew, apt to expound as a doctor rather than appeal to the emotions like a Luther. Calvin " taught not with affected eloquence," Beza informs us, " but with such deep knowledge, with so grave and solid a style, that all who heard him were ravished with admiration." The Reformation restored to the heart that freedom which had been so long denied it, and, with the logical precision and severity of his race, Calvin furthered that freedom. For the Reformation was primarily a revival of religion, a renewal of man's unending yearning for communion with God. " The Reformation," to quote Bishop

---

[1] Throughout this chapter I feel much indebted to vol. v. of E. Doumergue's magnum opus, *Jean Calvin*. There is a bibliography of J. Calvin in G. Wolf, *Quellenkunde der Deutschen Reformationsgeschichte*, 2 vols., 1915-1916.

Westcott's words, "was the affirmation of individuality." But to secure this right to the individual the old doctrinal system had to be swept away and a new one built on its ruins —the new spirit had to express itself in new forms. The materials for the structure were no longer the Bible and tradition, but the Bible alone. The architecture of the building, however, depended on the character of the builders. And so we have Luther with his curious mixture of reliance on the letter of what pleased him and daring criticism of what did not; the English reformers with that remarkable combination of new and old determined by their political circumstances; and Calvin with the pitiless logic so characteristic of the French temper, so unassailable in his conclusions when his premises are granted.

When Francis I. sternly persecuted the Huguenots in 1534 and 1535, Calvin fled from France, first to Strasburg, then to Bâle. His ambition at that time was to lead a retired and studious life. The desire for seclusion had laid such hold on him that he did not even seek to become a preacher. Farel, another Frenchman, had begun the teaching of reformed doctrine in south-western Switzerland. The moment he heard that Calvin was in Bâle he came to visit the scholar who proclaimed: "I was wholly given up to my own interior thoughts and private studies." Farel explained to him how urgently Geneva required the services of such a well-instructed man. He pointed out that his own strength was failing and that his colleagues were all feeble. Calvin uncompromisingly refused. His health also was unequal to the labour, his character too unpliant for negotiation with adversaries. Moreover, he could serve the reformed faith far more effectually by his pen, and to that service he meant to devote his life. " I perceive what it is," rejoined Farel, "you are wrapped up in selfish love of leisure and books. May God's curse rest upon these studies, if you now refuse your aid to His Church in her time of need!"

The outcome of that interview is to be read in Calvin's nomination as " Teacher of Theology." His name occurs in the register of the Council of Geneva for September 1536, with the designation of " *iste Gallus.*" The work begun in Switzerland by one Frenchman, Farel, was crowned and completed by another, Calvin.[1]

If—it is a large if—John Calvin is *homo unius libri*, that book is undoubtedly his *Institutes of the Christian Religion*, 1536. But we refuse to admit that he is such a man, for with the signal exception of Machiavelli, and perhaps Bodin, no one during the sixteenth century is capable of facing such a problem as that of Church and State. From its opening decade to its closing one, all conceived Church and State as but two aspects of one and the same problem. Therefore it is as indispensable to read Calvin's commentaries, sermons and letters as his great *Institutes*, if we are to grasp his conception in its entirety. For the *Institutes* is a theological masterpiece in which the State received incidental attention in the last chapter. Calvin himself would have repudiated the idea underlying our last sentence, for he would strenuously have contended that all his books deal with the organisation of Church and State.

The *Institutes* is inevitably founded upon the Bible, and there are many texts from it. Its author does not disdain to use quotations from such Fathers as St Augustine and Origen or from the classical writers. He peruses the writings of Plato, " the most religious and the most sober-minded," and Aristotle, of Cicero and Seneca. Was not his very first book a commentary on Seneca's *De Clementia*? Nor did he pass by the new writings discovered by the humanists. A curious proof shows how up-to-date his reading was. He used Themistius, and the lines he quotes in the *Institutes* had been published for the first time in Venice in 1534, two years before his own book had appeared. Seldom do we meet with a *magnum opus* after its author has turned fifty, though the names of Kant and Lamarck forbid us to generalise in this easy manner, but is there any other case of a man who wrote a work of such widespread influence as the *Institutes* when only twenty-six?

In 1539 and 1559 two new editions appeared, and in the

---

[1] *Cf.* L. Elster, *Johann Calvin als Staatsman, Gesetzberger und Nationalokonom—Jahrbücher für Nationalokonomie und Statisk*, xxi., 1878.

first of them the argument is amplified.[1] There is, however, no alteration in the texture of the thought. What was true when he was a student of twenty-six is equally true—no more and no less—when he is a statesman of fifty. They used to say of William Pitt the Younger that he was cast in a mould. So too was Calvin. The years deepened his experience—that was all. What he thought in 1536 he felt more keenly in 1559, and his iron rule in Geneva deepened his sense of the worth of his system. Beza noted this when he remarked: "In the doctrine he taught in the beginning, he remained constant to the end: he changed nothing (*nihil prorsus*)."[2] What did the circumstance that his inflexible theories had broken down in Geneva under the stress and strain of life matter fundamentally? What if Farel and he were obliged to fly for their lives? A system is still a system, and his must stand. True to the character of his own country, there is in the *Institutes* a division and a systematisation, a logic and a penetration of conception, that moved not merely his own age but the succeeding ones. His sagacity and perspicacity in Biblical interpretation even yet command our admiration.

Before Calvin's *Institutes* there had appeared in 1521 the *Loci communes rerum theologicarum seu hypotyposes theologicæ* of Melanchthon, in 1525 the *Commentarius de vera et falsa religione* of Zwingli, the *Summaire briefve declaration d'aucuns lieux fort necessaires a ung chascun chrestien pour mettre sa confiance en Dieu et ayder son prochain* of Farel, and the two Catechisms of Luther. The labours of Calvin outdistanced them all. His is the one theological work that has left the deepest impression on the New World as well as the Old, for John Calvin his mark is visibly written all over the United States down to this very moment. Is not his spirit of asceticism discernible in the prohibition policy of our day?

Laws ought to be written. The *lex scripta* is " nothing but

---

[1] Köstlin, *Studien und Kritiken*, pp. 7-62, 410-486 ; Warfield, " The Literary History of Calvin's *Institutes*," *The Presbyt. and Reform. Review*, 1899, p. 194ff.

[2] *Opera*, xxi., p. 170 ; *Abstersio Calumniarum*, p. 263.

an attestation of the *lex naturæ*, whereby God brings back to
memory what has already been imprinted on our hearts." [1] Of
all the reformers perhaps Melanchthon laid most stress on
the *lex naturæ* or the *jus naturale*. He finds in it three main
divisions, concerning the worship of God, concerning the
formation of the State and the inviolability of the individual
persons guaranteed in the State, and concerning property. [2]
Calvin entertains the idea of natural law considerably, especially in his commentaries on Genesis and in his sermons on
Deuteronomy. He believes that there is an order of nature,
and that there is a right of nature, resulting from this order.
Indeed " the moral law is no other thing than the witness of
the natural law and of the conscience we have of it, which has
been graven by God in the souls of man." [3] With Aristotle he
holds that " man is by nature a social animal and by natural
instinct he is also led to favour and preserve this society." [4]
As the world would otherwise dissolve, " the sense of nature
says that we must obey princes." [5] The law of nature is inviolable and indestructible. [6] God can alter it, [7] but man cannot.
As the Church and State exhibit two aspects of the same
institution, so natural law and revealed law exhibit two aspects
of the same code. [8] The Decalogue, from one angle, is the law
of God, but from another it is the law of nature which God
has definitely revealed. [9] The conscience of man demands from
laws a natural equity. [10]

---

[1] *Commentary on the Psalms*, cxix. 52 ; *Opera*, xxxii., p. 236. *Cf.* xxvi.,
p. 674 ; xxvii., p. 568 ; xxxiv., p. 504 ; xxviii., p. 563.

[2] A. Lang in *Calvin and the Reformation*, p. 59. *Cf.* Melanchthon, *Opera*
(in *Corpus Reformatorum*), xxi., cc. 116ff., 391, 417 ; xiii., c. 7.

[3] *Institutes*, i., p. 238 ; *Opera*, xxiii., p. 586.

[4] *Opera*, i., p. 325. *Cf.* xxvii., pp. 143, 246, 290, 293, 414-415, 445,
450, 451.

[5] *Opera*, xxiv., p. 605.

[6] *Ibid.*, pp. 603, 662 ; xxvii., p. 686 ; xxix., pp. 49, 662, 725.

[7] *Ibid.*, i., p. 371 ; xxiv., p. 725 ; xxx., p. 168 ; xxxv., p. 400 ; xxxvi.,
p. 29.

[8] *Ibid.*, xxvii., pp. 568, 582 ; xxviii., pp. 61, 63, 77, 110. Cf. *The
Institutes*, I. iv. 4 ; II. viii. 1 ; III. ii. 22 ; IV. x. 15 ; xx. 16 ; *Opera*,
xxviii., p. 434.

[9] *Opera*, xxviii., p. 454.   [10] *The Institutes*, IV. xx. 16.

For the doctrine of the nature and origin of the State we have to investigate not with Machiavelli the sovereignty of the Prince, but the sovereignty of God [1] and the fall of man. Calvin's attitude led him to feel that God was in His heaven and therefore all was right with the world. With St Paul he could ask the question: " Shall the thing formed say to him that formed it, Why hast thou made me thus? Hath not the potter power over the clay, of the same lump to make one vessel unto honour, and another unto dishonour? " To Calvin and Luther, as to the Jew, the first idea in their theology was the greatness of God. The innumerable and inexplicable things of life are simply the whirling wheel on which the clay is changed and shaped till the potter's design is finally accomplished. Eastern nations realise the sovereignty of God : Western nations do not. In this respect Calvin was markedly Eastern in his mental affinities. To him the independence and the restlessness of the Westerner were utterly abhorrent. God is great, and it is not in our power to resist. God knows all, and, in spite of the saying of Alfonso of Castile, it is not in our capacity to criticise. We are His creatures, and are at His disposal. Has He sent good? Blessed be God. Has He sent evil? Blessed be God. We are the clay and He is the potter.

Belief in the sovereignty of God creates a majestic view of God, and this lies at the root of reverent religion. It also lies at the root of the making of strong men. There was only one thing the Calvinist feared, and that was sin. There was only one being he feared, and that was God. The Calvinist feared God with all his soul, and this exhausted his capacity for fear. The face of man he did not fear. What was man, even though he be a king, compared with the King of kings? Everything is *sub specie æternitatis*. Nor does the power of God mean the powerlessness of man. If Luther could say: " *Credo, ergo sum*," Calvin could say: " *Ago, ergo credo*." The belief in predestination formed the school of vigorous ecclesiastical and political life. God is active and energetic, and therefore his servant, man, must also be active and energetic. Order and obedience,

---

[1] Beyerhaus, pp. 51-55, 56, 60. *Cf.* Calvin, *Opera*, xxiv., p. 368; xxv., p. 644; xxix., p. 49; xxxv., pp. 150, 162; xl., pp. 685-687; xli., p. 446.

gravity and chastity, temperance in life and sobriety in thought are qualities every whit as valuable for the State as for the Church. Economy and industry lead on to property, and this in turn leads on to prosperity in the State as much as in the Church. The sovereignty of God might seem at first sight as if it would lean towards absolutism in politics, whereas it does nothing of the kind. The fear of God took away the fear of man. As no power comes from man, and as all power comes from God, all in His sight, kings and subjects alike, are equal. There is a halo around the heavenly King: there is none around the earthly king. The Calvinist ecclesiastical system acknowledges no head with right divine. There are simply representatives chosen by the people. The ecclesiastical republic in time leads on to a political republic. For when men have learned in ecclesiastical affairs to govern themselves through their elected representatives, the stage to representative government in the State is but a short one. James I. was never more right than when he uttered the words: " No bishop, no king."

The glowing activity and energy of Calvin, set in motion by the law of God, are plainly visible in every department of life. There is a cruel determination in the man, but it is inevitable. Is there any creature so cruel as a man obsessed by a fixed idea? For he sees nothing else: common humanity deserts him and he becomes nothing but an unrelenting will, the kind of Florence Nightingale that Mr Lytton Strachey has conceived. Through the Church he means to reform the State. Is his law merely valuable for the faithful? Is it not just as valuable for the State, and indeed for the whole social order? In this dogmatic attitude to law we have in germ the notion of the State according to the Lutheran and Calvinist conceptions. The Church stands supreme in her own domain, outside the jurisdiction of the State. The State may interfere when the Church excommunicates an erring member, but this provides the limit of his intervention. In a word, the Church appears as a free society, living and growing in the State. Profoundly as Calvin had studied his Bible, the outcome of his teaching for citizens was their equality, and this in spite of the fact that

passages like that of the " Parable of the Talents " plainly contradict the idea of the equality of all souls in the sight of God.
Still, God, by virtue of His sovereignty, had or had not elected
a soul to salvation for all eternity. This Divine election dissolved
all earthly distinctions. They were temporal, this eternal. A
peasant might be so elected : his lord might not be. The lord's
descent might be blazoned by heraldry : the peasant's name
might be written in the Lamb's Book of Life. At bottom such
ideas inevitably prepared the way for democracy.

The first conception in the Calvinist State is the sovereignty
of God, and the second the fall of man. The Fathers held stoutly
to the idea that the origin of the State was to be found in
Adam's transgression, and Calvin adopted this view fervently.
But for sin there would be no need for government. But for
sin each of us " bore the law in his heart." But for sin " all
constraint employed against us " would be useless. " Justice is
the remedy for this corruption that dwells in man." [1] " We
should be simply like beasts if there was no principality, if
there was neither justice nor rule ; we should not be simply
like savage beasts, but much worse. And why? " [2] Calvin
intimates that beasts conduct themselves after their own
orderly fashion, but men do not so conduct themselves. [3]

" Earthly justice " provides a " remedy " which is in
essence a Divine remedy. In devising absolution for the corruption of man the popes introduced " human extortion," for
Calvin feels as strongly as Luther the financial drains effected
by Rome. Calvin resumes his consideration of the origin of
the State. " It does not happen by the perversion of men that
kings and other superiors obtain their power on earth." [4]
For the State is a Divine institution. " God has established
the polity of this world." [5] " All the principalities of this world
are the figure and image of the kingdom of our Lord Jesus
Christ." Who does not know that this order is heaven's decree

---

[1] " Sermons on Deuteronomy," *Opera*, xxvii., p. 409.

[2] " Sermons on Deuteronomy," *Opera*, xxvi., p. 409; " Homilies on
Samuel," *Opera*, xxx., p. 487.

[3] " Sermons on Daniel," *Opera*, xli., pp. 350, 450.

[4] " Sermons on 1 Titus," *Opera*, liii., p. 132.   [5] *Ibid.*, p. 132.

(*nunc ordinem cælitus ordinatum*)? The Providence of God rules and governs all inferior matters, and especially kingdoms, principalities, and all States, with their magistrates and their administrators of justice.[1] In a word, the occasion of the State is human wickedness: the cause of the State is Divine. "God maintains principalities; He has no other reason except that He loves mankind. . . . In this He has declared His infinite love." [2] "Thus it is for us to love the earthly polity, as it is for us that it is such a mark of the goodness of God and of His fatherly love." [3] Still, he harks back to his first idea. We maintain the State, as we maintain law, simply on account of the wicked. "Until we are like the angels of paradise, we have need of some order and check, which keeps us in our place." [4]

With Calvin as with Luther, liberty and justification by faith go hand in hand. In his chapter on Christian Liberty, Calvin insists on the fact that the Christian is no longer under the yoke of the law, that the yoke of the law is removed, and that the Christian obeys freely. The emphasis, however, is not altogether placed on the same qualities. Luther dwells on the free and joyous mind possessed by God's children, reconciled with Him and living together here below in love. Calvin dwells more on obedience than on this freedom. The ascetic element is more marked in Geneva than it is in Wittenberg.

As man is detached from the world and attached to God, Calvin stresses the internal liberty of the soul more than the external liberty of the body. Still, the ordinary member of his communion could not draw a line of demarcation. He saw the Church at work in baptism, confirmation, Holy Communion, marriage, burial; and all her rites combined with her organisation impressed him. These sank into his being even more than the sermons, of which he heard far too many. Subconsciously the impression persists. As is the dogma, so is the

---

[1] "Homilies on Samuel," *Opera*, xxix., p. 658.

[2] "Sermons on Daniel," *Opera*, xli., p. 350; "Homilies on Samuel," *Opera*, xxix., p. 584; "Sermons on Deuteronomy," *Opera*, xxviii., pp. 409-410.

[3] "Sermons on Deuteronomy," *Opera*, xxvii., p. 449.

[4] "Sermons on 1 Timothy," *Opera*, liii., p. 134.

Church; as is the Church, so is the State. The Church, in fact, makes society, and society makes the State.

The head of the Church, the *unicus rex*, is Christ, a view common to Knox and Zwingli. If Christ is the Head, clearly there is no place left for the Pope. When, however, he abolishes the jurisdiction of the Pope, Calvin does not entertain the remotest idea of replacing him by the Saxon Prince with the Consistory to enunciate his demands. Princes most emphatically are not what Melanchthon deemed them to be, and that is *præcipua membra ecclesiæ*. Nor are they what Luther deemed them to be, *summi episcopi*. There is delegation in the Lutheran Church, but there is little of it in the Calvinist. The Lutheran rests content if the Church of which he is a member assures him of the ministry of the Word and the Sacraments. The Calvinist wants this assurance, but he wants very much more. For he wants the Church to be the field in which he must labour effectually in order to hasten the reign of Christ, the real Head of the Church. Such labour will be long and stern. Nothing is more characteristic of Calvin's letters than the military terms with which they are filled. We hear continually of armies and battles, of standards and soldiers.

If Christ is to reign in the Church—and this is vital with Calvinism—he must also reign in the State. In the Preface to the *Institutes* its author informs Francis I. that men " defame " evangelical doctrine when they describe it " as aiming at nothing else than to wrest the sceptres of kings out of their hands, to overturn all tribunals and seats of justice, to subvert all order and government, to disturb the peace and quiet of society, to abolish all laws, destroy the distinctions of rank and property, and, in short, to turn all things upside down." [1] The circumstance that he dedicates his book to a king shows the absurdity of these charges. His last chapter in it analyses the mode of civil government. Calvin was quite right to defend himself, yet we are by no means sure that if Francis I. could have pierced the veil of the future he would have remained

---

[1] *Institutes*, i., p. 4 (1845 ed.). Cf. *Opera*, xv., p. 759; xvi., pp. 612-613; xvii., pp. 715-716, 656; xviii., pp. 38-39, 82, 176, 344-345, 378, 427-428, 437, 580-581, 619-620; xix., pp. 121, 409, 410, 412.

satisfied with this *apologia*. M. Imbart de la Tour [1] has proved that even in the early sixteenth century France was turning into a centralised monarchy with a leaning to Gallicanism. What was the French King to think of the view that the Church possessed the right to develop her proper functions without any interference on the part of the State? Francis I. could perceive that with such a right her members also possessed the power of moulding her destiny. If they mould her destiny why can they not mould that of the State? If they can secure equality in the Church, why not go on to secure it in the State?

Calvin was far too methodical a Frenchman to rest satisfied with talk merely about rights. He proceeded to create machinery for the employment of these rights, and he also proceeded to create machinery for the punishment of those who violated them. Luther was not enough of an ecclesiastical statesman to perceive the necessity of machinery for the preservation of law, order and, above all, of discipline in a newly organised body. With statesman-like instincts, Calvin felt fully determined that discipline must take its part in the purging of the offender. The spirit of Calvinism is as vague as the character of a nation. The fact of Calvinism is in no wise vague, and one of the institutions that differentiated it sharply from Lutheranism is that it had resolutely determined that it should have Discipline. Men might talk as they pleased about their rights, but Calvin resolved that they should bear in mind their duties. If they did not, then his Discipline should bring them to their senses. His genius for an ordered coherence had methodised the incoherence of Luther. His mind was set on unity, not on divinity, and by virtue of his genius and his mind he compelled the clashing churches who owned allegiance to the Calvinist creed to become a highly organised body. In a word, he was a lay Pope.[2] Indeed he was that most formidable of all popes, a Pope by birth, not by election.

---

[1] *Cf.* his three illuminating volumes on *Les Origines de la Réforme*.
[2] Calvin, *Opera*, xvi., pp. 83ff., 333ff., also *Bulletin du Prot. français*, pp. 1859, p. 72.

What the Discipline meant is clear from the following extracts from the Registers of the Genevan Council from 1545 to 1547 [1]:

"A man who swore by the ' body and blood of Christ' was condemned to sit in the public square in the stocks, and to be fined.

"Another, hearing an ass bray, and saying jestingly, ' Il chante un beau psaume,' was sentenced to temporary banishment from the city.

"A man was sentenced to the *amende honorable* for saying in church, at the moment of the benediction of the Communion, ' Taisé vos, y est prou prié.'

"A young man, presenting his bride with an account-book, said: ' Tenez, madame, voici voitre meilleur psaume.' Another, a working-man, for saying in a wine-shop: ' S'il y a un Dieu, qu'il me paie mon écot '; both had to undergo penalties. A young girl, in church, singing the words of a song to the tune of the psalm, was ordered to be whipt by her parents.

"Drunkenness and debauchery were visited with more severe penalties; adultery more than once with death. Prostitutes who ventured back to Geneva were mercilessly thrown into the Rhone. Cards were altogether prohibited. Rope-dancers and conjurers were forbidden to exhibit. Usury was restricted, no higher rate of interest being allowed than 6 per cent."

It would be perfectly easy to multiply these entries, but enough has been given for us to realise that Calvinism meant Discipline; it meant duties that must be taken seriously. Among these duties lay the election of the minister. Is he to be elected by the whole Church, by other ministers, by the elders, or by a single man? The last alternative Calvin decisively rules out, for what right has the magistrate to own such a power? The Apostles, he reasoned, did not by their own voice determine the election. The Bible plainly shows that they presided over the elections in order to lead the people to come to a

---

[1] I take these from the convenient summary in M. Pattison, *Essays*, i., 302-303.

suitable choice. They declared who the minister was to be, but at the same time the people ratified their choice by raising their hands in approval. Calvin proposes a plan, and on its behalf he invokes the authority of the primitive Church, the decree of the Council of Antioch that nothing be done against the will of the people, and even the authority of Leo X. Practically his plan amounted to this, that in Geneva the clergy chose, the political authority ratified their choice, and the election was put before the congregation, who were in no wise bound to receive this election as a matter of course. Their ratification did not resemble that of an English Chapter when a Dean or Bishop is sent to it. Obviously, the Church had ample training in ecclesiastical elections, and this training led her members to bethink themselves of its use in political elections.

Calvin insists on the authority of the minister. The Prince must support him in his criticism, for otherwise he is a *deterrimus tyrannus*, and his reign is nothing but a " criminal sacrilege " (*scelestum sacrilegium*).[1] The only limit on the power of the minister is the Word of God.[2] He cannot order his flock to carry out what that does not authorise. Of course the minister must have complete liberty to preach to the magistrate as well as to the citizen.[3] This freedom is vital. " Let us remember that in church the Word of God obtains such a sovereign authority that neither the sacrificers nor the kings nor the princes nor their council are at all privileged nor dispensed in any wise (from its observance) any more than other (folk), as if their life was not subject to the Word of God." [4] In fact, all the powers claimed by an Isaiah or a Jeremiah were claimed by Calvin on behalf of his ministers, and this claim was urged in an age when there was no liberty of the Press.

Liberty must not degenerate into licence. The Anabaptists commit this mistake, for they " try to pervert it. They are like brigands, and we must reckon them the enemies of the salvation

---

[1] 1557, *Opera*, xxxi., p. 769 ; xli. p. 408.
[2] " Sermons on Deuteronomy," *Opera*, xxvi., p. 318 ; xxix. p. 229.
[3] " Lessons and Familiar Expositions on the Minor Prophets—Amos ii. 12."
[4] " Commentary on Hosea v. 1, and on Micah iii. 10."

of men. They war on one another, when we see that they force themselves to come to a horrible confusion." [1] " It is true that they pretend to be spiritual ; but they are devils who endeavour to pervert all humanity, and to throw it into such horrible confusion that it would be better that men should become brute beasts or men-wolves than to have such a mixture." [2] Calvin is convinced that there must be order. God means that there should be " some sensible sovereign among his people." What " nature teaches," " what has been followed by nature in all the world and approved by the mouth of God . . . when we see what God has thrown out of order so as to show us political order, we must come to the conclusion that he approves of it ; for otherwise he would not allow it. . . . Let us know by this that it is a matter of which he approves." [3] In short, " Our Lord takes so much interest in earthly polity that He means it to be maintained and to see justice in the life of men. Human blood is precious to Him, for men are formed in His image ; but He does not spare so much a man who has turned against civil order, that he is stoned and dies." [4]

If there are subjects as troublesome as the Anabaptists, at the other end of the scale there are rulers who are tyrants. What is to be their fate? Calvin frankly admits that subjects are not the only folk to disturb " the order of justice." Sometimes the magistrates, charged with maintaining it, " exercise rather a barbarity and tyrannical cruelty than a legitimate domination, and prove themselves to be ravening beasts." Calvin knew France and Switzerland too well not to admit the truth of this impeachment, but he is so much a man of order that he prefers tyranny of any sort whatsoever to anarchy. Europe had barely recovered from the demoralisation due to the Black Death and indeed to certain aspects of the Renaissance. A settled land with orderly government is so much in his mind that he can write : " There never was, and we could not think of a tyranny so cruel and unlimited in which there

---

1 " Sermons on Deuteronomy," *Opera*, xxvii., pp. 409-410.
2 " Sermons on 1 Timothy," *Opera*, liii., p. 135.
3 *Opera*, xxviii., p. 445.
4 *Opera*, xxvii., p. 455, " Sermon civ. on Deuteronomy."

was not some sort of equity. For God does not permit that this order should be so overthrown by the wickedness of men that we should not perceive some traces of it." [1] " Whatever excesses there may be with princes, still the goodness of God surmounts them so that He does not altogether allow that the polities and ordinances that He has instituted should be completely thrown into confusion." [2] " We see even when tyrants dominate that there are grave corruptions, yet that is more tolerable than if there were no order. Let us put as in a balance one tyrant or several, who exercise every form of cruelty, who pillage some and murder others and who commit many other serious wickednesses under the guise of justice ; on the other hand, let us put a people who have no chief, no magistrate, no authority, but are all equal : it is certain that there will be graver and more horrible confusion when there will be no preeminence than there will be with the most exorbitant tyranny in the world." [3]

Calvin was so impressed by the vocation of man in private life that he extended this cardinal idea to public life, reaching towards a view of the State that is not unlike the Platonic. The State has a moral content ; it has an immanent morality, allowing men to lead a good life within its range. In fact, the State possesses a vocation every whit as much as the Church herself, for is not the State, under another aspect, fundamentally the Church? In the considered judgment of Calvin the State cannot turn aside from morality, from the law of God, for in so turning it commits suicide. Here is the parting of the ways with Machiavelli, who simply regards the State as serving our interests devoid of all share in the nobler existence that Calvin insistently claims for it. With Machiavelli and with the Jesuits the State is a means to an end. Nor is it altogether without significance that in 1541 Calvin, recalled from exile, directs the Puritan State of Geneva, and in 1541 Loyola is elected general of the new Society of Jesus.

It is fundamental to grasp the Calvinist conception of the

---

[1] " Commentaries on 1 Peter ii. 14."
[2] " Sermons on Daniel," *Opera*, xli., p. 352.
[3] *Opera*, liii., " Sermons on 1 Timothy," p. 131.

Christian State, for this forms his outstanding contribution to
political thought. It is this conception that renders Calvinism
such a tremendous factor in seventeenth-century thought, not
only in Holland and Old England but also in New England.
The Christian State, in Calvin's opinion, is a creation of God
exactly like the Christian Church. They are two creations of
the same Author. These two creations can be autonomous and
independent without ceasing to possess a concurrent common
activity. The State is not Christian because the Church compels
it to be so. The Church is not Christian because the State
compels it to be so. By virtue of their origin and their nature,
the State and the Church are obliged to observe the same law,
which comes from God, their common Creator.[1] At first sight
this seems like the ideas of Innocent III., but this is not really
so. With Innocent the Church is the sun and the State the
moon. With Calvin the Church and the State are each suns.
The difference of the two is the essential matter with Innocent :
the equality of the two is the essential matter with Calvin.

The French thinker considers the union that at first existed
between Saul and Samuel. " Let us realise," he tells us, " that
God rules the governments of the world, so that he means
that there should be kings, princes, magistrates and men
pre-eminent by their dignity who preside over others and bear
the sword, and serve as God has ordained. And on the other
hand let us recognise that God has constituted the Church
a spiritual government, that of the preaching of the Word, to
which all ought to be submissive, and against which no rebellion
ought to be tolerated : all men of whatever condition must allow
themselves to be governed by it, as sheep by a shepherd, hearing
his voice only, and following him everywhere he calls them.
These two orders constituted by God are not at all repugnant,
like water and fire, which are contrary ; but these are matters
conjoined, so that the one taken away, the other suffers much ;
as if we damage an eye in anyone, the other eye suffers seriously
by the blow ; so that if an arm is cut, the other suffers seriously,
and cannot alone suffice for the work of the two." [2] It was

---

[1] *Opera*, xxvii., pp. 454-455, " Sermon civ. on Deuteronomy."
[2] *Opera*, " Homilies on 1 Samuel," pp. 659-660.

therefore, Calvin considers, an excellent union (*optima societas*) when Saul associated himself with Samuel, the prophet of God. On the other hand, when he separated himself from Samuel and " dared without him to undertake something," all he did was unfortunate and detestable.[1] At times we feel not far removed from the conception of the *societas perfectas*.

The intimate bond between Church and State comes out in a hundred ways. We look on territory as settled by treaties. Calvin thinks that " we do not dwell on the earth by chance, but on the place on which it has pleased God to set us." [2] Behind the treaties the thinker discerns the conflict that leads to them. Here he notes one grand difference between the State and the Church. The former employs force, whereas the latter employs freedom. " The Church has no sword to punish malefactors, and no commandment to constrain them, no prisons, no fines, no other punishments which the magistrates customarily employ." [3] Ecclesiastical power rests on liberty. " Besides it is not merely that, but he who has sinned is punished willingly because by a voluntary chastisement he declares his penitence." [3] The Lutherans thought that when the civil power turned Christian, this difference ceased to exist. Not at all, thought the French statesman. " The magistrate has not appeared in the Church." [4] Indignantly he denounces " the blasphemies " that have named Henry VIII. as " sovereign head of the Church," and he also denounces the Papacy when it becomes Cæsaropapacy.[5]

If the civil power is excluded from authority in the Church, ministers are similarly excluded from authority in the State. " There is no doubt that Jesus Christ meant to exclude ministers of the Word from earthly lordship over people when He said : ' Kings rule over people, but it is not so with you.' " [6] In the spirit of Henry II., he denies the clergy all jurisdiction, all

---

[1] *Opera*, " Homilies on 1 Samuel," pp. 659-660.
[2] " Sermons on Deuteronomy," *Opera*, xxviii., p. 685.
[3] 1543, IV. xi. 3.
[4] 1543, IV. xi. 4.
[5] " Commentaries on Amos vii. 13," IV. xi. 10-12.
[6] IV. xi. 8.

exceptional immunity. On this score he sharply criticises the Pope and his priests, taking occasion to show that " the ancient bishops " themselves " have not reckoned that their right was in any wise infringed, if they were subject to lay judges in civil cases."[1] " As for the ministers of the Word of God, in their persons, in their character as men, they are subject to the laws, and they render obedience to the magistrates, and they pay them honour and reverence."[2]

The powers of Church and State are distinct: they are not different. They are not separate, for they are by their nature conjoined. The State is no mere police State, concerned merely with the keeping of contracts. The State aspires to guide the citizen in his efforts to realise himself to the utmost of his capacity. The State is as much concerned with our duty towards God as with our duty towards our neighbour.[3] The State must look after " idolatry, blasphemies against the name of God and against His truth, and other scandals of religion."[4] " The policy God has instituted in the world procures us three benefits: that we can lead a peaceful life; that God is served and honoured; that the life of man is upright."[5] Three things, and three things only, really matter. They are peace, religion and uprightness.[6] Why, inquires Calvin, has God established the powers that be? It is in the first place " that we should live," as St Paul said, " in all piety." What does this word piety mean? It is in essence the honour of God, when there is a religion pure and holy among us. By this the magistrates are proved to be such when they bear not the sword in vain against those that trouble the Church, against all heretics, against those who disseminate errors and false opinions, against those dreamers under the influence of Satan who to-day seek that

---

[1] IV. xi. 15 : " Nihil lædi se ac suum ordinem judicarunt, si subjicerentur."

[2] *Opera*, liii., " Sermons on 1 Timothy," pp. 223-224.

[3] IV. xi. 3, 16; "Sermons on Deuteronomy," xxvi., pp. 576-577; "Sermons on 1 Timothy," liii., p. 142 ; " Homily xxvi. on 1 Samuel vii.," *Opera*, xxix., p. 532ff.; Letter to Lord Somerset, *Opera*, xiii., pp. 64-67 ; Letter to the King of Poland, 1554, *Opera*, xv., p. 335.

[4] *Opera*, i., pp. 229, 230; IV. x. 3.

[5] *Opera*, liii., " Sermons on 1 Timothy," p. 130.

[6] *Ibid.*, p. 134.

we should bestow an unchecked licence upon those who seek to overthrow the truth and upon those who break the unity of the faith and the peace of the Church. " And yet we behold mortal man who will suffer the truth of God to be slandered, that men should mock at Him, and that the order He has given among men should be abolished. And is this tolerable? The magistrates assuredly realise what condemnation there will be on their head, and the dreadful vengeance that awaits them, unless they take care to enforce [this order] so as to maintain the honour of God, which consists [in this], that pure religion has place and power among men." [1]

Calvin entertains not the shadow of a doubt that princes and magistrates " are lieutenants of God." [2] Public servants generally and kings particularly are designated " sons of God." [3] Indeed they are called " God." [4] All their authority is " jurisdiction as delegated by God." [5] Of course the establishment of the authority of the King does not in the smallest degree detract from the authority of God, Whose servant the King is.[6] To-day we believe in obedience to the powers that be solely on utilitarian grounds, with the result that on a fresh weighing of the claims of utility we may upset the *status quo*.

The Calvinist knew better than we. For he realised that authority is sometimes superhuman, something sacred. It is so contrary to the nature of man to obey, that while and when he obeys a particular action of God is necessary. For obedience is due to the intervention of the Holy Spirit.[7] Submission to such a power receives a dignity that is all its own. Man obeys man not on his knees but as a free man. The subject renders his loyalty to the King who is God's representative on earth, and such loyalty assumes a grand and noble character.

Calvin draws a distinction between the office and the man

---

[1] " Sermons on 1 Timothy," *Opera*, liii., pp. 140-141.
[2] " Sermons on Job," *Opera*, xxxiii., p. 162.
[3] " Homily in 1 Samuel," *Opera*, xxix., p. 617.
[4] " Commentaries on the Psalms," *Opera*, xxxiii., p. 160.
[5] 1555, *Opera*, xxv., p. 644.
[6] 1552, l., p. 397 ; xxxv., pp. 152, 229 ; xxxvi., p. 626 ; xl. pp. 662, 707.
[7] " Sermons on Deuteronomy," *Opera*, xxix., p. 228.

who exercises the office.[1] He may be a Nero, he may be "the declared enemies of God," even "devils incarnate." At the same time we must be careful not to "accuse God when we see the men they make." [2] Fundamentally "all power comes from God, for God stretches out His hand to whom He will, and according to His pleasure He creates a man king and ruler. All these therefore who have the right of the sword and public power are slaves of God, even if they exercise tyranny and are brigands (*latrones*)." [3] They may be "lieutenants of God" in their public capacity, but they may simultaneously be "brigands."

The Frenchman believes in sovereigns because he believes in God, but there is little of the halo of Divine right around them. In nothing is the absence of the historical sense more apparent than in his refusal " to inquire too curiously by what right each Prince rules." The providence of God bestows kingdoms, and Divine sovereignty estops all questioning. The authority of the Prince is essentially *de facto* : the *de jure* sovereign is no concern of his. The authority of the Prince is the authority of fact. Common sense is apparent in the injunction that "when there is a change of empire, the engagements of the subject cease." Such common sense is most uncommon, and was conspicuously absent in the Revolution of 1688. Loyalty to the King—and loyalty to God—requires that the Christian " exposes his life in order to defend his Prince." The tone of Calvin is lukewarm, for we learn that if a stranger invades one's country, it would be perfidy not to oppose him, not to succour the Prince, according to the oaths he has taken. If, in spite of these efforts, the invader wins, "the subject is released from the obligations of his oath, because it is not in the power of the people to set up princes. It is to God alone that it belongs to change rulers according to his pleasure. And as all power resides in God alone, then when a Prince reigns, the people must not obstinately persist

---

[1] *Opera*, vii., p. 83 ; xxvii., p. 78, " Sermons on 1 Timothy " ; *Opera*, liii., p. 130, " Sermon lxxiv. on Deuteronomy."
[2] " Sermons on Daniel," xli., p. 352.
[3] " Prælections on Jeremiah," xxvii. 6, *Opera*, xxxviii., p. 544.

in not submitting to him, as to a legitimate Prince, seeing
he has been divinely appointed." [1] Take the case of Daniel
in Babylon, " how he had good right to deem the King an
odious man, if he had not paid reverence to this great power,
that God had given him! Thus let us learn by the example
of the prophet to pray for our adversaries who want to ruin
us; and above all pray for tyrants, if it is the will of God that
we should be subject to them. For though they were unworthy
that folk should practise any duty of humanity towards them,
yet since they possess no superiority save by the permission
and good will of God, let us bear their yoke peaceably, and
this not merely to avoid their indignation, as St Paul warns
us (Romans xiii. 5), but for the sake of conscience. Otherwise
we should be rebels not only against them, but even against
God." [2] There is enough in this teaching to justify our agreement with the remark of Tocqueville that Christianity commands us to render to Cæsar the things that are Cæsar's, but
discourages the question whether Cæsar is entitled to such
obedience.

The sovereignty of God is paramount. Order and obedience
are due to it tolerably unquestioningly. God acts in him who
commands and He acts in him who obeys. Man is man because
he bears the image of God. Authority is simply the particular
image of God in man. The Prince, the magistrate, bears
this august mark in special fashion. When a military officer
attempted to seize the staff of office of a Genevan syndic, the
magistrate simply said: " This staff has been given me not
by you but by God and the people, to whom I shall return it
and not to you." [3] In the spirit of St Thomas Aquinas, Calvin
argues that this is why animals obey man, why the citizen
obeys the magistrate. " When men ask why it is that princes
are so well obeyed though they still rule with grave immoderation . . . that yet they are maintained in their dignity and
persist in it.~The reason is that God has them in His hand
and that He has engraven such majesty that they must obey,

---

[1] "Prælections on Jeremiah," *Opera*, xxix., p. 158.
[2] *Opera*, xl., pp. 665-666.
[3] Bonivard, *Advis* (1865 ed.), p. 139.

although they practise immoderation and cruelty often. And in fact, how is it that beasts fear men? It is on account of the image of God that is engraven in them." [1] Is the law of nature also at work? " When people submit to kings, princes, magistrates and great folk, and receive from them laws, and suffer themselves to be condemned, it is certain that this happens by a movement and a divine instinct, which inspires in men this fear, without which it is certain that they never would submit to others. . . . We know what ambition is innate in each man, and how much each is greedy of rule : it is absolutely contrary to our nature to place our heads under the yoke of another." [2]

If the people have their duty towards the King, he in his turn has his duty towards them. For the social pact, the social contract, is in existence. Louis XIV. could declare: " *L'Etat, c'est moi.*" Such a notion does not enter the mind of Calvin, who is much more of the opinion of Frederick the Great, who declared that he was the first servant of the State. In fact, the benevolent despot of the eighteenth century is not an inappropriate description of the sovereign this thinker depicted. The King reigns " in general for the common good " (*in commune populum commodum*). To think that the world has been created for kings and princes is to misconceive the entire position, for " they are rather created for the world." [3] In their quality as " vicars of God " they must display themselves to men "as an image of Providence, safeguarded [with] the kindness, sweetness and justice of God." If they prevaricate, they are twice " cursed," for they injure not only men but also God.[4]

Calvin is anxious to set forth the duty of the people, and he is no less anxious to set forth the duty of the sovereign. In his earliest work, his edition of Seneca's *De Clementia*, in 1532, he even then laboured to show the true functions of rulers,

---

[1] " Sermons on Daniel," *Opera*, xli., pp. 349-350.
[2] " Homily in 1 Samuel," *Opera*, xxix., p. 660. Cf. *Opera*, xli., pp. 396-397, 415 ; "Sermon vii. on Daniel," ch. vi.
[3] " Sermon cxiii. on Job," xxxi., *Opera*, xxxiv., p. 656.
[4] *Opera*, IV. xx. 6.

and with the passing of the years this idea strengthened. They possess power " on this condition, that they work and even serve the common good of the people, as if God had placed the burden on their shoulders to sustain the common estate." [1] Practically this is in the editor's mind already in 1532. His discussion then of the theory of the tyrant betrays an anti-despotic tendency. Then he also thought that " this great Roman Empire [of Nero] was in reality a great brigandage (*vere magnum latrocinium*)." Why? Because it lacked liberty.

The diversity of governments Calvin reckoned to be the will of God. Unlike Machiavelli, he indulges in speculations on the best form of government.[2] He is opposed to universal monarchy [3] in general and to the Holy Roman Empire in particular.[4] Subconsciously nascent nationalism was at work, and it influenced him more than readers sometimes think. Yet he does not estimate highly hereditary monarchy, which indeed he reckons the worst form of government.[5] Indeed from 1536, the date of the first edition of the *Institutes*, to 1559, the date of the last, his hostility to monarchy seems steadily to grow. We learn that kings achieved their ends by " frauds and finesses " [6]; that they ceaselessly devise new taxes [7]; that the greatest kings are the worst [8]; and that among them " he is the most powerful who can be styled the rich son of a celebrated brigand." So far as we can judge, Calvin's ideal form of government is a representative one, resting on the election of the magistrates by the people—that

---

[1] *Opera*, xxv., pp. 629-630. Cf. *Institutes* (1543), xx., p. 7; *Opera*, i., p. 1105.

[2] *Opera*, i., pp. 232-233.

[3] 1543, p. 601; IV. vi. 8, 9.

[4] 1561, " Prælections on Daniel," ii. 5, *Opera*, xl., pp. 597-598; *Opera*, xl., Prolegomena.

[5] Cf. *Opera*, xli., pp. 4, 227; xxix., pp. 4, 684-685; xxx., pp. 281, 294, 426; xxvii., p. 479; xxxiii., p. 503; xxxiv., p. 138; xxxviii. pp. 322, 383; xxxix., p. 4.

[6] " Commentary on Isaiah," *Opera*, xxxvi., p. 665.

[7] *Ibid.*, p. 573.

[8] *Ibid.*, pp. 168, 332; chap. viii. 7, and xix. 4. Cf. *Opera*, xxv., p. 592; xli., pp. 415, 418; xxxii., p. 56; xxxi., p. 451.

is, by the "common voice of all."[1] Here we must be careful. For though he employed the word people, he obviously means the chosen people, a considerable restriction of the franchise. The *plebs* is not the people: it is the populace. It would be easy to go through his voluminous writings and gather phrases proving that he employed such shibboleths—not shibboleths to him—as liberty, fraternity and equality. We learn that liberty is "an inestimable benefit (*inestimabilis bonus*),"[2] and that "Christ is the only head of the Church, and no constraint can be exercised over the conscience Christ has made free."[3] We learn, however, that this liberty must be safeguarded by the right of the Church to excommunicate.[4] For fraternity, it is sufficient to quote the statement that "humanity is a single family, created by one blood,"[5] though members of the family found a warmer welcome in Geneva when they adhered to the doctrines of Calvin than when they did not. Calvin's doctrines, much as he loved discipline or despotism, powerfully promoted freedom. Luther's doctrines, much as he loved freedom, powerfully promoted despotism.

Calvin stood on stronger ground when he spoke of equality. The laity are equal among themselves, the pastors are equal among themselves. The laity and the pastors are also equal among themselves.[6] The doctrine of the priesthood of the laity is answerable for much in the spread of democracy. Immediately the believers became popes with the infallible word of God in their hand. How could the reformer debar

---

[1] "Commentary on Hosea i."; "Commentary on Amos vii. 13," *Opera*, ii., p. 1098; iv., p. 1134; *Institutes* (1559), IV. xx. 8. *Cf.* "Commentary on Micah v. 5," *Opera*, x., p. 120; xliii., p. 374. *Cf.* also H. D. Foster's thoughtful account of "Calvin's Programme for a Puritan State in Geneva," *Harvard Theological Review*, i., pp. 423-424, 1908.

[2] *Opera*, xxix., p. 544; xxx., p. 185.

[3] *Ibid.*, i., p. 204. *Cf.* vii., p. 83; xxix., p. 619; "Homily xxxv. in I Samuel x."

[4] "Commentaries on I Corinthians v. 4."

[5] "Commentary on Acts xvii. 26." *Cf.* "Sermon cvi. on Deuteronomy xvii.," *Opera*, pp. 479-480; "Commentary on Philemon 4," *Opera*, xxvii., pp. 608, 622; xxvi., p. 9; lii., p. 474; "Commentary on Thessalonians iii. 5."

[6] "Commentary on Titus ii. 11," *Opera*, lviii.-lix.; for the "Sermons on Jacob and Esau," *Opera*, xxxiv., pp. 657, 658, 660.

them from a voice in the State when he allowed them a voice in the Church? For if they were fitted to be entrusted with eternal affairs, were they not fitted to be entrusted with temporal? As the doctrine of justification by faith bestowed free pardon on believers, their God was their Father. Since He was not a despot, their king could not be one. How could the great revolutionary—for such, in spite of his conservatism, he became—allow the sovereignty of conscience and refuse his followers all share in the sovereignty of their country? No doubt the infant Lutheran Church of the sixteenth—like that of the first—century remained in a condition of subservience to the ruler. The Calvinist Church was in no such condition. The Reformed Church of 325 was no more the Church of 125 than the Church of 1725 was that of 1525. The day which saw the slave and the master signify their membership of the Body of Christ by kneeling side by side, to partake of the rite of Holy Communion, witnessed the beginning of the movement which one day was to give to the former a share in the government of their common country. After the Massacre of Vassy, Theodore Beza, alluding to a current proverb, remarked significantly to Antony, the King of Navarre: " Sire, it is in truth the lot of the Church of God, in whose name I speak, to suffer blows and not to return them. Yet I also take leave to remind you she is the anvil that has employed many hammers." [1] If the hammer of the absolute Pope ceased to be wielded, the same fate awaited the hammer of the absolute Prince.

As the congregation was sovereign in form, it might become —and did become—sovereign in substance. As the faithful received religious liberty, they went on to claim political. There is only one liberty, and it is liberty of conscience. All other forms of liberty are its offspring. " Quand on commence à douter en religion," Chateaubriand acutely points out, " on doute en politique. L'homme qui cherche les fondements de son culte ne tarde pas à s'enquérir des principes de son gouvernement. Quand l'esprit demande à être libre, le corps aussi veut l'être. Cela est une conséquence toute naturelle." Free religious and free political life are ultimately inseparable.

[1] *Histoire Ecclésiastique*, ii., p. 6.

There is not a real break in the line of political thought from the *Franco-Gallia* of Hotman to the Declaration of Independence of 1776. As the one proclaimed the political liberty of the French of the sixteenth century, so the other proclaimed the political liberty of the American of the eighteenth. The line of succession runs from Martin Luther to John Calvin, from John Calvin to Philippe de Duplessis-Mornay, from Philippe de Duplessis-Mornay to John Knox, from John Knox to John Milton, from John Milton to John Locke, and from John Locke to Alexander Hamilton

Obviously the view that every layman is a priest is of the most far-reaching order. So Calvin conceived it when he speaks at the same time of the election of ministers and magistrates.[1] Both were elections, and the fact that one was for the Church and the other for the State was frankly immaterial. His view tends to be that the government of a country by elected magistrates is, on the whole, the best. True, kings succeeded judges, but these kings were given to the Israelites " to torment them." [2] " Let the people elect." [3] Let men be returned " by the common voice of the people." [4] Still, it must always be borne in mind that all authority, in the last resort, comes from God. Hence he writes in 1563 that " to elect one's magistrates is not granted to all : it is a prerogative with which God has thought fit to please the chosen people." [5]

The Old Testament contains the old pact of God with men, and the New Testament contains the new pact of God with men. No doubt the *pactum subjectionis* on the part of man rests largely on voluntary submission, on consent. If whatever the sovereign permits he commands, whatever the people suffer they obey. To the federally-minded Calvin such a conception proved peculiarly attractive. To him the Old Testament resolved itself into the Old Covenant, with the

---

[1] *Opera*, liv., pp. 35-36 ; xxvii., pp. 411, 413 ; liii., p. 451 ; " Sermon xxxvii. on 1 Timothy," pp. 475-476. *Cf.* " Sermon civ. on Deuteronomy," *Opera*, xxvii., pp. 458-459.

[2] *Opera*, xxvii., pp. 459-460. [3] *Ibid.*, xxvii., pp. 410-411.

[4] *Ibid.*, xliii., p. 374. *Cf.* Jourdain, *Excursions historiques et philosophiques à travers le Moyen Âge* for a study of "La Royauté Française et le Droit Populaire."

[5] *Opera*, xxiv., p. 610.

historical development of the contract of God with men.[1] Did He not conclude contracts with the patriarchs, with Adam, Noah, Abraham and others?[2] When Calvin thinks of the individual, the theory of predestination is in his mind. When he thinks of the mass of individuals, the theory of contract is in his mind. Legally speaking, he feels strongly that the pact concluded by God with men differs in degree, not in kind, from that concluded by man with man.[3] This contract with God is mutual.

The legality of Calvinistic theology comes out in a thousand ways. It comes out, for instance, in the importance that such theology attached to the Pauline epistles as contrasted with the Gospels, for the Apostle to the Gentiles was as familiar with Roman law as Calvin himself. The sixteenth-century theory of the Atonement attests what a strong hold the notion of agency exerted on the thoughtful. Nor is this a matter of surprise when we grasp what a large share this theory of contract occupied in Reformation thought. For from theology it readily passed to politics after the middle of this century. How easy the transition was is obvious when we note that as there is a contract between God and men, there is—or there may be—one between men and men in general, and between men and their Prince in particular. The contract in the Church is the signing of the Confession of Faith. What happens explicitly in the Church happens implicitly in the State. The Confession of Faith, 1537, contains a social pact on the lines of what Calvin conceived to be the pacts of the Old Testament. True, it was mainly religious, but those were the days when religion was politics and politics was religion. A civil ordinance commanded under pain of exile " all burghers, inhabitants and subjects to swear to guard and observe " this coeval covenant. Calvin consistently defended it with an appeal to the covenants made by the Israelites under Moses, Josiah, Asa, and "the

---

[1] " Commentary on Galatians iii. 15 " ; " Commentary on Jeremiah xxxi. 32," II. x. 1, 20; *Opera*, xxxviii., p. 687.

[2] " Commentary on Luke i. 55 "; " Commentary on Galatians iii. 17 "; " Commentary on Genesis xii. 3," *Opera*, xxiii., pp. 124, 148, 177, 193, 234-235.

[3] " Sermon cxliii. on Deuteronomy xxvi.," *Opera*, xxviii., pp. 286, 513; xxvii., p. 146.

admirable defenders of liberty, Ezra and Nehemiah."[1] Is not this contract the precursor of the Scots Covenant, 1638, the English Solemn League and Covenant, 1643, and the covenants of New England?

Calvin takes trouble to show that the implicit attitude in the State is, on consideration, really explicit. Take the choice of Saul as the first King of Israel. Much that is not recorded in Holy Writ appears in the new exegesis. We learn, with perhaps an air of surprise, that the Israelites " agreed to his appointment," that " they approved of his office," that they gave their " good will," that in a solemn assembly they " consented," and that " there was a mutual duty of the Prince towards his subjects."[2] If a man so little carried away by imagination as his exegete could find all this in the narrative in 1 Samuel, what did not the imagination find in it?

When the contract had been concluded, Calvin was sanguine enough to hope that it would be fulfilled. Francis I. bitterly persecuted the Huguenots. In 1555, in 1557, in 1559, and five times in 1561, Calvin advocated passive obedience. He disapproved of the Conspiracy of Amboise in 1560. Coligny naturally pressed him to countenance resistance. In a letter of 16th April 1561 Calvin sensibly showed that " if he shed a single drop of blood, rivers of it would spread over the whole of Europe." Reluctantly he grants that if " princes of the blood " resist, and if " the Courts of Parlement join in their resistance," all " good subjects " could " lend them a hand." A single prince of the blood who is not " the first in degree " will not suffice to legitimise the revolt.[3] With all his democratic leanings, it is evident that Calvin could on occasion control them. His sense of law and order was too deeply rooted in him lightly to permit the shedding of blood.[4] Loyalty, in

---

[1] *Opera*, v., 319ff.; xxi., 206ff. *Cf.* an able article by H. D. Foster on " The Political Theories of Calvinists before the Puritan Exodus to America," *American Historical Review*, xxi., pp. 480-503, 1916.

[2] *Opera*, xix., pp. 635-637.

[3] *Ibid.*, xviii., pp. 427-428.

[4] *Ibid.*, xviii., 203, 208, 218, 230, 255, 268, 270-271, 773-774; xxix., p. 660; xli., p. 375; liii., pp. 133, 139; liv., pp. 555, 558; IV. xx. 22, 23, 25, 29, 775, 777-778.

spite of his tepid writing about it, was not wantonly to be thrown away. The after-history of the Huguenots attests how much such teaching influenced them, for, in spite of massacres and persecutions, they remained steadfast in their attachment to the Throne.

The long-continued persecution began at last to shake the faith of the reformer in the duty of obedience. Events were too much for him. " In a higher world," writes Cardinal Newman, " it is otherwise ; but here below to live is to change, and to be perfect is to have changed often." Gradually Calvin changes his attitude. Men suffer in their bodies and in their goods. For all that, they do not obey. They can disobey, for they can resist inwardly. Instead of passive obedience, he teaches passive resistance. True, the faithful are bound to obey up to a point. That point is reached when the command concerns the decrees of God. But all decrees, certainly during the sixteenth century, fundamentally bore on the decrees of God. Passive resistance reaches a limit when authority commands something immoral or irreligious.[1] Vague as these adjectives are, Calvin was in no wise inclined to interpret them too harshly. Luther [2] and Duplessis-Mornay [3] hoped for the superman, the providential saviour, to arrive for their succour, but Calvin was awake to the danger of such a being. His legal mind turned to the question of what class of the magistracy was likely to assist the persecuted. The constituted authorities in France were the inferior officials and the seldom-summoned States General. The King, from one angle, is a superior authority, though of course in the eyes of God all ranks of the magistracy stand on an equal footing.[4] Sovereignty comes from above, not from below. Authority cannot ascend from the people to the Prince simply because the people cannot confer what they do not possess. The sovereignty of God

---

[1] *Opera*, xxx., p. 72; xli., pp. 25-26; xxx., pp. 36-38, 72 ; IV. xx. 30 ; xiv., pp. 402, 507 ; " Prælections on Daniel vi. 22 " ; " Homily lxxii. on 1 Samuel xix." ; " Homily l. on 1 Samuel xiv." and " Homily lxvii. on 1 Samuel xiv."

[2] *Werke*, Weim. ed., p. 554; Erl. ed., 39, pp. 288, 289.

[3] *De la Puissance légitime au Prince sur le Peuple*, pp. 240-241.

[4] *Ibid.*, pp. 118-119; Calvin, *Commentaries on* 1 *Peter* ii. 14.

forms the real supreme factor, and the only factor that genuinely matters.

Inferior and superior officers are chosen by men, and this might seem to contradict the Calvinist conception. Not at all. Calvin provides us with an illustration to render his point clear. The farmer sows and waters his crop, but it is God that gives the increase. The condition of the crop is the sowing, though the cause of it is God. Similarly the condition of the election of officers is the will of the people, though the cause is the counsel of God. Calvin never will admit that the people of themselves are the cause of the sovereignty of the Prince, a sovereignty that must issue from above. Instead of lessening the power of the electors, Calvin strengthens it. For if they are simply the condition of the power of the Prince, he himself is in the same plight. In fact their authority is equal to his, for they and he alike are priests in the sight of God. The King is no longer anything more than an honorary *primus inter pares*, and one equal can certainly resist another equal.

No one can read the last paragraph of the *Institutes* without seeing that all the time the conscience of the subject is held, as it were, in reserve over the authority of the King. By the theory of natural right this weight attached to the monitions of conscience is increased. There is a contract. Woe betide the King if he break it! Had he not broken it by the series of massacres from Amboise to Vassy, and, above all, by the horrors of St Bartholomew's Day? Was it difficult for the persecuted Huguenot to dot the " i's " and stroke the " t's " of the last paragraph of the *Institutes*? There we read: " But in that obedience which we hold to be due to the commands of rulers, we must always make the exception, nay, must be particularly careful, that it is not incompatible with obedience to Him to Whose will the wishes of all kings should be subject, to Whose decrees their commands must yield, to Whose majesty their sceptres must bow. And indeed, how preposterous were it, in pleasing men, to incur the offence of Him for Whose sake you obey men! The Lord, therefore, is King of kings. When he opens His sacred mouth, He alone is to be heard, instead of all and above all. We are subject to the men who rule over us, but subject only in the Lord. If they command anything against Him, let us not pay the least regard to it, nor be moved by all the dignity which they possess as magistrates— a dignity to which no injury is done when it is subordinated to the special and truly supreme power of God."[1] He proceeds to give us the examples of Daniel: who did not commit sin when he refused to obey the impious decree of the king because the king had exceeded his limits; and of the Israelites: who did commit sin when they obeyed the decree of Jereboam to worship the golden calf. The last four sentences of the *Institutes* run in this fashion: " I know the imminent peril to, which subjects expose themselves by this firmness, kings being most indignant when they are contemned. As Solomon says, ' The wrath of a king is as messengers of death ' (Prov. xvi. 14). But since Peter, one of heaven's heralds, has published this edict, ' We ought to obey God rather than men ' (Acts v. 29), let us console ourselves with the thought, that we are redeeming the obedience which the Lord requires, when we endure any thing rather than turn aside from piety. And that our courage may not fail, Paul stimulates us by the additional consideration (1 Cor. vii. 23), that we were redeemed by Christ, at the great price which our redemption cost Him, in order that we might not yield a slavish obedience to the depraved wishes of men, far less do homage to impiety." Calvin's dedicatory epistle may have told Francis I. that its author was on the side of order, but if the French King pondered over these closing sentences he may well have wondered whose was to be the order. Was it to be the order of the King of France? Or, was it to be the order of the King of Geneva?

Our edition of the *Institutes* runs to some eighteen hundred pages, and is not a book to be read in an arm-chair by the fireside. The pamphlets of Luther consisted of a few sheets, and we can readily understand their wonderful circulation. But what are we to say to the circulation of the *Institutes*? Before 1620 there had appeared at least seventy-four editions, in nine languages, and also fourteen abridgments. Before the founding of New England there had appeared no less than

[1] Vol. iii., p. 553 (1845 ed.).

four hundred and thirty-five editions of some work of Calvin.
The Dutch, the Walloons, the Palatines, the Germans, the
French and the Huguenots perused the *Institutes* eagerly. In
England Bishop Sanderson, Charles I.'s chaplain, considered
the *Institutes* to be " the best and perfectest system of divinity." [1]
In 1578 the undergraduates must have been of a sturdy
mental build, for they were required to pass an examination
in it and also in Calvin's Catechism. In 1636 Laud admitted
that the *Institutes* " may profitably be read as one of their first
books in divinity," yet he feared the trend of it might influence
the men of New College unduly if they read it at a receptive
age or, as he phrased it, " too soon." He concluded : " I am
afraid it . . . doth too much possess their judgments . . . and
makes many of them humorous in, if not against, the Church." [2]
As nine editions of the *Institutes* appeared in English before
the outbreak of the Civil War, the apprehensions of Laud
are intelligible. As well as Sanderson and Laud, Hooker and
Milton, Harrington and Sidney, Locke and Rousseau all
perused it.

Calvin, confident in his power as the real ruler of Geneva,
could write : " Although the Lord takes vengeance on un-
bridled domination, let us not therefore suppose that that
vengeance is committed to us, to whom no command has
been given but to obey and suffer. I speak only of private
men. For when popular magistrates have been appointed to
curb the tyranny of kings (as the Ephori, who were opposed
to kings among the Spartans, or Tribunes of the people to
consuls among the Romans, or Demarchs to the senate among
the Athenians ; and, perhaps, there is something similar to
this in the power exercised in each kingdom by the three
orders, when they hold their primary diets). So far am I from
forbidding these officially to check the licence of kings, that
if they connive at kings when they tyrannise and insult over
the humbler of the people, I affirm that their dissimulation is
not free from nefarious perfidy, because they fraudulently betray
the liberty of the people, while knowing that, by the ordinance

---

[1] Sanderson, *Works*, i., p. 297.
[2] Laud, *Remains*, ii., p. 82 ; Wood, *Annals*, i., p. 193.

of God, they are its appointed guardians."[1] When the humble Huguenot felt his situation desperate, he was not over-inclined to leave the matter in the hands of sixteenth-century Ephori or Tribunes or Demarchs. He and his like took the matter into their own hands and rebelled. Such a spirit communicated itself to Puritans in Scotland like Knox and Buchanan, to Puritans in England like Penry and Cartwright, and to Puritans in New England like Bradford and Cotton, Hooker and Williams. " Let not Geneva be forgotten or despised," wrote John Adams, the second President of the United States; " religious liberty owes it much respect, Servetus notwithstanding."[2]

Before that miracle of style, the Authorised Version of the Bible, appeared in 1611, the Genevan translation had been the common Bible of the people for three-quarters of a century, going through over a hundred editions before 1617. Between 1560 and 1644 there were at least one hundred and forty editions,[3] numbers not unworthy of comparison with the success of the Lutheran version. Of the latter from 1530 to 1540 there were thirty-four Wittenberg editions and seventy-two reprints in other parts of Germany, and from 1541 to 1546 there were eighteen Wittenberg editions and twenty-six reprints. From 1534 to 1584 no less than a hundred thousand complete Bibles left the press at Wittenberg. Eighty-four original editions and two hundred and fifty-three reprints appeared in Luther's lifetime.[4] It is, therefore, the truth to say that the combined effect of the Lutheran and the Genevan versions was to flood Europe with the Bible. In the Genevan Bible there was a marginal commentary not illiberal. These notes *inter alia* dealt with contract and congregation, with the supremacy of God's Word, with the deposition of kings and with the duty of resistance to tyrants. What the *Institutes* failed to accomplish, that the Genevan Bible accomplished. Similar

---

[1] *Institutes*, iii., p. 552 (1845 ed.).

[2] J. Adams, marginal note in his "Discourses on Darien," *Works*, vi., p. 313.

[3] *Historical Catalogue of Bibles* (Library of the British and Foreign Bible Society), p. 61.

[4] *Cf.* Paul Pietsch's estimate in Luther, *Werke*, Weim. ed., " Deutsche Bibel," p. 2.

notes also appeared in Beza's edition of the Vulgate text of the New Testament, which ran into eighty-eight editions, and in Junius and Tremellius's *Biblia Sacra*.

John Calvin was the editor of the first printed edition of metrical psalms for church worship. Clement Marot translated thirty psalms and received a royal licence for them. Theodore Beza, Calvin's friend, wrote the metrical version of Psalm lxviii., which was to the Huguenots what Psalm xlvi. was to the Lutheran.[1] What the Psalms meant to the Huguenots, let Florimond de Rémond testify: " When the Catholics saw simple women seek torments in order to maintain their faith, and meet death, crying only on Christ their Saviour, or singing a psalm; when they saw the young virgins go to the scaffold as gaily as they would go to the bridal couch; when they saw men rejoice at the sight of the horrible preparations and instruments of death, and, half-burned and roasted, contemplate from the stake their impending tortures, standing firm as rocks among the billows of grief—in a word, dying with a smile— their hearts wept as well as their eyes." The Bible inspired the Calvinist, and he faced death as grimly as he faced life.

Beza,[2] Hotman and Duplessis-Mornay stood in such intimate relationship to Calvin that they may be called the most distinguished French pupils in his school. Beza is the friend and the collaborator of one whom he was proud to acknowledge as his master, whose successor he was as the head of the Calvinist churches. Beza's *Du Droit des Magistrats sur leurs Sujets*, 1574, is the most noteworthy of all the treatises produced by these three men. Behind the whole book there stands the law of nature. This law of nature gives birth to a right of nature that is imprescriptible and inviolable. We must obey princes " provided they do not command irreligious or iniquitous matters." Irreligious matters are those forbidden by the " first table of the law of God." Iniquitous matters are those contrary " to what each owes to his neighbour according to his private or public vocation." Plainly he thinks that obedience is not due to princes who order irreligious or

---

[1] *Cf.* my *Erasmus and Luther*, pp. 144-157, especially pp. 156-157.
[2] He presented the *Codex Bezæ* to Cambridge University.

iniquitous matters. Calvin, Hotman and Duplessis-Mornay are not in favour of tyrannicide. Beza proves to be the one exception. He did not condemn Poltrot, the assassin of the Duke of Guise. Beza wrote these grave words: " I do not approve of the opinion of those who, without any distribution or exception, condemn all tyrannicide, to which formerly Greece ordered so many honourable rewards."

With enormous erudition Hotman advances in his *Franco-Gallia*, 1573, to prove his thesis, that formerly France was governed by a monarchy of which the States General tempered the authority. This liberal tradition has been abandoned, and the sooner we return to it the better. The safety of the people is the supreme law. The liberty of holding general assemblies is part of the law of nations. Kings who limit this holy and sacred liberty must no longer be deemed kings, but the tyrants they undoubtedly are.

Like Beza, Duplessis-Mornay, in his *Vindiciæ contra Tyrannos*, 1579, takes as his premises the idea of God and the Decalogue. Antecedent respect for both forms the foundation of all States. Royalty must be—it only can be—elective, and he repeats the arguments of Hotman. There is a political contract either expressed or understood. His definition of a tyrant is the plain one to be found in Bartolus, and it is that the king who violates this contract is a tyrant. The rights of nature, the rights of the people, and the rights of civil law all agree in commanding us to take arms against such a monarch. Agreeing in their chief outlines as the *Du Droit des Magistrats sur leurs Sujets*, the *Franco-Gallia* and the *Vindiciæ contra Tyrannos* certainly do, yet we must not forget the fact that after 1559 Calvin and his three pupils preached the right of obedience under normal circumstances, just as they preached before 1560 the right of resistance under abnormal circumstances. Nor do these three main treatises by any means exhaust the anonymous pamphlet literature appearing before St Bartholomew's Day. Take a perfectly typical one, *La Politique, Dialogue . . . de l'Authorité des Princes et de la Liberté des Peuples*. In it we meet with the stock arguments that every power is of God, that there are sovereign laws of

God and nature, that there are deputies or ephors of the people, that there is a contract pledging the King to fulfil his function and prevent tyranny, and that if he violates this contract the ephors must carry out their bounden duty.

The Huguenots did not cease their exertions with the writing of pamphlets. Their national synod of 1560 presented a memorial to the Estates of France. Among the arguments employed we learn that " there will otherwise be no Security for the performance of any Contracts and Ordinances that may pass between the King and his subjects," and the synod asked the Estates to declare that under a queen-mother and a minor king, a situation not unlike the Scots one, " none other but the States of the Kingdom can nominate . . . Counsellors of State." Surely until this addition were made to the Estates, they would " not propose or answer anything," but would " appeal unto the next Assembly of the States." [1] Local consistory, district colloquy, provincial assembly and national synod— such were the steps by which the humblest congregation was linked up with the central body. As an *imperium in imperio*, these bodies ultimately developed all the functions of a State, for they were financial, administrative, legislative and military. Such was their position in 1559. By 1594 the organisation had reached a far more highly developed stage,[2] and so much was this the case that the Venetian Suriano wrote : " They [*i.e.* the Huguenots] have begun to spread among the populace the idea that the King has his authority from the people, and that the subject is not obliged to obey the Prince when he commands anything which is not to be found in the New Testament. And they are on the highroad to reduce that province to the condition of a democratic state like Switzerland." [3]

What Calvin's three pupils preached, William the Silent

---

[1] Quick, *Synodicon . . . or Acts of Reformed Churches of France*, i., pp. 12-13.

[2] Anquez, *Hist. Ass. Polit. Réf. de France*, pp. 62-66 ; Doumergue, *L'Origine de la Déclaration des Droits de l'Homme*, pp. 26-27. *Cf.* also Corbière, " De l'Organisation Politique du Parti Protestant en France en 1573," *Mém. Acad. Sc. Montpellier*, viii., 1886-1887.

[3] Whitehead, *Coligny*, p. 302.

practised. When Alva's persecution became too much for him he consulted Marnix Ste Aldegonde, who counselled him that " men have taken arms by the advice and authority of the Estates General of the country, which have a lawful vocation from God against an oppressor of the country and a sworn and irreconcilable enemy of all servants of God." Bred in Geneva, we can discern the hand of Calvin in these words of Marnix Ste Aldegonde: " If they reject a prince who is offered them for their defence against tyranny, they are ungrateful toward God, rebellious against His will and merit coming under the yoke."[1] Reluctantly William the Silent had come to accept such counsel. Was he not " one of the chief members of the Estates "? Indeed " the Estates have been instituted to put a check upon the tyranny of the Prince." Is it not evident that " the King is only inaugurated after having sworn to observe the law "?[2] So William came to think in 1572, and so he informed Queen Elizabeth.[3]

Formally William informed the Estates General of his conclusions. He told them that the ruler " by his oath purposes that in case of contravention we should not be longer bound to him." Besides, " between all lords and vassals there is a mutual obligation. . . . Among other rights we have this privilege of serving our dukes as the ephors served their kings in Sparta—that is, to keep the royalty firm in the hand of a good prince and to bring to reason him who contravenes his oath." Then comes the conclusion that would have rejoiced the heart of Hotman: " The assembly of estates, a bridle and bar to tyranny hated by tyrants, and loved by true princes, is the sole foundation of a State."[4] And this is put forth at

---

[1] Groen van Prinsterer, *Archives . . . d'Orange Nassau*, vii., pp. 277-285. Here I glean much from H. D. Foster, " Political Theories of the Calvinists," *Am. Hist. Rev.*, xxi. 481ff., April 1916.

[2] Kervyn de Lettenhove, *Les Huguenots et les Gueux*, iii., pp. 177-182.

[3] It is worth stating that the Netherlands pamphlets stress the rights and duties of the Estates. *Cf.* such pamphlets as *Discours Sommier*, and *Remonstrance en forme de Complainte et Doléance à MM. les Deputes des Estats Généraux* (1579).

[4] *Apologie de Guillaume de Nassau* (ed. Lacroix), pp. 85, 101, 102ff., 118; English translation in the *Phenix*, i., pp. 449-538. On the influence of the *Vindiciæ contra Tyrannos*, *cf.* Pirenne, *Histoire de Belgique*, iv., c. 3.

a time when everywhere, even in England, the kings of all
countries are increasingly potent and the States General of all
countries are increasingly impotent.

As the Scots dethroned their Queen Regent, so the Dutch
dethroned their King. Scotland was the first country to get
rid of their Prince and the Netherlands was the second. Its
natives in 1581 put forth their Declaration of Independence
of the yoke of Philip II. in a remarkable document. Its
preamble points out that " all mankind know that a prince
is appointed by God to cherish his subjects, even as a
shepherd to guard his sheep. When, therefore, the Prince
does not fulfil his duty as protector ; when he oppresses his
subjects, destroys their ancient liberties, and treats them as
slaves, he is to be considered, not a prince, but a tyrant. As
such, the estates of the land may lawfully and reasonably
depose him, and elect another in his room." " God did not
create the people slaves to their Prince, to obey his commands,
whether right or wrong, but rather the Prince for the sake of
the subjects. . . . When this [tyranny] is done deliberately, un-
authorised by the States, they may not only disallow his authority,
but legally proceed to the choice of another prince for their
defence. . . . This is what the law of nature dictates for the
defence of liberty . . . more justifiable in our land . . . for most
of the Provinces receive their Prince upon certain conditions,
which he swears to maintain ; which, if the Prince violates, he is
no longer sovereign."[1] In accordance with their natural and
civil rights the Estates of the Netherlands depose Philip II., on
the ground that the contract, by his conduct, has been annulled.

Four German publicists, Bareus and Zanchius, Alstedius
and Althusius, adopt the attitude of Beza, Hotman and
Duplessis-Mornay. In true Calvinistic spirit Pareus maintains
that " the proper and first cause of the magistrate is God
Himself ; but men are the proximate causes."[2] In almost the

---

[1] Dutch Declaration of Independence, translation in Somers' *Tracts*, i.,
p. 323ff. *Cf.* M. Lossen, "Aggaüs Albada und der Kölner Pacifications-
congress im Jahre 1579" (*Raumer-Riehl Hist.*), Taschenbuch, 1876.

[2] Pareus, *Comm. Rom.* (1617), p. 1059; Duplessis-Mornay, p. 96. *Cf.*
South, *Sermons*, i., p. 471.

exact words of Calvin he proceeds to show that " subjects not private citizens, but appointed as inferior magistrates, may justly, even by arms, defend the commonwealth and Church or religion against a superior magistrate." The reason is that " even the higher magistrate is subject to Divine laws and his commonwealth." In his *Tenure of Kings* Milton adopts the teaching of Pareus on the right of deposition of kings in these words: " They whose part is to set up magistrates, may restrain them also from outrageous deeds, or pull them down; but all magistrates are set up either by Parliament or by electors, or by other magistrates; they, therefore, who exalted them may lawfully degrade and punish them." [1] As Milton quotes Pareus, so Pareus quotes his master Calvin with a reverential air.

Zanchius, on his exile from Italy, became professor at Strasburg and Heidelberg. He had lived at Geneva, and had imbibed sound Calvinist doctrine. With classical and Scriptural examples in his mind, he urged the duty of resisting a superior magistrate who commands evil, for such resistance is not resistance to a power ordained by God. Obedience to God takes precedence of any obedience to man. " If for the sake of religion," Zanchius holds, " you oppose yourself to the King, you oppose yourself not to power but to tyranny, and unless you so oppose yourself you act contrary to Divine and human law." [2] Alstedius maintained the subjection of all to the *lex naturæ* and to the Bible; obedience to laws rather than kings; the right of the entire body of subjects to resist tyrants upon violation of oath; the function of the ephors or estates of the realm to appoint, judge and depose the King, and exercise *summa auctoritas*, especially in extraordinary taxation. [3]

The spirit of Calvinism is thoroughly at work in the mind of Johannes Althusius (1557-1638), who studied law at Geneva with Denys Godofred. A Calvinist elder in the church at Emden, Althusius was a courageous magistrate in that town. For thirty-six years professor of law at Herborn, there is naturally a legal spirit in his *Politica Methodice Digesta*, 1603.

---

[1] Pp. 1063-1066; Milton, § 60.
[2] *Opera Theologica*, iv., pp. 799-801.
[3] I use Forster's summary in *Am. Hist. Rev.*, xxi., p. 500.

The expression of his thought is dictated by his belief, and accordingly in him we have the use of the Bible in determining the outward form of Church and State. There is the usual admiration for Jewish law in general and the Decalogue in particular, and of course the Old Testament prevails over the New. The examples he selects seem to illustrate a priori processes of thought, for he so conceives political doctrine as stoutly as any monarchomachs. A free contract between already existing minor corporations creates the State, and free choice settles the form of government. What effects the union of the Sovereign and the people is merely Nature and, through her, God. There are, in his judgment, two contracts: the contract of society and the contract of government. By the governmental contract the people, conditionally or unconditionally bestow all or part of their powers upon the ruler. By the social contract they contract as individuals with one another— the developed view Rousseau came to hold. Althusius obviously had reached such a view.[1] Of course in the background of these contracts stand the ephors. If the Sovereign breaks the contract between him and the people he *ipso facto* loses his Divine authority, and the people exercise the Divine will in deposing him.[2] The treatment of the tyrant by Althusius and Mornay is identical.

The contract is as present to the mind of John Knox as to Johannes Althusius. In 1558 he addressed a letter to the commonalty of Scotland, desiring the Estates and nobility, as well as the commonalty, to " compel your Bishops and Clergy to cease their tyranny and answer by the Scriptures of God."[3] From covenants in general, and Asa's in particular, he gathers in his *Appellation*, " the first, That no idolater can be exempted from punishment by God's law. The second is, That the punishment of such crimes, as idolatry, blasphemy, and others, that touch the Majesty of God, doth not appertain to kings

---

[1] *Cf.* Maitland, Intro. to Gierke's *Political Theory of the Middle Ages*, xxiii.

[2] O. Gierke, *Johannes Althusius und die Entwicklung der Naturrechtlichen Staatstheorien*, pp. 29-30, 31, 34, 56-58, 69.

[3] *Works*, iv., p. 524 (ed. Laing).

and chief rulers only, but also to the whole body of the people, and to every member of the same, according to the vocation of every man, and according to that possibility and occasion which God doth minister to revenge the injury done His glory." [1] In his *Second Blast* he concludes that " most justly may the same men depose and punish him that unadvisedly elect." [2] Of course no idolater ought to receive public office, and a prince who becomes an idolater should be opposed, and such opposition is just.[3]

In his interview with Mary Queen of Scots in 1561 she charged him with disloyalty as a subject, and the conversation turned to the contract theory. " Think ye," inquired Mary, " that subjects having power may resist their princes? " " If their princes exceed their bounds," was the bold reply.[4] It was old doctrine with him, for in 1544 in a letter from the Continent he wrote: " Let a thing here be noted, that the Prophet of God sometimes may teach treason against kings, and yet neither he, nor such as obey the word spoken in the Lord's name by him, offend God." [5] As Elizabeth and Mary were both opposed to him, he had written that *livre de circonstance*, *The First Blast of the Trumpet against the Monstruous Regiment of Women*. Had there been a Lady Jane Grey reigning either in London or in Edinburgh, it never would have appeared. Bodin, who lived in the land of the Salic law, held precisely the same opinions. " Women," thought Bodin, " ought to be removed as far as possible from the majesty of government ; for the rule of women is contrary to the laws of nature, which has given men prudence, strength, greatness of soul, and force of mind to govern, but to women has denied these gifts." [6] Elizabeth naturally called the author of such sentiments Badin. Bodin and Knox agree in thinking that the laws of nature and

---

[1] *Works*, iv., p. 501.
[2] *Second Blast*, p. 540.
[3] *Works*, iv., p. 539.
[4] *Works*, ii., p. 372. *Cf.* ii., pp. 434-461. *Cf.* Milton, *Tenure of Kings*, § 35.
[5] *Works*, ii., pp. 539-540. *Cf. Ibid.*, p. 372.
[6] *De Republica*, p. 1154 (ed. Franc., 1591). *Cf.* pp. 1155-1157.

the laws of God combined with the teaching and example of pagan and Christian antiquity are decisive in this matter.

The rule of Mary offended Knox, and he urged her deposition. He asked " The Brethren of the Christian Congregation "[1] to affirm that " to bridle the fury and rage of Princes in free kingdoms and realms . . . appertains to the Nobility, sworn and born Counsellors of the same, and also to the Barons and People, whose votes . . . are to be required in all great and weighty matters of the commonwealth." Queen Mary fell, and with her fall sovereigns could read the writing on the wall.[2] When James Boswell's father was asked what the execution of Charles I. had effected, his reply was: " Faith, it made kings gar [know] that they had a lith in their neck." The deposition of Mary made them realise that they had a lith in their rule. This lith is perfectly perceptible in the *First Book of Discipline* and in the *Second Book of Discipline*. The First Book laid down that all, rulers and ruled, were subject to discipline; that this discipline involved the suppression of idolatry in all its forms; and that there was punishment to be enforced on all who disobeyed the superintendents of the Kirk.[3] The Second Book, published in 1581, pursues every whit as vigorously the objects of the First. The minister commands: the magistrate obeys. Why? Because the authority of the former flows directly from God, and his authority overrules the latter in all matters agreeable to the Word of God. And what was not agreeable to this Word?[4] The resolution of the General Assembly required kings to promise to defend " the true religion . . . as they are obliged . . . in the law of God . . . in the eleventh chapter of the second book of the Kings, and as they crave obedience of their subjects so the bond and contract to be mutual and reciprocal in all times coming betwixt the Prince and God and his faithful people according to the word of God."[5] What the General Assembly resolved

---

[1] Knox, "History of the Reformation in Scotland," *Works*, i., p. 411.
[2] *Ibid.*, pp. 424, 432, 442-443, 448, 450.   [3] *Ibid.*, ii., p. 183ff.
[4] Second Book, pp. 2-7, 14-15.
[5] Knox, *Works*, ii., p. 458, " The bond betwixt the Prince and the People is reciprocal."

the Scots Parliament formally passed in 1567—that is, the duty of the resistance of the subject to his Sovereign, in case of necessity, became part and parcel of the law of the land.[1]

George Buchanan, in his *De Jure Regni apud Scotos*, 1579, furnished theoretical justification for the policy Knox pursued. Buchanan's leading idea was that kings exist by the will and for the good of the people. There is a contract with ephors and the people to enforce it. Therefore kings may be brought to account for misgovernment, and with Beza he agrees that under certain circumstances tyrannicide is justifiable. As Milton justified the execution of Charles I. in his *Defence of the People of England*, so Buchanan in his book justified the deposition of Mary. His is a party pamphlet which met with a large measure of success, though a squib produced during the English Civil War noted the similarity of the doctrine of *De Jure Regni apud Scotos* with that laid down by the Jesuit Mariana in his *De Rege et Regis Institutione* :

" A Scot and Jesuit, hand in hand,
    First taught the world to say
That subjects ought to have command,
    And monarchs to obey."

The English were slower, because less logical, than the Scots to adopt the teaching of Geneva. Theirs is a land of precedent, and in the year 1399 they had one to their hand without leaving their own shores. Still, a wanderer like Peter Martyr at Oxford, a Puritan like Christopher Goodman, a Bishop like John Ponet of Winchester, a divine like Thomas Cartwright, all betray, in differing fashions, the influence of the Pope of Geneva. Peter Martyr agreed with Calvin in teaching active resistance : he did not agree with Melanchthon in teaching merely passive resistance.[2] In common with the three French pupils of his master, he held that the private man may not revolt, for that was a duty reserved for the ephors

---

[1] *Acts of the General Assembly* (Bannatyne Club ed.), i., p. 109; *Acts of the Parliament of Scotland*, iii., pp. 11-12, 14, 23-24, 39.

[2] *Loci Communes* (1576 ed.), 4th Div., Locus xx., §§, 11-13, pp. 1086-1087.

and Roman tribunes or the Imperial electors. Undoubtedly private folk may use force to oblige a prince "to fulfil conditions and compacts (*pacta*)" to which he has taken oath.

Christopher Goodman (*c.* 1520-1603) was once Lady Margaret Professor of Divinity at Oxford, though his views drove him into exile at Frankfort and Strasburg. From Geneva he issued his defence of Wyatt's Rebellion, entitled, *How Superior Powers ought to be obeyed of their Subjects, and wherein they may lawfully be by God's Word disobeyed and resisted.* In 1558 it appeared with Knox's *First Blast of the Trumpet*, and both bitterly attacked the government of women in general and of Mary in particular. The violence of both pamphlets displeased even their own side. Calvin pronounced Goodman's book "somewhat harsh" and to "be handled with caution," though "admitted to be true."[1] Obedience is due, in Goodman's eyes, to superiors on the ground that they help the subject to defend God's laws. "If they will do so, and keep promise with you according to their office, then do you owe them all humble obedience. If not, you are discharged, and no obedience belongeth to them: because they are not obedient to God."[2] This quotation Milton embodies in his *Tenure of Kings*.[3] Goodman entirely disapproves of passive obedience and approves of the resistance of idolatry by force. With Ponet and Melville, Goodman holds that people were not "created of God to serve their kings." On the contrary, "their kings [are] appointed of God to preserve His people, whereof they are but a portion and a member."[4] The heads of the Church adjudge whether monarchs are or are not carrying out God's ordinances. With Cartwright and Bellarmine, he believes that the subject must primarily obey the Church and secondarily the State. A heretic may rule, but he is no true king. How can such execute the commands of the Church? And the execution of such commands is his bounden duty. With Ponet, though not with Calvin, Goodman maintains that "it appertaineth

[1] *Original Letters*, 1537-1558 (Parker Society), ii., p. 771.
[2] *How Superior Powers*, etc., pp. 44ff., 60, 110, 118, 139, 189.
[3] Milton, ii., p. 308 ; Goodman, chap. x., p. 139.
[4] *How Superior Powers*, etc., p. 149.

not only to the Magistrates and all other inferior officers to see that their Princes be subject to God's Laws, but to the common people also."[1]

John Ponet (*c.* 1514-1556) was a classical scholar who was a student of Italian and German literature.[2] He was also a mathematical and physical scholar who was no mean theologian. On Mary's accession he was deprived, and is said to have fled to the Continent. Stow, however, preserves the tradition that he took an active part in Wyatt's Rebellion. Eventually he found his way to Peter Martyr at Strasburg. In 1556 he published his *Short Treatise of Political Power,* of which John Adams declared that it contained " all the essential principles of liberty which were afterwards dilated on by Sidney and Locke."[3] Ponet follows John of Salisbury in advocating the doctrine of tyrannicide. He permits it " where just punishment is either by the whole State utterly neglected, or the Prince with the nobility and counsel conspire its subversion." He allows the private man to exercise this terrible right provided he " have some surely proved motion of God."[4] Of course he holds that all powers come from God, and that all other officers are merely His ministers. The laws of God and the laws of nature bind men, and the former comprehend the latter. " Men ought not to obey their superiors that shall command them to do anything against God's Word, or the laws of nature." " Kings may not make laws without the consent of the people," nor " dispense with them." With Calvin he stoutly holds that " As among the Lacedemonians certain men called Ephori were ordained to see that kings should not oppress the people, and among the Romans the Tribunes were ordained to defend and maintain the liberty of the people . . . so in all Christian realms and dominions God ordained means, that the heads . . . should

[1] *How Superior Powers,* etc., p. 146.

[2] On his views *cf.* L. Cardauns, *Die Lehre vom Widerstanderecht des Volks gegen die rechtmässige Obrigkeit im Luthertum und im Calvinismus des* 16. *Jahrhunderts,* pp. 37-40.

[3] Adams, *Works,* vi., p. 4.

[4] *Cf.* chaps. i., ii., iv. and vi. Cf. *Zurich Letters* (Parker Society), i., p. 124. *Cf.* M. Lossen, *Die Lehre vom Tyrannenmord in der christlichen Zeit.,* p. 24.

not oppress the poor people . . . and make their wills their laws . . . in France and England's Parliaments." Triumphantly we meet with the statement that " Kings, though they be the chief members, yet they are but members, no other are the people ordained for them, but they are ordained for the people."

Thomas Cartwright, sometime Lady Margaret Lecturer on Divinity in Cambridge University, launched the idea that Episcopacy was not primitive. What he found with this mark was a Church in the hands of ministers and elders, with synods, national and provincial. The Presbyterian ideal is foreshadowed. Nor is Cartwright any more democratic in England than Calvin is in Geneva. The prime duty of the people, in the mind of the English divine, is unquestioning obedience to the officers of the Church. " Theirs not to reason why, theirs but to do or die " is no inappropriate sentiment for them. The Word of God, Cartwright held, was superior to any law or command of man. There was a definite creed and an equally definite form of church government to be found in it by the discerning, and that creed and that form must for ever bind man. If there was a faith, it was a faith delivered *once for all* to the saints. His ideal of private life was as ascetic and his ideal of public life was as theocratic, or rather bibliocratic, as that of Bernard of Clairvaux himself. Man was a " worm," mere clay in the hand of the Divine Potter, to be moulded as He deemed best. He, however, had delegated His earthly power to the Church. The Church therefore commands, and the State meekly obeys. As in Spain the Inquisition handed over the culprit for punishment by the State, so the synod also handed him over to the State.[1] In Cartwright's *Second Reply* this is the procedure recommended. In his *Second Admonition to the Parliament* we learn, in no dubious language, that it is the imperative duty of the magistrate to visit with severe punishment those who affect to despise the chastisement of the Church.[2] Nor must the magistrate ever relax his efforts to put down relentlessly all idolatry.[3] Aristotle thought that the State ranked prior to the

[1] *Demonstration of Discipline*, p. 75.
[2] *Declaration of Discipline*, pp. 13, 187.
[3] *Second Reply*, cxv.ff.; *Second Admonition to the Parliament*, p. 49.

individual, and Cartwright fervently believed that the Church ranked prior to the State.[1]

France, the Netherlands, Germany, Scotland, England and New England all attest how seminal were the ideas scattered broadcast by Calvin in his letters and sermons, in his commentaries as well as in his *Institutes*. The rest of the things he saw and the dreams he dreamt are they not written in the history of Europe? The great reformers are immortal, but the immortals form in nowise a republic. There are many ranks among them, and Calvin towers among these ranks. The tide of affairs during the sixteenth century was setting steadily towards absolutism, and the man who fundamentally altered the direction of the current was the great Frenchman. In his volume on the Reformation, Michelet entitles the closing paragraph, " Europe saved by Geneva." Let those who want to scan the estimate of so sober a scholar as Mark Pattison turn to his *Essays*.

" The polity of Calvin was a vigorous effort to supply that which the revolutionary movement wanted—a positive education of the individual soul. Crushed under the weight of a spiritual aristocracy on the one side, and ground down by the huge machine of administrative monarchy on the other, all personal freedom, all moral attributes, had nearly disappeared among the people on whom this superincumbent mass pressed. To raise the enfeebled will, to stir the individual conscience, to incite the soul not only to reclaim its rights, but to feel its obligations; to substitute free obedience for passive submission —this was the lofty aim of the simple, not to say barbarous, legislation of Calvin. The inquisitorial rigours of the Consistory encouraged, instead of humbling, independence. Government at Geneva was not police, but education; self-government mutually enforced by equals on each other. The power thus generated was too expansive to be confined to Geneva. It went forth into all countries. From every part of Protestant Europe eager hearts flocked hither to catch something of the inspiration. The Reformed Communions, which doctrinal discussion was fast splitting up into ever-multiplying sects, began to feel in

---

[1] *Reply to Whitgift*, p. 144.

this moral sympathy a new centre of union. This, and this alone, enabled the Reformation to make head against the terrible repressive forces brought to bear by Spain—the Inquisition and the Jesuits. Sparta against Persia was not such odds as Geneva against Spain. Calvinism saved Europe."[1]

REFERENCES

Banke, H., *Die Probleme der Theologie Calvins*, Leipzig, 1922.

Baur, J. A. F. *Johann Calvin (Religionsgeschichtl. Volksbücher*, iv. 9), Tübingen, 1909.

Beyerhaus, G., *Studien zur Staatsanschauung Calvins mit besonderer Berück-sichtigung seines Souveranitätsbegriffs* (Bonwetsch & Seeberg's Neue Studien, 7), Berlin, 1910.

Borgeaud, C., *The Rise of Modern Democracy*, London, 1894.

Cadix, M., *L'État, sa Notion et ses Rapports avec l'Église d'après Calvin*, Paris, 1900.

Choisy, E., *La Théocratie à Genève au Temps de Calvin*, Genève, 1897.

Crue, F. de, *L'Action Politique de Calvin hors de Genève d'après sa Correspondance*, Genève, 1909.

Devisme, J. T., *Des Principes d'Organisation Ecclésiastique de Calvin et leur Application à Genève et en France*, Strasburg, 1838.

Doumergue, E., *Jean Calvin*, Lausanne, 1899-1917, especially vol. v.

Doumergue, E., etc., *Calvin and the Reformation*, New York, 1909.

Doumergue, E., *Les Démocraties modernes*, Paris, 1921.

Goguel, G., *Le Réformateur de la France et de Genève, Jean Calvin*, Toulouse, 1863.

Henry, P., *Das Leben Calvins*, Hamburg, 1835-1844.

Hundeshagen, K. B., *Ueber den Einfluss des Calvinismus auf die Idee vom Staat und staatsbürgerlicher Freiheit*, Berne, 1842.

Kampschulte, F. W., *Johann Calvin, seine Kirche und sein Staat in Genf.*, Leipzig, 1869.

Knodt, E., *Die Bedeutung Calvins und des Calvinismus für die protestantische Welt im Lichte der neueren und neusten Forschung* (Vorträge der theolog. Konferenz zu Giessen, 30), Giessen, 1910.

Köstlin, J., *Calvins Institutio nach Form und Inhalt in ihrer geschichtlichen Entwicklung: Studien und Kritiken*, Gotha, 1868.

Lang, A., *Die Bekehrung Johannes Calvins (Studien zur Geschichte der Theologie und der Kirche*), Leipzig, 1897.

Lang, A., *Johannes Calvin* (Schriften des Vereins für Reformationsgeschichte, 99), Leipzig, 1907.

Murray, R. H., *Dublin University and the New World*, London, 1921.

---

[1] M. Pattison, *Essays*, i., p. 306ff.

CALVIN AND HIS *INSTITUTES*

Schulthess-Rechberg, G. von, *Der Kardinal Jacopo Sadoleto. Die Beziehungen Calvins und H. Bullingers*, Zürich, 1909.

Stähelin, E., *Calvin's Leben und ausgewählte Schriften*, Elberfeld, 1863.

Tissot, F., *Les Relations entre l'Église et l'État à Genève au Temps de Calvin*, Lausanne, 1874.

Weber, G., *Geschichte Darstellung des Calvinismus im Verhältniss zum Staat in Genf. und Frankreich.*, Heidelberg, 1836.

Zahn, A., *Die beiden letzten Lebensjähre von Johannes Calvin*, Leipzig, 1895.

CHAPTER IV

BODIN AND THE THEORY OF SOVEREIGNTY

JEAN BODIN (1530-1596) was born in Angers, possibly the son of a Spanish Jew, in the *douceur angevine*, that left no impression on the severe texture of his character. He studied law at Toulouse, becoming a professor at that university, and educated himself both as jurist and as humanist. In 1561 he came to Paris to try his fortune at the Bar, meeting with but indifferent success. Learning in general and humanism in particular attracted him so ardently that he threw up his legal career. In 1566 he published his *Methodus ad Facilem Historiarum Cognitionem*, and in 1568 his *Réponse à M. de Malestroit touchant le Fait des Monnaies et de l'Enchérissement de Toutes Choses*. These established his reputation as a learned man with solid judgment. Attaching himself in 1571 to the Duc d'Alençon, the brother of Charles IX., he became inevitably immersed in the party of the Politiques. In 1576 he became Advocate of the King at Laon, for the future his home, and the same year he married, and was elected to represent the Vermandois as one of the deputies for the Third Estate at the Estates of Blois.

A student of political science, Bodin was no mere man of the closet. With vigorous faith and independent energy, he devoted himself in his public life to such matters as the advocacy of tolerance, the placing of country above party and above theology, and in fact showed himself actuated by those principles that distinguished the Politiques.[1] He stoutly opposed at Blois men like Versoris, a Paris advocate, who imperiously asked the King to recommence at once the wars waged in the name of religion and who insisted that the unity of the kingdom was to be found in obliging all to hold the faith of the majority of Frenchmen. Bodin at Blois fought hard for pacification, and experienced the hot opposition of Versoris, who later was to be one of the principal founders of

---

[1] Forneron, *Les Ducs de Guise et leur Époque*, ii., p. 191.

the League.[1] Nor, in spite of his position, was Bodin simply an official of Charles IX. In a couple of questions he opposed the royal will at the Estates, and triumphed. He sought for the appointment of a commission of a dozen members to sift the *cahiers* of the Estates and he moved for the alienation of the royal demesne in order to pay the expenses of the wars. " Le roi," maintained the Vermandois representative, " n'était que simple usager du domaine. . . . Quant au fonds et propriété du dit domaine, il appartenait au peuple." [2] Losing the favour of the King by his policy, he re-entered the service of the Duc d'Alençon, now Duc d'Anjou. In 1577 he published in French his magnum opus, *Six Livres de la République*, achieving immediately name and fame for its author. Visiting England in the suite of the Duc d'Anjou in 1579, he met with a Cambridge professor lecturing on a Latin translation of his work. This was so wretched that he turned it into Latin himself, and it appeared in 1586, and is the edition usually used.

If one were forced to select a text to describe this thinker, the following expresses the changelessness in his mental outlook : " As it was in the beginning, is now, and ever shall be, world without end." What he said in his *Methodus* he resays in his *Réponse à M. de Malestroit*; what he said in his *Réponse à M. de Malestroit* he resays in his *République*. If in his *Théâtre de la Nature* he pleads passionately for the influence of the stars on human destiny, if he can fix firmly the date of the birth of the world on 15th September [3] as completely to his satisfaction as Usher fixed it to his, if he pleads passionately against the system of Copernicus, his *Heptaplomeres* pleads no less passionately for similar issues. If there are theories of climate, of ideal government, and of revolution in his *Methodus*, we meet with the same views presented in his *République*. He is coherent in the views he expounds at such length, but he is also confused to a degree remarkable even during the sixteenth century. Changelessness, coherence and confusion are the

[1] Bodin, *Les Six Livres de la République*, p. 485 (1593, Lyons ed.).
[2] Baudrillart, *J. Bodin et son Temps*, p. 125.
[3] *Méthod.*, viii., p. 363 ; *Rép.*, IV. ii., p. 379ff.

characteristics of Bodin: the changelessness is in thought, the coherence in idea, and the confusion in expression.

From pasquinade and pamphlet he reaches philosophy. Confusing as his writing is, Bodin earnestly sought order and harmony in everything in heaven and earth. Hence he attached importance to secret and mysterious correspondences between the world of feeling and the world of perception. Did not the stars in general and the succession of phenomena in particular relate themselves secretly to numbers? A Pythagorean like Bodin did not entertain the least doubt on this head.[1] Gebhart insists that even the most enlightened minds of the Middle Ages were dominated by such a symbolism, which became the " catégorie maîtresse de leur pensée." [2] It certainly dominated Bodin, who perceived in numbers the key of the world and who perceived in events arithmetical relations. We smile at his naïve belief, and yet we may see in it—if we take trouble —that its follower shared the mediæval horror of hazard, of anarchy, of the desire to witness matters ordered in a rational world " pour faire entendre que les choses humaines ne vont pas fortuitement." If he were humanist and jurist, he was also Pythagorean and astrologer. Nor was he singular in his belief in astrology. For jurisconsults like Alciat [3] and Charondas le Caron, magistrates like Nicolas Rémy and de Lancre, surgeons like Jean Wier and Ambroise Paré shared the belief Bodin expressed in his La Démonomanie, which also attests a faith in sorcery as strenuous as that of Alciat himself. Did not Sixtus V. launch his Bull Coeli et terrae creator Deus against magic and kindred matters in 1585? Bodin argued that if God and man multiplied laws against sorcery, is not this a proof of its existence? For legislation is not passed for something altogether imaginary.[4]

Emphatically a man of the Renaissance, Bodin exhausted the sources of antiquity. With the eagerness of the explorer of new territory and with the intrepidity of a soldier he combined

---

[1] Fouillée, La Philosophie de Platon, ii., p. 28.
[2] Gebhart, L'Italie mystique, p. 300.
[3] Opera, ii., p. 424 ; iv., p. 560.
[4] Démon., Preface, p. 35. Cf. his Théâtre, IV. xvi., p. 778.

a lack of discernment in the value of the books he read. As a
Puritan was to read his Bible, in which any one text was quite
as good as any other, so this French scholar read the classical
historians. The charming fictions of Livy [1] or Herodotus
meant as much to him as the scientific writing of Thucydides.
Like so many men of the New Learning, he developed a
veneration for classical sources, and thus was not a little blind
to the worth of the work he read. He was as willing to submit
to the influence of Plato as he was unwilling to submit to that
of Aristotle. The mystical aspect of Platonic thought exercised
a strong appeal over his mind. " Platon," he informs us,
" (qu'Aristotle vraiment surpasse en subtilité comme esprit
plus raffiné), a eu cependant de plus belles lumières et de plus
certaines cognoissances de la diuinité et des esprits immortels,
lesquelles sans la grace de Dieu il n'eust iamais acquises." [2]
That Plato was the god of the Renaissance is a commonplace
of criticism. The Academy of Florence professed the warmest
admiration for this deity, and Bodin certainly burned incense
at his shrine. From the great Greek he borrows the idea [3] that
science leads us to a knowledge of God [4]; that religion forms
the social cement [5]; that the end of polity is neither happiness
nor even well-being but the good life of the citizens [6]; that
atheists ought not to be convinced but punished [7]; that numbers
exercise an obscure but potent force on destiny [8]; and that
the stars are inhabited by intelligent beings. [9] Nor is this
last belief foolish to one who believes in the cyclical theory
of history. At bottom the Stoic rested on the conception of
wisdom, which has not produced practical perfectibility, but
which has given men the law of life. This wisdom embraced
the world above as well as the world below. Heaven was quite
visible any clear night, and there were all the souls of men till

---

[1] *Cf.* Bodin, *Rép.*, IV. vii., p. 452 ; V. vi., pp. 553, 559-560.

[2] *Hept.*, v., p. 361.

[3] Here I use the convenient summary in Chauviré, *Jean Bodin*, p. 176.

[4] Plato, *Republic*, vii. (Aime-Martin ed.), p. 321.

[5] *Laws*, xii. (Coll. du Panthéon littéraire), p. 408.

[6] *Ibid.*, iv. and v., pp. 248, 254, 269.

[7] *Ibid.*, x., pp. 354, 357.

[8] *Republic*, vii., pp. 314-320.   [9] *Laws*, xii., p. 408.

another conflagration of this world began another process in its evolution. Posidonius provides occupation for them. Were they not watching the stars go round? Such a prospect evidently inspired Virgil, who, in the *Georgics*,[1] tells us that he covets not the stimulus of the past, though he does covet the understanding of the sciences: he seeks to grasp the " ways of the sky and the stars.".It inspired Cicero [2] and it inspired Seneca.[3] No doubt this attitude is not so disinterested as it seems. Were not the movements of the stars secretly connected with the life of man? Was there not a hidden bond between astrology and astronomy?

The general influence of Plato is perfectly discernible in Bodin's mental horizon: so, too, is the particular influence. There is, for instance, a striking similarity in their views [4] on the nature of punishment [5]; the inequality of the law in different cases [6]; the leaning of absolute equality towards the creation of worse inequality at the expense of merit [7]; the tendency of excessive inequality, on the other hand, in the distribution of riches to civil convulsions [8]; the danger of absolute power to the moral health of the despot [9]; and the disadvantages of democracy and the advantages of legitimate monarchy.[10] Nor do we in the eyes of either Plato or Bodin come to the individual when we deal with what seems purely private. For to both of them the family forms the foundation of State. Both agree on the necessity of an inalienable patrimony, the inferiority of women,[11] the right of the State to the education of children,[12] and the share to be taken by music in the life of the people.[13]

---

[1] *Georgics*, ii. 475-492.
[2] *Tusc. Dis.*, i. 44-45; *De Rep.*, vi. 16.
[3] *Ad Marciam de Consoll*, 25.
[4] Again I use Chauviré's summary, p. 176.
[5] Plato, *Laws*, viii.
[6] Plato, *Politics*, p. 407; Aristotle, *Nicomachean Ethics*, v. 10.
[7] *Laws*, vi., p. 277.
[8] *Ibid.*, v., p. 261; *Republic*, viii., pp. 362-368.
[9] *Laws*, iii., p. 238.
[10] *Politics*, pp. 404, 408.
[11] *Laws*, v., p. 271; *Republic*, v., p. 207.
[12] *Laws*, vii., p. 306.
[13] *Republic*, v., p. 214. *Cf.* Bodin, *Rép.*, IV. ii., p. 392.

BODIN AND SOVEREIGNTY

Aristotle had been seated on a pedestal throughout the Middle Ages, and Bodin deliberately removes him from it. His main complaint against him is that he thoroughly misconceived the nature of Platonic thought. Yet the singular thing is that Bodin himself is far more Aristotelian than Platonic in his political conceptions. As Aristotle examined the constitutions of many countries, so Bodin covered the whole range of European history. The truth is that he was educated in the tenets of the schoolmen, and these tenets were impregnated with the teaching of the Stagirite. We are influenced by writers who repel us as well as by those who attract us, and the influence of Aristotle over Bodin was potent even if it was repellent.[1] Nor does Bodin confine his attention to such masters as Plato and Aristotle. In his *Methodus* he makes use of the ideas of such writers as Tacitus and Polybius, Appian and Denys of Halicarnassus, Plutarch and Suetonius.[2] The *Georgics* and the *Pharsalia* are almost as familiar to him as Philo and Plotinus, Proclus and Porphyry.[3] His acquaintance in not a few cases is minute. Thus from Polybius he borrows his disapproval of the mixed State and his views on the use of religion to the statesman.[4]

With the schoolmen he had much more than a bowing acquaintance, and he really knew such jurists as Bartolus and Baldus, Alexander and Alberic de Rosate, Paulus de Castro and Fellinus. The decisions of the judges as well as the registers of *Parlement* he had diligently perused. For instance, he had read *Les Registres du Parlement de Paris, intitulé les Ordonnances Barbines*, and quotes Nicolas de Bohier, who had published a collection of the decrees of the *Parlement* of Bordeaux, and Pierre Bellugne, an authority on the law of Aragon. His exact knowledge of the law of Rome inspired him with the deepest respect for it.[5] Inevitably he stoutly

---

[1] Bodin's debt is clear if we read Aristotle, *Politics*, i. 1, 5, 35; 5, 1-3; ii. 1, 17; 2, 9; 4, 12; 6, 7; iii. 4, 1; 5, 2-5, 11; 10, 4; iv. 1, 5; 2, 3; 8, 3; 9 all; vi. 1, 5; 5 all; viii. 3, 1, 2, 7; 7, 7; 8, 6; 9, 1, 8, 15.
[2] *Method.*, iv., pp. 61, 65, 69, 74, 77.
[3] *Hept.*, iii., p. 204; vi., p. 460; *Th. Nat.*, iii. 2, p. 421; iii. 14, p. 570ff.
[4] *Polybius*, vi. 1, 3, 9.　　　　[5] Yet see *Method.*, p. 3.

opposed the pretensions of the canonists: their policy and their law were anathema to him.[1] His nascent nationalism originated with him as ardent hostility as Du Bois's to the claims either of the Pope or the Holy Roman Emperor. For him as a Frenchman these two claimants to international sovereignty are simply foreigners. He, for his part, upholds the absolute sovereignty of France by the King thereof.[2] What pleases the Prince had the force of law, but the Prince must be his Prince. He must be neither Pope nor Emperor. Persian and Greek, Egyptian and Hebrew[3] jurisprudence he has pondered as well as Frank[4] and English, German and Italian, but none of them command such whole-hearted admiration as the Twelve Tables of Rome[5] and the *Institutes* of Justinian.[6]

The learning of such sixteenth-century scholars as a Rainolds or a Scaliger amazes us, and so too, though of course on a lower plane, does Bodin's. He reads the statutes of Poland,[7] the form of the investiture of the Duke of Carinthia, the customs of Muscovy and Tartary.[8] Does he not peruse Sigismund of Herberstein's *History of Muscovy*, and even Tritheim and Francis Alvarez's *History of Ethiopia*? For each separate country he has historian after historian whom he consults. For Italy he has Paul Jove and for Venice he has Bembo and Sabellico, Coccio and Contarini; for Florence he has Guiccardini; for Germany he has Sleidan; for Nürnberg he has Conrad Celtes; for Scotland he has Hector Boetius and for England Polydore Virgil. Legislation always interests him, and he inquires particularly into the customs of Naples and Milan, Ferrara and Venice.[9] Above all, he is intrigued by the annals of the Swiss republics. Is there a cantonal sovereign? Is there a federal sovereign? Does sovereignty belong to the canton till such time as all the cantons meet? Indefatigably he investigates treaties in order to throw light on the problem of the relations

---

[1] Yet see *Rép.*, I. ix., p. 132; vi., p. 736.
[2] See especially *Rép.*, I. ix., p. 132.
[3] *Method.*, pp. 4, 5. *Cf.* Guttmann, pp. 14-23, 46-63.
[4] *Rép.*, VI. vi., pp. 718, 722.   [5] *Ibid.*, III. v., p. 307.
[6] *Method*, p. 3.   [7] *Rép.* p. 93.
[8] *Ibid.*, p. 33.   [9] *Ibid.*, pp. 93-96.

of the States.[1] The old world dominated by the Holy Roman Empire had remained a shell since 1348, and now the shell was visibly smashing up. What was to take its place?

There had been cosmos in Europe, and now there was chaos. There must be a way out of the chaos, and it was for the intelligence of Bodin to find it. If Plato and More dreamed dreams and saw visions, surely it was reserved for him to bring down to mother earth some conception, turning shadow into substance. An ordered comity of nations is what he envisages, and plainly the empiricism of Machiavelli is not of the slightest avail to him. *La Raison d'État* is all very well, but a mere policy of expediency stood self-condemned in the eyes of our thinker. There is from the point of view of the Italian no political science, and there can be no political science. From such pragmatism the mind of Bodin stands in utter revolt. He must write his *République* in order to fight the teaching of *The Prince*. What had the statecraft of Catherine de' Medici accomplished for her adopted country?[2] St Bartholomew's Day spoke eloquently on the worth of a policy of expedients. The measured judgment of Bodin is: " Quant au sçavoir, je crois que ceux qui ont accoustumé de discourir doctement, peser sagement et résoudre subtilement les hautes affaires d'estat s'accorderont qu'il [*i.e.* Machiavelli] n'a pas sondé le gué de la science politique, qui ne gist pas en ruses tyranniques qu'il a recherchées par tous les coins d'Italie."[3]

For Bodin there has been an indissoluble marriage between politics and religion, and he cannot bear the divorce that Machiavelli intended to effect. For him at least Machiavelli " mis pour fondemens des Republiques l'impieté et iniustice, blasmant la religion comme contraire a l'estat."[4] Machiavelli recommends the Prince to pursue perjury and perfidy, covering both with the cloak of loyalty. To Bodin, however, " le pariure est plus execrable que l'atheïsme, d'autant que

---

[1] Generally cf. *Method*, x.; *Rép.*, I. ii., p. 12; ix., p. 140; II., p. 610; III. ii., p. 169; V. iii., p. 507; VI. iii., p. 649; V., pp. 686, 705; VI., p. 719.
[2] Weill, *Les Théories sur le Pouvoir Royal en France pendant les Guerres de Religion*, p. 160.
[3] *Rép.*, Preface. [4] *Ibid.*, p. 3.

l'atheïste qui ne croit point de Dieu ne luy fait pas tant d'iniure, ne croyant point qu'il y en ait, que celuy qui sçait bien et le pariure par moquerie."[1] Has not the Italian writer " met pour vn parangon de tous les Roys le plus desloyal fils de prestre qui fut onques : et lequel neantmoins auec toutes ses finesses fut honteusement precipité de la roche de tyrannie haute et glissante, ou il s'estoit niché, et enfin exposé comme vn belistre a la merci et risée de ses ennemis ? "[2] In blunt English, Cæsar Borgia proved a failure. But what if he had succeeded?

Walter Bagehot used to say that if you wanted approval in the House of Commons—he was speaking of two generations ago —all you had to do was to speak in favour of economy ; if you wanted disapproval, all you had to do was to speak in favour of a particular economy, for all the folk interested in it at once sprang to their feet to attack you. Similarly, we note that when men attack Machiavellianism they proceed on general grounds. When, however, it comes to a particular point, some of the expedients might readily have come out of the pages of *The Prince*. Bodin will not do wrong, yet he must somehow succeed in his schemes for the welfare of the State. His advice is to calculate coldly the chances of the scheme in hand, and then act promptly to ensure success. Nothing is more to be dreaded than an abortive operation. If the means employed do not justify the end achieved, they at least excuse it. Q. Gallius conspired against the Emperor Augustus, who pardoned him publicly and had him privately killed. " Mais la plus part," Bodin informs us, " qui auoit bonne opinion de la clemence naturelle d'Auguste n'estimoit pas qu'il eust voulu en vser ainsi : et les plus fins excusoient cela."[3] Is the gulf yawning between Machiavelli and Bodin so extremely wide when it comes to practical matters? With the latter force creates right. He thinks that the false princes are those " qui se despartent des promesses qu'ils ont faictes a leur disaduantage, estans contraincts par les vainqueurs."[4] For any man " sçait assez que la plus part des traictes de paix se font par force, ou par crainte du vainqueur, ou de celui qui est le plus puissant : et

---

[1] *Rép.*, V. vi., p. 258.   [2] *Ibid.*, Preface, p. 2.
[3] *Ibid.*, IV. vii., p. 443.   [4] *Ibid.*, V. vi., p. 659.

quelle crainte y a t il plus iuste que de perdre la vie ? " [1] Lady
Macbeth is not the only creation in the annals of the sixteenth
century who would do right, and yet would wrongly win. If
the sovereignty of the end does not dominate Bodin to the
extent to which it dominates Machiavelli, still it is by no means
absent.

For Bodin there is natural religion as well as revealed, and
indeed at times in his *Heptaplomeres* he comes close to the
opinion that the former is the generalised conception of which
the latter forms the particular. Obviously such an opinion
leads straight towards toleration, and Bodin did not belong
to the Politiques without imbibing this manifestation of their
spirit. With a breadth of view unusual during the sixteenth
century he holds that " les diversités d'opinions ne doivent pas
le troubler, pourvu tu aies dans l'esprit que la vraie religion
n'est pas autre chose que le regard d'un esprit pur vers le vrai
Dieu." [2] Is it not enough for man if he can in any wise attain
to the religious stature of Socrates and Plato, and the noble
men of antiquity? [3] Did not Alexander Severus unite in his
oratory images of Abraham and Orpheus, Hercules and
Jesus? " Pour moy," we learn, " afin de ne blasmer personne,
i'ayme mieux approuuer touttes les religions que d'en cond-
maner vne, laquelle seroit peut estre la veritable." [4] The spirit
of the wars of religion is as alien to him as it is to L'Hôpital.
Bodin's conclusion is memorable : " Aussy i'entre volontiers
et sans repugnance partout dans les temples des Iuifs, des
Mahometans, des Chrestiens, mesme des Lutheriens et des
Zwingliens, afin de nestre pas accusé d'atheïsme ou destre vn
seditieux capable de troubler la tranquillité de la republique.
Ie reconnois touttesfois que ce que i'ay ie tiens du chef ou
maistre de tous les autres Dieux : qui nous empescheroit donc de
mesler nos prieres en commun afin de toucher ce pere commun
de la nature et cet autheur de touttes choses, si bien qu'il nous
conduise tous dans la connoissance de la vraye religion." [5]

---

[1] *Rép.*, V. vi., p. 659.   [2] *Ibid.*, V. i., p. 478.
[3] *Hept.*, vi., p. 601ff.   [4] *Ibid.*, vi., p. 673.
[5] *Ibid.*, vi., p. 675. The *Heptaplomeres* remained in manuscript till Guhrauer
published extracts of it in 1841, and Noack the whole of it in 1857.

The speakers in the *Heptaplomeres* testify to the views entertained by its author. There are Curoni the Catholic and Curce the Zwinglian, Frederich the Lutheran and Octave the Mohammedan, Toralba, the devotee of natural religion, with Salomon the Jew and Senamy, the worshipper at all shrines, be their altars what they may. Compared with Sir Thomas More our author is dull indeed, but the *Utopia* is not a whit more broadminded than the *Heptaplomeres*. What, after all, is gained by disputes about theological questions? The Sorbonne rang throughout the sixteenth century with them, and a visitor to it, when informed of this, dryly asked what had been settled. Wearied with the vanity of it all, Curoni cries, when the matter was no less than the divinity of Christ, " C'est tousiours a recommencer."[1] The peace of God passed by such controversialists. Bodin sought it and found it : " Et apres s'estre embrassez mutuellement en charité, ils se separerent. Et depuis ils vescurent ensemble dans vne vnion admirable, dans vne pieté et dans vne façon de vie exemplaire, prenans leurs repas et estudians tousiours en commun. Mais on ne parla iamais plus de religion, encor que chacun soit demeuré ferme et constant dans la sienne, ou ils ont perseueré iusques a la fin et dans vne saincteté toute manifeste."[2]

Bodin, who limits himself almost wholly to combining the ideas of Plato and Aristotle with those of Machiavelli, lays down the principle that men follow the pursuit of a chimera when they seek the realisation of the ideal. " When I speak of the flourishing state of a republic, I do not mean that it has arrived at the height of perfection."[3] Bodin displays a fondness for definition, and Grotius notes that he cares more for words than for things. Giving an excessive importance to the classical writers, he ranks Homer and Hesiod high, and the melancholy of these two poets attaches itself to Bodin himself. His thought remained immovable. When a young man he defended the astrological view that numbers influence the destiny of man, and when an old man he still defended this view. As a young man he attacked the Copernican system, and as an old man he persisted in his attack. Is there a philosopher's stone? He is

---

[1] *Hept.*, vi., p. 527.   [2] *Ibid.*, vi., p. 684ff.   [3] *Rép.*, iv.

not sure : Nature guards her secrets closely. If God and man
legislate against sorcery, this of itself proves the existence of
sorcery. Tolerant as he is, Bodin regards atheism as a crime
to be punished.[1] The compass, geographical discovery, astronomical laws, the invention of artillery—these are sufficiently
striking witnesses of the progress in his day. Bodin, however,
deems that printing only deserves comparison .with the discoveries of antiquity.[2] Like Montaigne, he is as much impressed
by the novelty of the ideas of his day as by their truth. The
stranger the tale of the traveller the more he—and Montaigne
—is pleased.

Anticipating the Pragmatists, Bodin thrusts to the one side
all means of attaining knowledge save experience, which is
" maistresse de toute certitude." [3] On the other hand, he can
hold that our senses deceive us, that our reason is unworthy
of trust. " L'entendement descouure et fait iugement de l'erreur
des sens. . . . La raison est donc comme le reigle de Polyclète,
par laquelle on corrige les erreurs des sens, s'ils ont failly en
quelque chose : et laquelle n'a pas tousiours faute de l'aide
d'iceux en ses diuines operations." [4] It is easy to see why he
finds it hard to know God, why he believes in mystical experience.[5] In theory Bodin, like More, advocates freedom of
thought : in practice he falls back on authority. Like Machiavelli, he believes in witchcraft, and he disbelieves in the
discoveries of Copernicus and Galileo. He returns to the Bible,
" laquelle nous préferons a toutes les raisons que l'on pourroit
alleguer a l'encontre." [6] There is a pæan on progress in his
Methodus, but it is plainly inconsistent with the tenor of his
fundamental thought.[7] God, he proclaims, is free to act as
He pleases, and Bodin draws the conclusion that accordingly
the laws of nature are not fixed.[8] If the laws are not fixed, he

[1] *Rép.*, vi., p. 590 ; *Theatrum Naturæ*, p. 5.
[2] *Method.*, vii., p. 360ff.
[3] *Theatrum Naturæ*, II. ix., p. 350 ; III. xii., p. 553.
[4] *Ibid.*, IV. ix., p. 685.
[5] *Démonomanie*, Preface, p. 17ff.
[6] *Theatrum Naturæ*, II. vi., p. 261 ; *Heptaplomeres*, iii., pp. 172-173.
[7] *Methodus*, vii.
[8] *Theatrum Naturæ*, I. iii., p. 31ff.

wonders if there is the possibility of scientific knowledge. In spite of his beloved Plato the science of government barely advances.[1]

The range of Bodin is encyclopædic. His *Methodus* provides us with a philosophy of history, his *Réponse à M. de Malestroit* with an outline of political economy, his *République* with political philosophy, his *Heptaplomeres* deals with the world of religion, and his *Amphitheatrum Naturæ* with the world of science. Not indeed that their author for one moment confines himself in each of these books to their main topics. On all these matters he has much to say in the five books, and he says it the moment a thought strikes his mind. He is eminently unsystematic and confusing. Scaliger, one of his critics, justly remarked that the contents of a chapter rarely answered to the title the author gave it.

The *Methodus*, published in 1556, provides us with his grasp of the knowledge of history. Its full title, *Methodus ad Facilem Historiarum Cognitionem*, renders this point of view clear, and his attitude to history is not unlike that of Sir John Seeley, who regarded it as a school for statesmen. It is a point of view as old as Commines, the father of modern history, and Machiavelli and Guicciardini, who all conceived that the main task of history was the teaching of the attainment of political success. The aim of these men, and of the brothers Pithou and Pasquier, Hotman and L'Hôpital, was not the investigation of knowledge but the increase of their zeal for their country. Bodin, therefore, from this angle inaugurated nothing new. He simply regarded history as a means to an end, and that end the welfare of the State, the French State. There is no attempt at disguise in the preface to the *Methodus*, where we learn *de facilitate, oblectatione, et utilitate historiæ*. Nor is Bodin without followers in the delusions contained in these words, for the whole German school of history of the last three or four generations looked on history from the purely national, the purely utilitarian, standpoint. It is easy to condemn Bodin, but is it so easy to condemn Treitschke? Apart from the research of the latter, what separates him from his French ancestor?

---

[1] *Methodus*, vi., p. 377.

History is indeed light labour if it simply means drawing morals to suit the State, but is it light if it means the search after truth?

History Bodin regards as true narration or description. This leads him to divide it into human, natural, and divine. Human history has man for its subject, as natural history has the physical world, and divine history God. The materials of history, in the widest sense, are all *consilia, dicta, facta* of mankind. Human history changes, but *plus ça change, plus c'est la même chose*. Behind all its incessant mutability there are principles, and these principles Bodin diligently seeks. With one of the accepted ones he effects a break, for he rejects the notion of a Golden Age in the past. This argues no mean capacity on his part, for to a man who knew his classics as intimately as he such was the orthodox view. Most of us to-day are inclined to regard progress as a matter of course. Knowledge expands, we think, and there is no reason why it should not continue to do so indefinitely. This was not so with the Greeks. They, for the most part, conceived on the contrary the possibility of a process of deterioration, a cycle or a succession of cycles. The majority thought that there had been a Golden Age, but it is long since past. Moreover, there seems to have been the feeling that this age was distinctly dull. Beyond the Pillars of Hercules once existed Plato's "Atlantis": it is now lost to the sight of men in the depths of the sea. In it innocence and happiness reached the highest possible stage: the utmost man can expect is to return, however distantly, to this stage. This view possessed a great practical value, for it kept men from that fanciful and foolish idealising which is the curse of the modern world. Similarly there had once been a complete body of knowledge: the past knew far more than the present can ever hope to know. What George Meredith called "the rapture of the forward view" was for the most part denied to the classical writers. Bodin, therefore, exercised no mean intellectual courage in rejecting the current of opinion held by the authors he admired so reverently.

Bodin argues that history should proceed from the universal to the particular, that a general view of history should precede the investigation of any country or period. He spends space on rather unoriginal remarks on the qualities of the ideal historian, the rules to be attended to in ascertaining historical facts and in judging of historical evidence, the sources of the prejudices often displayed by historical writers, combined with a reasoned survey of the merits and the demerits of ancient and modern historians. His chief lack is a lack of distinction. Here and there we discern gleams of originality, as when he anticipates Ranke in holding that the true ideal of history is a plain and exact exhibition of what actually occurred. "Historia nihil aliud esse debeat quam veritatis et rerum gestarum veluti tabula." There is another gleam of better things in his resounding attack on a jurist like Cujas on the ground that he is a mere interpreter of Latin texts, not a searcher of scientific truth. No study of Roman law, Bodin argues, however complete or accurate, can give more than a partial notion of law. It is absurd to do as Cujas does when he makes Roman law identical with or the measure of universal law. There is a universal law, in which all the different—and differing—codes of law have their root and rationale. To reach this universal law the historians as well as the jurists must be consulted, in order that Persians and Egyptians, Greeks and Hebrews, Germans and English may all find the niche into which they fit alongside the Roman one. We can forgive Bodin much of his diffuseness and more of his confusion for the stress he lays on the conception of universal law, the knowledge of which can be reached only through the methodical study of history as a whole.

He received the idea of universal law just as he rejected that of a Golden Age. Mankind had so grown since its primitive stage that " if that so-called Golden Age could be revoked and compared with our own, we should consider it iron." [1] New laws and new customs, new institutions and alas ! new errors characterise the changing history of mankind. The crest of the wave is sometimes higher and the trough is sometimes lower, but the general level is undoubtedly steadily—if slowly— rising. Machiavelli deems that our moral progress is stationary, whereas Bodin holds that it is advancing.[2] Men speak of the

---

[1] *Methodus*, vii., p. 353.   [2] *Ibid.*, vii., p. 356.

good old days, but if we could but return to those days we
should feel that we were living among wild beasts.[1]

In the age of the Reformation it was not easy to be just to
the past if it were not that of classical antiquity, and it is the
signal merit of Bodin that he is just to the past. The accepted
survey of history was based largely on the prophecies of Daniel,
that never-failing resource of the cranks of all ages, and this
survey divided our annals into four periods corresponding to
the Babylonian, Persian, Macedonian and Roman monarchies,
the last of which was to survive to the Day of Judgment. For
this time-honoured division Bodin suggests three great periods,
the first two of which lasts about two thousand years. During
the first period the South-Eastern peoples proved predominant;
during the second the Middle or Mediterranean peoples; and
during the last the Northern nations who wrought the decline
and fall of the Roman Empire proved predominant. This acute
division actually anticipates that advanced by Hegel.

The interest of Bodin's three periods is not confined to the
fact that he was bold enough to break with current notions. In
fact it consists in the circumstance that he takes into account
both psychological and climatic considerations. Thus we learn
that the note of the first period is religion, of the second
practical sagacity, and of the third warfare and inventive skill.
Climatic considerations occupy some space in his *Methodus*
and more in his *République*. Though Montesquieu proudly inscribed on his *Esprit des Lois* the epigraph, "*Prolem sine matre
creatam*," we ask: Is it true? Much of it concerns itself with
the influence of climate on character, and here he has certainly
been anticipated by Bodin, who in his turn has been anticipated
by Hippocrates and Aristotle, Plato and Polybius. Bodin
towers over them all till we come to the eighteenth century.
For he has been at pains not merely to lay down such vague
teaching as that physical circumstances determine national
characteristics, but he has also applied this knowledge with a
wealth of insight that forms by no means the least feature in
his originality.

While we are surprised at the importance Bodin attaches

---

[1] *Methodus*, vii., p. 361.

to climate, we are no less surprised at the fashion in which he connects the stars with it. At bottom, however, he is desirous of arriving at an order and a unity in the universe. The world above and the world below must be interdependent, and astrology undoubtedly furnishes one of the links in the chain connecting them. It is easy, *à la* Macaulay, to criticise this thinker, but we feel more anxious to grasp his mentality. His mystical mind induces him to note correspondences where others would not dream of seeing them. Behind all such correspondences he traces the outline of the order that will one day lead to the formulation of scientific law. Like his predecessor Machiavelli, he is persuaded that the trend of events marches westward. In this march the men of the South and of the North play the rôles climate allows them. Climate is all important, for he perceives that " l'Espagnol redouble son appétit et ses forces passant d'Espagne en France," that " le François deuient languide et dégousté passant en Espagne : et s'il veut boire et manger comme en France, il est en danger de ne pas le faire longue " [1]; that " les armées des peuples de septentrion s'allengorissent venant au païs méridional," and that " comme il s'est veu des sept mille Espagnols qui passèrent en Allemaigne sous l'empereur Charles-Quint." [2] He seeks a reason for these differences, and no doubt he urges the share taken by Venus and Saturn, by Jupiter and Mercury.[3] He also puts forward a scientific reason in accordance with the knowledge of his time. " Tout ainsy que, en hiuer, les lieux sousterrains et les parties interieures des animaux retiennent la chaleur qui en esté s'éuapore : ainsy est-il des peuples septentrion qui ont la chaleur interieure plus vehemente que ceux du païs meridional : laquelle chaleur faict que les forces et puissances naturelles sont plus grandes ès vns que non pas ès aultres : qui faict aussi que les vns sont plus affamez, déuorent et cuissent mieulx que les vns que les aultres, pour la froideur de la region, qui resserre la chaleur naturelle."

The influence of climate on the character of particular

---

[1] *Rép.*, V. i., p. 466 ; *Meth.*, v., p. 100.
[2] Cf. *Rép.*, V. i., p. 481.
[3] *Meth.*, v., p. 124f., p. 135 ; *Rép.*, V. i., pp. 480-481.

peoples is then set out at length. We read that " le peuple de
Septentrion le gaigne par force et le peuple de Midy par
finesse," and that " ceux du milieu participent médiocrement
de l'un et de l'aultre ; c'est pourquoi ils ont establi les grands
Empires qui ont flory en armes et en loix." There is nothing
amazingly novel in these speculations in our day, but they were
most amazingly novel in Bodin's, when Calvin was laying down
that the boundaries of countries are entirely a matter for God
and when his view of grace was teaching the nothingness of the
character of man. Here comes a thinker who lays down that
there are natural forces at work at least as potent as those of
predestination. Doubtless man is the creature of God, but he
is none the less the creature of climate.

Bodin proceeds to inform us that " les peuples meridionaux
sont foibles, petits, noirauts." [1] As well as the stars, the four
humours, phlegm, blood, anger, melancholy, have their appropriate work. The extreme North is phlegmatic, the extreme
South melancholic. " Or Galen confesse que la pituite rend
l'homme pesant et lourd : le sang ioyeux et robuste : la cholere
actif et dispos : la melancholie constant et posé : et, selon qu'il
y a plus ou moins des quatre humeurs meslés ensemble, autant
y a de varietés." [2] The influence of climate on manners emerges.
Wherever Venus sheds her influence—that is, in warm countries
—there we have polygamy, while in temperate countries we
have monogamy.[3] " Encores auons nous vne différence notable
entre le peuple meridional et septentrional, c'est a sçauoir que
cestuy cy est plus chaste et pudique, et le meridional fort
lubrique : ce qui leur audient a cause de la mesme melancholie."
In Germany, on the other hand, men and women bathe together,
and there is no cause of jealousy. " Et neantmoins les peuples
de midy et sont si passionnés, qu'ils meurent souuent de ceste
maladie." [4] Climate, in Bodin's judgment, will explain such a
phenomenon as the greater ferocity of the Muscovites compared with the Moroccans. Men of the South " y vont d'vne
impetuosité brutale, et comme bestes sans raison." This race

---

[1] *Rép.*, V. i., pp. 464, 467 ; *Meth.*, v., p. 99.   [2] *Rép.*, V. i., p. 471.
[3] *Ibid.*, pp. 475-476.
[4] *Ibid.* ; *Meth.*, v., pp. 114-116.

is " cruel et vindicatif, pour la nature de la melancholie, qui presse les passions de l'ame d'vne violence extreme, et employe son esprit a vanger sa douleur." " Ceux qui sont fort subiects a cest humeur la deuiennent plus souuent furieux que les autres, s'ils n'ont moyen d'assouuir leurs affections." [1]

Man's position in the Arctic, the temperate and the tropical zones will explain much in his mental characteristics. With Commines, he agrees that men of the North possess force, while those of the South possess finesse. " Si bien on prend garde aux histoires de tous les peuples, on trouvera que les grandes armées et puissances sont venues de Septentrion : les sciences occultes, la philosophie, le mathématique et aultres sciences contemplatives sont venues du peuple meridional ; et les sciences politiques, les loix, la jurisprudence, la grace de bien dire et de bien discourir ont pris leur commencement et origine aux regions metoyennes et tous les grands empires y ont esté establis." [2] Our author sets to work on these lines, and explains why the Roman Empire grew. " Les Romains ont bien estendu leur puissance sur le peuples de Midy et d'Orient ; mais ils n'ont pas beaucoup gaigne sur les peuples d'Occident et de Septentrion, quoiqu'ils fussent victorieux de tous les aultres peuples : néantmoins ils employoient toutes leurs forces, et avoient bien faire à soustenir l'effort, et parer les coups des peuples de Septentrion, qui n'avoient ny villes murées, ny fortresses, ny chasteaux, comme dict Tacite parlant des Alemans." For a moment he envisages all the kingdoms taking their due position as part of an ordered whole. The men of the North come with their contribution of the mechanical arts of life, the men of the Middle with their skill in diplomacy, in jurisprudence and politics, and the men of the South with their visions. Each zone brings its due share, and the whole becomes truly rich when all the shares blend into one.[3]

Montesquieu ascribes the immutability of religion, manners, custom and laws in India and other Oriental countries to

---

[1] *Rép.*, V. i., pp. 472-473 ; *Meth.*, v., pp. 111-113, 121.
[2] *Rép.*, V. i., p. 467.
[3] *Ibid.*, p. 480 ; *Meth.*, v., pp. 124-127, 136.

their warm climate.[1] Buckle attributes a highly wrought imagination and gross superstition to all people, like those of India, living in the presence of great mountains and vast plains, knowing nature only in its overpowering aspects, which excite the fancy and paralyse the reason. He finds an early predominance of reason in the inhabitants of a country like ancient Greece, where natural features are on a small scale, more comprehensible, nearer the measure of man himself.[2] Treitschke ascribes the absence of artistic and poetic development in Switzerland and the Alpine lands to the overwhelming aspect of nature there, its majestic sublimity which paralyses the mind. He proceeds to show that, by contrast, the lower mountains and hill country of Swabia, Franconia and Thuringia, where nature is gentler, stimulating, appealing and not overpowering, have produced many poets and artists.[3] Such speculations of Treitschke, of Buckle and of Montesquieu are all ultimately traceable to the seminal notions Bodin scattered with so lavish a hand. Take these passages of his. " Mais le plus notable changement particulier est la différence des lieux montueux et des plaines et des vallées tournées vers le Septentrion ou vers le Midy en mesme climat; en pareille latitude, voire en un mesme degré, qui cause une merveilleuse différence entre les uns et les aultres. . . . Il ne fault donc s'esmerveiller si le Florentin qui est exposé au Levant et au Midy, ayant les montagnes à dos du cote de Septentrion et de Ponent, à l'esprit beaucoup plus subtil que le Vénitien. . . . Les peuples de Septentrion ou qui demeurent aux montagnes, fiers et guerriers, se fians en la force de leur corps, veulent les estats populaires, ou du moins les monarchies électives; et ne peuvent aisement souffrir qu'on leur commande par braverie." The Swiss are also a case in point, for they " vivent en toute liberté, sans seigneur, non pas pour l'asseurance des lieux naturellement fortifiez, mais d'autant que leur naturel est sauvage et ne se peut apprivoiser aisément. . . . Celuy donc s'abuseroit fort qui voudroit changer l'estat

---

[1] *Esprit des Lois*, Bk. XIV., chap. iv.
[2] *History of Civilisation*, i., pp. 86-106.
[3] *Politik*, i., p. 225. *Cf.* the whole chapter on " Land und Leute."

populaire des Suisses et des Grisons et aultres montaignards en monarchie : car iaçoit (bien) que la monarchie soit beaucoup meilleure en soy, si este que la subject n'y est pas si propre." If anyone seeks to measure the advance contributed by our philosopher, let him turn to the speculations of the schoolmen, and attempt to bridge the gulf between Bodin and them. Bodin and Althusius, by this advance, absolutely annihilated the aims and, above all, the methods pursued by mediæval thinkers on politics. Before Vico and before Montesquieu, Bodin practically proclaimed that all knowledge is knowledge of relations, a truth that was regarded even in the eighteenth century as heresy.

In 1566 M. de Malestroit published his *Paradoxes*, dealing with the influence of money. He attributed much importance to the depreciation of the currency, conceiving that because a cask of wine used to sell for four livres and then sold for twelve it was therefore genuinely three times as valuable. He assumed that the precious metals are the true and just standard of the cheapness or the dearness of commodities. In 1568 Bodin published his *Réponse aux Paradoxes de M. Malestroit touchant l'Enchérissement de Toutes les Choses et des Monnaies*, and in 1578 his *Discours sur le Réchaussement et la Diminution des Monnaies*. Bodin refused to entertain the notion that the amount of money in circulation constituted the wealth of the community. Money had no fixed value from year to year, but was constantly changing. Therefore Malesdroit's idea of its fixity was a pure paradox. Bodin is perfectly clear that it is desirable to standardise the value of money, for he notes clearly all the evils flowing from the opposite policy. Mercantilist as he is, nevertheless he realises that it is quite useless to forbid the exportation of the precious metals. He almost seems to see how their action equalises price. For if money goes to one neighbourhood, attracted by the high prices prevailing, traders send goods there in order to take advantage of these prices, with the result that they fall. He ably analyses the law of demand and supply. A believer in a strong monarchy, he cordially endorses a policy of paternal government. The State can, ought and must stimulate the commerce of the country.

There must be high taxes on foreign manufactures and low duties on raw materials and articles of food. Public finance he calls the sinews of the State, and he bestows much space upon it, reckoning an equable system of taxation among the greatest of boons. In spite of his devotion to Plato, he vigorously defends the system of private property. It may very well be that, as More felt frightened of the excesses of men like the Anabaptists, so Bodin felt frightened. Be that as it may, he is certainly clear in thinking that a man must possess property to develop personality, if we translate his thought into the language of our day. Montaigne taught that "il ne se faict aucun profit qu'au dommage d'autruy,"[1] and in fact the tenet that the gain of one was the loss of another constituted a leading feature of Mercantilist policy. Bodin had so far emancipated himself from such ideas that he held the precisely opposite opinion, perceiving with the utmost lucidity that both parties gained by the exchange of commodities. What is true when two men exchange goods is equally true when two nations exchange goods. He assailed the proposition that the gain of one nation is necessarily the loss of another, a view that is even to-day without weight in the financial policies of all countries save England.

Important as the work of Bodin is in many directions, there is no direction in which it is so important as in the theory of sovereignty.[2] So long as the Holy Roman Empire survived, so long was it impossible to contemplate any such theory. Nationality may be no more than nascent, but there must be some feeling that one's country is somehow not quite the same as other countries. In fact, we come to the notion that we owe a duty to our State that we owe to none other. There may be an Emperor, but he is distant. There is a King, and he is near. Once the King is in possession with his army, not merely of soldiers but also of officials, then it is possible to contemplate sovereignty in the concrete. The King is there, functioning before our very eyes. The Emperor is wandering about, the Pope is in Rome, but the King of Bodin is in Paris, and he is

---

[1] *Essais*, LIV. i., chap. 21.
[2] *Cf.* Meinecke, *Die Idee der Staatsräson*, p. 70ff.

emphatically Bodin's sovereign. His *République*, published in 1577, is essentially a treatise on his conception of the State, for this is what he means by the *République*, the commonweal. No doubt there are climatic and economic considerations at work, but fundamentally " la vraie felicité de la République et d'un homme seul est tout ung." We are not far from Platonic thought throughout the sixteenth century, and Bodin feels, with Plato and Aristotle, that man is naturally born to be a citizen. The impulse to political society exists by nature in all men. Man does not invent the State in order to satisfy this impulse. He has this impulse because his end is the State, and is only to be realised in the State. Emphatically " La République est un droict gouuernement de plusieurs mesnages et de ce qui leur est commun avec puissance souveraine." That the " droict gouuernement " must possess " puissance souveraine " was the crying need of France in the throes of the wars of religion. In his preface the author fights those " qui, sous voile d'vne exemption de charges, et liberté populaire, font rebeller les subiects contre leur princes naturels, ouurant la porte a vne licentieuse anarchie, qui est pire que la plus forte tyrannie du monde."

The " mesnage " of his definition of the commonwealth is the family, composed after the Roman model, the father possessing the old *patria potestas*.[1] Man governs woman just as the State governs the several families of which it is composed. "Dieu," we learn, " l'a establie par edict exprés." Living in the land of Salic law, we can understand Bodin's position, which he strengthens by an appeal not only to the laws of God and those of nature but also the laws of the Romans, the Thracians and the Lombardians. His " mesnage " is " vn droict gouuernement de plusieurs subiects, sous l'obeïssance d'vn chef de famille, et de ce qui luy est propre." [2] This chief is the king of the home. Without any assignment of cause the husband can divorce the wife.[3] Bodin shows us " le chef de famille sortant

---

[1] *Rép.*, I. iv., p. 20ff. Rabelais and Ayrault had the same conception of fatherly authority.

[2] *Rép.*, I. ii., p. 7.

[3] *Ibid.*, I. iii., pp. 17-19; V. ii., p. 500; VI. vi., p. 739; *Th.*, III. vi., p. 452; III. xiv., p. 578. *Cf.* Chauviré's ed. of the *Hept.*, pp. 565-566.

de sa maison ou il commande pour traiter et negotier avec les autres chefs de famille de ce qui leur tousche à tous en general ; alors il depouille le tiltre de maistre, de chef, de seigneur pour estre compaignon, pair assoice avec les aultres." With Bodin and Vico the State grew out of the family. Precisely as in classical Rome, the father held himself responsible for the acts of his son, punishing him as he pleased, " sans que les magistrats en puissent prendre congnoissance." Many reasons have been given for the fall of the Roman Empire. Bodin adds to them, for in his considered judgment it was because paternal power has gradually been *laschée*, and that there had been no longer the *rares et beaux* examples of filial piety that used to adorn the annals of the metropolis of mankind.

How slowly individualism emerged during the sixteenth century is clear in a hundred ways. Take one of them. To the Church we oppose the State, and to the State we oppose the individual. Such a position was utterly out of the ken of our philosopher. To him there was no such thing as an individual, standing in complete isolation. There was a family, a conception he could grasp, but how could anyone be outside all obligations of the household? The family is " la vraye source et origine de toute république et membre principal d'icelle," [1] and this is so despite the views of Plato in the past and More and the Anabaptists in the present. Such men with their views " chassent l'amour s'entre le mari et la femme, l'affection de enuers les enfans, le reuerence des enfans enuers les pères, et la bienueillance des parents entr'eux, ostant la proximité de sang, qui les vnit du plus estroit lien qui peut estre . . . d'autant que la nature d'amour est telle, que plus elle est commune, et moins a de vigueur." [2] Bodin is not so inhuman as some of his *obiter dicta* might suggest. He utterly breaks with the classical tradition on the question of slavery. The Greeks held that the slave was incapable of the good life, and the Romans held similar views modified by the fact that physically they were superior to the slave. Bodin doughtily attacks the opinion of Aristotle that slavery is in accordance with natural right. The grand argument of such men he deems to be the generality

---

[1] *Rép.*, I. ii., p. 7.   [2] *Ibid.*, III. vii., p. 332.

of the institution, " car toute chose contre nature ne peut estre de longue durée." Slavery, in his judgment, is neither natural nor necessary, indicating that it is against nature, " d'asservir les sages aux fols, les ignorants aux hommes entendus, les meschants aux bons." Bitingly he writes that " la seruitude sera naturelle quand l'homme fort, roide, riche et ignorant, obeïra au sage, discret et foible, quoy qu'il soit poure." [1] On social, moral and economic grounds Bodin indicts slavery. Socially it promotes tyranny and the tyrannical temperament; morally, it gives rise to a set of desperate men, not the stuff out of which men manufacture good citizens; and economically, such labour does not pay. Bodin congratulated Henry II. and Charles V. on their freeing the Peruvians. Nevertheless, it is not wise to be over-hasty with the emancipation of the serfs. Before obtaining their freedom they must be taught a trade, for fear they die of hunger, " affriandés de la douceur d'oisiueté et de liberté." [2]

In our day we are alive to the importance of origins: in fact, we are sometimes obsessed by them. The sixteenth-century mind, in spite of the Renaissance and the Reformation, tended to fall back on the *status quo*. This is perhaps the reason why Bodin, like Burke, stands aloof from such matters as the origin of monarchy. By whatever means it comes into being, by whatever motive, he is as careless as Hobbes, Locke and Rousseau are careful. Suffice it for him that it exists. Its origin and its forms are simply accidental. The all-important question is: " In whose hands is the sovereign power? "

In chapter ten Bodin proceeds to analyse the marks of sovereignty. The first mark is " la puissance de donner loi à tous en general et à chacun en particuler . . . sans le consentement de plus grand ni de pareil ni de moindre pue soi." This anticipation of the famous definition of sovereignty given by John Austin plainly has a pedigree which he, like all the members of the utilitarian school, ignored. If Baldus is the first to say " *Rex est imperator in regno suo*," he is not the last who holds it. Bodin proceeds to reason that whatever the Sovereign permits he commands. Do men say that custom, the legislator

---

[1] *Rép.*, I. v., p, 35.   [2] *Ibid.*, p. 46.

and the magistrate stand in the way of such a definition? Not at all. For we read that " la loi, fidele au vieil esprit des legistes et a la cause de l'unité, la loi peut casser les coutumes, et la coutume ne peut deroger à la loi. . . . Le législateur n'est tel que par délégation de la souveraineté." Nor is the magistrate a sovereign. His labour is to interpret and to apply the law, and " de la ployer soit en douceur, soit en rigeur, pourvu qu'il se garde bien de la casser en la ployant."

The second mark of sovereignty is " décréter la guerre ou de traiter la paix." Of course generals possess power in the field, but it is a delegated power. Behind them stands the Monarch.

The third mark is " d'instituer les principaux officiers." The Law Courts, the Colleges, the local Estates and the like, appoint men, but this right of election is subject to confirmation on the part of the Sovereign.

The fourth mark " c'est a savoir le dernier ressort qui a toujours été l'un des principaux de la souveraineté." In the last resort he comes to the people, and he plainly declares that there are sometimes abuses of position, usurpations of sovereignty. He allows tyrannicide. But what he gives with one hand he withdraws with the other, for he declares that the King of France, who is legally absolute, can in no wise be called a tyrant. If a sovereign Prince relaxes his power over his subject or his vassal, he *ipso facto* constitutes this subject a sovereign. It is, in the opinion of Bodin, imprudent in the highest degree to allow a subject to attain such a position. It is, in fact, derogating from sovereign power, always a calamity at home and even more so abroad.

The fifth mark is " la puissance d'octroyer grâce aux condamnes par-dessus les arrêts, et contre le rigueur des lois, soit pour la vie, soit pour les biens, soit pour l'honneur, soit pour le rappel du ban." He looks askance at the powers of bishops and of certain provincial governments in this respect. He furnishes a reasoned defence for the infliction of the death penalty. It serves as a deterrent, it safeguards society, and the Bible authorises it. There are other rights of sovereignty to which he alludes, such as the right of coinage, of the imposition of taxation, and the like. But he who makes law, decrees peace and war, institutes the principal officers, realises the ultimate spring of his authority and the power of pardon is an undoubted Sovereign. Such a monarch stands forth proudly despite your Holy Roman Emperor and despite your Pope. Within his realm all bow down to him, and without the realm he bows down to no one.

Is the *Leviathan* of Hobbes standing before us? For there can be no doubt that as Hobbes was stirred by the civil war of his day, so Bodin was stirred by the civil wars of his days. He is the first to define *Majestas*: " c'est la puissance absolue et perpetuelle d'une Republique." Is the Prince *legibus solutus*? Is the position that " quod principi placuit legis habet vigorem "? By no means. The laws of nature step in to impose not a few restrictions, and so too do the laws of God. In fact it seems as if these two sets of laws bring about a state of affairs not unlike Cromwell's fundamentals with which he thought Parliament might not tamper, or not completely dissimilar from the restrictions of a federal constitution. Bodin sedately sets down that " quant aux lois divines et naturelles, tous les princes de la terre y sont subjects et n'est en leur puissance d'y contrevenir. . . . Et par ainsi la puissance absolue des princes et seigneuries souveraines ne s'étend aulcunement lois naturelles ; et, par exemple, il ne peut voler, et il doit respecter ses promesses et exécuter les obligations par lesquelles il s'est engagé. Il est oblige, comme chacun, par sa conscience morale ; il est même d'autant plus rigoureusement tenu de ces obliga- tions morales que ses facultés légales sont plus larges et Sénèque dit bien ' Cæsari cum omnia licent, propter hoc minus licet.' "

Bodin draws no sharp line of demarcation between the *jus naturale* and the *jus gentium*. The former is the essence of all civil laws, the totality of the principles recognised by all peoples, which depends in the last resort on a universal juridical ideal. Such a law blends so readily with ordinary civil law that no one can say where the one ends and the other begins. He fought the notion that the Prince can be brought to account before the bar of the *lex naturæ*, " car il est bien certain, en termes de droit, que si la convention est du droit naturel, ou de droit commun à tous les peuples, et l'obligation et l'action seront de même nature."

The conception of the fundamentals comes out more clearly in the statement that sovereignty is formally limited " par les lois qui concernent l'Estat du royaulme et de l'establissement d'iceluy, d'autant qu'elles sont annexées et unies avec la couronne . . . le Prince n'y peut déroger, comme est la loi salique." As he need not respect the civil law and customs of his country, the Prince evidently may commit iniquity, but not injustice. On the other hand, he must not put an end to the meetings of the Estates or of the *Parlements*. Still, his sovereignty dominates them, not they him. He has no patience with those who think that " les estats du peuple sont plus grands que le Prince." Still, " il est bienséant à un Prince souverain de garder sa loy." Besides, " qu'en cela se congnoit la grandeur et maiesté d'un Prince souverain, quand les Estats de tout le peuple sont assemblés, présentant requestes et supplications a leur Prince en toute humilité, sans avoir aulcune puissance de rien commander ny décerner, ny voix délibérative ; ainsi ce qu'il plaist au Roy consentit ou dissentit, commander ou défendre, est tenu pour loy, pour édict, pour ordonnance." The *pater patriæ* is to assume a kindly attitude towards his Estates. They are perhaps necessary good institutions though occasionally they are necessary evil ones. All the time, however, we feel that in Bodin's opinion the Prince is the power. He may, if he pleases, possess impartial advisers. He may, if he pleases, impose taxes impartially on nobles and *roturiers* alike. Is there anyone or any institution to constrain him to adopt the excellent schemes Bodin propounds? Is there a magistrate or a set of magistrates? Are there either local Estates or the Estates General? There is no one and no institution to control him. There is not a vestige of a practical limitation anywhere to be found in Bodin's writings. It is as vague as the feeling of the French Revolutionary Assembly that public opinion would put an end to all laws contrary to the general weal. Bodin, little as he meant it, is the literary father of absolutism. He might have been the father of constitutional monarchy—had he possessed the vestige of the idea of a

constitution. The Sovereign is really *legibus solutus*. The Greeks
and the English possessed political instinct, but Bodin was
wholly devoid of it. Whatever the period may be the historian
narrates, he really writes the history of his own period, his
own time. Whatever the Sovereign may be to the publicist,
he really is to Bodin his own King.

The forms of the commonwealth are monarchy, when the
sovereign is one; aristocracy, when it is a small number;
democracy, when it is the majority. The thinker dismisses
anarchy as a temporary condition,[1] and a mixed condition he
deems impossible and incompatible.[2] He is keenly aware of
the difference in the spirit of sovereignty. The rule of Nero
differed as much from that of Trajan as did the rule of Louis XI.
from that of Louis XII. He proceeds to analyse the three sorts
of monarchy. The first, " royale ou legitime, est celle ou les
subiects obeïssent aux loix du monarque, et le monarque aux
loix de nature, demeurant la liberté naturelle et proprieté des
biens aux suiects." The second, " seigneuriale, est celle ou le
prince est faict seigneur des biens et des personnes, par le
droict des armes et de bonne guerre, gouuernant les suiects
comme le père de famille ses esclaues." The third, " tyrannique,
est ou le monarque, mesprisant les loix ne nature, abuse des
personnes libres commes d'esclaues, et des biens des suiects
comme des siens." [3] How far does this classification enable
him to detect when the spirit of sovereignty alters? Plainly,
" le tyran est celuy qui, de sa propre auctorité, se faict Prince
souuerain, sans election, ny droict successif, ny sort, ny iuste
guerre, ny vocation speciale de Dieu." He is, however, too
honest with himself not to face the difficulty boldly. " Voila
les differences les plus remarquables du roy et du tyran : qui ne
sont pas difficules a connoistre entre les deux extremités d'vn
roy tres iuste et d'vn tyran tres meschant: mais il n'est pas aisé a
iuger quand vn Prince tient quelque chose d'vn bon roy et d'vn
tyran." [4] That is, when we require guidance, we are given none.
There is no difficulty—Bodin certainly experiences none—in
saying that the King respects the homes of his subjects, the

[1] *Rép.*, iii., pp. 309-310.　　[2] *Ibid.*, II. i., pp. 177, 185.
[3] *Ibid.*, ii., p. 191.　　[4] *Ibid.*, ii., p. 204.

rights of nature, and the like. How in the world are we to attach definiteness to such vague terms? Such a consideration does not seem to occasion any trouble to Bodin. Like his own Plato, he lived in a balloon which never allowed him to obtain more than a glimpse of anything. True, he caught a commanding view of the theory of sovereignty, but of the practice thereof a fog, mental or otherwise, obstructed his vision.

There are drawbacks to monarchs. There are such obvious ones as the change in policy with each new reign and the difficulties of minorities and regencies.[1] In spite of them, " le principal point de la République, qui est le droit de souve-raineté, ne peut subsister, à parler proprement, sinon en la Monarchie; car nul ne peut estre souverain en une République qu'ung seul : s'ils sont deux on trois, ou plusieurs, pas ung, n'est souverain d'autant que pas ung seul ne peut donner ny recevoir loy de son compaignon." The theory of sovereignty, in Bodin's eyes, is simply monarchy in general and French monarchy in particular. The elections of the Popes and the Holy Roman Emperors suffice to demonstrate to him that such a method is not expedient.[2] He shrewdly notes that the Roman Empire was only happy under the Antonines, who transmitted their heritage by adoption.

The *République* is a *livre de circonstance*. It is written for the express purpose of preserving royalty. " Quand j'ai vu les sujets s'armer contre leurs princes ; des livres mêmes, vrais brandons de guerre civile, paraître, ou l'on nous apprenait à précipiter ces princes, don du ciel à la terre, du haut de leur trône sous prétexte de tyrannie : quand j'ai vu saper les idées sur lesquelles reposent, je ne dis pas ce royaume, mais tout ordre social ; alors j'ai affirmé qu'un homme de bien, un citoyen vertueux ne saurait attenter à son prince, si tyran fût-il, par quelque voie que ce pût être ; qu'il fallait en laisser la punition à Dieu et aux autres princes. Et je l'ai prouvé par la loi humaine, la loi divine et la raison." [3] St Bartholomew's Day marked all by way of attraction or by way of repulsion.

---

[1] *Rép.*, IV. vii., pp. 451-452.
[2] *Ibid.*, VI. iv., pp. 681, 683, 688-689.
[3] *Rép.*, the Dedication to the Comte de Dampierre.

Bodin knew his classics far too well not to remember Brutus and Cassius, Aristogeiton and Harmodius, and how was he to cast a stone at Poltrot de Méré? He is forced to agree with Calvin and Hotman that " c'est chose tres belle et magnifique a vn prince, de prendre les armes pour venger tout vn peuple opprimé par la cruanté d'vn tyran."[1] There are two cases where the Prince is not absolute, as in Venice or the Empire, and when he is. In the former case " il n'appartient a pas vn des suiects en particulier, ny a tous en general, d'attenter a l'honneur, ny a la vie du monarque, soit par voye de faict, soit par voye de iustice, ores qu'ils eust commis toutes les meschancetés, impietés et cruautés qu'on pourroit dire."[2] In the latter case, the status of the Prince is that of the father of his people. Can we conceive of a son judging and then killing his own father? " Il est bien licite de ne luy obeïr pas en chose qui soit contre la loy de Dieu ou de nature, s'enfuïr, se cacher, parer les coups, souffrir la mort, plustost que d'attenter a sa vie, ny son honneur."[3] Such is the bounden duty of citizens towards the monarchs of France, Spain and England. Not without reason he joins issue with the Protestant pamphlets which, in excusing regicide, really undermined the foundations of all order in the kingdom. " De respondre aux obiections et arguments friuioles de ceux qui tiennent le contraire, ce seroit temps perdu ; mais tout ainsi que celuy qui doute s'il y a vn Dieu merite qu'on luy face sentir la peine des loix, sans vser d'argumens : aussi font ceux la, qui ont reuoqué en doute vne chose si claire, voire publié par liures imprimez que les suiects peuuent iustement prendre les armes contre leur prince tyran, et le faire mourir en quelque sorte que ce soit : combien que leurs plus apparens et sçauans theologiens (Luther, Caluinius, *In Ioann* et *Institut*, cap. vlt., lib. 4, sect. 31) tiennent qu'il n'est iamais licite, non pas seulement de tuer, ains de se rebeller contre son Prince souuerain, si ce n'est qu'il y eust mandement special de Dieu, et indubitable."[4]

---

[1] *Rép.*, II. v., p. 209.

[2] *Ibid.*, p. 210. *Cf.* Douarche, *De tyrannicidio apud scriptores decimi sexti sæculi*, p. 54.

[3] *Rép.*, ii., p. 213.   [4] *Ibid.*, p. 212.

On behalf of aristocracy Bodin pleads the existence of the just mean. It is neither the government of one nor of all. Moreover, it seems sound that " la puissance de commander en souveraineté soit baillée aux plus dignes : or la dignité ne peut estre qu'en vertu ou en noblesse, or en biens, ou ès trois ensemble." Yet, when examined, this turns out to be a monarchical argument, for among the most worthy " il y en tousjours quelqu'un qui surpasse les aultres, auquel la souveraineté, par mesme argument, seroit due." Besides, aristocracy creates division. " On a tousjours veu que plus il y a de testes en une seigneurie, plus il y a de disputes et moins de résolutions."

On behalf of democracy we learn that there is the excellence of its ideal with its end, equality. Like a skilful advocate, he allows this form of government credit for many excellences : " On peut dire que l'Estat populaire est le plus louable, comme celuy qui cherche une équalité et droiture en toutes loix, sans faveur ny acception de personnes ; et qui réduit les constitutions civiles aux les loix de nature : car tout ainsy que nature n'a point distribué les richesses, les estats, les honneurs, aux uns plus qu'aux aultres ; aussi l'Estat populaire tend à ce but— la d'esgaler tous les hommes, ce qui ne peut estre faict sinon en esgalant les biens, les honneurs et la justice à tous, sans privilège ny prérogative quelconque : comme fit Lycurgus." He speaks of equality in terms that might have come from the mouth of Rousseau himself. Unlike Plato, he believes that democracy is a stable form of government, and that it produces great men. On the other hand, he shows by the aid of examples that equality is a dream, if a beautiful one. The people is neither capable of governing the State nor of choosing men to do so. The history of Athens attests that democracy ends by banishing virtue. The League of his day is scarcely a more winning case. The greatest of all the objections lies in the confusion between Mine and Thine, a confusion that seems inherent in democracy.

Bodin concludes that of the three forms of government the monarchical is much the best. The King in fact is God on earth. He is not the mere *primus inter pares* that mediæval

France deemed him to be. He stands serenely alone in a dignity that no mere peer can approach. Not only does he provide us with five marks by which we can identify the real Prince, but he is also careful to provide us with six marks by which we can detect the varying types of subordination.

There is the tributary prince: " il retient tout droit de souveraineté"; the prince " qui est en protection; the sovereign prince of one country and a vassal of another prince for another country; the simple vassal, who is not the subject of him from whom he holds his fief; the liege vassal, who is not subject; and the prince who is subject and justiciable by another on a personal title.

With five marks on one side and six on the other, it is easy to note the supremacy of the sovereign: " Le Prince de la patrie es tousjours plus sacré et doit être plus inviolable que le père, estant ordonné et envoyé de Dieu." His Divine Right is unmistakable, for " le plus grande seureté d'un Prince souverain est qu'il faut qu'on croye qu'il est sainct et inviolable."

The Sovereign of Bodin embraces in his person all the functions of the State. There ought to be a Senate, as it is useful to him. This Senate is the legitimate assembly of the councillors of the State, in order to give advice to those who possess the sovereign power in every commonwealth. Age and experience are the qualities required in the composition of the Senate, as well as sound judgment and counsel. The right of proposing ought to belong to each member, with a complete independence. He considers the office should continue for life. How little he was of a constitutionalist is evident from the stress he places on the following: " Le Senat est establi seulement pour donner advis et non pas pour commander . . . et, s'il avait puissance de commander ce qu'il conseille, la souveraineté serait au Conseil, et les conseillers d'Estat au lieu de conseillers seroient maistres, ayant le maniement des affaires et puissance d'en ordonner à leur plaisir : chose qui ne se peult faire sans diminution, ou pour mieulx dire, éversion de la maiesté, qui est si haulte et si sacrée qu'il n'appartient a subjects, quels qu'ils soyent, d'y toucher, ny près ny loing."

The agents of the Sovereign he divides into two classes: officers and commissaries. The first have charge of ordinary business, the second of extraordinary. For the powers of the commissaries he ransacks classical history, finding precedents in the Dictatorship in general and in the form Pompey received it for five years in order to end the war with the pirates. The proconsuls and the pro-prætors of the Empire provide him with further illustrations of the duties of these commissaries. They existed "auparavant qu'il eust offices establis. Car il est bien certain que les premières républiques estoient régies par main souverainne sans loix, et n'y avoit que la parole, la mine, la volonté des Princes pour toutes loix, lesquels donnoyent les charges en paix et en guerre à qui bon leur sembloit, et les révoquoyent aussitost, s'ils vouloyent, afin que le tout dépendist de leur pleine puissance, et qu'ils ne fussent attachés ny aux loix, ny aux coustumes." Now plainly, these commissaries left the door wide open to absolutism. If anyone cares to turn from the precepts of Bodin to the practice of Henry VIII. he will find a world of difference between them. Bodin clearly thought that the English King was a sovereign, for he says so. Henry VIII. never got rid of Parliament even in his most absolutist days. The forms of liberty were preserved though the spirit inhabiting them was tyrannical. When he died, Parliament still lived, and in happier days could breathe the spirit of freedom. In France, on the other hand, the commissary class gave rise to that centralisation which ultimately abolished the States General. The shadow of freedom disappeared before the substance of the commissary. As Charles V. and Philip II. overthrew the free constitutions of Castile and Aragon, so the French kings overthrew the might of the States General. The fact that from 1614 to 1789 it never met is an eloquent one, testifying, in another shape, that Bodin was the literary parent of absolutism. Hear him as he informs us that " les estats aristocratiques et justes royaulmes sont maintenus par la médiocrité de certains estats, corps et communautés bien réglés." In the fashion in which James I. attempted to treat Parliament, the French monarch was, with an air of condescension, to allow the States General to exist in a powerless condition. Of course he will take care to regulate all the Estates, local and general, and "maintenir en médiocrité."

In his eleventh and twelfth chapters Bodin discusses Parliament and Magistracy, and the fourteenth treats of Revolutions. Did it ever strike him that if the common folk had not an organised outlet in order to express their thoughts they might resort to an unorganised one? The essence of a revolution consists in a change or displacement of sovereignty. The causes of revolutions are a contest arising between the claimants on the failure of the posterity of princes, inequalities in wealth, oppression, the ambition of a commander, alterations in laws, the admission of unworthy men to high office, the absence of the middle classes, and the like. His analysis is strongly reinforced by the many examples he adduces. He ransacks classical and modern times, and in the course of his remarks he undoubtedly illumines the past. Trying to ascertain general principles, underlying revolutions, he comes to the conclusion that " quelques fois aussi le peuple est si bizarre, qu'il est presque impossible de la tenir dans un estat, que tost après, il n'en soit ennuyé ; comme on peut dire des anciens Athéniens, Megariens, Samiens, Syracusains, Florentins et Genevois." Behind all these causes we are conscious of the presence of the spirit of liberty and of equality, especially of the latter.

Changes of government are most desirable when least felt. The change which goes on gradually is more tolerable, whether it be from evil to good, or good to better. He is conscious that the most dangerous moment for a bad government is that in which it begins to amend. In addition to diagnosing the disease, he is also able to prescribe suitable remedies. Revolutions can be prevented by refusing to bestow upon the same man, with the supreme dignity, the supreme command. Each State is a law to itself. The first rule for maintaining States is to grasp the nature of the particular State, and the causes of the maladies peculiar to it. If it be dangerous to change laws frequently, it is in like manner every whit as dangerous to change magistrates, whose appointments should continue for life. On the other hand, the Sovereign ought to bear in mind that he can influence legislators by placing conditions, offices, and all other rewards of virtue, in public view, and by sharing them among his subjects according to their merits. Can this end be achieved by bestowing office in perpetuity? If the magistrate is irremovable, does he not secure practical immunity? Bodin is perfectly clear that he who distributes honours and offices among a small number of individuals, which is inevitable when they are conferred for life, kindles jealousy in one towards another.

That sovereignty requires sanction is a fundamental assumption with Bodin. As he refuses to admit the contract theory of government, inevitably he means the sanction of the State. The supreme power remains vested in the Great Leviathan of Hobbes. Men speak of the force of right, but as a Frenchman he felt the right of force to be used in the troublous times in which he lived. Abroad the necessity is quite clear. " Il est certain en matière d'estat qu'il faut estre le plus fort ou des plus forts ... autrement on seruira tousiours de proye a la discretion du vainquer." [1] " Si l'on discute sur l'exécution d'un traité, quand il y n'a plus d'excuses, le plus fort en matière d'estat ne laisse pas tousiours de le gaigner, et le plus foible a tort." [2] At home the necessity is equally clear. " On sçait bien qu'en telles guerres [*i.e.* the civil wars] les plus foibles ont le tort, et que les plus forts declarent tousiours les autres ennemis de la patrie." [3] When these wars at home are ended, the judge requires sanction to enforce his decrees. " En matière d'estat, qui est maistre de la force il est maistre des hommes et des loix et de toute la Republique." In sentence after sentence he pushes this point home. " Mais en termes de droit, il ne faut pas, disoit Papinian, auoir esgard a ce qu'on fait a Romme, mais bien a ce qu'on doit faire." [4] " Il n'est pas icy question de sçauoir qui est le plus fort, mais seulement s'il est licite droit." [5] There is Platonism in all that our philosopher writes, but it is a Platonism founded firmly on fact. There is an implicit account of sovereignty in Plato and Aristotle, and this implicit account becomes quite explicit with Bodin. What does he care for the

[1] *Rép.*, V. vi., p. 553. [2] *Ibid.*, p. 570.
[3] *Ibid.*, I. iv., p. 26. [4] *Ibid.*, i., p. 187.
[5] *Ibid.*, V. v., p. 211.

Sir Thomas Mores, men who create a world of fancy in which there is no force? He, for his part, has nothing but scorn for " ceux qui nous escrit de la République, sans aucune congnoissance des loix ni di droit commun, ont laissé les principes, voulans bastir de beaux discours en l'air sans fondement aucun."[1] He has his foundations laid, and they are laid in the force that supports the authority of the Sovereign.

Bodin was not a literary Melchizedek. Who indeed is? In 1519 appeared *La Grande Monarchie de France*, by Claude de Seyssel, a loyal servant of Louis XII. He esteems the monarchical State to be the best, and he arrives at his considered judgment by surveying what he called the democratic government of Rome and the aristocratic one of Venice. Then he glances at the monarchies, and of them all the French is easily chief. There is order in the State, dignity with the King. There is care for religion, for justice. In a word, it forms the ideal of paternal government with just enough independence on the part of corporations to keep the balance true. The freedom of these corporations, the limitations set on royal authority by the existence of old institutions, the class of clergy, and the class of magistrates all sustained this feeling of independence. Seyssel notes checks on the power of the Sovereign in the existence of episcopacy, the existence of the Law Courts, and the existence of past policy. What the sovereigns of the past have accomplished moulds what the Sovereign of the present is accomplishing.

Bayle calls Michel de L'Hôpital one of the greatest men of his time, and none will quarrel with this verdict, for he was one of the wisest and one of the most attractive men of his generation. A man of wide learning and of infinite patience, he was so free from partisanship that his school of thought prepared the way for the Politiques. Extremists on either side loathed him: posterity loves him. He was a noble figure in an ignoble generation. Catherine de' Medici appointed him Chancellor at a time when St Bartholomew's Day was still in the dim distance. At the end of eight years pressure was brought to bear on her, and L'Hôpital had to retire. Toleration

---

[1] *Rép.*, I. vi., p. 51.

he desired with all the ardour of his great soul, but it was not to be in his day. He laboured for the Edict of Nantes, and other men entered into the fruit of his labours. His *Traité de la Réformation de la Justice* pleads that justice constitutes the very noblest attribute of the Sovereign, and is likewise the most important. In his *Harangue aux Etats d'Orléans* he ventures to point out to Assembly that the two institutions, Church and State, need not be absolutely coincident. " Many," he held, " may be citizens, who are not even Christians." He pleads with them to remember that their work is to settle the bases not of religion but of the body politic ; he prays them to support the King as one who stands between and above parties. He maintains stoutly the absolute power of the King, who, though he acts on the advice of his counsellors, is not obliged to follow their plans. He notes the old custom of convoking Estates and the tie they form between the citizens and the monarch. L'Hôpital advises the King to preserve neutrality in the question of religion. Nobly this Turgot of the sixteenth century emphasises the circumstance that " c'est une chose convenable au devoir et office du roy d'aimer and procurer non seulement la prosperité exteriorure de ses sujects, mais principalement le salut de leurs ames et paix en leur conscience : or la conscience est de telle nature qu'elle ne peult estre forcée, mais doibt estre enseignée, et n'estre point domptée, ny violée, mais persuadée par vrayes et suffisantes raisons. Et mesmes la foy seule estre [estant ?] contraincte elle n'est plus la foy." [1]

Du Haillan and Louis LeRoy wrote works that left some mark on the mind of Bodin. The former believes in the existence of fundamental laws, inviolable by the Prince, points out the harmonious hierarchy of the orders in France, and approves of the Salic law. The latter teaches pretty much what Bodin teaches on such matters as the duties of the States General, the functions of the *Parlement* of Paris, the revolutions in neighbouring cities, the excellence of the ancient

---

[1] Coll. de Poissy, 1st September 1561 (i., pp. 470-471). *Cf.* the parallel sentiment in Bodin, *Rép.*, IV. vii., p. 455.

laws, the dangers of change, the air of restfulness given to a country by a regulated royalty, and the like.

There are traces of Seyssel and L'Hôpital, of du Haillan and LeRoy in the mind of our author, but the man himself furnished not a little of his own mental nutriment. Dull and confused as his works may be, no one can peruse his *magnum opus*, the *République*, without discerning contact with a seminal mind. De Thou esteemed it as a vast and profound work " in quo . . . omni scientiiarum genere non tincti, sed imbuti ingenii fidem fecit." Publicists like Paruta and Loyseau read it admiringly. The theologians of the League attacked it with all the powers of vituperation at their command. Among these, Possevin, del Rio and Guillaume Roze united in solid condemnation of it. To make up for this abuse there is the measured approval of Montaigne, who held that he " est un bon autheur de notre temps, accompagne de beaucoup plus de judgement que la tourbe des escrivailleurs de son siècle, et merite qu'on le juge et considere." Such judgment and such consideration he received from Grotius, Pufendorf and Hobbes. After the fashion of the seventeenth century, Sir Robert Filmer borrowed in a wholesale manner from Bodin, who thus exercised his sway over the gentlemen of the period.[1] Bodin emphatically cleared the conception of sovereignty as it had not been cleared before, and this constitutes his crowning achievement.[2] Three politics there are : monarchy, aristocracy and democracy ; and of these the first is by far the best and the greatest. " Mixed forms " of government are simply idle conceits. Nor does his work cease when he turned the attention of the Parliaments of the seventeenth century to this burning problem. What he could not do himself he did through another. For not the least of his glories is that the *République* is the father of the *Esprit des Lois*.

---

[1] *Cf.* Knolles's translation.

[2] W. A. Dunning, " Bodin on Sovereignty," *Pol. Sc. Quarterly,* ii., pp. 82-104 (1896).

BODIN AND SOVEREIGNTY

REFERENCES

Barthélemy, Le Comte Edouard de, *Étude sur J. Bodin*, Paris, 1876.

Baudrillart, H., *J. Bodin et son Temps*, Paris, 1853.

Bloch, J. S., *J. Bodin, ein französischer Staatsmann und Rechtslehrer*. (Separat-Abdruck aus A. Bruhl's *Populär-wissenschaftlichen Monatsblättern*, Jahrg. 1), Prag, 1881.

Bodin, J. de Saint-Laurent, *Les Idées Monétains et Commerciales de Jean Bodin*, Bordeaux, 1907.

Chauviré, R., *Jean Bodin, Auteur de la " République,"* Paris, 1914.

Dock, A., *Der Souveränetätsbegriff von Bodin bis zu Friedrich der Grosse*, Strasburg, 1897.

Errera, P., *Un Précurseur de Montesquieu*, Paris, 1896.

Feugère, L., *Caractères et Portraits Littéraires du XVIᵉ Siècle*, Paris, 1859.

Fosses, C. des, *J. Bodin, sa Vie et ses Œuvres*, Angers, 1890.

Fournol, E., *Bodin, Prédécesseur de Montesquieu*, Paris, 1896.

Guttmann, J., *Bodin in seinen Beziehungen mit dem Iudentum*, Breslau, 1906.

Hancke, E., " Bodin, eine Studie über den Begriff der Souverainetät " (*Untersuchungen zur Deutschen Staat-und Rechtsgeschichte de Gierke*), Breslau, 1894.

Jacquet, *De Historiarum cognitione quid senserit Jo. Bodin*, Paris (n.d.).

Landmann, M., *Der Souveränetätsbegriff bei den franzosichen Theoretiken von Jean Bodin bis auf J.-J. Rousseau*, Leipzig, 1876.

Meinecke, F., *Die Idee der Staatsräson*, München and Berlin, 1924.

Molinier, V., *Aperçus historiques et critiques sur la Vie et les Travaux de J. Bodin, sur sa Démonomanie des Sorciers*, Montpellier, 1867.

Renz, F., *Jean Bodin : Ein Beitrag zur Geschichte der historischen Methode im 16. Jahrhundert* (Lamprecht, *Geschichte*, Unters. iii. 1), Gotha, 1905.

Seton-Watson, R. W. (Ed.), *Tudor Studies*, London, 1924.

CHAPTER V

CALVIN'S DISCIPLES

WHAT Erasmus meant in the world of religion, the Politiques meant in the world of politics, and the causes of the failure of Erasmus and the Politiques are pretty much the same. Like all parties, the Politiques had their men of thought and their men of action, their Erasmuses—on a small scale—and their Colignys. Thinkers like the Chancellor L'Hôpital and the historian de Thou, and pamphleteers like Beza, Hotman and Duplessis-Mornay belonged to their ranks. They had adopted to the Huguenots the same attitude as the humanists had adopted to the Reformation before the year 1520. The men of action were the aristocrats and the bourgeoisie. The real leaders of the Politiques were the Montmorencys, and men of their high rank were enabled by their possessions in Languedoc to link up the Huguenots from the Alps to the Atlantic. The Politiques were the Moderates, the cultivated men and the earnest thinkers, who leaned to the new opinions in theology. Detesting violence on a wholesale scale, they pleaded for toleration. One-third of the nobility and one-eighth of the population belonged to the Huguenots. The former constituted its backbone, for they provided the cavalry, the important arm of the sixteenth century in France. Three motives actuated them: one was their religion; another was their desire to preserve their privileges, and a third was their opposition to the steady increase in the centralisation of all authority. If they were the military strength, they were the political weakness. The rank and file require a leader, but a leader of the middle class suits them far better than a man of the upper classes. A Luther or a Zwingli, a Knox or a Cromwell, has consequently achieved a far larger measure of success than a Coligny or a Condé or a Henry of Navarre. The peasantry and the legal profession were hostile. The former had suffered from the tyranny of the nobility, the latter regarded themselves as the champion of Gallican liberties, and they resented intruders into a domain that was peculiarly their own.

The Renaissance came to France divorced from religion but married to life of the Italian type. The Renaissance came to England divorced from life of the Italian type and married to religion. If anyone wishes to grasp the comparative failure of the Politiques in France and the comparative success of the Puritans in England, let him compare the literatures of the two countries during the sixteenth century. Let him read Ronsard and Du Bellay, and let him then read Sidney and Spenser, and he will not be long in perceiving that in France the spirit of poetry is pagan, whereas in England it is informed by the spirit of religion.

The success of Catherine de' Medici [1] combined with the failure of the Politiques resulted in many matters, and one of them was St Bartholomew's Day. Recent investigation tends to reduce most numbers of the past, but in this case the tendency has been to increase the estimate. In a sane chapter Mr Whitehead reckons that over ten thousand perished.[2] Lord Acton had put the total lower, but he was unacquainted with the bulk of the Spanish papers, and knew of the correspondence of the Nuncios only by a few stray dispatches published by Mackintosh and Theiner. Whatever the numbers may be, the cruelty cannot be reduced. The sixteenth century was a hard age, but even it was appalled by the madness of the massacre. A distinguished savant like Ramus and a lawyer like La Place were no more spared in 1572 than Lavoisier in 1794. If Catherine de' Medici had no need of such men, neither had the Republic any need of chemists. The bead-roll includes the wisest, and it includes the greatest and the best, for on it are inscribed Briquemault and de Caumont, Cavagnes and Coligny, Guerchy and Lavardin, Pilles and Teligny, and La Rochefoucauld. In the measured words of Lord Acton, it is pleasant to realise that it was only in Spain and Italy, where hearts were hardened and consciences were corrupted by the Inquisition; in Switzerland, where the Roman Catholics lived

---

[1] *Cf.* L. Jordan, "Niccolò Machiavelli und Katharina von Medici," *Historische Vierteljahrschrift* (1903), vi., pp. 338-356; P. van Dyke, "Machiavelli und Katharina von Medici," *Historische Vierteljahrschrift* (1916), pp. 33-45.

[2] Whitehead, *Gaspard de Coligny,* chap. xvii.

in suspicion and dread of their Protestant neighbours; among ecclesiastical princes in Germany, whose authority waned as fast as their subjects abjured their faith, that the massacre was welcomed as an act of Christian fortitude.

Gregory XIII. felt so delighted with the news that he exclaimed that the events of 24th August were more agreeable' to him than fifty victories of Lepanto.[1] On the evening of the 5th or 6th the guns of the Castle of St Angelo fired a triumphal salvo, and the illumination of Rome ceased only with the 8th. On that day the Pope, accompanied by thirty-three cardinals and all the ambassadors, attended a crowded service of thanksgiving in the French Church of St Louis.[2] Above the principal entrance to this church hung a cloth of purple silk, and on it shining in letters of gold the Cardinal of Lorraine had composed a Latin inscription. It explained to all and sundry the joy of Charles IX., the Most Christian King, who, burning with zeal for the Lord God of Hosts, now that the heretics and public enemies had been suddenly cut off as by an avenging angel, augured well from this happy success, and, joining his prayers to theirs, was present in spirit in this the church of his ancestor, St Louis. Another French cardinal, Pellevé, chanted the mass, and the choir sang gleefully Psalm xxi. Gregory XIII. proclaimed a solemn jubilee, struck a medal to commemorate the massacre, and ordered Vasari to paint frescoes of such items of 24th August as the throwing of the body of Coligny from a window, to be executed on the walls of the Vatican. There was other matter on the walls of the Vatican had the eyes of the Pope been but able to grasp it. The handwriting on the wall might have revealed to him that rebellion on the part of the reformers had now ample justification. True, such teaching had been implicit in the teaching of John Calvin, but the difference 1572 made was that now it was explicit. How grave a change was wrought is obvious in the conversation of Coligny with Charles IV. on the very eve of St Bartholomew, when the Admiral assured

---

[1] Paris, *Bibl. Nat.*, 16,040,192 (Ferralz, Rome, 11th September).
[2] La Mothe-Fénelon, vii., p. 341. *Cf.* Philippson, *Deutsche Zeitschrift für Geschichtswissenschaft*, 1892, p. 135; Gregorovius, vii. 642.

him of his unalterable devotion to the Crown. After Coligny's murder his rooms were rifled and his papers carried to the King. Among them were reminiscences of "the late religious troubles in the kingdom" that he had written during the last two years. His enemies were bitterly disappointed to find in them nothing disloyal and everything loyal. The wars of religion had been largely religious wars down to 1572, but after that fatal date they assumed a political character. Calvin had, on the whole, taught obedience to the powers that be, and such obedience had been faithfully rendered. Now the whole matter had been fundamentally changed, and men felt that their old world had come to an end. The Huguenot realised that he was an outlaw, and he naturally began to question the law, and the fountain of the law, the King. Why should the Sovereign be hereditary, why should he not be elective? From whom did he derive his power? Was it not from the people? If he abused his power could he not be deposed, could he not be resisted? Was there any point now in discussing the merits of toleration? Pamphleteers of the rank of Beza (1519-1605), Hotman (1524-1590) and Duplessis-Mornay (1549-1623) now step on the scene to explain the meaning of St Bartholomew's Day.[1] The force of argument had been advocated, but now it was the turn of the argument of force. These three thinkers may have lit the match—set fire to the powder magazine. They did not make the powder; that was the function of Catherine de' Medici. They were rather driven to build freedom than eager for it.

[1] There are full bibliographical lists of the pamphlets of the French wars of religion in Lelong, *Bibliothèque Historique*, ii. 233-354, Nos. 17,757-19,557, and in the sale catalogue of the Coste Library (Lyons, 1854), Nos. 1575-2066. *Cf.* A. Tilley, *Studies in the French Renaissance*, pp. 294-320; E. Armstrong, *English Historical Review*, vol. iv. (1889), pp. 13-40; K. Glaser, "Beiträge zur Geschichte der politischen Literatur Frankreichs in der zweiten Halfe des 16. Jahrhunderts" (*Zeitschr. für franz. Sprache u. Litteratur*), xxxix., p. 240ff. The important pamphlets are to be found in Simon Goularts' *Mémoires de l'Estat de France sous Charles IX.* (1576). *Cf.* also Hauser, *Les Sources de l'Histoire de la France*, vol. iii., and the *Catalogue de l'Histoire de France*, i., p. 281ff. Notices of the individual writers are in Haag, *La France Protestante*. *Cf.* W. A. Dunning, "The Monarchomachs," *Pol. Sc. Quarterly*, 1904.

Their influence was not merely literary but also institutional. The working of Presbyterianism in the Old World constituted the true training of democracy in the New.

What Mutianus meant to his circle of admirers, what Melanchthon meant to Camerarius, what Montaigne meant to La Boëtie, what Goethe meant to Schiller, what Blücher meant to Gneisenau, Theodore Beza (1519-1605) meant to John Calvin. Beza gained by the friendship. He saw many sides to a problem, he was well aware of the many shades of meaning to be taken out of what seemed a simple passage in the Bible. Like not a few many-sided men, Beza was fearful, irresolute, inclined to compromise. The reformer saw summits and abysses : his friend also saw the plain lying between them. He proved an admirable corrective to the fearlessness, the resoluteness, the uncompromising spirit of Calvin.

Like Calvin, Beza was a Frenchman sprung from the ranks of the old nobility. Casual contact with Melchior Wolmar affected him just as deeply as it affected Calvin. For thanks to Wolmar's suggestion Calvin abandoned the study of the Code of Justinian for that of the Code of the Sacred Law. Thanks also to Wolmar's suggestion young Beza in 1535 entered the University of Orleans, not the University of Paris, in order to devote himself to civil law. Familiarity with the Old Testament is apt to disguise the fact that it really is, to a large extent, up to the prophetical books, a survey of the Mosaic law and its actual working. The conception of a covenant, of a contract if you like, is never very far away from its pages. Among many other matters this will account for the intense strain of legality in the Huguenot party. Soldiers and sailors, commanders and divines, as well as legists, all insist on ascertaining the legal basis of their action. Nowadays, like Frederick the Great when he invaded Silesia, we are content to act, afterwards devising reasons for our action. Not so during the sixteenth century. The first thing that the Huguenot sought—when it came to deeds—was to find out his right, his power. This will explain why, before 1572, when the right of resistance was discussed, there is invariably stress laid on the circumstance that the King is favourable or unfavourable. If he is not, then the Huguenots must fall back on the heir. If the heir is not favourable, then they must fall back on the princes of the blood. If they are not favourable, then they must fall back on the magistrates. There must be some authority before 1572 and there must be some show of authority after 1572. The task of the Huguenot in defining tyranny was by no means easy. A king might be guilty of some oppressive acts. Did these invariably turn him into a tyrant? A Leaguer or a Jesuit had a far easier task in defining the tyrant, for either simply assumed he was a heretic. Obviously it was quite straightforward in determining whether this was so or not, for all not belonging to the communion of Leaguer or Jesuit were heretical. The Huguenot assumed that in a rough-and-tumble world occasionally there would be tyrants to despoil their goods and to tax them severely. None of these things vitally mattered till a command conflicted with the laws of God. Then resistance was inevitable. Yet the resistance must be as constitutional as possible.

In 1548 we find Beza in Paris, meditating a treatise on the Salic law,[1] an odd law at all times when we consider the part taken by French women in general and by Catherine de' Medici in particular. Besides, what marks out the French Reformation in one way is the enormous interest in it taken by women of high degree. Enforced idleness in a jail converted Coligny and enforced idleness in an illness converted Beza in 1548, and then he set out for the Mecca of Protestantism, Geneva, in 1548. There he met Calvin, and at once fell under the sway of that masterful personality. Teacher and taught met to begin that intimacy that grew with the passing of the years.

In 1549, the date of the first Book of Common Prayer, the Académie of Lausanne called Beza to the office of professor and preparer of men for the pastorate. Unwilling so soon to part from his new friend, Beza took time to consider the offer.

---

[1] Baum, *Theodor Beza*, i., p. 33. Perhaps here we may say that it is tempting to agree with Dr Armaingaud's *Montaigne Pamphlétaire*, who sees in the French satirist a Huguenot writer of the school of Calvin. But we regard Dr Armaingaud's case as wholly unproven.

Calvin persuaded him to accept, and for nine years Beza discharged his duties with zeal and efficiency. Thirty miles separate Geneva from Lausanne, and the intercourse between Calvin and the new professor continued. Among his colleagues was François Hotman, the distinguished jurist and political philosopher. There is much reason for thinking that the pamphlets published after 1572 were the work of a group of men of whom Beza and Hotman formed the outstanding members. The magnetism of Beza attracted so many to the Académie that from a mere handful of students the number increased to close on seven hundred.[1] There were, however, dissensions in the Church, and it was dissensions like these that go far to explain the ruin of the Huguenots. Recalled to Geneva, he became in 1558 Calvin's coadjutor and Rector of the University of Geneva. The Divinity School, the Medical School and the Law School were all flourishing, though we are not surprised to learn that the study of law attracted more than the study of medicine.

The needs of his own country called him to Court in 1561, where he met with a warm reception from Catherine de' Medici. She treated him with flattering familiarity, summoned him to her private room, and drew him on to discuss his beliefs with her.[2] She even went so far as to hold *Prêches*, as the Huguenots called their form of worship, in her own apartments, with all the Court for congregation. At the Colloquy of Poissy, 1561, Beza spoke on many matters touching on obedience. " It is true," he admitted, " that we teach that our first and principal obedience is due to our God, Who is the King of kings and Lord of lords. But if our writings do not suffice to clear us from such a crime laid up to our charge (as disloyalty to our Sovereign), we shall bring up, Sire, the example of very many lordships and principalities, and even kingdoms, which have been reformed according to this same

---

[1] Baum, *Theodor Beza*, i., p. 519.
[2] *Cf.* Suriano's Dispatch, 8th September 1561, p. xlvi., vol. vi. of *Dispatches*, edited by Sir H. Layard (Publications of Huguenot Society of London); Baum, ii., pp. 45-54; Calvin, *Opera*, xviii., p. 674; Beza, *Histoire Ecclésiastique*, i., p. 551.

doctrine. These will suffice us as good and sufficient testimony for our acquittal. In short, we take our stand respecting this matter on what Saint Paul says in the thirteenth chapter of Romans, where, speaking of temporal government, he expressly enjoins that every soul be subject unto the higher powers. 'Nay,' Saint John Chrysostom says on this passage, 'even were you an apostle or an evangelist, for that such subjection does not derogate from the service of God.' But if it has happened, or if it should hereafter happen, that some, covering themselves with the mantle of our doctrine, should be found guilty of rebellion against the least of your officers, Sire, we protest before God and your Majesty, that they are not of us, and that they could not have more bitter enemies than we, according as our poor condition permits.

" In fine, Sire, the desire we have to advance the glory of our God, the obedience and very humble service due to your Majesty, our affection for our native land and specially for the Church of God—these have brought us to this place in which we hope that our good God and Father, continuing the course of His lovingkindness and mercies, will confer upon you, Sire, grace such as that which He conferred on the young King Josiah, two thousand two hundred and two years ago ; and that under your happy government, Madam [Catherine de' Medici], assisted by you, Sire [the King of Navarre], and the other and excellent princes of the blood and lords of your council, the ancient memory shall be revived of that renowned Queen Clotilde, who served of old as the instrument of God to give the knowledge of Himself to this realm. Such is our hope. For this we are ready to employ our lives, to the end that, rendering to you very humble service in a matter so holy and praiseworthy, we may behold the true golden age in which our Lord and Saviour Jesus Christ shall be worshipped by all with one accord, as to Him belong all honour and glory for ever. Amen." [1]

That these hopes were not destined to be realised the Massacre of Vassy and the outbreak of the first Religious War all too soon demonstrated. In Condé's name he wrote a reasoned

---

[1] Speech, 9th September 1561.

protest against such proceedings, and in the course of it he maintained that the foes of his religion " have engaged in writing to introduce foreign arms, which means, in plain talk, to give the kingdom to be the prey of its enemies. On the contrary, I do not ask to retain my arms, I do not make use of the king's money, I do not call foreigners to enter the kingdom, and have declined those offered to me. God is my witness that I have begged them not to come and to prevent others from coming, either for or against us." [1]

To Geneva Beza returned in 1563 after an absence of twenty months, and his welcome from Calvin was peculiarly cordial.[2] On Calvin's death the following year he became—so far as any human being could—his successor. The professor resumed his labours on the New Testament, producing his edition of the Greek text of the New Testament in 1565. Between this year and 1604 he produced no less than nine editions of the New Testament. He was the owner of two valuable manuscripts—the Codex Bezæ (D) of the Gospels and Acts and the Codex Claromontanus of the Pauline Epistles. Besides, he had access to the collations made by his printer, Henri Estienne, for his father Robert. The study of the New Testament was one method of raising the problem of authority. The principle of authority had received rude assaults at the hand of Luther. In his denunciation of indulgences he had appealed from Tetzel to the Pope. At the Diet of Augsburg he appealed from the Pope ill-informed to the Pope better informed, and then from the Pope to a Council. Did not the Councils, especially on papal primacy, contradict one another? When the verdict of a Council was used against him he appealed to the Scriptures. When these did not support his position he appealed to selected passages from them. Even this was not final. In the last resort he appealed to the conscience of the individual Christian. It is remarkable that the heralds of revolt, not only in Germany but also in France and Switzerland, are at first friars and priests : the day of laymen like

---

[1] *Mém. de Condé*, iii., pp. 395-416, for the whole of this measured utterance.
[2] On Beza's work, *cf.* C. Borgeaud, *Histoire de l'Université de Genève, l'Académie de Calvin*, vol. i.

Calvin and Melanchthon was later. The Church came to be no more than a community of Christian believers wherever they were to be found. With the people, however, the new authority he gave them was a translation of the Bible in their own speech. This he interpreted with such an infallible accent that he became the Pope of the Protestants.[1]

When Simmias demanded " a word from God " to confirm the speeches of Socrates he expressed what all men felt. This " word from God " Luther gave his followers. The Gospel came to the peasant in the sixteenth century, and exercised over him the influence which the philosophers' doctrine of the rights of man exercised over the French peasant in the eighteenth.[2] It fostered those habits of critical examination of fundamental truths which constitute the very mainsprings of revolt. The Bible had been known through the medium of the Church, which constituted itself the sole interpreter thereof. It was not, therefore, the competing authority it at once became. A monopoly of salvation has always been fatal to its holders, and no less fatal to the cause of toleration. The possession of the Bible delivered the Lutherans and the Calvinists from such a pressing danger. Luther and Calvin might claim to be infallible; their claims, however, were examined by the only bar of reason then applicable to the masses, and that was the sacred record. Once upon a time a man was forced to use faith alone, whereas now faith and reason were open to him.

It came as a shock of surprise to the reader to note that in the Bible St Peter made mistakes and was rebuked accordingly, thus showing little sign that either he or his successors were infallible. It was difficult to think that the extortionate cardinals were in the line of succession from one who had neither silver nor gold. It was no less difficult to see in the New Testament the precedents for the worship of the Virgin Mary or the Saints, the celibacy of the clergy, the use of indulgences, the

---

[1] Luther, *Tischreden* (*Kroker*), No. 4. *Cf.* Philipp Melanchthon's *Letzte Lebenstage*, p. 38.

[2] *Cf.* G. Bonet-Maury, *Le Protestantisme français et la République aux XVIᵉ et XVIIᵉ Siècles*, Société de l'Histoire de Protestantisme Français, May-June, 1904.

veneration of relics and the like. Between the purity and simplicity of the meeting at the upper room at Jerusalem and the then growing architectural and artistic beauty of St Peter's there was a difference sufficient to provoke inquiry.

St Bartholomew's Day came to Beza, in spite of warnings he addressed to Coligny, with a shock of surprise. He counselled Prince Henry of Condé and Henry of Navarre to hold on to their faith,[1] and he counselled the reformers in distant England. On the strength of rumours he wrote on 27th June 1566 to Bishop Grindal: " I have yet to learn by what right, whether you look at the Word of God or at the ancient canons, the civil magistrate is authorised to introduce new rites in churches that have been constituted or to abrogate old ones; what right bishops have, without the advice and consent of their body of elders, to ordain anything novel." [2] On the other hand Bishop Sandys wrote to Gualter at Zurich on 9th August 1574: " Our innovators, who have been striving to strike out for us a new form of church, are not doing us much harm; nor is this new fabric of theirs making such progress as they expected. Our nobility are at last sensible of the object to which this novel fabrication is tending. The author of these novelties, and after Beza, their first inventor, is a young Englishman, by name Thomas Cartwright, who they say is sojourning at Heidelberg." [3] Whitgift complained of Beza's attempts to impose Genevese discipline on all the churches.

The reading of the Bible and the preaching of the sermon drove home to the hearts of the people the new message; so too did the new hymns they sang. Andrew Fletcher of Saltoun saw deeply into human nature when he wrote: " I know a very nice man . . . that believed if a man were permitted to make all the ballads, he need not care who should make the laws of a nation." [4] Luther and Beza realised as profoundly as Fletcher that the hymns of a country were more important than its laws.

---

[1] *Lettres Missives de Henri*, IV. i., p. 351.
[2] *Tract. Theol.*, iii. pp. 209-213.
[3] *Zurich Letters*, p. 466 (Parker Society).
[4] An Account of a Conversation concerning a Right to Regulation of Governments (1703).

The whole German nation sang itself into Lutheran doctrine. According to Herder, "Germany was reformed by songs." [1] Hans Sachs saluted Luther as the nightingale of Wittenberg. What hymns accomplished for Germany the Huguenot Psalter of Beza and Marot accomplished for the Calvinist churches wherever they met. The poetic genius of Clément Marot wedded to the spiritual insight of Theodore de Beza formed that admirable Psalter that has left its impress on the Huguenots. What the forty-sixth psalm meant to Lutheranism the sixty-eighth psalm meant to Calvinism. Beza served the learned by his edition of the Greek Testament, but he served not merely the Huguenots but all Christendom by the noble version Marot and he published of the greatest poetry in the whole range of the Old Testament.

His *Life of Calvin* forms a tribute of love and admiration paid to the memory of one he adored. Nor is his *Histoire Ecclésiastique* a whit behind it in affording us clue after clue to recapture the spirit of the age. Within three years of the publication of his *Confession of the Christian Faith* there were six French editions printed in Geneva alone. Translated into English and Italian, the Church of Rome placed it on the Index. Even in 1685, the year Louis XIV. saw fit to recall the Edict of Nantes, the Archbishop of Paris warned his clergy in a special circular-letter that it was a dangerous book. [2] More germane to our purpose, however, is his treatise, *Concerning the Duty of Punishing Heretics*, published in 1554. This treatise links together the names of Erasmus and Luther, of Beza and Castellion. For there is an after-history to Luther's *Von welltlicher Oberkeyt* in Switzerland. There Sebastian Castellion, under the name of Martin Bellius, published in 1554 his plea in favour of toleration, entitled *Traicte de Hérétiques*. Castellion's object is twofold. He seeks to answer two questions. One is, What is a heretic? The other is, How must we treat him? Here are the names he invokes, and they are a strange medley, on behalf of his thesis: Luther, Brenz, Erasmus, Sebastian Franck, Lactantius, Caspar Hedio, John Agricola,

---

[1] *Kalligone*, Part II. iv.
[2] Baum, *Theodor Beza*, ii., p. 83.

Otto Brunfels, Conrad Pellican, Urbanus Rhegius, St Augustine, St Chrysostom, St Jerome, Cælius Secundus Curio, Sebastian Castellion, Georg Kleinberg and Basil Montfort.

The passage Castellion quotes from Luther is taken from *Von welltlicher Oberkeyt*. The doctrines of the two domains, the Kingdom of God under Jesus Christ and the kingdom of the world under the magistrate, were calculated to allow the existence of toleration—when each authority may not trespass on the field of the other. Castellion is not content with such an argument in his favour; he proceeds in his noteworthy book to quote from Luther's sermon on the Tares and the Wheat, which obviously proclaims the danger and the difficulty of detecting the heretic.[1]

Castellion makes use of two works of Erasmus, the first of which he wrote in 1526 against the Sorbonne, entitled *Supputatio Errorum Bedæ*.[2] It substantially develops the same conception of the Church and the State as the *Von welltlicher Oberkeyt*, for Erasmus draws a distinction between ecclesiastical and secular pains and penalties. " Is this to disarm the Church? " Erasmus asks indignantly, and he answers his own question : " Dare I [remove] from the bishops their authority to teach, correct and excommunicate? What right have they beyond these functions? What laws of the Church are they of which I am reminded in this connection? Is a bishop one who only knows how to bind, throttle, torment—burn? " The passage attracted the attention of the Sorbonne, notably of Beda, who passionately attacked it, and in 1527 the hostile Sentences of this body were promulgated, condemning certain opinions as heretical.[3]

On 4th November 1529 Erasmus wrote a " Letter to the would-be Evangelists," protesting that he does not take from the Prince the power of the sword that Christ and the Apostles had recognised. There is room for severity against two grave heresies—where they assume a blasphemous character—it is his usual limitation on toleration—and where they take a

---

[1] Luther, *Werke*, Erl. ed., ii., pp. 80-83.
[2] *Cf.* Erasmus, *Commentaries on St Matthew's Gospel*, chap. xiii.
[3] Proposition 32.

seditious form.[1] Still he maintains in his *Declarationes ad censuras Lutetiæ vulgatas sub nomine Facultatis Theologiæ Parisiensis* that in spite of the Sorbonne his interpretation of the parable of the Tares and the Wheat is true. Castellion does not quote from this document, but he takes his second excerpt from the *Apologia adversus articulos aliquot per monachos quosdam in Hispania exhibitos*.[2]

Stung by the stain left on the fame of Calvin through his consent to the burning alive of Michael Servetus, at Geneva, on 27th October 1553, Beza wrote the following year his treatise *Concerning the Duty of Punishing Heretics by the Civil Magistrate : in Answer to the Medley of Martin Bellius and the Sect of the new Academics*. In it he proves himself a whole-hearted defender of his friend Calvin, and Servetus is not a man struggling towards truth but "of all men that have hitherto lived the most impious and blasphemous."[3] He stoutly argues that heretics are to be punished. These heretics are neither Jews nor Turks, but Christians who simply follow their own—perverted—judgment. That such men ought to be punished "no one—to my knowledge at least—has been found thus far to call in question, with the exception of these new Academics."[4] It is of paramount importance that doctrine should remain safe. If false doctrine attacks the Church it must be removed, even at the cost of a severe operation. The Bible is perfectly clear on this point, for it contains laws against blasphemers and false prophets. Are the acts of Moses, Asa and Josiah all to be neglected? Is not he that will not hear the Church to be regarded as a publican and a heathen? Were not the heretics Philetus and Hymenæus given over by the Apostles to be buffeted by Satan? To Beza "such men appear to act more absurdly than if they were to deny that sacrilegious persons or parricides ought to be punished; since heretics are infinitely worse than all such criminals."

---

[1] *Cf.* his letter to Duke George of Saxony, 12th December 1524.

[2] *Opp.*, ix., col. 1054d, 1057d and 1058a.

[3] *De Hæreticis a Civili Magistratu Puniendis* (*Tractationes Theologicæ*), i., p. 85.

[4] *Ibid.*, i., p. 143.

Who is to punish the heretic? The civil magistrate and none else.[1] The chief end of man, according to the Scots Catechism, is to glorify God, and the chief end of society, according to Beza, is to honour God. Therefore the magistrate must deal sharply with all who refuse to render Him the honour that is His rightful due. By the sword (*jure gladii*) he must coerce the factious and pertinacious despisers of religion. Ministers of the Church cannot themselves enforce this discipline; otherwise there would be a confusion, a mingling, of the power of the sword and that of the keys. Obviously, then, it is the duty of the civil magistrate. Such a Christian magistrate will not tolerate the dissensions of the citizens in secular affairs. Why should he tolerate them in religious affairs? For of course the things that are not seen are eternal, and therefore infinitely more valuable than mere temporal affairs. Is it not obvious that if the ministry intrude on the office of the magistrate, as the Roman Antichrist has done, there is the gravest danger of dire confusion as the outcome of commingling what God has separated? If the pastors err, if the shepherds become transformed into wolves, what is to happen? Some will say, " Let a Council be convoked and let it compel the unruly to submission." But who is to summon the Council? Clearly it is the office of the civil magistrate, for we must not forget the injunction of the Apostle, Let every soul be subject to the higher powers.[2]

What is the punishment to be? The penalty of the heretic is death. Why not? All races execute men for parricide and voluntary homicide, for blasphemy and sacrilege. In accordance with mediæval notions Beza leaves those outside the Church to God, Who will enlighten them in His own good time. Those within the Church who are heretics stand in a wholly different position. If they are punished as they deserve, is there any punishment meet for their crime—one of the most serious in the category of the Church? A man who slays another attacks the common weal. A man who prepares the corruption of the Church starts something that will result in the everlasting

---

[1] *Cf.* Bonnard, *Thomas Éraste*, pp. 142-149.
[2] *Ibid.*, i., pp. 143-145.

destruction of an infinite number of men. Therefore to preserve human society as well as to vindicate the glory of God such a man ought to receive the severest penalty the magistrate can inflict.[1] " In fine," concludes Beza, " I do not hesitate to affirm that those princes do their duty who adopt as examples for their own imitation these laws of God, by establishing, if not the very same kind of penalty, yet certainly the very same measure of penalty, and who, as against factious apostates, enact some form of capital punishment for horrible blasphemy and crime. For the majesty of God should be held to be of such moment among all men, through the everlasting ages, that, whoever scoffs at it, because he scoffs at the very Author of life, most justly deserves to be put to death by violence. This I say, this I cry aloud, relying upon the truth of God and the testimony of conscience. Let my opponents shout until they are hoarse that we are savage, cruel, inhuman, bloodthirsty. Yet shall the truth conquer and show at length that those deserve these epithets who, in their preposterous or insincere zeal for clemency, suffer the wolves to fatten upon the life of the sheep rather than do their duty in vindicating the majesty of God." [2] It is a relief to turn to Beza's *Icones*, published in 1580, in which he draws the images or portraits of such men as Wyclif and Hus, Jerome of Prague and Savonarola, Erasmus and Reuchlin, Francis I. and Budé, Scaliger and Robert Étienne, Marot and Michel de l'Hôpital, and the sketch of the noble Politique makes us a shade hopeful that the spirit of the *De Hæreticis a Civili Magistratu Puniendis* did not altogether cling to its author to the very end.

Of the three disciples of Calvin, Beza is the one in whom the change wrought by St Bartholomew's Day is most palpable. He belonged to the aristocracy, and his original tone of thought is far removed from revolution. On 1st January and 21st October 1561 he counsels submission to authority, and even so late as 1594 he gave this advice.[3] The Massacre of Vassy, 1562, altered him, and that of 1572 was to alter him far more. Yet

---

[1] *De Hæreticis*, i., p. 151. [2] *Ibid.*, i., p. 155.

[3] *Opera*, xvii., p. 638; 1st January 1561, xviii., pp. 1-2; 21st October 1561, xix., p. 68.

even in the former year he is so shaken by the horrors the Duke of Guise inflicted at Vassy that he meditates resistance. He did all that lay in his power to obtain an edict granting some measure of relief for the Huguenots, granting what Calvin called *tolerabilis libertas*. He hoped for peace, but after 1562 is not war possible? The Guises have violated the edicts of the King, they have murdered the faithful, and they plainly seek to compass the entire destruction of the faithful. What is the course to pursue? Undoubtedly, in accordance with his legalism, he must appeal to Condé, a prince of the blood, to the magistrates, to the great seigneurs and the nobility of France.

Between 1562 and 1572 much water flowed under the bridge. In 1574 Beza published his *Du Droit des Magistrats sur leurs Sujets*,[1] one of the most important and one of the most far-reaching of all the pamphlets that appeared after the fatal 24th of August. In size it amounts to no more than eighty-five pages, but who can estimate the effect of the propositions enounced? For its author laid down these principal theses:

There is no other will than that of God alone, Who is everlasting and immutable, the standard of all justice. To Him alone we owe absolute and unconditional obedience. Divine and natural law limits the power of the ruler. The people whom He has been pleased to allow to themselves to be governed, either by a prince or by some chosen lords, are more ancient than their magistrates, and therefore the people is not created for the magistrates, but on the contrary the magistrates for the people.[2] There is a mutual obligation between Prince and people. All resistance of the subject against his superior is neither unlawful nor seditious. Just resistance by arms is contrary neither to the patience nor the prayers of Christians. All must oppose themselves to those who mean to usurp domination over their fellow-citizens, or others not subject

---

[1] It appeared in Latin in 1576. *Cf.* Cartier's study of it in the *Bulletin de la Société d'Histoire et d'Archæologie de Genève*, ii., pp. 187-206; *cf.* also Lelong, *Bibl. Historique*, ii., p. 763, Nos. 27, 120; Lenglet, *Méthode Historique*, iii., p. 53; Bayle, *Dissertation sur le Livre de Junius Brutus*, xii., Dict., xv., p. 136.

[2] Here, as in some other matters, he anticipates Rousseau.

to them. The representatives of the people are above kings. These representatives or others ordered to serve as a check to sovereigns can and must repress sovereigns in all possible ways when they turn tyrant. The public good and the rights of nature are superior to those of individuals, even to those of the Sovereign. The unjust usurper of domination can become a legitimate and inviolable magistrate, becoming so voluntarily in consenting to the right by which legitimate magistrates are created. When persecuted for religion, men can defend themselves by arms with a good conscience. In a word, these theses assert that sovereignty rests with the people. They exist before any magistrate; they are superior to any magistrate, and they own and ought to exercise the right to revolt in case of need. He finishes his book with an appeal to Divine justice : " Quant à cette manière de gens qui ne servent au monde que pour le faire regorger de sang innocent, abusant des princes de la seule ruine desquels ils s'aggrandissent . . . je les remets, non point tant à leur conscience, d'autant que la plupart n'en a plus, qu'au tribunal de celui de la Souveraineté de Justice duquel le temps et l'effet montrera qu'ils n'auront pu s'exempter." [1]

The first complete theory of political Calvinism is presented to us in *Du Droit des Magistrats sur leur Sujets*, rendering explicit what was but implicit in the thought of the Pope of Geneva.[2] There is a *mutua obligatio* between the King and the people. Beza tells us something about it, and Hotman provides us with some additional details of its nature. The people, as a body, can claim rights under this contract. The people, as individuals, can claim no legal rights. Beza and Hotman implicitly hold that the city or the district holds itself responsible for the protection of true religion, a position entirely in keeping with that federalist tinge that coloured the teaching of Calvin himself. The mediæval conception of estates reinforced this federalism that characterised the outlook of all

---

[1] *Du Droit*, p. 521.
[2] Fickler (1578) and Beccaria (1594) attacked it. *Cf.* Lossen, p. 215ff. Did Beza contribute to the *Réveille-Matin*? The reasoning in it resembles that of *Du Droit*. On the Roman Catholic version of *Du Droit*, produced by Fickler, *cf.* Lossen, *Sitzungsber. du München Ak.*, i. and iii., 1885, p. 245.

the Huguenot Monarchomachi. There are many associations or estates in the State, which is no more than the highest of them all. Implicitly such a conception ran entirely counter to the growing absolutism of the Crown.

The rights of nature are invoked in order to justify the position taken up. There are such rights of nature, and they are inviolable and imprescriptible. By virtue of them we must obey princes " provided they do not command irreligious or iniquitous matters." The irreligious matters are those forbidden by the " first table of the law of God." The iniquitous matters are those contrary " to what each owes to his neighbour according to his private or public vocation." For Beza natural right is summarised in the Decalogue. He is in no wise concerned with, say, the question of social contract raised by Rousseau. He is, however, concerned to show that there is a civil contract enshrining the Decalogue.[1] Such a contract, he would say with Hooker, cannot be abrogated, so far as the people are concerned. Such rights as this contract guarantees are, by nature, inalienable. In fact, the natural right of the nation is always reserved, explicitly or implicitly. At the same time he is as much against anarchy as he is against Anabaptism. " I detest," he owns, " seditions and all confusion as horrible monsters." [2]

In his desire to check tyranny effectively he distinguishes between three categories of persons. First, there are quite private people who cannot, in their private capacity, oppose their force to the force of the tyrant. They must suffer the yoke.[3] Then come inferior magistrates, officers of the kingdom rather than of the King, and among them he reckons dukes, marquises, counts, mayors, consuls, eschevins and the like. It is open to them to oppose the manifest oppression of the people. Above the private persons and the inferior magistrates stand the representatives of the people, who are the sovereign guardians of the rights of the people. They serve as the real check to the Sovereign, and must repress him when he turns tyrant.[4] Nor

---

[1] *Du Droit*, pp. 352, 367-369.
[2] *Ibid.*, pp. 355, 357.
[3] *Ibid.*, p. 357.
[4] *Ibid.*, pp. 259, 352, 358-359, 369.

is this a mere precept, for Beza proceeds to enumerate the cases where countries have got rid of their kings when they refused to accept the conditions laid down.[1]

Calvin, Hotman and Duplessis-Mornay are not in favour of tyrannicide. Beza forms the one outstanding exception, for, in common with the Jesuits, he is in favour of it. Melanchthon leans to it.[2] And when Poltrot assassinated the Duke of Guise Beza did not condemn him.[3] " I do not," admits Beza, "approve of the opinion of those who, without any distinction or exception, condemn all tyrannicides, to whom Greece formerly offered so many honourable rewards." [4] That *Du Droit des Magistrats sur leur Sujets* had a ready sale is evidenced by the fact that there were a dozen editions in French or Latin before 1608. Its seed fell on ground prepared for it by the events of 1572.

François Hotman's family came originally from Breslau. His father had been " Master of the Waters and Forests " and counsellor or judge of the *Parlement* of Paris. His son François was the eldest of his eleven children, and his talents as a lad promised a career of exceptional brilliancy for him. Besides, after the fashion of those days, he could succeed to his father's position in the *Parlement*. When only fourteen he went to study law at the University of Orleans, the university of Calvin, Beza and Budé. Within three years he had become a doctor of laws, and, proceeding to Paris, he was with the great jurisconsult, Dumoulin, the advocate of national independence and Gallican liberties. Admitted to the Bar, he pleaded with marked success. The study of jurisprudence attracted him more than the practice of law, and accordingly he began to lecture in 1546 on his favourite subject. Among his students was Étienne Pasquier, who in after years counted it one of the greatest pieces of good fortune that ever befell him that he was permitted at this time to be among Hotman's admiring audience. The lecturer was keen-witted enough to discern

---

[1] *Du Droit*, pp. 359, 365-367. *Cf.* Troeltsch, *Soziallehren der christlichen Kirchen und Gruppen*, pp. 687-693.
[2] *Opera*, iii., p. 1076.
[3] *Ibid.*, xviii., p. 2 ; xix., pp. 20-22. [4] *Du Droit*, p. 354.

the merits of the contract theory. He could see that it embodied the notion that law and government were based on consent, that it emphasises the moral aim of the State, that with its recognition of the rights of the individual it recognises the rights of others, and that it builds upon the law of nature, which all sixteenth-century men accepted. In spite of all this, Hotman, one of the ablest jurists of his day, ignores the contract conception. He knew far too much about the beginnings of law to accept it. The truth is that this conception is unhistorical and illogical, assuming a knowledge of law utterly outside the ken of primitive man.

Tertullian never wrote a greater truth than "semen est sanguis Christianorum." The martyrdom of such Huguenots as Anne Dubourg stirred Hotman so deeply that, to the disgust of his family, he threw away all his prospect of a great career in order to join the Reformed faith. His father practically disinherited him and his family poured reproaches on him for his conduct. Obliged to leave France, he sought an asylum in Geneva. In 1549 he held a chair of Latin at Lausanne, and in 1555 he proceeded to Strasburg, where he resumed his old studies with an astonishing reputation. All the time he is working behind the scenes for the faith he held so dear. In 1560 appeared his *Epistre envoiée au Tigre de la France*.[1] In this short pamphlet of ten pages he attacks with concision and with conciseness Charles de Guise, Cardinal de Lorraine, the "Tigre" whom his brother was serving. The orations of Cicero against Catiline gave him the model for his assault on one whom he justly looked on as mainly responsible for the misfortunes of his country. Nevertheless Charles de Guise was an accomplished man of letters, a judicious art patron, a fashionable preacher, and, above all, owned a most capable head for statesmanship.

In 1560 Hotman is in the service of the King of Navarre, Antoine de Bourbon, and then in that of his brother, the

---

[1] Baird, *History of the Huguenots*, i., p. 445ff. *Cf.* Hanke, *De Script. rer. Rom.*, i., p. 249 ; ii., p. 387. Hotman may have contributed to the *Réveille-Matin*. Cf. *Ep. Hot.*, 441 ; Lenient, *La Satire en France*, ii., p. 30 ; Elkan, *Die Publizistik der Bartholomäusnacht*, p. 57.

Prince of Condé. His old interests still claim him, for he teaches in the schools of Valence and Bourges. St Bartholomew's Day left its mark also on him. On 30th October 1572 he wrote from Geneva to Bullinger: " Hier soir, je suis arrivé ici, sauvé par la providence, la clémence et la miséricorde de Dieu, échappé au massacre, œuvre de Pharaon. . . . Je ne puis dans ma tristesse écrire davantage. Tout ce que je puis dire, c'est que cinquante mille personnes viennent d'être égorgées en France dans l'espace de huit or dix jours. Ce qui reste de chrétiens erre la nuit dans les bois; les bêtes sauvages seront plus clementes pour eux, je l'espère, que les monstres à forme humaine. . . . Les larmes m'empêchent d'écrire davantage. Souvenez-vous de moi dans vos prieres." He confides in Walther on 4th October: " Ma femme a été enlevée et en proie à toutes sortes de violences. Tous nos bien ont été pillés. Jamais, que je sache, les fureurs de Satan ne se sont dechainées avec tant de force contre les gens pieux ! " On 8th November he tells Bullinger: " Ce n'est pas seulement la perte de nos femmes et de nos enfants qui nous afflige, mais la ruine incroyable de nos Églises au delà de tout ce que nous aurions pu craindre."

In Geneva the exile meditates over the destinies of his country and of his Church. In 1556 he could write to Bullinger, " Je vous recommande Genève : c'est la mère des martyrs de France, qui lui rendent temoignage devant Dieu," but all the time *la patrie, sa patrie*, tugged at his heart-strings. In spite of this, the care of the churches and the freedom of worship are always in his thoughts. On 17th June 1574 he wrote an indignant protest to Walther, " La reine mère s'est emparée du pouvoir alléguant une parole du roi, comme si l'on pouvait disposer par un testament de ce qui n'est pas à soi ! Qui peut ignorer, pour peu qu'on connaisse notre besoin, que le droit de gouverner dans les interrègnes appartient aux États généraux et au Conseil." The sentiments the jurisconsult expresses in his writings he really thinks and feels. With his legal studies almost in the foreground in 1578 he set out for Bâle. His *Anti-Tribonian* provides us with a lively indictment of the disastrous legal and political effects of perusing Justinian. It is in French history, not Roman, that French law can best be understood. In Bâle he was grieved by the violent quarrels between the Lutherans and the Calvinists, quarrels that embittered his existence.[1] His home life was, however, happy, for his wife was *dimidium animæ meæ*. She, alas! fell a victim to the plague, and her husband had not the heart to continue the struggle. Shortly before his death he told Strennius: " Tels ont été mes destins que je puis dire avec le patriarche : Les jours de ma vie ont été courts et mauvais. Cependant mon courage n'est pas si abattu, et je m'abandonne pas tellement à la tristesse et au deuil, que je ne sois soutenu par la confiance en cette félicité que Dieu dan sa clémence et sa bonté, nous a promis après cette misérable vie. Je sais que l'infortune est l'inseparable compagne de la piété, et Christ, lorsqu'il nous a appelés a lui, ne nous a pas promis des richesses et des dignités, mais sa croix et des afflictions sans terme. D'ailleurs, je reconnais qu'il nous envoie son Esprit, qui nous console dans tous nos chagrins et dans tous nos périls. C'est là, il faut l'avouer, la suprême béatitude et le souverain bonheur que les philosophes anciens ont cherché dans des choses légères et périssables." [2]

Facts like these are vital for the understanding of the *Franco-Gallia*, the book Hotman wrote in 1573,[3] when he was feeling to the full the experiences of St Bartholomew's Day. Beneath the outward calm of the mind discussing the State of ancient France, we are always conscious of the heart seething with indignation at the fate of men and women he

---

[1] The Council of Geneva refused to allow the publication of the *Franco-Gallia* or Beza's *Du Droit* (*Registres du Conseil*, vol. lxviii., 7th July, 23rd October 1573, pp. 145, 185, 208-209). Beza intervened on behalf of the *Franco-Gallia*, and it then appeared in 1573. On the political theory of the Huguenots *cf.* E. Armstrong's fine article in *English Historical Review* (1889), vol. iv., pp. 13-40. Glaser ably analyses the *Franco-Gallia* in *Beiträge z. Gesch. d. polit. Literatur Frankr. Ztsch. für Francös Sprache*, Bd. xxxix. (1912), p. 240. On Dareste's discovery of two hundred and fifteen letters of Hotman, cf. *Rev. Hist.* (1876). *Cf.* H. M. Baird, *English Historical Review*, 1892; P. J. Blok, "Correspondance de F. Hotman," *Arch. Musée Teyler* (1911).

[2] *Epis.*, p. 243.

[3] Hotman, *Epis.*, p. 111.

had known and loved. He dedicates his book to Frederick, Count Palatine of the Rhine, and his dedication breathes the spirit of patriotism, anticipating the work of Richelieu, who was the first to make every Frenchman realise that he belonged to *la patrie*. He has a fine definition of the French, which takes us by surprise when we remember that it was penned in 1573 [1]: " Comment que ce soit, et quel accident que c'ait esté, qui ait donné ce nom aux François, quant à moy je suis content de croire, et suis bien d'accord, que ce fut cette gentille rencontre, de bon et heureux présage, dont il prit son origine, de sorte que dès lors ceux là portèrent méritoirement et proprement le titre de François, que ayans abatu la domination des tyrans, se maintindrent en liberté honeste, mesme sous l'authorité des voys." [2] Here the cosmopolitan accents of an Erasmus are replaced by a new nascent nationalism. The State of Machiavelli is one for which we can intrigue : the State of Hotman is one for which we can live and—if need so require—die. Read the burning words of the dedication of the *Franco-Gallia* : " C'est une parole ancienne, très illustre prince, que ' la patrie est partout où l'on se trouve bien,' parole attribuée à Teucer, fils de Telamon, et approuvée par beaucoup de siècles. Car c'est le fait d'une âme forte et élevée, parait-il, que de supporter, avec une fermeté tranquille, même l'exil, au même titre que les autres adversités, et de mépriser les injustices de la patrie ingrate, comme on ferait des injustices d'une marâtre. Mais je pense qu'il en doit être tout autrement. Car, si c'est crime et une impiété de ne supporter qu'avec impatience les habitudes et les rudesses de ses parents, à combien plus forte raison de la patrie, que tous les sages, d'un commun accord, ont placée toujours avant les parents ! Il est vrai, un homme qui n'a souci que de son repos et qui ne pense qu'à ses aises, mesure l'amour de la patrie aux avantages qu'elle lui procure. Mais cette solicitude tout égoïste est une partie de cette inhumanité qui est le propre des épicuriens et

---

[1] *Franco-Gallia*, pp. 271-272. *Cf.* E. Cougny, " François Hotman, la France-Gaule," *Mémoires de la Société des Sciences morales, Lettres et Arts de Seine-et-Oise,* 1574.
[2] *Franco-Gallia*, p. 288.

des cyniques, école d'où sortit cette parole feroce : Moi mort, que la terre soit anéantie par le feu ! . . . Il y a dans les âmes douces et généreuses un amour inné de la patrie, amour qui ne peut en être arraché qu'avec les autres sentiments humains. Cet amour, Homère le montre réalisé dans Ulysse, qui préfère à toutes les délices, et même au royaume offert par Calypso, Ithaque, sa patrie, un pauvre nid d'aigles, suspendu aux flancs des rochers escarpes.

> " Nescio qua natale solum dulcedine cunctos
> Afficit, immemores nec sinit esse sui."

There is possibly no better source than the letters of Hotman for discerning the beginnings of the new nationalism to which the *tres magi* of Bacon, Henry VII. of England, Louis XI. of France, and Ferdinand the Catholic had given the form of each kingdom that made it possible. If Bodin provides us with a theory of sovereignty, we are by no means sure that Hotman does not provide us with that spirit of love to Sovereign and country which was one day to inspire all Frenchmen with that devotion to *la patrie* which so distinguishes France.

Hotman is a patriot, who feels on this account the sorrows of his country all the more keenly. Calvin is to him *amantissime domine, mi pater* : there is also *la patrie*.[1] Perhaps we ought to bear in mind the circumstance that he was an exile as well as a Huguenot. He warns us as he begins his *Franco-Gallia*[2] that " D'abord, il faut prendre garde de mettre sur le compte de la patrie une faute dont elle n'est pas coupable. A Rome et en d'autres lieux, il y a eu de monstreueux tyrans." Here there is, we may feel certain, a side-glance at the mad Charles IX. and the terrible Catherine de' Medici. He proceeds to inform us that " Ces tyrans ont accablé de toutes sortes de tourments, non seulement les gens de biens, mais même les citoyens qui avaient bien mérité de la patrie. Ces criminelles folies, faut-il en rendre la patrie responsable ? On sait la cruauté de l'Empereur

---

[1] Dareste, *Essai sur F. Hotman*, p. 4 ; Calvin, *Opera*, xii., p. 717. *Cf.* xiii., pp. 22, 37, 60, 265, 548 ; xiv., pp. 344, 357-358, 397, 413-414 ; xvii., p. 73.
[2] *Cf.* Waddington, *Revue Historique* (1893), li. On Hotman's general position *cf.* Treumann, pp. 54-57, 59, 60.

Macrinus : Julius Capitolinus l'appelle le Boucher, parce que
sa maison dégouttait de sang humain comme une boucherie
du sang des animaux. Des historiens signalent bien d'autres
tyrans : comme l'ecrit le même Julius Capitolinus, à cause de
leur cruauté, l'un fut appelé Cyclope, l'autre Busiris, un autre
Scyron, un autre Typhon, un autre Gygès : engagés dans cette
voie, ils ne purent sauveur leur empire que par la cruauté.
Est-ce une raison pour les bons citoyens ne veuillent plus
avoir de soin ni de sollicitude pour la patrie? Bien au contraire,
c'est une raison de plus de venir au secours de la patrie quand
elle est opprimée, misérable, et implorant l'assistance de ses
enfants : c'est une raison de plus de rechercher de toutes parts
les remedes salutaires à ses maux. Et cependant, qu'elles sont
heureuses les contrées favorisées de bons et doux princes :
Oh qu'ils sont heureux les citoyens auquels il est permis de
vieillir tranquillement sous un gouvernement paternel, dans les
demeures de leurs pères et de leurs enfants ! "

The spirit of patriotism has diverse origins, and one of them
has been by the way of war. The fierce national pride of Spain
came in part from her long struggle with the Moor, who had
been in Spain from 711 to 1492. The fierce national pride of
France came in part from the Hundred Years' War with
England. It is, however, perfectly plain in the writings of
Hotman that the civil wars of the sixteenth—and even of the
seventeenth—century did not a little to stimulate that intense
feeling for *la patrie*. Take such a passage as this from the
beginning of the *Franco-Gallia* : " Il fut un temps aussi où,
vers notre Gaule franque, les jeunes gens studieux accouraient
de toutes les contrées de la terre et s'empressaient vers nos
Academies, comme vers le centre bien approvisionné de tous
les arts libéraux : maintenant ils se detournent d'elle avec
horreur, comme d'une mer infestée par les pirates, comme
d'une contrée où règne une monstrueuse barbarie. Ce souvenir
me brise le cœur. Depuis douze ans, l'incendie de la guerre
civile désole et ravage notre patrie infortunée ; mais ma douleur
est d'autant plus amère quand je vois que beaucoup de mes
concitoyens sont spectateurs oisifs devant cet incendie, comme
autrefois Néron devant Rome en flammes ; qu'il en est d'autres

qui, par leurs paroles et par leurs livres, attisent les flammes, et que, pour les éteindre, presque personne n'accourt. Je n'ignore pas combien ma condition est modeste, humble même. Mais personne, que je sache, ne répudie le zèle de celui qui, dans un incendie, apporte son petit seau d'eau. J'espère aussi que personne, parmi les vrais amis de la patrie, ne méprisera mon humble secours dans recherche des remèdes, à nos communs malheurs."

The pail of water he brought to extinguish the flames was a book of two hundred pages, glowing with a fervent feeling on behalf of national sovereignty. The influence of the Renaissance is apparent throughout, for are there not one hundred and fifty pages consisting of pure classical quotations? We are, however, conscious the whole time that it is with a late phase of the Renaissance we are concerned, for Hotman is no cosmopolitan either of the Erasmian or the Goethe type. First and last, and all the time, he is a Frenchman whose soul is on fire to save his country. The sources of writers are always of outstanding importance. It is noticeable, for example, how often Hotman appeals in confirmation of his views to Seyssel's *La Grand Monarchie de France*, published in 1519. Seyssel plainly regards a monarch like Louis XII. as his ideal. For though absolute in theory, he limited himself in practice, and indeed there were the three checks of religion, justice and " police " to order his doings.

Freeman taught the unity and the continuity of history in his day, and Hotman taught it in his. True, Freeman taught it critically, fully aware of the value or the want of value of the document he was using. Hotman taught it uncritically, with no sense of the value of the evidence he employed. Whether a speech was or was not delivered, whether an election was or was not historically accurate, whether in fact his incidents were or were not trustworthy—these were all questions outside his ken. The circumstance that he could appeal to the ancient history of France or Germany furnishes testimony to the point that he believed in the continuity of history, and this is no mean achievement for a man of the sixteenth century. The past to him was not a time of the mere shuffling of kites and crows:

the past was vitally part and parcel of the present. In another matter he did not resemble Freeman, for to him most—if not all—roads led away from Rome. What were the precedents at Rome or in Germany? The answer to this question is never long out of his mind. When, however, the question of electing kings arises, he does not mention those of the Roman epoch, because Rome, according to him, subdued Gaul. Nor can we ignore the circumstance that, in addition to consulting Cæsar and Tacitus, he also consults Sidonius and Gregory of Tours, Eginhard and Otto of Freisingen, ending with Commines and Joinville.

Gaul was part of the Roman Empire, and in those far-off days it was ruled by a single man. The cities, we learn, were governed by a general assembly of delegates. Tacitus reckons sixty-four of these cities. Under the chief ruler there were other chiefs. Behind the governors of the city, behind the kings and behind the ruler, there was the National Assembly or States General, the fount of authority. The subjects of the King are not serfs.[1] The extent of the power of the people is, he thinks, obvious from a remark of a native Gaul that the multitude exercised no less authority over the King than the King over the multitude. There are many precedents quoted, of Casticus, King of the Sequani, of Ambiorix, King of the Eburi, and of many another. The authority of Plato and Aristotle, of Cicero and Polybius, is invoked in order to buttress the charming—and fanciful—picture that Hotman draws. Then comes some curious philology, with no less curious speculations on the original language of the Gauls. There is a trace of discernment in the remark, thrown out quite casually, that the Bretons preserve the remains of the original language spoken by the Gauls. The word Frank of course means free. *Francisisia* is the synonym of asylum, and *francisare* is the act of emancipation. Franks, in this sense, he proudly claims his ancestors to be. Nor does kingly authority in the least degree detract from this freedom. " For it is not servitude," we read, " to obey a king, nor are they to be esteemed slaves that obey him ; but these rather who submit to the caprice of a tyrant, a robber, or a

---

[1] *Franco-Gallia*, p. 288.

murderer, as sheep submit to the butcher, are truly to be called by that most vile name of slaves. Thus it was that the Franks always had kings, even when they professed themselves maintainers and defenders of freedom; and when they set up kings, they set not up tyrants and murderers, but guardians, overseers, protectors of their own liberties." [1]

Of course the Franks never gave away their liberties. They made and unmade their kings; in the last resort the annual meeting of the National Assembly exercised its sway, and in the background we perceive the whole time the sovereignty of the people. Hotman does not want a purely elective royalty. He shows that in France the sons succeeded their fathers by " prerogative." " The people possessed a sovereign authority not only to elect their kings, but also to repudiate the sons of the kings, and elect strangers." [2]

The King ruled over willing subjects. The proof advanced is that he had no army, for the good will of his men was amply sufficient to defend him. The National Assembly or council used to say to the sovereign [3] : " We who are as good as you, and are more powerful than you, elect you King on such and such conditions. Between you and us there is One with greater authority than you " [4]; and such an oath was actually tendered by the Aragonese to their monarch. This oath Beza, Hotman and Mornay all quote in vindication of their position. [5] The examples of Hilderic, of Chlodowig and of others are offered for our attention. No doubt some strong kings, Hotman is too honest not to admit, contracted the rights of the National Assembly which really flow from the *jus gentium*. [6] We never go far from the law of nature. Still, such a king is a tyrant. The essence of a tyrant is that he employs his royal office for his own aggrandisement, not for the benefit of his subjects.

---

[1] *Franco-Gallia*, p. 37.
[2] *Ibid.*, p. 293.
[3] On the Aragonese precedent *cf.* A. Perez, *Relaciones* (Paris, 1598), fol. 29 ; Prescott, *Ferdinand and Isabella*, I. lxxxvi. (Introduction).
[4] *Franco-Gallia*, p. 85.
[5] Baird, *Amer. Hist. Rev.*, i., p. 621.
[6] *Franco-Gallia*, p. 86. *Cf.* pp. 309, 310.

Of course this is the position of Calvin, Beza and Mornay. It is also true, Hotman notes, that Hugh Capet, by turning temporal dignities into permanent, restricted the authority of the National Assembly. Nor can the Pope elect the King of the Franks.[1] A case like that of Pepin is in no wise to the point. For we glean that what really happened then was that the French removed the incompetent Childeric and installed the competent Pepin in his stead. All that Pope Zachary did was to approve of what the Franks had already accomplished.

At all times and in all places the National Assembly, the States General, preserves the commonweal.[2] Chapter seventeen is worth reading for the sake of noting how Hotman ingeniously applies his seven instances to prove the sovereignty of the people. The learning displayed is considerable, and the insight is even more considerable. The inevitable conclusion is that " our ancestors left to the King his own privy councillors to care for his personal affairs; they reserved for the public assembly the choice of the older men that were to consult together and point out to the King the mode of administering the kingdom." [3] The King is mortal, the kingdom immortal. Bodin's seven instances attest the truth of such a view. The people controlled the kings of the Capetian race. The reign of Louis XI. interposes a formidable obstacle in the way of accepting Hotman's ideas, and he thinks that even over this monarch the authority of the council was occasionally memorable. At the same time he frankly avows that Louis XI. was a tyrant, and that his tyranny redounded not only to his own infamy but also to the ruin of his people as well. " However this may be," he concludes, " it is evident that less than a hundred years have elapsed since the liberty of France and the authority of the solemn assembly were in vigour, and in vigour against a king weak neither in age nor in mind, but already forty years old and possessed of such greatness of intellect as plainly never was found in any other king of ours. Thus it may be understood that our commonwealth, founded and established in liberty, retained for more than eleven hundred years that free and venerable constitution (*statum*) which it

---

[1] *Franco-Gallia*, pp. 112, 113.   [2] *Ibid.*, pp. 87, 88.   [3] *Ibid.*, p. 130.

possessed, even by force of arms, against the power of tyrants.''
The States General provides the remedy for all the political
evils which France inherits.[1] Formerly it governed *la patrie*:
it does not now. The sooner France returns to political sanity
the better, but the only road is through the action of the States
General.

What is the conclusion of the whole matter? Why does
Hotman expend so much learning on the state of the Franks?
Is he a mere antiquarian? By no means. The whole book is
dictated by the practical needs of men after 1572. Clearly,
if Hotman's thesis is true, important consequences follow.
Sovereignty resides in the nation, and such sovereignty is
absolute. To the people belong the right of governing, and
if they delegate their authority to the magistrate he is obviously
responsible to them. The conclusion is irresistible. The people
possess the right to depose the King, even by force of arms.
" Je trouve très-vraies," triumphantly concludes the author,
" ces antiques paroles de Marc Antoine. Bien que les séditions
soient fâcheuses, quelques-unes sont justes et presque néces-
saires : mais alors celles-là sont très-justes et très-nécessaires
quand le peuple opprimé par la cruauté d'un tyran réclame le
secours de l'assemblée légitime des citoyens." [2] Such a conclusion is a trumpet call to action, and as such the Huguenots
took it. The insight of Hotman is apparent in every line of his
book. Through his plea for the Huguenot cause he can rise
to a survey of the loss of liberty in France. The dissension of
the French he justly regarded as the occasion of it. The causes
lay deeper. They were the changed character of the States
General, which represented the national want of cohesion, the
class divisions and the absence of local government. Contribut-
ing causes were the idea that the essence of the Sovereign lay
in himself, not in his office, and the loss of the official character
of the nobility, with its inevitable outcome in the growth of
bureaucracy.

The concluding chapters of this book are devoted to the
Salic law and the authority of *Parlements*. The Salic law

---

[1] *Franco-Gallia*, pp. 304, 306, 313, 315-316.
[2] *Ibid.*, p. 126.

meets with his unmitigated satisfaction. We read of the enor-
mities of such feminine rulers as Clotilde, mother of the kings
Childebert and Clotaire; of Fredegonde, of Brunehaut; of
Plectrude, widow of Pepin; of Queen Judith, mother of Charles
the Bold; of Queen Blanche, mother of St Louis, and of Isabella,
wife of Charles VI. As we read the author's remarks on these
women we are really reading his characterisation of Catherine
de' Medici, for she is never out of his mind, and she it is
who inspired him, as Mary inspired Knox, to denounce the
monstrous regiment of women. Hotman excludes women
from power, but he aims at Catherine de' Medici. Hotman excludes an unworthy king, but he aims at replacing Charles IX.
by his brother François de Alençon, the friend of Coligny.

Parlements, in Hotman's eyes, are courts of justice, pure
and simple, and as courts they have their due place in the
constitution. That is all he is willing to concede to them.
When they usurp the functions of the National Assembly the
author—with Gentillet—lavishes his fierce criticism on them.
The name *parlamentum* rightfully belongs to the National
Assembly, and the *Parlements* are encroaching on the functions
of the Assembly, thereby impairing and imperilling its legitimate
place in the constitution. Besides, what are we to think of
Parlements when we find the *Parlement* of Paris approving of
the massacre of 1572? Its president, Christopher de Thou,
actually praised the monarch for the successful dissimulation
he had practised towards the Huguenots. On more than one
occasion the *Parlement* of Paris had bowed in obsequious
submission to Charles IX.

Before the days of critical scholarship the *Franco-Gallia*
enjoyed a resounding reputation. There was enough in the
coronation oath of the King to render plausible the history that
Hotman placed at the service of the Huguenots. The conception of contract, however, he leaves to the one side. Besides,
for 1572 it is not quite so fanciful as we are inclined to imagine.
A trained jurisconsult like him would not pronounce rashly:
it was not in his nature to do so. In the spirit of Fustel de
Coulanges he wrote in reply to attacks: " Qu'ils prouvent
que mes citations sont fausses; jo ne dis rien, moi. Je laisse

parler l'histoire ; je suis un simple compilateur." He was more, much more than that, for the doctrine of the *Franco-Gallia* acted as dynamite in the closing decades of the sixteenth century. It supplied the Huguenots with that legal and historical basis for which they always longed since the awful deed of Catherine de' Medici. Written in *bonne foy*, it produced conviction in the mind of the reader as much by its sincerity and by the passion beating in the heart of the author as by its then matchless erudition. His book had a fate not uncommon in those days, for if it provided strength to the Huguenots it also provided strength to the League. The passion and the enthusiasm of the *Franco-Gallia* gave it such a widespread circulation that Michelet thinks that no such success was reached till the days of Rousseau. Fénelon's *Plan de Gouvernement*, 1711, is substantially an echo of Hotman's plea for the restoration of the authority of the States General. That austere lawyer, John Selden, quotes Hotman no less than twenty-five times, and there are references to the *Franco-Gallia* in Milton's *Defensio Prima* and *Defensio Secunda*,[1] in Sidney's *Government*,[2] and in Thomas Hollis's *Memoirs*.[3]

The last of Calvin's three disciples is Philippe de Duplessis-Mornay (1549-1623). Born at the château of Buhi, he belonged to an old family of nobility, allied to some of the most illustrious in the kingdom. His mother, not his father, leaned to the Reformed doctrine, and his first teacher was a Protestant minister. As a child he read the Gospels for himself, and openly embraced Calvinism. His father wished him to become a page at Court, but the lad developed pronounced literary tastes. At the University of Paris for four years he regularly worked fourteen hours a day. The reading of Church history and the Fathers attached him more warmly to the creed to which he had given his youthful devotion. So firm was his attachment that he resolutely declined the prospects of a rich abbacy and a bishopric. In 1567 he fought on the side

---

[1] *Defensio Prima* (1651), p. 212.

[2] Chap. ii., sect. 30.

[3] *Memoirs*, ii., Appendix. On the influence of the *Franco-Gallia*, *cf.* Dareste, *Essai sur Hotman*, p. 76 ; Chauviré, *Jean Bodin*, p. 256.

of Condé, and indeed there were three men within him, for he was soldier, theologian and statesman. All roads for the Protestant in those days led to Geneva, and accordingly we find Mornay there. At Heidelberg, as became a Huguenot, he studied law, and in Italy he studied history and archæology. Escaping assassination on St Bartholomew's Day by a miracle, he took refuge in England, where he attracted the attention of Elizabeth. La Noue pressed him to return to France, where he once more took up arms. Fighting with Henry of Navarre, he was present at the battles of Coutras and Ivry. He saw in Henry the hope of the Huguenot, the man raised up by God to defend the Evangelical faith. " Ceux qui aident," he wrote in his *Memoirs*, " le roi de Navarre aident la cause de Dieu en sa personne." [1] The day came when Henry had to settle the question, Was Paris worth a mass? Sully advised him that it was, but how could Mornay tender any such advice? He warmly agreed with d'Aubigné that " it was better to be King of a corner of France, serving God, and assisted by those of tried fidelity and love, than reign precariously under the heel and domination and at the bidding of the Pope."

An ardent pamphleteer, Duplessis-Mornay had long occupied himself, both in theory and practice, with the question of resistance to tyranny. Before 1577 he composed his *Vindiciæ contra Tyrannos*,[2] and in his dedication he announces that the book he published in 1579 is in essence a reply to Machiavelli's *Prince*.[3] Machiavelli threw over natural law, and Mornay no less completely, like Calvin's other disciples, adopted it. Like

---

[1] *Mem.*, iv., p. 182.

[2] On the original title page it stated that the book was printed at Edinburgh, but it was really printed at Bâle by Thomas Guérin. Its editor was the friend of Mornay, Pierre Loyseleur. It was composed in 1574 or 1576 at latest. In 1692 Bayle attributed it to Hubert Languet. In 1876 Max Lossen proved that Mornay was its author. Waddington agrees in the *Revue Historique*, 1893, p. 65ff. Cf. *Revue des Deux-Mondes*, 1848, xxi., p. 736ff., on *La Politique du Calvinisme en France*, Duplessis-Mornay; G. Garrisson, " De la Politique du Calvinisme en France," *Revue des Deux-Mondes*, February 1848; and M. Lossen, " Die Vindiciæ contra Tyrannos des angeblichen Junius Brutus," *Sitz. K. bayr. Akad. ph.-h. Kl.* (1887), i. p. 215.

[3] There are eight references to Machiavelli in the Preface.

Hotman, he refers to women of the type of Athaliah and Brune-haut, but no one is in doubt that Catherine de' Medici is the real ruler with whom he is concerned. In principle, Mornay is much more advanced than Hotman, but in application of principle he is more conservative. Employing the evidence of the Bible, he analyses the nature of tyranny, and he confirms his conclusions by the law of nature, moral and political philosophy, and by civil law and Imperial rescripts. If the idea of contract is the most important of the contributions bequeathed by the Romans to the thought of mankind, Mornay inherited not a little of this legacy. As an outcome of his study, reinforced by his perusal of Beza's *De Jure Magistratum* and Hotman's *Franco-Gallia*, he puts before us general grounds of rights against tyrants. There are four questions, and the first three are of permanent interest, while the fourth is of passing. The questions are: (1) Whether it is the duty or the obligation of subjects to obey a prince's ordinances when contrary to God's law. (2) Whether they may lawfully resist a prince who is setting aside God's law or laying waste his Church. If so, to whom, by what means, and to what extent is it lawful? (3) Whether and how far they may resist a prince who is oppressing or ruining a State. To whom is this lawful, by what means, and by what title? (4) Whether it is the right and duty of princes to inter-fere on behalf of neighbouring peoples who are oppressed on account of adherence to the true religion, or by any obvious tyranny. The essence of Hotman's book lies in the illustrations, not in the argument. The essence of Mornay's book lies in the argument, not in the illustrations. The first question is, Is a subject bound to obey a prince who enjoins what is contrary to the law of God? Clearly the whole question of the nature of the contract is at once raised. Like Beza, Mornay sets out with his foundations of God and the Decalogue, which form the foundation of all States. To Mornay there is for right ruling a triple contract on which all government depends: the contract between God and the King, that between God and the people, and that between the people and the King.[1] All other govern-ments, like those of Russia and Turkey, are not *imperia sed*

---

[1] Pp. 38, 52, 54.

latrocinia. In true mediæval spirit Mornay conceives the relation of God to the earth as that of a feudal lord to the *coloni* and the *emphyteutæ*. The governors are *Dei beneficiarii et clientes*, and they receive their investiture from God. Divine right and popular sovereignty are not in the least exclusive of each other. " Princes are elected by God and installed by the people." [1] Royalty must be and only can be elective, and he repeats the points urged by Hotman. He also repeats the points raised by Beza on natural right. When the political contract is not expressed, it is understood.[2] We hear much more about the duties of the governors than about their rights. For Mornay takes the ground that the more ample the estate which the vassals enjoy the larger their sense of the debt they owe. Kings are but God's vicars, and has God made them sovereigns without reserving His sovereign rights? Such a question answers itself. Kings are nothing but the vassals of the King of kings. Mornay pursues the matter to its logical conclusion. Just as a vassal may forfeit his fief, so—arguing in the spirit of Wyclif—a king may forfeit his—if he neglects God and allies himself with God's enemies.

Like all the Calvinist writers, Mornay, the ablest of them, does not mean to include everyone under the head of the people. There is the people as distinguished from the populace, and it is the former, the elect, with which he is primarily concerned. The people has also entered into a contract. They have sworn to be God's people, and all their conduct must be in accordance with this oath. If the King orders conduct unbecoming a godly man, is it not quite clear that such a command cannot be obeyed? The king, on his side, has broken the contract. By stratagem and by war—if need be—the King must be brought to a becoming frame of mind. If he is not, the nobility, the representatives of the people in the States General, and the magistrates must step in to exercise their plain duty of resistance to such orders on the part of the Sovereign. Old

---

[1] P. 241. *Cf.* p. 96.

[2] P. 194. *Cf.* generally Lossen, " Vindiciæ contra Tyrannos," *Sitzungsberichte der philosoph-philologischen und historischen Classe der k. b. Akademie der Wissenschaften zu München*, 1887.

Testament precedents are invoked to show that the controlling principle is the covenant or contract. God elected Israel to be His peculiar people, and they on their part prepared an agreement to worship Him exclusively. On the creation of royalty this covenant was confirmed. In a word, King and People are co-contractors to maintain the worship of God. " The People is obliged to the Prince on condition : the Prince is obliged to the People purely and simply. Yet if the Prince does not keep his promise, the People is at liberty, the contract rescinded, and the right, the obligation, annulled." [1]

From the question of obedience Mornay passes on naturally to discuss the question of resistance. Is it lawful, so runs the second question, to resist a prince who is violating the law of God and laying waste the Church? As far back as the early days of the fourteenth century Bartolus held that a king who violates the contract is a tyrant. There are two sorts of tyrants. The first is the titleless tyrant who takes possession of the kingdom by main force and evil practices. Against this tyrant there is no difficulty for Mornay in establishing the right of resistance.[2] " Natural right teaches us and commands us to maintain and guard our life and liberty, without which life is not life, against all injury and violence." [2] It is a clear case of legitimate defence. " The rights of nature, of people, of civil laws, command us to take arms against such tyrants." [3] At the same time we must remember that the titleless tyrant changes to a tyrant with a title if he wins the consent of the people.[4]

The second class of tyrant is the ruler who of set purpose oppresses his people. He has received the kingdom by election or by succession, but he governs it against right and equity. Still, Mornay is anxious to keep criticism within limits, for, after all, are not kings mere men? He may at times misgovern, but is there a purpose behind his misgovernment? Does he despise the law? Does he injure the people? Does he spoil the kingdom? If he does these things, then undoubtedly he is a tyrant.[5] Even then the private man has no *locus standi*. If

[1] Pp. 184-185, 222. [2] P. 208. [3] P. 209. *Cf.* p. 242.
[4] Pp. 214, 216. [5] P. 217.

warnings are useless, if the King is truly a tyrant, then it is for the nobility, the representatives and the magistrates to discharge their duty. Now " not only is tyranny a crime, but it is the chief and the climax of all other crimes." " If the brigand and the sacrilegious are reckoned infamous, if men sentence them to death for their deeds, could we invent a punishment great enough for the crime of tyranny?" Who can doubt that here the heart of Mornay can be felt beating? Who can doubt that here we have Charles IX. and Catherine de' Medici brought vividly before us?

The Old Testament provides instance after instance where kings enforced the worship of God on their subjects and where subjects enforced it on their kings. Here he asks his third question : To what extent is it lawful to resist the Prince who is oppressing and destroying the State? His answer really turns on the point that though God chooses the King, the people install him. The history of the Israelites, of the ancient Greeks and Romans, of the French monarchy, all alike agree in demonstrating the soundness of this conclusion. " No one is born a king ; no king can exist *per se* or can reign without a people. But, on the contrary, a people can exist *per se* and is prior to the King in time." Is not the monarchy hereditary in France? True, but the people voluntarily limit their choice of a king to a single family.

The people possess the right to resist the tyrant, but each individual possesses no such right. For Mornay perceives that the concession of such a right leads to pure anarchy. The people is not—he is emphatic on this point—is not *hoi polloi*, and the people is not a particular individual.[1] For the individual the only duty is submission. The people, in short, means the people organised with legal and legitimate representatives.[2] We must be on our guard not to be led away by a Theudas or by a Barcochba, or an Anabaptist of Münster.[3] Of course God can call an individual like Moses, but such a call is clear and unmistakable. " What are private folk to do if the King constrains them to serve idols? If the magistrates, into whose hands folk have consigned their authority, or, if the

---

[1] P. 61.   [2] Pp. 62, 63.   [3] Pp. 86, 87.

magistrates of the places where the private folk live oppose themselves to it, they obey their leaders and employ all means, as servants of God, to aid the holy and laudable enterprises of those who legitimately oppose evil." Otherwise, they are to support bad princes and pray for better.[1] If, however, the magistrates fail to discharge their duty, then the only resource available is flight.

The fourth question is: " Is it the right and duty of princes to interfere on behalf of neighbouring peoples who are oppressed on account of adherence to the true religion, or by any obvious tyranny? " Here Mornay entertains no doubts, and returns an unhesitating affirmative. The action of Elizabeth of England and of the Protestant princes of Germany in aiding the Huguenots meets with warm approval. There is a difference here between the position of Duplessis-Mornay and that of Calvin. Calvin no more than Bismarck controlled events: they plainly controlled him; but he protests against this control. The disciple, unlike the master, seeks to find a reason for this control, and finds it. The truth is, that between Calvin and Duplessis-Mornay there stands St Bartholomew's Day. It is a pregnant fact that within a decade after 1572 Beza's *Du Droit des Magistrats*, Hotman's *Franco-Gallia*, Mornay's *Vindiciæ contra Tyrannos*, Gentillet's *Discours sur le Moyen de bien Gouverner et Maintenir en bonne Paix un Royaume, contre Nicholas Machiavel*, the *Réveille-Matin*, the *Tocsain*, the *Franc-Turquie*, or *Anti-Machiavel*, and the like, all appeared. The Church of Calvin had stretched from Geneva to Paris, and far beyond the French capital. Imbued with the spirit of this extension, Mornay dreams of human fraternity, a dream that was destined to slumber till 1789. The dream, however, is enshrined in the pages of the *Vindiciæ contra Tyrannos*. Hence Duplessis-Mornay can furnish a reasoned answer to the fourth question on the broadest of grounds. If the Church is Catholic, why should not members of her from England and Germany come to the succour of their distressed brethren in France?[2] For are we not all one body? If the brethren are truly fraternal, they will assist as a matter of course.[3] Everywhere we must

---

[1] Pp. 238, 239. [2] Pp. 246, 247. [3] Pp. 254, 255.

fight religious oppression, and everywhere we must fight civil
and political oppression.[1] Where religious fraternity ceases,
human fraternity ceases. The Jew is not only neighbour to
the Jew but to the Saracen, and indeed to everyone else.[2]

In spite of a provincial accent there is a tone of true
Catholicity in the concluding paragraphs of the *Vindiciæ
contra Tyrannos*. Duplessis-Mornay stoutly holds that " Pour
ce, dit Cicéron, que tous les hommes ont une mesme nature
humanine, nature prescrit et ordonne qu'un homme désire et
procure le bien de l'autre quel qu'il soit, seulement pour ceste
cause qu'il est homme ; autrement il faut que toute association
humaine périsse. Et pourtant, comme la justice a deux fondemens, le premier qu'on ne fasse tort à personne, le second
qu'on aide à chascun, si faire se peut ; aussi il y a deux sortes
d'injustice, l'une de ceux qui font tort à leurs prochains, l'autre
de ceux qui, pouvans empescher le mal, néanmoins laissent
leurs prochains accablez sous iceluy. . . . Oyez l'avis des philosophes payins et politiques, qui ont beaucoup plus sainctement
parlé en cest endroit que plusieurs chrestiens de nostre temps.
. . . Le prince qui regarde, comme en passant le temps, les
forfaits du tyran, les massacres des innocens, lesquels il pourroit
conserver, pour certain, en prenant son plaisir à une escrime
si sanglant, est d'autant plus coulpable que de tyran mesme ;
et celuy qui fait entretuer les autres et plus homicide que ceux
qui tuent." [2]

Recalling the saying of Terence, " Homo sum ; humani nihil
a me alienum puto," he proceeds to remark : " Après avoir en-
core flétri le sophisme de ceux qui repoussent toute intervention
pour secourir les peuples souffrants, mais pratiquent toutes les
interventions pour piller voisins et s'emparer de leur pays." [3]
There surely is a new spirit in the last words : " Brief, si
l'homme se fait loup contre son prochain, qui empesche,
suivant le proverbe, que l'homme ne soit un Dieu à l'homme ?
. . . Et pour clorre ce discours en un mot : la piété commande
qu'on maintienne la loy et l'Église de Dieu ; la justice veut
qu'on lie les mains aux tyrans ruineurs du droit et de toute

[1] P. 257.   [2] Pp. 258-261.   [3] P. 262.

bonne police : la charité requiert que l'on tende la main et qu'on
releve ceux qui sont accablez." [1] After 1572 the Huguenots,
for the most part, had ceased to plead on behalf of toleration.
Catherine de' Medici taught them that they must fight if they
were to win freedom to worship God. Duplessis-Mornay,
however, remained true to the political creed of the Politiques,
for he ceased not to urge ably and eloquently the virtues of
toleration. This quality is present in his *Exhortation aux Estates*,
which makes a direct appeal to the Roman Catholics to exhibit
clemency.

The *Vindiciæ contra Tyrannos* met with a resounding success.
It was reprinted seven times before 1608. Two English
editions appeared during the Civil War and the Revolution,
and were inevitably quoted in Parliament. Fifteen other works
of Duplessis-Mornay were published in England before 1617.
William Barclay devoted two whole books of his *De Regno et
Regalia Potestate adversus Monarchomacos*, published in 1600, to
a refutation of the principles of the *Vindiciæ contra Tyrannos*.
He is cited, for instance, in a petition to Parliament in 1593.
Nor does John Milton disdain to employ a reference to Mornay
in his *Second Defence of the People of England*. Ponet and
Harrington, Sidney and Locke all speak with respect of this
French thinker. Mornay's influence was not confined to the
Old World. In far-distant Connecticut Thomas Hooker quoted
the *Vindiciæ contra Tyrannos*, and John Adams, in his *Defence
of the Constitution of the Government of the United States*, deemed
the pages of the *Vindiciæ contra Tyrannos* valuable. Mornay's
concluding section lifts it out of the dust of the temporal into
the serene air of the eternal.

Calvin's disciples had accomplished their destiny. The main
current of the last half of the sixteenth century had been
steadily flowing in the direction of absolutism. The large
current of public opinion which they formed acquired its force
and volume only by degrees. [2] The reaction against royalty
during the second quarter of the seventeenth century is partly
the outcome of their writings. The fundamental change of
conviction they wrought proceeded slowly and gradually, and

---

[1] P. 264.   [2] Treumann, *Die Monarchomachen*, p. 8.

CALVIN'S DISCIPLES

has been in this respect like the gradual rising of the tide that was to engulf Charles I. and—for a time—the young Louis XIV. The contract theory lies behind the English Revolution of 1688, the American Revolution of 1775 and the French Revolution of 1789.

REFERENCES

Ambert, J., *Duplessis-Mornay*, 1549-1623, Paris, 1847.

Baird, H. M., *Theodore Beza*, New York, 1899.

Baron, J., "Franz Hotman's Antitribonian," *Ein Beitrag zu den Codificationsbestrebungen von xvi. bis zum xviii. Jahrhundert*, Bernæ, 1888.

Baum, J. W., *Theodor Beza, nach handschriftlichen Quellen dargestellt*, Leipzig, 1843-1852.

Becker, H., *Loys le Roi*, Paris, 1895.

Blocaille, E., *Étude sur Fr. Hotman*, Dijon, 1902.

Buisson, F., *Sebastien Castellion, sa Vie et son Œuvre* (1515-1563), Paris, 1892.

Cartier, A., *Les Idées Politiques de Theodore de Bèze*, Genève, 1900.

Chevruel, H., *Hubert Languet*, Paris, 1852.

Cougny, E., *Fr. Hotman, La France-Gaule*, Paris, 1874.

Dareste, R., *Essai sur François Hotman*, Paris, 1850.

De Felice, F., *Lambert Daneau*, Paris, 1892.

Desjardins, A., *Les Sentiments Moraux au XVIe Siècle*, Paris, 1887.

Douarche, A., *De Tyrannicidio apud scriptores sæculi decimi sexti*, Paris, 1888.

Ehinger, L., "Franz Hotman, ein französischer Gelehrter, Staatsman und Publicist des xvi. Jahrhunderts," *Historische Gesellschaft, Beiträge*, etc., Neue Folge, Bd. IV., Hft. 1, Basel, 1839.

Elkan, A., *Die Publizistik der Bartholomäusnacht*, Heidelberg, 1905.

Gerold, C. T., *Duplessis-Mornay et son Influence Politique sur l'Église Réformée la France*, Strasbourg, 1861.

Heppe, H., *Theodor Beza, Leben und ausgewählte Schriften*, Elberfeld, 1861.

Labitte, C., *De la Démocratie chez les Prédicateurs de la Ligue*, Paris, 1841.

Laski, H. J. Ed., *A Defence of Liberty against Tyrants*, London, 1924.

Leber, M. C., *De l'État réel de la Presse et des Pamphlets depuis François Ier*, Paris, 1834.

Lemaire, A., *Les lois Fondamentales de la Monarchie française d'après les Théoriciens de l'ancien régime*, Paris, 1907.

Lenient, C., *La Satire en France ou la Littérature Militante au XVIe Siècle*, Paris, 1886.

Lossen, M., *Die Lehre von Tyrannenmord in der christlichen Zeit.*, München, 1894.

REFERENCES

Lureau, H., *Les Doctrines démocratiques chez les Écrivains Protestants Français de la seconde moitié du XVIᵉ Siècle*, Bordeaux, 1900.

Martin, P. F., *Un Chrétien du XVIᵉ. Siècle, Duplessis-Mornay*, 1899.

Méaly, F. M., *Les Publicistes de la Réforme sous François II. and Charles IX.*, Dijon, 1903.

Moussiegt, *Les Théories Politiques des Réformées au XVIᵉ Siècle*, 1899.

Pears, S. A., *The Correspondence of Sir Philip Sidney and H. Languet*, London, 1845.

Pertuzon, T., *Vie de Théodore de Bèze et son Ministère à Genève*, Strasbourg, 1836.

Picard, A., *Theódore de Bèze : ses Idées sur le Droit d'Insurrection et son Rôle pendant les Premières Guerres de Religion*, Cahors, 1906.

Platzhoff, W., *Die Theorien von der Mordbefeugnis der Obrigkeit im xvi. Jahrhunderts*, Berlin, 1906.

Polenz, C. von, *Geschichte des französischen Calvinismus*, Gotha, 1857ff. (vol. iii. analyses political writings).

Reusch, F. H., *Beiträge zur Geschichte des Jesuitenordens*, München, 1894.

Ricard, L. X., *L'Esprit Politique de la Réforme*, Paris, 1893.

Sayous, A., *Études Littéraires sur les Écrivains Français de la Réformation*, Paris, 1854.

Schaeffler, A., *Duplessis-Mornay considéré comme Theologien*, Strasbourg, 1849.

Schlosser, F. C., *Lèben des Theodor de Beza und des Peter Martyr Vermili*, Heidelberg, 1809.

Tilley, A., *Studies in the French Renaissance*, Cambridge, 1922.

Touchard, G., *De politica Huberti Langueti Vita*, 1899.

Treumann, R., *Die Monarchomachen. Eine Darstellung der revolutionären Staatslehren des xvi. Jahrhunderts* (1573-1599), Leipzig, 1895.

Viguié, A., *Les Théories Politiques Libérales en France. Étude sur la Franco-Gallia*, Strasbourg, 1879.

Viollet, P., *Histoire du Droit Civil Français*, Paris, 1905.

Waddington, A., *De Huberti Langueti Vita*, 1888.

Weill, G., *Le Développement du pouvoir Royal en France pendant les Guerres de Religion*, Paris, 1891.

CHAPTER VI

LEAGUERS AND JESUITS

THE Politiques had been the party of the moderates, the League the party of the immoderates. The Politiques had been fervently patriotic : that indeed had been their *raison d'être*. The tendency of the League was, from the very first, to join an alliance with Philip II. of Spain, then the most powerful monarch alive. The Jesuits and the Guises are the leaders who ally themselves with a reformed and reinvigorated Papacy with the all-powerful Spanish monarchy behind it. In 1562 Prosper de Sainte-Croix tells us that " her Majesty is going towards Blois, so as to be nearer the Huguenot forces, because she fancies they will be able to counterbalance those of the League." [1] 1576 witnessed the definite foundation of the League. Its objects appear in its articles. The first states that it is an association of Catholic princes, lords and gentlemen with a view to the restoration and upholding of the sole supremacy of the Catholic, Apostolic and Roman Church. The second professes to support Henry III., but this support is to be in subordination to the coming States General. The third article seeks the restoration to the Provinces of the realm and the provincial Estates of such rights and privileges as they had in the days of " the King Clovis, first Christian King, together with still better and more profitable liberties and franchises, if such can be found." The oath to be taken on joining " The Holy Catholic Association " sets the authority of the League above even that of the Sovereign.

The Ligue was in form a federation of nobles and Jesuits to defend the Roman Catholic religion. Its motto was " une foy, une loy, un roy." In reality the death of Alençon left Henry of Navarre heir to the throne, and the Ligue was determined at all costs to prevent the accession of a Huguenot. An alliance with Spain was indispensable if this object was to be achieved. The claims of hereditary succession must be attacked if its members were to make any progress with the people. Thus we

---

[1] *Cimber et Danjou*, I. vi., p. 54.

have the singular result that the League was anti-national and was democratic: anti-national because it sought the support of Spain, and democratic because it sought to champion popular rights, to make the *vox Dei* the voice of Guise. Its programme was to redress taxation, to re-establish *Parlements* as something more than Law Courts, and to ensure the calling of the States General at least once in every three years. Like the Huguenots, it resisted stoutly the growing centralisation of all authority. The right to the throne, the Leaguers held, did not lie in lineage. The right to the Crown was elective, and, like the election to the Holy Roman Empire, it was open to any orthodox member of the Church. The people could make or unmake a monarch. The pact by which the throne was held "lay between the King, the People and God." If the King failed to observe the pact, it was simply justice to depose him, for " he and his officers were merely the ministers of the People." Sixtus V. naturally grew restive when he ascertained that Ligueurs desired appointments in the Church to be decided by popular election. The Ligue stood for nationalism whereas it was anti-national. The Ligue stood for democracy whereas it was aristocratic. The Ligue stood for religion whereas it was Jesuit-ridden. It was essentially a selfish body in the Church, and it was every whit as selfish in the State.

For us the interest of the Ligue, with its thirty thousand members, centres in the doctrines advocated. Faced with the existence of an Anglican like Elizabeth on the throne of England and faced with the existence of a Huguenot heir, Henry of Navarre, to the throne of France, its members received new illumination on hereditary right. They came to think that thrones cannot be transmitted by strict hereditary right; that their form of kingly divine right was the doctrine that no heretic could reign; and that the Church owned ultimate authority in matters of succession. In fact, all the questions raised by Calvin and his disciples are raised by the Leaguers and by the Jesuits. Is monarchy based on hereditary right? or on the will of the people? or on the sanction of the Church? To the first question there must be an unhesitating negative, but to the other two, especially in combination, the answer was just as decisively affirmative. Hotman's arguments supplied the Ligue precisely with the ammunition it required. Just as the Huguenots were dropping these arguments the Ligueurs picked them up. Calvinism during the days of the Ligue staunchly sustained royalty. " Dieu," Duplessis-Mornay said in 1586, " prend en main la cause des roys et se tient blessé en leurs personnes." [1] Nor does he stand alone. For we meet with Calvinist *apologias* for monarchy, placing it on a logical basis. The theory of regicide—it was mainly Beza's—was repudiated, and there were loud protestations from the Huguenots when Jacques Clément assassinated Henry III. In fact, the Huguenots and the Ligueurs changed sides, with differences. The former believed in the free examination of religious doctrine; the latter did not. Both agreed in the free examination of political doctrine. The former approved as heartily of absolutism as the latter approved of democracy. The Ligueurs justly reproached the men they termed the " new " Huguenots with substituting the conception of hereditary monarchy for the sovereignty of the people.

It is the fashion of all proselytes to go to extremes, and therefore the Ligueurs became more democratic than the Huguenots had ever been. We now learn that " le peuple fait les rois, il les peut desfaire comme il les a crées." [2] The Calvinist doctrine had been that it was God who created the Sovereign, but now we see more advanced views. Henry of Navarre is told that " la couronne de France n'est point hereditaire, mais elective . . . ; nous obeïssons aux rois et non tyrans." [3] In company of the great Jesuit, Bellarmine, we travel backwards past Machiavelli to the days of Gregory VII., Innocent III. and Boniface VIII.

No one who reads M. Labitte's book on *De la Démocratie chez les Prédicateurs de la Ligue* can remain in any sort of doubt on the vast influence exercised by the priest in politics. Among them we reckon such men as Boucher, Roze, Guincestre and Pigenat. Jean Boucher is easily chief of them all by the number

---

[1] *Mém. de la Ligue*, i., p. 79.
[2] *Ibid.*, iii., p. 528.
[3] *Dial. du Mah.* (Ratisbon ed., 1726), iii., pp. 403, 409.

of his writings and by the fierceness of his zeal. The historian, de Thou, who belonged to his family, approves of his learning but disapproves of his ferocity and of his temper. Voltaire describes him as " seditieux emporté jusqu'à la démence." Men used to speak of Cavour as a statesman of prudences combined with imprudences. Boucher had all the imprudences that gave him weight with such an extreme body as the Ligue. His ambition led him from the Chair of the Humanities at Reims to Paris, and in December 1580, at the age of thirty, he became *recteur* of the University. Nor was he satisfied with an academic position, for he also was appointed curé of St Benoit, where he soon made himself felt. In 1587, under the inspiration of Boucher, the Faculty of Theology had decreed " qu'on pouvoit ôter le gouvernement aux princes qui ne remplissent leurs devoirs, comme l'administration à un tuteur suspect." Henry III. ordered the doctors of the Sorbonne and the preachers to appear at Court,[1] and he addressed them: " Vous êtes motoirement malheureux et damnés," he said, " vous avez calomnié votre légitime roi, ce qui est défendu par l'Ecriture. Je sais votre belle résolution, à laquelle je n'ai point eu égard, parce qu'elle a été faite après déjeuner par trente ou quarante maîtres-ès-arts crottés qui, après grâces, traitent des sceptres et couronnes. Sixte V. a envoyé aux galères des religieux de Saint-François qui avaient médit de lui ; je pourrais faire le pape ; mais je vous pardonne à la charge de n'y retourner plus." Boucher had termed the King a tyrant, and Henry in turn termed him " le plus méchant de tous," and the charge was perfectly true. The usual Huguenot grounds for regarding the monarch as a tyrant are that he possesses no title to the throne, and that if he does he governs his subjects entirely for his own benefit. Boucher adopts these grounds, and adds another, for he holds that an heretical king is a tyrant. Of course he thinks that the Pope possesses the power of releasing subjects from their allegiance. In fact a king, as such, acquires no status until he receives the consecration of the Church. The Huguenots were always uncertain when a

---

[1] Félibien, *Hist. de Paris*, ii., p. 1165; Fleury, *Hist. Eccles.*, xxxvi., p. 133 ; Lestoile, *Journ. de Henri*, iii., p. 234ff.

king was a tyrant. The Leaguers and Jesuits were always certain, for was not a tyrant a heretic?

Boucher's *Histoire tragique de Gaveston* created a sensation on its appearance.[1] It is a translation of Walsingham's account of Gaveston, the favourite of Edward II., and Boucher brings the account up to date. There is an almost incredible impudence in some of the current allusions. Take one of them. "Ainsi finit Gaveston; nous en espérons autant, quand il plaira à Dieu vous chasser, comme un proditeur de la patrie, de ce royaume, ou bien (de peur que ne retourniez comme fit Gaveston) de vous oster de ce monde." In 1588 his *De justa Abdicatione Henrici tertii* informed the learned of what he conceived to be the situation of France at that moment. His conclusions, true to the spirit of Gregory VII., are that—

(1) The right of deposition of the King is double: one belongs to the Church and the other to the people.

(2) The Pope or his representatives can abrogate the laws, change the constitutions, provided they unbind the people from the oath of obedience and that they warn the human flock saved by Christ to trust in a most sure guardian. This proposition seems so simple, so natural, to Boucher that he does not rely on reasons, but gives nothing but historical examples.

(3) The sovereignty of the people cannot be contested. It is the people who make kings; the right of election is superior to the right of heredity, and even when a king has been elected the commonwealth still preserves its power. The people have the right of life and death over kings. Monarchy is only, as with Beza and his fellow-writers, a mutual contract, and we must maintain the old French formula: " Mettre les rois hors de paige." In this fashion the Crown has passed from the Merovingians to the Carlovingians, and from the Carlovingians to the Capetians.

Then comes the application of these three points to Henry III. He is, we learn, " parjure," " assassin et parricide," " meurtrier-sacrilegé," " fauteur d'hérésie," " schismatique,"

---

[1] On Boucher and his pamphlets *cf.* K. Glaser, *Zeitschr. für franz. Spr. und. Lit.*, xiv. (1917-1919), p. 299ff. *Cf.* Krebs, 121ff.

"simoniaque," "sacrilège," "magicien," "impie," and "anathême." The people ought to exercise their deposing power because the Sovereign is "perfide," "lésé la majesté de la république," "tyran et ennemi de la patrie," "cruel," "inutile au gouvernment," "adultère," "coupable de tous les vices," and "condamné de sa propre bouche."

It is not a little startling to ascertain that the *De justa Abdicatione Henrici tertii* won a large measure of approval when published. The Faculty of Theology of Paris University unhesitatingly recommended it as a work of edification. True, the style is lively and the illustrations forcible, but there is a total want of considered judgment about every line of it.

The fame of Boucher continued to grow to such an extent that the University of Paris chose him as Vice-Chancellor,[1] and men openly spoke of him as the true king of the Ligue.[2] In spite of threats from Mayenne he continued to negotiate with Parma in the interests of the Infanta. In truth, the firm supporter of Boucher was not the young Duke of Guise but the great Philip II. himself. Anxious for the Duke of Guise to marry the old Infanta, Boucher naturally makes light of the Salic law. The fundamental law of France is not the Salic law. "La loi fondamentale d'un estat est de n'avoir qu'une religion, la catholique, et de régler tout à ce niveau, fût-ce mesme la loi salique."[3] Put plainly, this means that the States General can summon the Infanta Isabella to the throne of France.

The leading idea in Boucher's political philosophy is the union of theocracy with democracy, the union of the old papal supremacy of the Middle Ages with the popular sovereignty of the Calvinists. In the States General, chosen by the people, he sees, as Hotman sees, the supreme power to lie. The monarchy is their work: "Les Estats ont le roy en jurisdiction directe de leur authorité souveraine et puissance naturelle. . . . Ce sont eux en qui, naturellement et originairement, reside la puissance et majesté publicque qui faict et establit les roys qui sont par le droict des gens et non de droict divin

---

[1] Du Boulay, *Hist. Univ. Parisiens*, vi., p. 808.
[2] *Journ. de Henri*, iii., p. 315a.
[3] *De justa Abdicatione*, pp. 584, 595.

et de nature." [1] The purport of the following passage is unmistakable: " La puissance de lier et de délier demeure aux peuples et Estats qui sont éternellement gardes de souveraineté, juges des sceptres et royaumes, pour en estre l'origine et la source ; comme ceux qui ont faict les roys, non par nécessité ou constrainte, mais par leur franche volonté, estant en eux de choisir de plusieurs sortes de gouvernement celuy qui leur est le plus utile. Et si bien tel surtout et le plus ordinairement celuy de monarchie (comme aussi nous l'advouons pour ce que la vérité est telle), ne laisse pourtant ceste liberté de demeurer ès peuples pour choisir de leur plein grec este forme de gouvernement, mesme pour destituer et changer les roys selon que le cas y eschet : estant en tout véritable que c'est des peuples que sont les roys et non des roys les peuples, veu que le peuple est la base sur le roy pose." There is, we freely admit, nothing particularly novel in these views if they come from a Huguenot, but they come from the king of the Ligue, and possess therefore an importance all their own. [2]

According to Bayle, Roze [3] was quite as extreme in his views as Boucher. Eloquent and ambitious, Roze was able to fill the churches where he preached. [4] Chaplain to the King, in 1583 he was consecrated as Bishop of Senlis. [5] Deserting his benefactor, Henry III., he turned over to the Ligue, becoming one of its most fiery supporters. The official positions held by Roze and Boucher gave them at all times commanding influence in Paris and in the provinces. The Jesuit Guincestre believed in audacious statements as firmly as either Roze or Boucher. He made little of the death of Catherine de' Medici because she was inclined to favour the heretics. [6] He preached against " la vie, gestes et faicts abominables de ce perfide tyran Henry

---

[1] De justa Abdicatione, pp. 249, 263.   [2] Ibid., p. 250.
[3] Le Duchat, Lelong, F. Daniel and Anquetil identify Roze with Rossaeus. Cf. Labitte, De la Démocratie de la Ligue, p. 295ff.; Reusch, Beiträge zur Geschichte des Jesuitenordens, p. 27; Schlosser, Die Lehre vom Widerstandsrecht, p. 52.
[4] Davila, i., p. 382; ii., p. 333.
[5] Gallia Christiana, iii., p. 1023.
[6] Félibien, Hist. de Paris, ii., p. 1175; Lestoile, Journ. de Henri, iii., p. 279a.

de Valois" against whom he "desgorgea une infinité de vilainies et injures," saying *inter alia* that he invoked devils.[1] All the *curés* of Paris, save three, belonged to the Ligue, and Guincestre powerfully backed the teaching of these men. One of them Guincestre informed : " Vous avez conscience de rien ; moi qui consacre chaque jour, en la messe, le précieux corps de Notre-Seigneur, je ne me ferais aucun scruple de tuer le tyran, à moins qu'il fût a l'autel, et ne tînt une hostie en main." [2] At the Notre-Dame, Pigenat eulogised the Guises, and then brusquely asked his congregation if there was not one of them zealous to revenge the death of the great Lorrainer with the blood of the tyrant who condemned him to be massacred.[3]

The teaching of men like Boucher and Roze, of Guincestre and Pigenat, permeated not merely the congregations but also the colleges. In 1561 in the college of Lisieux we meet with Jean Tanquerel, a bachelor of divinity, defending the following thesis : " Savoir, s'il est en la puissance du pape d'excommunier un roy et donner son royaume en proye et d'affranchir les sujets du serment de fidélité qu'ils ont en luy, quand d'ailleurs il se trouve qu'il favourise les hérétiques." [4] Nor is Jean Tanquerel by any means a solitary student. The religious orders, the *curés*, and the doctors of the Sorbonne all stood solidly behind the Ligue. Paris, as always, proved to be the chief scene of the popular frenzy, and indeed we know nothing quite like it in our annals, not even the temporary madness over Dr Sacheverell. The Duchess of Montpensier openly patronised the preachers, boasting that through them she exercised more influence than her brother Henry through his armies.[5] The death of Henry of Guise enabled the Ligue to throw off its outward regard for monarchy, and it put forth all its democratic tendencies.

---

[1] Matthieu, *Hist. des dern. Troubles*, p. 182. Cf. *Sat. Ménipp.*, i., pp. 156-157 ; Lestoile, *Journ. de Henri*, iii., p. 285a.

[2] Lestoile, *Journ. de Henri*, iii., p. 289b.

[3] Fleury, *Eccles. Hist.*, clxxviii. § 79; Félibien, ii., p. 1176; Lestoile, *Journ. de Henri*, iii., p. 283a.

[4] Pasquier, *Œuvres*, 89a.

[5] Lestoile, pp. 244a, 241ff.

With the exception of Lorraine, the rest of France shared the madness of Paris. A few prelates, the Archbishop of Tours for instance, tried to control their priests, but the priests utterly broke away from their control. The chapter of the cathedral of Rheims forbade *curés*, under the penalty of excommunication, to give absolution to any of their parishioners who refused to sign the Ligue.[1] Of course Jacques Clément, the Dominican, was proclaimed from every pulpit as " le bienheureux enfant de Dominique, le saint martyr de Jésus-Christ."[2] If any dared to stigmatise as regicide the hero who had delivered France " de ce chien Henri de Valois " the preachers marked him down as a fit example for popular vengeance. Clément, as a matter of fact, consulted the theologians of his order, and they advised him that he could rightly slay a tyrant.[3] Finding the sermons she heard not sufficiently violent, the mother of the Duchess of Montpensier harangued the people on the joyful news that the tyrant was dead. Madame de Montpensier received the mother of Jacques Clément, and in sermons the congregation were invited to look upon her as the mother of a martyr.[4] In churches candles were lit before statues of Clément himself.

Sixtus V. rejoiced as keenly over the murder committed by Clément as Gregory XIII. rejoiced over St Bartholomew's Day. Anquetil tells us that " il [*i.e.* Sixtus V.] s'echappa dans la première joie que lui causait la fin violente de Henri de Valois, jusqu'à la comparer, pour l'utilité, a l'Incarnation du Sauveur, et pour l'héroïsme du meurtier, aux actions de Judith and d'Eléazar."[5]

Seven days after the death of Henry III. the Ligue put its teaching into practice, for it proclaimed the Cardinal de Bourbon King under the title of Charles X., a title as real as that of our own Henry IX. Meanwhile the deed of Clément was fully

---

[1] *Conseil salutaire*, p. 51.
[2] Mezeray, *Hist. de France*, iii., p. 659.
[3] *Ellinger*, pp. 405, 406.
[4] Lestoile, *Journ. de Henri*, iv., p. 3 ; Saint-Foix, *Essais sur Paris*, iii., p. 63.
[5] *Esprit de la Ligue*, iii., p. 94.

exploited. Bourgoing presented his view of the " Estrange mort de Henri de Valois, advenue par permission divine." [1] To him the act is one of Divine vengeance. An angel, according to him, appeared to Jacques Clément, showing him a naked sword, and saying : " Je te viens acertener que par toy le tyran doit être mis à mort." In the issue we are assured that " l'ame du meurtrier n'avoit laissé de monter au ciel avec les bienheureux." By the year 1589 it is quite plain that the pamphleteers of the Ligue have inextricably bound together the sovereignty of the Pope and the sovereignty of the people.

The democratic views of the Ligue might have passed muster, for were there not mediæval French precedents pointing in the same direction? What did not pass muster was the anti-national policy, for how could an alliance with Spain be other than against the best interests of France? This weak joint in the Ligue armour was exposed by Michel Hurault, grandson of Michel de l'Hôpital, in his *L'anti-Espagnol*. The author openly proclaimed that Philip II. had corrupted the preachers and the Jesuits, who were all acting under his orders. The Duke de Nevers, whose Catholicism was undoubted, gave a rude shock to the Ligueurs by his *Traité de la Prise d'Armes*. Mayenne plucked up courage to administer summary chastisement to the Seize in 1591, the leading spirits of the Ligue, for their murder of President Brisson. The Politiques also began to raise their head. Jacques Gillot, a councillor of *Parlement*, was a wealthy and important member of this party, and gathered at his house such men as Florent Chrestien and Jean Passerat, Pierre Pithou and Pierre LeRoy, and Nicholas Rapin. They were all scholars or men of scholarly instincts, revolted by what was happening in their country. In 1593 appeared their joint work, the *Satire Ménippée*. No less than four editions were demanded in less than three weeks. In the sixth edition the title was changed to *Satyre Ménippée de la Vertu du Catholicon*, and its success afforded a welcome proof that the people of Paris were becoming somewhat tired of the Ligue. Seven speeches hold up to ridicule the ambitious aims of men like Mayenne, who wants to be king ; of the Archbishop of Lyons,

---

[1] *Archiv. cur. de l'Hist. de France*, Ser. I., vol. xii., pp.384-395.

Pierre d'Espinac, who wants a cardinal's hat; of Rieux, who seeks amid the general disorder the opportunity of plundering his neighbours; of the Bishop of Senlis, Guillaume Roze, who also wants this hat; and of the Cardinal Legate, who seeks to advance the interests of Spain and those of the Holy See. The tone of the satire suggests what a curse the self-seekers have been to their country. After all, *la patrie* ought to count as a force in the lives of men. It threw ineffaceable ridicule on such men as Boucher and Guincestre. We encounter "les curez des grosses paroisses avec soufflets d'orgues dont ils souffloient au derrière de plusieurs manants qui se laissoient emporter au vent. D'aultres se tenoient tout debout le gueule bée et ouverte, et les dits curez leur souffloient en la bouche et les nourrissoient de vent." [1]

How much satire undermined the prestige of Rome is plain to all who turn over the leaves of Sebastian Brandt's *Ship of Fools*, the *Vadiscus* and other pungent writings of Ulrich von Hutten, the *Epistolæ Obscurorum Virorum* of Crotus Rubianus and others, the *Facetiæ* and the *Triumphus Veneris* of Heinrich Bebel, and the *Pantagruel* and *Gargantua* of Rabelais. Is satire the price mankind pays for freedom? Its roll of service includes the assaults of Luther on the monks, of Bacon on the schoolmen, of Pascal on the Jesuits, of Butler on the Puritans, of Voltaire and Anatole France on superstition, and of Bentham on lawyers. Shaftesbury was the opponent of enthusiasm— that is, fanaticism—which, like all convictions, he would have exposed to the test, not of persecution, but of wit and humour. Satirists like Rapin realised the sagacity of this expedient. The *Satire Ménippée* circulated on all sides, creating and moulding public opinion in a direction in no wise favourable to the Ligue. Rapin parodies Roze so skilfully that the discourse the Bishop of Senlis is supposed to have delivered is a veritable masterpiece. What the battle of Ivry effected for Henry of Navarre on the field, the *Satire Ménippée* effected in the minds of men. In spite of Boucher, the thoughtful did not like the idea of the young Duke of Guise marrying the old Infanta Isabella, and they

---

[1] *Satire Ménippée* (Nodier's ed.), p. 196.

doubted if Boucher was right in rejecting the Salic law as fundamental. The folios of Claude de Seyssel and Guillaume Postel, of Pasquier and Pierre Dupuy, and of Antoine Loisel were once more taken down, and the arguments in favour of this law re-perused. On the other side were ranged the preachers, Jean Guyard and Antoine Hotman, brother of François. The learned read the folios and the unlearned the *Satire Ménippée*, and the outcome was that all alike desired a peaceful solution. The prospect of endless wars of religion pleased no one. When Henry of Navarre discovered that Paris was well worth a mass, the days of the Ligue were numbered. His decision disposed of the contract theory in France down to the days of Rousseau. Heredity—not contract—was the principle Henry IV. came to represent.

Men like the Jesuit Guincestre had been among the main supports of the Ligue, and it is not a little interesting to find the most undemocratic body in the world, the Jesuits, advocate advanced democratic doctrine.[1] Such views can be found in the *Controversia Anglicana* of Becanus, the *Commentarius Exegeticus* of Gretser, the *Apologia pro Henrico Garneto* of Eudæmon-Joannes, the *Next Succession to the Crown of England* by Doleman, who really was Parsons, and the *Defensio Ecclesiasticæ Libertatis* of Adam Tanner. Parsons, like Boucher, urges that James I. should be set aside in favour of a Roman Catholic. Tanner supports the Pope in his quarrel with the Venetian Republic. These are all pamphlets of more or less fleeting interest. Of another order are such works as the *De potestate summi Pontificis* (1611) of Bellarmine, the *De Rege et Regis Institutione* (1599) of Mariana, the *De Justitia et Jure* (1593 [pt. i.] ; 1600 [pt. ii.]) of Molina, and the *De Legibus ac Deo Legislatore* (1612) of Suarez, a man who stands for sheer ability in the same rank as Bellarmine. All these writers pretty well agree that the Church is the most perfect of all governments. The author of the Church is Christ, Whose vicar is the Pope. Hence He

---

[1] *Cf.* the fine article of J. N. Figgis in *The Transactions of the Royal Historical Society*, New Series, vol. xi. (1897), pp. 89-112; Ranke, *Die römischen Päpste in den letzten vier Jahrhunderten*, ii., p. 123ff., and his *Zur Geschichte der politischen Theorien*, *Sämt. Werke*, xxiv., pp. 223-236.

refused to allow the people to make Him a king, for His power was from above.[1] When He said that His kingdom was not of this world He thereby indicated the plenitude of power given to the Pope immediately from God. Though the cardinals elect the Pope, his real election comes from God.[2] This will help men to grasp the position that as Christ is the real King of all States, other sovereigns are to look on the interference of the Pope simply as the action of another subordinate, whose position is yet higher than theirs.[3] There are utilitarian reasons for the existence of the secular State: there are none for the existence of the religious State. At the head of the Church stands the infallible Pope, whose power is absolutely unlimited.[4] He is *legibus solutus*, and may not, like the people of Calvin's disciples, alienate the *plenitudo potestatis*. With an eye on the history of the Middle Ages it flits across the mind of a writer like Santarelli that it is just possible that the head of the Church may turn heretic and may, therefore, require the judgment of the Council.[5] Such a thought is dismissed as unworthy, and the Black Army of Roman Catholicism, then as now, regard the Pope as infallible.

As is the moon to the sun, as is the body to the soul, so is the secular State to the religious State of the Jesuits. Though Osorius [6] denies that government is a consequence of the Fall, other writers like Salmeron stoutly uphold this patristic notion.[7] The end of the one State is temporal peace, and the end of the other eternal happiness. Is there any possible comparison between them? Besides, did not Jeremiah plainly say: " I have set thee above nations and kings, to build up and break down "? Did not St Peter receive the two swords which Christ said were enough and not too much? Was not Abel the first priest and

---

[1] Santarelli, *Tractatus de Hæresi*, i. 31-32.

[2] Jean de Salas, *Disputationes in Primam Secundæ S. Thomæ*, viii. 3. *Cf.* Dante, *De Monarchia*, iii., whose view is the same.

[3] Eudæmon-Joannes, *Apologia*, p. 81.

[4] Osorius, *Conciones*, iii., p. 42.

[5] Santarelli, *De Hæresi*, i. 31, 5.

[6] *Conciones*, iii., p. 39. *Cf.* Jean de Salas, in *Thomam Aquinatis Quæstiones*, vii. § 1.

[7] *De Justitia et Jure*, Tr. v., disp. 46; Tr. v., disp. 22.

Cain the first king? Does not the Old Testament testify to the superiority of priests over kings? Since the advent of Christ there is a contract, explicit or implicit, by which none but orthodox rulers are acceptable. Does not the baptismal vow come under the heading of a contract authorising the Church to depose heretical kings?

The tone of the Jesuit authors towards the secular State is as disapproving as it is approving towards the religious State, yet Suarez presents the State as a secular institution. The tyranny of the Sovereign is the object of their perpetual dread. As Machiavelli separated his aspects of the State in practice, so the Jesuits separated theirs in theory, for no writers have more acutely analysed the temporal and the spiritual powers. They allow the King as law-maker and the clergy to stand outside the jurisdiction of the secular judge. The power of the Pope is unlimited and comes directly from God. The power of the King is limited and comes only indirectly from God. " Rex est minister Dei, et reipublicæ pro-rex "—such is the doctrine taught. Hence every sovereign comes originally from popular appointment. There is a tacit revolt against the Aristotelean notion that men come together in the State in order to realise the good life which otherwise is not possible. Such a view conflicts with the perfectness of the Church. The Jesuits deem that God drives men to union, and from this union unconsciously comes political power. Lessius, however, declares that the commonwealth can have no dominion over the lives and property of its subjects, for that they have not themselves, and cannot therefore resign to the community.[1]

Political power lies with the people, who are by nature all free and equal. Is Adam an obstacle to such a view?[2] Not in the least. For is it not obvious that the patriarch possessed economic, not political, power? The whole community possesses power, which it exercises through the King or the ruling body it elects. Such a condition is more often implicit than explicit.

---

[1] De Justitia et Jure, II. c. iv., d. 10. Cf. Molina, Tr. iii., diss. 1 ; Jean de Salas, vii. § 2.

[2] Adam Tanner, Defensio Libertatis Ecclesiæ, II., cc. iii., iv.; de Salas, Disput., vii. § 2, 114.

Medina thinks that since a republic is instituted solely for the common good, this is to be regarded as a sort of fundamental law; and this is pretty well the general tone on the subject. One matter in this implicit contract requires attention. It is to be assumed that the Sovereign belongs to the orthodox faith. Becanus mentions as well the definite original contract between King and people.[1] The sovereignty of the people precedes all actual rule and it forms a part of the *jus gentium*. Hence it is easy to justify the deposing power. As a matter of fact, since St Peter is to feed the sheep of the Church, is it not perfectly certain that such a command carries with it the exclusion of the wolf from the State? Why did Christ say that He came not to send peace on earth but a sword, to divide the son from the father, if the Church is not to be able to separate sovereigns from subjects when the need arises?

Clearly if we allow the deposing power we also allow tyrannicide. There are two classes of tyrants—usurpers and despots. Usurpers may be slain at sight, despots may not be. The whole commonwealth must expressly or tacitly condemn them, though the tacit condemnation opens up a wide field. Mariana asks in his *De Rege et Regis Institutione*, published in 1599: Is it right to kill a tyrant? He answers Yes. In default of statesmen " this right belongs to each individual who means to risk his life for the benefit of the State." [2] Later he asks: Is it lawful to poison a tyrant? Yes, it is lawful, but it is to be given to him in such a fashion that he is not aware of it; for if he is, it is suicide, and suicide is a sin.[3] The Jesuit Bonarsans tried to stir up the Romans to assassinate Henry IV. He did not, however, find a warrior to raise his arms against " this savage beast." [4] The Jesuit Rossaeus defined the tyrant to be killed. He is simply a tyrant. Now a " heretic is every king who mixes himself with ecclesiastical questions, who does not chase from the Church the heretics, who does not prevent the meetings of heretics." [5] As the outcome of such teaching Jean Chastel endeavoured to assassinate Henry IV. in 1594. He

---

[1] Becanus, *Controversia*, 150. *Cf.* Krebs, 6off., 141ff., 146, 207, 212.
[2] *De Rege*, i. 7 ; Ellendorf, p. 403.   [3] Ellendorf, p. 406.
[4] *Ibid.*, p. 409.   [5] *Ibid.*, p. 416.

merely wounded him on the lip. Meanwhile a Jesuit published his *Apologie pour Jehan Chastel, Parisien, exécuté à mort, etc., par François de Vérone*. According to this author, Henry was only a self-styled king: he was really a heretic. Now anyone possesses the right to murder a heretic. Take the decree of *Parlement* in 1560 as a proof of this, for the then President, Le Maistre, allowed anyone to kill a Huguenot. Moreover, the Sorbonne in 1589 decided that the French, without any scruple of conscience, could arm themselves against the King, and that each individual could kill him.

The Jesuits take up the ideas of Gregory VII., and drive them to as great extremes as Boucher and Roze. With the Dominicans, they violently affirm the purely natural foundation of the State and the civil power. They take up this conception simply to abase the State and to exalt the Church. Molina and Mariana, Bellarmine and Suarez stand at the head of these curious monarchomachs among the Jesuits. From Gregory VII. onwards the Church considers the State as the work of the devil and of sin. The Church is holy, founded by God. From this holy Church the State, which was conceived and born of sin, takes the legitimisation of its being. From paganism the Middle Ages took over the idea that the origin of the State is to be sought in an instinct of nature or of the human will. The most impassioned supporters of natural right are the Dominicans and the Jesuits. In their views they tend to fall back on the law of nature—that is to say, a conception of the State that is largely philosophical, largely civil and lay. The secularism of these writers is only too transparent. They all, especially Mariana, write like men of the world to whom theology is almost an accident. Their theorists agree, on the whole, that the civil commonalty rests on natural right; that in virtue of natural right, sovereignty belongs to the commonalty; and that the right of sovereignty precedes the commonalty, authorised and compelled by the law of nature to delegate it. Suarez sums up the general position: " A Deo tanquam naturalis juris auctore. Deus, per legem naturalem. Jure naturali, ergo a Deo." All power comes from God means that God is the Author of nature, whence all power comes. Once formed, no individual can prevent the commonalty from being sovereign. Nothing comes from the will of men, but everything comes from the nature of things.[1] Like Grotius, Suarez is willing to allow the commonalty to change or alienate its sovereignty. In a sense it is all natural right, but in another sense it is theocracy, and Gierke is quite right in noting its theocratic foundation.[2]

To the Jesuits there is eternal law in accordance with the Divine nature, and all other law ultimately comes from it. There is natural law implanted in the instincts of man. A fifteenth-century writer, Gabriel Biel, took occasion to point out that God is the Author of natural law only in the sense that He is the Author of reason. Vasquez, curiously enough, makes the natural law independent of God.[3] His position depends on the fact that he regards natural law as the embodiment of reason, not of caprice, taking up the attitude of the average man to the reign of law in science till Henri Poincaré upset it. The *jus gentium* is not quite the same as the law of nature. There are natural liberty and equality in the former, and both are absent in the latter. The *jus gentium* is not so much natural as positive, for all those things which belong to the law of nations were first only matters of civil law, but by degrees spread to other nations and States. As soon as anything was invented and accepted by any one man or region, it then was only a matter of civil law, not of the law of nations. According to Jean de Salas, the *jus gentium* was the sovereign act of the whole human race at its entering upon a common life, and may not be repeated without common consent.[4] On the other hand, the position of a Grotius is taken up by that notable thinker, Francis de Victoria, and Suarez,[5] Lessius[6] and Castro-Palao,[7] who assume that the *jus gentium* owes its force to custom, thus resting on common consent and the practice of civilised nations.

---

[1] Gierke, *Johannes Althusius*, p. 67. *Cf.* p. 68, n. 30.
[2] Gierke, *ibid.*, p. 68, n. 30.
[3] *Commentarii*, disp. cl. 3.   [4] *De Legibus*, vii. 2, 3.
[5] *Ibid.*, ii. 19.   [6] *De Justitia et Jure*, Bk. II., c. ii., d. 3.
[7] *Theologia Moralis*, Tr. iii., disp. 1, p. 3.

Suarez wrote an immense work in ten books, entitled *Tractatus de Legibus ac Deo Legislatore*, published in 1612. He assumes the existence of the law of nature that has been recognised by the most eminent philosophers of paganism, by St Paul, St Augustine and St Thomas Aquinas. He takes up the position that Christ was the true Light that lighteth *every* man that cometh into the world. No one, not even the Pope, can abrogate or enfeeble a single one of its precepts.[1] Some of its commands are imperative and some permissive, and accordingly he proceeds to distinguish the two classes. The State possesses the right to determine the conditions of property, to make laws regulating contracts and wills. " The nation," he thinks, " can renounce a right for a greater good." [2] Clearly it can sacrifice the rights of individuals for what it regards as the common good. In following natural law, Suarez practically takes from men their rights, leaving them simply their duties. The punishment of heretics he regards as unjust from the point of view of natural law, but just—or at least legitimate—from the point of view of the practical needs of society.[3] The Church, as the perfect State, must be able to invoke the secular arm of the State in order to punish the unfaithful and the heretic. She is an institution equipped with all that is necessary to a self-contained body, perfect in organisation, in institutions, and in the Divine right to everything necessary to the carrying out of her temporal ends.[4] War is right against the enemy abroad, and it is right against the enemy at home. Slavery seems to him to be a sort of penalty pronounced by the law of nations against those who take up arms in order to wage an unjust war,[5] a position to which Dominic Soto was utterly opposed.

The positions taken up by Suarez are tolerably common to all the Jesuits of the sixteenth century. He defends the people against the Sovereign, he defends the poor against the rich, he defends liberty against absolutism, and he teaches the

---

[1] *De Legibus*, Bk. II., chap. iv. § 8. *Cf.* Krebs, pp. 49, 149.
[2] *De Legibus*, Bk. II., chap. xiv. § 20.   [3] *Ibid.*, Bk. III., chap. xi. § 10.
[4] Robertson, *Regnum Dei*, pp. 251, 254ff., 257, 274, 281, 322, 346.
[5] *De Legibus*, Bk. II., chap. xviii. § 9.

doctrine of tyrannicide. With Calvin, he holds that all power comes from God,[1] and he also holds that the people possess sovereignty. " Civil power," he teaches us, " springs from natural right; but the determination of the measure and the form of government of this power is left to the will of men." [2] On monarchy he bestows approval, though the monarch must never forget that he is the delegate of the people, not the representative of God. Consequently all the ruler's acts must be in accord with public opinion. When men speak of hereditary rights in a monarchy, all they mean, when we examine the statement, is the persistence of common consent to the advantage of the ruling dynasty, or the translation of the mandate of the people from a prince to his descendants. For every dynasty presupposes the existence of a first prince who has received his authority from the nation. The pact between prince and people forms the basis of civil society. The case of Adam is not pertinent, for he refutes Filmer by anticipation in showing that Adam possessed patriarchal—not political —power. The pact does not permit the people to change or depose their prince, for Suarez holds with Calvin the supreme sovereignty of God.

The democratic doctrines of Suarez are the common property of his fellow-Jesuits. So far as we know, the first of them to proclaim the sovereignty of the people is Lainez, the second General of the Order, at the Council of Trent, in the sitting of 20th October 1562. Afterwards it appeared in 1598 or 1599 in the *De Rege et Regis Institutione* of Mariana, the greatest of the Jesuit writers.[3] This work is dedicated to Philip III., the son and successor of Philip II., and, at Loyasa's suggestion, was written for the political education of the future king. In it Mariana embodies conclusions he had formed when he was writing his well-known *History of Spain*. " The people," holds Mariana, " can force the King to obey the laws which they have decreed. They possess the right of overthrowing the

---

[1] *De Legibus*, Bk. III., chaps. ii. and iii.
[2] *Ibid.*, Bk. III., chap. iv. § 1.
[3] *Cf.* Cirot, *Mariana historien* (Paris, 1905); Sommervogel, *Bibl. de la Soc. de Jésus*, v., pp. 557-559.

Crown, disobeying the King and punishing him with death, if it is necessary." [1] Nor is the view of Rossaeus's *De Justa rei Publicæ in Reges impios et Hæreticos Auctoritate*, published in 1592, in any wise different from that of other members of the Society of Jesus. Take some quotations. " From what has been said on the origin and the power of kings, it follows that the power of Christian kings is limited; that they are set over the citizens and the State so that the people can extend, restrain, change, and, if circumstances demand it, completely suppress their government and institute another, under another form." [2] Here is the origin of civil power in the eyes of Rossaeus: " The civil power springs from human right and does not come from nature, but from the customs of the people." " It is neither God nor nature that orders it [*i.e.* the government], but only the will, the caprice, the free decision of the people." What renders power legitimate " is the solemn act of coronation by the bishops." [3] The perfect State dominates the whole situation.

Like the judicious Hooker, Suarez desires to see no law passed unless with the acceptance of the people : public approbation is essential. [4] From the consideration of laws there is an easy transition to the breaker of them, notably the chief breaker, the tyrant. On tyrannicide he holds two different doctrines in his *Treatise on Laws* and in his *Defence of the Catholic Faith*. In the third book of the *Treatise* he keeps strictly to the opinion of St Thomas Aquinas. [5] Against a legitimate king who orders unjust things, who proclaims iniquitous laws, there is no other course save passive resistance, for an iniquitous law is not really a law. Against a usurper, against a tyrant, in the classical acceptation of the term, the right of the nation will allow us to use force against such a common enemy. Still, submission is better than revolt provided that the oppression is not intolerable; for insurrection itself is often a thousand times worse than tyranny. The *Defence of the Catholic Faith* takes a more advanced position. [6]

---

[1] Ellendorf, p. 374.　　　　　[2] *Ibid.*, p. 393.
[3] *Ibid.*, p. 383.　　　　　[4] *De Legibus*, Bk. III., chap. ix. § 4.
[5] *Ibid.*, Bk. III., chap. x. §§ 7 and 8.　[6] Bk. VI., chap. iv. §§ 5-7.

In it he maintains that a tyrant or a usurper, whatever his conduct may be, can be killed by the first citizen if there is no other means of curtailing his power. The decisive words are: " Hunc tyrannum quod titulum interfici posse a quacunque privata persona, quæ sit membrum reipublicæ quæ tyrannidem patitur, si aliter non possit rempublicam ab illa tyrannide liberare."

When the legitimate Sovereign abuses his power there are two cases to be distinguished. In violating the laws he may prove a menace to one's own folk, one's son or daughter, or he may prove a menace to the State itself. In practice the distinction of the two cases amounts to nothing, for both, we are taught, can legitimately fall under the steel of the assassin. If our property is attacked we can, in view of the dangers to the public peace, abandon our claims. If the State is attacked, then murder, private murder, is legitimate when it offers the sole means of deliverance. " Et tunc certe licebit," so run the words, "principi resistere etiam occidendo illum, si aliter fieri non possit defensio." [1]

In his *De Rege et Regis Institutione*, published in 1599, Mariana sets out with an account of man in a state of nature—unique in sixteenth-century thought—that might readily have been found in the pages of Rousseau.[2] In order to overcome the disadvantages of this state, men submitted to the leadership of a man of capacity.[2] Few and simple laws came into being because there was doubt about the impartiality of the monarch and there was also doubt if men could control their passions. Since then laws have increased in number and complexity till " we are as much burdened by laws as by vices." [3] In order to have society there must be laws and a personal ruler. Democracy is possible and plausible,[3] but royalty possesses advantages. Kings originally possessed absolute power because such power was required for the repression of war and of anarchy. When, however, they abused their authority, society imposed on them the check of law. Absolutism, in the opinion

---

[1] *Defence of the Catholic Faith*, Bk. III., chap. iii. § 8. *Cf.* especially Bk. IV., chap. viii.

[2] *De Rege*, Bk. I., chap. i. [3] *Ibid.*, Bk. I., chap. ii.

of Mariana, is the fruit of brigandage. Far from sharing the common admiration of Cæsar and Cyrus, and Alexander the Great, he looks upon them with horror.

Hotman and Suarez are at one in lamenting the decline of the Estates in France and in Spain respectively. The latter pleads for the Estates of the Realm where bishops, nobles and representatives of the cities can meet together.[1] Such Estates formulate and guarantee the law of the land, which controls the Sovereign, and they regulate taxation, succession to the throne, and the religion of the State. He assigns a prominent part to the bishops.[2] He is careful to show that the Prince is under the fundamental laws of the realm, the restraints imposed by public opinion, the laws of nature and the laws of God.

There is not a little in Book III. to remind us of chapter eighteen of *The Prince*. The analysis of the aims and methods of royal activity provides us with matter for thought. You can have peace at home at the price of war abroad, and war abroad is therefore desirable. Normally a just cause for the outbreak of war can be found, but whether it can or cannot, we must provide occupation for our soldiers, and the readiest method is to allow incursions into foreign lands. True, they may pillage unrighteous cities, but, if necessary, they may also indulge in pure piracy and brigandage.[3] The Prince must, at all costs, maintain the good will of his subjects. Hope and fear are, in his judgment, as potent as Machiavelli deemed them to be. Actual rewards and punishments do not aid the Prince much, but the expectation of such rewards and punishments is very effective. If a subject seeks what you cannot give him, do not send him away in a state of despair. Suggest that it may be possible—some day—to bestow upon him what his soul covets.[4] With Machiavelli he is in thorough accord in delegating all unpleasant duties to officials and in reserving all pleasant ones to be performed by the King in person. Occasionally there will be popular tumults, for such is human nature. Let them be suppressed by the most ruthless officials, and then visit the latter with severe penalties for any possible

---

[1] *De Rege*, Bk. I., chap. viii.　　[2] *Ibid.*, Bk. II., chap. viii.
[3] *Ibid.*, Bk. III., chap. v.　　[4] *Ibid.*, Bk. III., chap. xv.

infraction of their duty, and " thus all the wickedness will be punished and yet the people will remain well disposed towards the Prince." With Louis XI., Mariana agrees that a prince who knows not how to dissimulate knows not how to reign. In principle, our author will not allow that it is right to lie or to deceive, but a lie or a deception is a present help in time of trouble. His words are : " Mentiri et fallere nunquam principi concedam ; sed nisi consilia tegere didicerit, omnibus etiam noxiis benignitatem ostentare, multis sæpe difficultatibus implicabitur."

We reserve for the last his discussion on the question, "An tyrannum opprimere fas est ? "[1] Resistance can be defended on the grounds of the sovereignty of the people and of the natural sense of mankind, as exhibited in history. Tyrannicide is stoutly defended. Of the murder of a tyrant—that is to say, of a usurper—there is no difficulty. Jesuit theologians and philosophers are in thorough agreement that the tyrant can be killed by the very first comer without any sort of process, without the intervention of a court of justice or of a political assembly, above all when the assemblies of this class have been destroyed. Nor is there any need to consult public opinion, for such a government should not be permitted to exist for a single day. Sacred and profane history attest the righteousness of tyrannicide. Are there not the examples of Ehud and Judith? If men require more examples, are there not Thrasybulus, Timoleon, Harmodius, Aristogeiton and Brutus? At the beginning of the fifteenth century Jean Petit justified the murder of the Duke of Orleans, but Mariana condemns his doctrine because he had argued " quasi tyrannum opprimere fas sit privata auctoritate. Quod non licet."

The question of the legitimate king is far more delicate. Such a king, when he turns tyrant, has *ipso facto* lost the good will of his subjects. If he persists in ruining the State, the assembly of the people must warn him of the danger of deposition he is incurring. If their warning remains unheeded, then,

---

[1] *De Rege*, Bk. I., chap. vi. *Cf.* Buchanan, p. 38 ; Rossaeus, cap. ii. and iii. ; Boucher, Lib. III., cap. xv. ; Danaeus, 42 ; Salm., p. 82 ; *De Jur. Mag.*, p. 232ff. ; Salamonius, p. 82 ; *Réponse Apologetique à l'Anti-Coton*, p. 31.

though not till then, the private individual may exercise the terrible right of tyrannicide. Such a man deserves well of his country. "Præclare cum rebus humanis ageretur, si multi homines forti pectore invenirentur, pro libertate patriæ vitæ contemptores et salutis."[1]

It is but a short step from the theory of Suarez and Mariana to the practice of Clément the Dominican and Ravaillac, of Louvel and Cadoudal, of the Gunpowder Plot. According to Mariana, by the assassination of Henry III. sovereigns can "learn, by this memorable teaching, that impious projects do not remain without vengeance." Mariana represents the murderer as "Æternum Galliæ decus." Mariana indeed deems Clément "has made for himself a great name by assassinating Henry III. He has avenged murder by murder, and washed the blood of the Duke of Guise in the blood of the King."[2] In 1610, on the assassination of Henry IV. by Ravaillac, the *Parlement* of Paris condemned Mariana's teaching as insidious, impious and heretical. In spite of the democratic theories of Suarez and Mariana, by their advocacy of tyrannicide they undid all the good that the rest of their writings did. What is the benefit of transferring power to the people if at the same time this power is really given to any man with a dagger or with a revolver? The State is thus placed at the mercy of the first fanatic who wished, for any reason, to remove the rulers of the country. Such doctrine is not democratic: it is anarchic. The Secret Councils of Venice and Rome countenanced political assassination. We now know that Gregory XIII. pardoned beforehand those who attempted the murder of Queen Elizabeth.[3] Nor is this a plan of the past. For the Nihilists of Russia and the Sinn Feiners of Ireland successfully employed it. There is no distinction, however, in favour of political assassination. Murder is murder. No refinement

---

[1] *De Rege*, Bk. II., chap. vi.; J. M. Prat, *Recherches Historiques et Critiques sur la Compagnie de Jésus*, p. 242ff.; Lossen, p. 55.
[2] *Ibid.*, Bk. I., chap. vi. *Cf.* Krebs, pp. 47, 49, 51, 60-61, 65-66, 108ff., 121, 134, 167, 169, 174-175, 177, 182, 189.
[3] A. O. Meyer, *England and the Catholic Church under Elizabeth*, pp. 270-272.

of sophistry, no tricks with truth, can condone these offences against the laws of God and man. At all times and in all places they should be denounced and unflinchingly punished. Those who gain power by political assassination, and who employ or suffer murderers to be employed, are more guilty—in the eyes of the statesman as well as the moralist—than the men and women themselves.

We are by no means sure how far Jesuit doctrines are in any wise democratic. Their writings during the sixteenth century always impress us as pure *livres de circonstance* to a greater degree than any other writings. They are reactionary, not revolutionary. They were democratic in the reign of Henry III. because the Sovereign was against them, and therefore they were against the Sovereign. Were they against the absolutist sway of a Louis XIV.? Then they preached absolute submission to the man who proudly proclaimed himself, in Voltaire's words, "L'État, c'est moi."

REFERENCES

Butler, Sir G., *Studies in Statecraft*, Cambridge, 1920.

Döllinger, I. von, and Reusch, F. H., *Die Selbstbiographie des Cardinal Bellarmin*, Bonn, 1887.

Döllinger, I. von, and Reusch, F. H., *Geschichte der Moralstreitigkeiten*, Nördlingen, 1889.

Douarche, A., *De Tyrannicidio apud scriptores sæculi decimi sexti*, Paris, 1888.

Eberings, *Historische Studien*, Berlin, 1906.

Egger, *Études d'Histoire et de Morale sur le Meurtre Politique*, Torino, 1866.

Ellendorf, J. O., *Die Moral und Politik der Jesuiten*, Darmstadt, 1840.

Figgis, J. N., *The Divine Right of Kings*, Cambridge, 1914.

Franck, A., *Réformateurs et Publicistes, Dix-Septième Siècle*, Paris, 1861.

Gerkrath, L., *Franz Sanchez*, Wien, 1860.

Gierke, O. von, *Johannes Althusius und die Entwicklung der naturrechtlichen Staatstheorien*, Breslau, 1913.

Grisar, H., *Iacobi Lainez Disputationes Tridentinæ*, Innsbrück, 1886.

Heron, D. C., *An Introduction to the History of Jurisprudence*, London, 1860.

Huber, J. N., *Der Jesuitenorden nach seiner Verfassung und Doctrin, Wirksamkeit Geschichte characterisirt*, Berlin, 1873.

Kaltenborn, K. von, *Die Vorläufer des Hugo Grotius*, Leipzig, 1848.

REFERENCES

Krebs, R., *Die politische Publizistik der Jesuiten und ihrer Gegner in den letzten Jahrzehnten vor Ausbruck des Dreissigjährigen Krieges*, Halle, 1890.

Labitte, C., *De la Démocratie chez les Prédicateurs de la Ligue*, Paris, 1841.

Lenient, C., *La Satire en France ou la Littérature Militante au XVIe Siècle*, Paris, 1886.

Lossen, M., *Die Lehre von Tyrannenmord in der christlichen Zeit.*, München, 1894.

Lureau, H., *Les Doctrines démocratiques des Écrivains Protestants Français la seconde moitié du XVIe Siècle*, Bordeaux, 1900.

Mueller, H., *Les Origines de la Compagnie de Jésus : Ignace et Lainez*, Paris, 1898.

Platzhoff, W., *Die Theorien von der Mordbefeugnis der Obrigkeit im XVI. Jahrhunderts*, Berlin, 1906.

Raderus, M., *De vita Petri Canisii de Societate Jesu, Sociorum e Germania primi, Libri tres*, München, 1614.

Reusch, F. H., *Der Index der Verbotenen Bücher*, Bonn, 1885.

Reusch, F. H., *Beiträge zur Geschichte des Jesuitenordens*, München, 1894.

Saitta, *La Scolastica del Secolo XVIe e la Politica dei Gesuiti*, Torino, 1911.

Schlosser, J., *Die Lehre vom Widerstandsrechte der Untertanen gegen die legitime Fürstengewalt bei den Katholiken des 16. Jahrhunderts*, Bonn, 1914.

Tilley, A., *The Literature of the French Renaissance*, Cambridge, 1904.

Werner, K., *Franz Suarez und die Scholastik der letzten Jahrhunderte*, Regensburg, 1861.

Wiskemann, D. H., *Die Lehre und Praxis der Jesuiten*, Cassel, Herzefeld, 1858.

Weill, G., *Les Théories sur le Pouvoir Royal pendant les Guerres de la Religion*, Paris, 1892.

CHAPTER VII

BRITISH SPECULATORS

THE ancients and the mediævalists ignored an idea which permeates the whole of our social philosophy, the idea of progress. Not only the philosophers but even the lawyers of antiquity and of the Middle Ages erred, as the founders of the great religious orders erred, in trying to substitute uniformity for variety, tradition for invention, and stability for movement. In these respects we have outgrown the wisdom of Greece and the sagacity of Rome. We may, however, find matter for thought in the reflection that the freest and most enlightened nations of antiquity, the nations rich beyond all others in vigour and originality of individuality, understood by freedom something quite different from that which the term conveys to our ears. The mediæval ideal, like the classical, lay in the past, and the best hope for men was to recover something of what they had once possessed. In the twentieth century the Golden Age is fondly believed to be coming, but in the fifteenth and sixteenth centuries all thinkers looked backwards.

The opening up of a new continent, the discovery of new planets, and the export to Europe of the new silver created a ferment which left the minds of men ready to receive fresh impressions. The results of the labours of Columbus and Copernicus are familiar to all, but the part that the muleteer of Potosi played is sometimes forgotten. He was travelling along a steep mountain-side. His mule slipped, and in his anxiety to save himself he clutched at a bush, which yielded a little to his pressure. The tearing up of some of the roots disclosed a mass of silver, and in this seemingly accidental fashion the metal once more altered the destinies of mankind. In the domain of matter, cause and effect exercise a widespread and well-nigh irresistible influence. The silver comes to Europe, raising prices, making labour dear, and thereby changing the tillage system to pasturage. In the agricultural world men are upset, and as the cake of custom is irretrievably smashed they are not so unwilling to hear strange doctrines as their fathers would have been.

The age was powerfully attracted to the study of mathematics and astronomy, and in the latter subject the writings of three such Germans as Cardinal Nicholas Krebs, named Cusanus, from Cues, near Treves, of Regiomontanus and of Georg Peuerbach, the most eminent astronomer of his time, were notable. Long before Nicholas Copernicus, Cusanus demonstrated the fact of the earth's motion and its rotation on its axis. Regiomontanus and Peuerbach were true scientific observers and calculators. The former wrote a work on the planets which the latter edited; it fell into the hands of Copernicus, inducing him to devote his life to astronomy. What they failed to achieve through their own labours they achieved through the labours of another. Indeed this is a characteristic of their work. In his factory at Nürnberg, Regiomontanus produced astronomical instruments, globes, compasses and maps. Nürnberg sea-compasses were among the most famous in Europe, rivalling the reputation of its maps. Regiomontanus improved the astrolabe, invented Jacob's staff and founded the scientific annual called *Ephemerides*. The improved astrolabe and Jacob's staff enabled men to calculate distances by ascertaining the height of the sun. Columbus, Vasco da Gama and Magellan could not have succeeded in their ventures had it not been for the assistance afforded them by this astrolabe and Jacob's staff. When Columbus and Vespucci sailed for the shores of India, they brought with them the calculations which Regiomontanus had worked during the thirty-two years for his *Ephemerides*. By his employment of these calculations Columbus predicted an eclipse of the moon in the West Indies. Among the pupils of Regiomontanus were Martin Behain and Bernard Walther, who proved a generous patron. Behain of Nürnberg was a cosmographer and a navigator, who at sea verified information that had reached him. For example, he traced on his map the route to the East Indies, round the Cape of Good Hope, six years before its discovery by Vasco da Gama. Magellan was chivalrous enough to admit that he found the Straits, afterwards given his name, on a map of Behain's, and it was this map which suggested to him the idea that it might prove a route to the Molucca Islands.

In the geographical discoveries of the century Regiomontanus could claim that he and his pupils had a share. He could also justly claim that he was among the earliest to perform experiments. Not content with his own work, he laboured to found a school, or at least a system. He devised problems for his students and offered prizes for their solution.[1] He lectured on his results to the citizens of Nürnberg, for he was anxious that all educated men should share his knowledge. Fortunately for him, Bernard Walther was wealthy, and he enabled Regiomontanus to establish a printing press with the object of producing learned mathematical and astronomical works [2]; he also published the first popular almanac. Walther built for him the first good observatory in Europe, equipping it with the best instruments of the day. Regiomontanus was the first astronomer, at least of the Western world, to calculate the size, distance and orbits of the comets, thus enlarging the scientific horizon of men.

The scientific spirit of men like Cusanus, Peuerbach and Regiomontanus took generations before they affected other thinkers, and generations more before they touched the middle classes. " The die is cast," wrote Kepler, " I have written my book. It will be read ; whether in the present age or by posterity matters little. It can wait for readers. Has not God waited six thousand years for one to contemplate His works?" Adam Smith's *Wealth of Nations* was published in 1776 : Free Trade was not completely in force till 1846. Edmund Burke dissected all the arguments in favour of the Penal Laws with incomparable force from 1760 to 1787 ; they were not abolished till 1829. A generation passed before the poetry of either Wordsworth or Browning was at all widely read. Even to-day it is a generation and a half before the thought of Cambridge or Oxford reaches the mind of the educated man : in the sixteenth century it was probably three or four generations. In one respect this century was fortunate. The geographical discoveries produced such far-reaching results that they com-

[1] J. Ashbach, *Geschichte der Wiener Universität*, i., p. 533.
[2] There is a list in A. Ziegler, *Regiomontanus*, pp. 25-37.

pelled men to listen to the astronomer: the crust of prejudice in their brain, the cake of custom in their life, was so rudely broken that the shock obliged them to receive the new as well as the old. What Darwin accomplished in the nineteenth century by his *Origin of Species*, what Newton accomplished in the eighteenth by his *Principia*, Columbus and Copernicus accomplished in the sixteenth. On the natural man matters immediate, like the work of Vasco da Gama and his fellow-geographers, exercise more influence than matters remote, like that of Regiomontanus and his fellow-astronomers.

To the voyages of Amerigo Vespucci, Sir Thomas More (1480-1535) owes the form of the imaginary commonwealth he described in 1515 and 1516. He tells us that the traveller who had "joyned himselfe in company with Americke Vespuce" remained in South America with some four-and-twenty companions. They roam through many countries and at length make their way westwards home by land and sea. The imaginary traveller is Hythloday, or Expert in Nonsense; and in his wanderings his attention directs itself to the island of Utopia, or Nowhere. Here the injustice and inequality dominant in the Old World are quite unknown, and the vision of the perfect State he sees is one which surely would in many ways have satisfied the soul of Plato. More, the best man of his time, stands out against the background of eternal truth as he points the way to justice, which reigns supreme in his imaginary island. He longed with intense earnestness to see a true community—not a rich and educated aristocracy existing side by side with poor ignorant peasantry—one people, prosperous and educated through all its different classes. This yearning for the weal of all humanity marks the advance of the Utopian ideal on the Greek. Progress is seen most distinctly in the growing recognition of the dignity of man and woman. On the other hand, the Athenian love of art, of beauty, is sadly wanting in the island.

The moral code of Utopia allows of suicide, divorce and slavery under certain restrictions. No one is allowed to kill himself without public authority, but in cases of incurably painful disease the priests and the magistrates recommend the

patient to find his way out of life. Divorces are granted for
adultery and for the "intolerable wayward manners of either
party," the guilty party in that case living ever after in infamy,
and single. Breakers of wedlock are reduced to slavery; if such
slaves prove unruly they are put to death "as desperate and
wild beasts." Simplicity reigns in the Utopian institutions.
The laws, writes Hythloday, the mouthpiece of the future
Lord Chancellor of England, are very few; so that "every
man is a cunning lawyer." He shows himself three centuries
in advance of his age by stigmatising the Draconian legislation, which, in this country till the commencement of the last
century, hanged a man for stealing goods to the value of forty
shillings. The end of all punishment he declares to be reformation, "nothing else but the destruction of vice and the saving
of men." He has also a clear anticipation of our ticket-of-leave
system.

Hythloday is a warm advocate of communism. More himself raises objections; but his mind appears to be spoken
through the mouth of the Portuguese mariner, for, like Plato,
More prefers public duties to private, and is somewhat im-
patient of the importance of relations. To Platonic inspiration
is due the impassioned argument in favour of community of
goods. To the *Republic* is directly traceable the leading feature
in the constitution of the happy island—namely, equality in all
things—and this is also the cardinal tenet of the Socialism of
our day. Do the more revolutionary passages of the *Utopia*
express the author's real convictions? This is of course a
difficult question to decide. But it is beyond controversy that
the publication of the story of Ralph Hythloday opened the
first chapter of modern Socialism. According to Michelet,
Vico (1668-1744) wrote not for his own age, but for that
which was to dawn half-a-century after his death; not for the
eighteenth century, but for the nineteenth. Similarly More
wrote not for his own age, but for that which was to dawn
for Winstanley and the Diggers a century after his death;
not for the eighteenth century, but for the nineteenth and
twentieth. The import of More's book lies above all in the
freedom with which it examined and criticised principles which

nearly all political treatises assume. It boldly put forward the assumption that society might be conceived in some radically different form. While the Reformers were calling on the civil powers to arm against the downtrodden peasants of Germany, More was earnestly pleading the cause of the workers. Social and political arrangements are tested by the convenience and claims of the working classes. The recognition of the community as a social organism, the proclamation of the right and duty to work, the State organisation of production, the abolition of coinage, are all articles in the Socialistic creed. Promulgated in the *Utopia*, they have set in motion a train of speculation of which the full effects are not yet seen.

More is as well aware of the virtues of toleration as L'Hôpital or Spinoza. Some of the Utopians adore the sun, others the moon, others a star, others a deified man—the philosophers among them—a Great Unknown. But they all acknowledge one supreme Deity, called Mithras. All manner of religious opinions are tolerated, except those that deny the immortality of the soul or the retributive justice of God in the next life. Heretics on either of these two points are excluded from holding office; otherwise they may go unmolested, but they are not allowed to argue on behalf of their opinions before an ignorant multitude. They are excluded because their views are deemed to be degrading to mankind and therefore to incapacitate those who hold them from governing in a noble temper. Utopus, the first king of the island, ordered toleration " as not knowing whether God, desiring manifold and diverse sorts of honour, did not inspire sundry men with sundry kinds of religion." Moreover, the people were " persuaded that it is not in a man's power to believe what he list. No, nor they constrain him not with threatenings to dissemble his mind and show countenance contrary to his thought. For deceit and all manner of lies they do marvellously detest and abhor."

What we may call the Church by law established teaches three articles: that there is a God, that the soul of man is immortal, and that God will reward the good and punish the wicked. The priests are " of exceeding holiness, and therefore few," thirteen only in each city, with a bishop at their head;

they are chosen by the people by ballot. Besides religious ministrations, they instruct the young and superintend public morals, and their rebuke, like the *nota* of the censors of the Roman Republic, carries with it deep disgrace. Religion found its centre in the family rather than in the congregation ; each household confessed its faults to its own natural head, the patriarch. The Christians of Utopia were in doubt whether they could not elect their own priests, thus dispensing with apostolic succession or with the authority of a bishop consecrated by the Pope—points of the very essence of Catholicism.

More's attitude to toleration is most clearly seen in the following : " King Utopus made a decree that it should be lawful for every man to favour and follow what religion he would, and that he might do the best he could to bring others to his opinion, so that he did it peaceably, gently, quietly and soberly, without hasty and contentious rebuking and inveighing against others. If he could not by firm and gentle speeches induce them into his opinion, yet he should use no kind of violence, and refrain from displeasant and seditious words. This law did King Utopus make not only for the maintenance of peace, which he saw through continual contention and mortal hatred utterly extinguished ; but also because he thought this decree should make for the furtherance of religion. Though there be one religion which alone is true and all others vain and superstitious, yet he did well foresee that the truth of the one power would at last issue out and come to light. But if contention and debate should be continually used—as the worst men be most obstinate and stubborn, and in their evil opinion most constant—he perceived that then the best and holiest religion could be trodden underfoot and destroyed by most vain superstitions. Therefore all this matter he left undiscussed, and gave to every man free liberty and choice to believe what he would."

The sentiments are fine, but they are not a whit more fine than those of Tertullian, who lived thirteen hundred years before Sir Thomas More. In a remarkable passage Lord Acton succeeds in showing not only that in the early part of the sixteenth century More did not stand alone in his belief, but

that his belief was practised on a fairly wide scale from about
1510 to 1530. In England and in Germany no doubt the old
persecuting spirit was not exorcised, but in many other countries
it was. Erasmus warmly extols the light and liberty which he
found in Rome in 1515. This is all the more surprising when
we remember that the *Encomium Moriæ* had been published
in 1512, censuring bishops, cardinals and popes. Leo X.
displayed very great tolerance, accepting the dedication of
Erasmus's edition of the Greek Testament.

Across the Channel the Inquisition found its powers severely
curtailed, and the French bishops refused to bring before it
those who were accused of heresy. Even Lutheranism was
allowed to spread with the connivance of the Court of Francis I.,
and for many years the converts persisted in regarding the
King as their defender. In Savoy the unfortunate Waldenses
were given a quiet time. Undoubtedly the Hapsburgs continued to persecute, though it is worthy of remark that in 1526
Ferdinand permitted the existence of the principle *cujus regio,
ejus religio*, and that in 1532 Charles V. spoke nobly of the
rights of conscience. The tendency to toleration may also be
witnessed in other fragments of the Holy Roman Empire.
In Denmark the Diet of 1527 assigned equal rights to Protestants and Roman Catholics. In spite of the evil memories
of the Hussite Wars, in 1512 the Bohemian Roman Catholics
and the Utraquists made an agreement in perpetuity that the
rich and poor of both Churches should enjoy freedom unrestrained. In Venice the members of the Greek Orthodox
Church worshipped God as their conscience dictated. The
laws of Emmanuel the Great protected the Judaising heretics
from the fury of the Portuguese mob. The fall of Granada
removed the remains of political power from the Moors, yet,
powerful as Torquemada was, Ferdinand the Catholic refused
to allow the Inquisition to claim them as under its sway. The
last instance is not perhaps quite fair. Society did not acknowledge the same obligations to a Turk as to a Christian. Toleration was not so readily shown to him who deviated from the
faith into which he had been baptized, though it might be
displayed to others.

More, then, was not exceptional in advocating the cause of toleration. In the fourteenth century theological thought and intellectual speculation were much more free than in the sixteenth. He had the example of thinkers in the past, and he had also the example of the practice of the present. He was, however, partly old and partly new. In the latter capacity he thought first and last of truth, while in the former he cared for good and evil. He is a memorable instance of the truth of Coleridge's aphorism that " he who begins by loving Christianity better than truth, will proceed by loving his own sect or Church better than Christianity." Toleration was ideal; but what if it brought evil as well as good, if it destroyed the unity of the Church he loved, if it achieved the disintegration and misery of his country?

When More wrote the *Utopia* he had no personal experience of heretics or of the assaults they might make on life and property, though his knowledge of contemporary history should have enlightened him. When he became Lord Chancellor, the sack of Rome, the horrors of the Peasant Wars, and the Anabaptist ideas altered his views. Then were advocated such doctrines as that a simple agreement between man and woman is all that is necessary to wedlock; that the baptism of a child of Christian parents is not only superfluous but even wrong; or that the murder of Archbishop Sudbury by the mob was a righteous act. " Friend Roper," he said wistfully, " I pray God that some of us, high as we seem to sit upon the mountains, treading heretics under our feet like ants, live not to see the day when we gladly would wish to be at league with them, to let them have their churches quietly to themselves, so that they would be contented to let us have ours quietly to ourselves." It is plain that he regarded England and Europe as on the brink of " red ruin and the breaking up of laws." In the true spirit of the More of later days Burke maintained: " I will not enter into the question how much truth is preferable to peace. Perhaps truth may be far better. But as we have scarcely ever the same certainty in the one we have in the other, I would—unless the truth were evident indeed—hold fast to peace which has in his company charity, the highest of the virtues." [1] To the Irish thinker as to the English the secular and the lay elements were fundamentally one. " In a Christian commonwealth," declared the former, " the Church and the State are one and the same thing, being different integral parts of the same whole." [2] Both were alike in regarding the utter dependence of national life and its continuity on religious consciousness, without which, to use the language of Burke, " no one generation could link with another " and " men become little better than the flies of a summer." The paradox in Plato which declares that it is in vain to expect any man to be a great statesman unless he cares for something greater than politics applies to both.

To draw a parallel between the attitude of More to the German Reformation and that of Burke to the French Revolution is tempting and profitable. Each regarded the movement of their day as religious and proselytising. Each perceived intuitively that there could be no peace between the new spirit and the old, and each desired to use force to crush the former. Nothing is so much in the mind of both as the conception of harmony and organic unity, and nothing is so much removed from it as forces making for confusion and disorder. Both believed in the moral government of the universe, and both felt certain that the Reformation and the Revolution respectively would not only subvert political institutions but would rob the world of its faith. Both saw the men of the new régime call in question the obligations of society, civil and religious, and both shrank from the right of revolution, advocated in the sixteenth and in the eighteenth centuries respectively.

To More civilisation and order were tolerably synonymous. He might hold views, advanced for his day, upon the distribution of property, the domestic relations, and the like, yet he held firm faith in civilisation based upon Catholicism. His mind realised in part the shock given to the principle of authority by the changes of the fifteenth century, while the whole man did not realise that the social system most urgently demanded reorganisation. Its foundations had been undermined by the events of 1348, and had been completely

---

[1] Speech, 6th February 1772.   [2] Speech, 11th May 1792.

undermined by those of 1492. The stones of the seemingly stately edifice had received a blow from which they could only hope to recover by fresh support. More's reading of history revealed a past devoid of radical changes. The living organism of human society had worked almost mechanically for hundreds of years. Its members, its circulation, its nervous system, and a sort of skin, consisting of its laws and institutions, seemed still the same. One is not altogether surprised to find that More was unable to see that a simultaneous set of changes had burst the worn-out skin. Dominated by the notion of unity, how could he adapt himself to the alteration from this idea to that of ceaseless flux? The law of status was going, the law of contract was coming. The environment which had once rendered a universal Empire and a universal Church necessary now rendered both an absolute impossibility. Man was no longer immutable, but mutable; one empire was replaced by many nations. In its essence the Reformation was individual-istic, and by consequence nationalistic. The centre of gravity was shifting from cosmopolitanism to nationalism. It is pathetic to note that More failed to perceive this momentous change, while Henry VIII. saw its signs. The noble-minded judge was fighting for an effete mediævalism, but his egotistic master proved the friend of progress. The tragedy of More's life—it was the tragedy of so many lives of the scholars of the Renais-sance—was that he builded not bettter but *other* than he knew, and set in motion forces whose outcome was destined to fill him with horror.

Law always lags behind public opinion, and the gap between the two was indefinitely widened in the early part of the six-teenth century because of the concentration and the accelera-tion of the forces of revolution. The Chancery Court, when it sentenced Bilney and Tewkesbury, Bayfield and Bainham to their terrible death, draped the scaffold for the Lord Chancellor himself. Another law court, the *Parlement* of Paris, when it refused to register Turgot's edict regarding the *corvée*, opened the prison door through which so many of the aristocracy of France passed to the guillotine. More's court endeavoured to control the new individualism, and in so endeavouring created intense feeling, leading to the awful persecution of the years to come.

The Christians were few in the reign of Nero and were comparatively numerous in that of Diocletian. The Politiques of the sixteenth century would have approved of persecution in the former instance and condemned it in the latter, because the cost of extirpating heresy under Diocletian would have been prohibitive. More agreed with Burke that " circumstances (which some gentlemen pass for nothing) give in reality to every political principle its distinguishing colour and discriminating effect." [1] In view of the altered circumstances More would have persecuted in both instances. The transformation wrought in him can be clearly seen in his relations to the censorship of books. Caxton did not venture to print a Bible in the vernacular because Wyclif's translation was forbidden. " On account of the penalties," remarks Sir Thomas, " ordered by Archbishop Arundel's constitution, though the old translations that were before Wycliff's days remained lawful and were in some folk's hands, yet he thought no printer would likely be so hot to put any Bible in print at his own charge, and then hang upon a doubtful trial whether the first translation was made before Wyclif's days or since. For if it were made by Wyclif, it must be approved before the printing." The dilemma was awkward, and Caxton avoided it by not publishing the Bible in the vernacular.

The *Index Librorum Prohibitorum* in England was established in 1526, thus preceding the first *Index* on the Continent by twenty-five years and that of Rome by thirty-three years. On 7th March 1528 Tunstall, Bishop of London, gave More the privilege of reading heretical works in order that he might confute them. The following year appeared the *Dialogue*. In it More departs from his tolerant principles, though he admits that in ancient times heretics were not punished till they became violent themselves. He attacks fiercely the heresies of Luther, which he plainly regards not as an error but as a crime. He vindicates the burning of heretics, " and showeth also that the clergy doth not procure it, but only the good and politic

---

[1] *Reflections on the French Revolution.*

provision of the temporalty." Traces, however, of his Utopian belief remain : " For in case the Turks, Saracens and Paynims would suffer the faith of Christ to be peaceably preached among them, and that we Christian men should therefore suffer in likewise all their sects to be preached among us, and violence taken away by assent on both sides, I nothing mistrust that the faith of Christ should much more increase than decay." In chapter fifteen his present conviction persuades him to declare " that princes be bounden to punish heretics, and that fair handling helpeth little with many of them."

William Tyndale (c. 1492-1536) at once issued *An Answer to Sir Thomas More's " Dialogue,"* and in 1532 appeared *The Confutation of Tyndale's Answer* in a portly volume of three hundred and twenty-six pages. The progress of Lutheranism is noted in the preface, which prays " our Lord to send us now some years as plenteous of good corn as we have had some years of late plenteous of evil books. For they have grown so fast and sprung up so thick, full of pestilent errors and pernicious heresies, that they have infected and killed, I fear me, more silly simple souls than the famine of the dear years destroyed bodies."

When the reformer turns politician, swift is his fall from his ideal. The fate of Wyclif, the fate of Savonarola, did not suffice to save More. From belief in toleration as a principle he came to look on it as an expedient. Goethe says that the condition of all greatness is devotion to an idea, and in this sense More was not great. The preface of the *Confutation* affords melancholy proof of the transformation of the writer : " Seeing the king's gracious promise in this point, I reckon that, being his unworthy chancellor, it apperteineth to my part and duty to follow the example of his noble grace, and after my poor wit and learning with opening to his people the malice and poison of those pernicious books, to help as much as in me is, that his people abandon the contagion of all such pestilent writing, may be far from all infection, and thereby from all such punishment as following thereupon doth oftentimes rather serve to make others beware that are yet clear, than to cure and heal well those that are already infected; so hard is that carbuncle catching once a core, to be by any means well and surely cured. Howbeit God so worketh and sometimes it is. Toward the help whereof, if haply it be incurable, then to the clean cutting out that part for infection of the remnant am I, by mine office, in virtue of mine oath, right especially bounden.

" Wherefore I reckon myself deeply bounden to show you the peril of these books whereof the makers have such mischievous mind that they boast and glory when their ungracious writing bringeth any man to death. And yet make they semblance as though they were sorry for it. And then Tyndale crieth out upon the prelates and upon the temporal princes, and calleth them murderers and martyr-quellers, dissimuling that the cruel wretch with his wretched books, murdereth the man himself, while he giveth him the poison of his heresies, and thereby compelleth princes, by occasion of their incurable and contagious pestilence, to punish them according to justice by sore painful death, both for example and for infection of others."

It is obvious that the More of the *Confutation* or of the coarse and scurrilous *Vindicatio Henrici VIII. a calumniis Lutheri* is no longer the More of the *Utopia*. The *Dialogue* proves that he often attended the examination of heretics. As Lord Chancellor he swore " to use all his power to destroy all manner of heresies." It was a duty he discharged with zeal and with more mildness than Mr Froude is willing to allow. As a judge he was obliged to enforce the statute *De Hæretico Comburendo*, and he cannot be held responsible for the law of the land. The stories of his cruelty to prisoners rest on the assertion of Foxe, and these seem to be untrustworthy. Mr Froude urges that in the case of Thomas Philips and John Field the Chancellor was guilty of illegal action. Mr Seebohm, however, has ably proved that the responsibility rests with the Bishop of London, and that the charge against Field was not heresy.

Henry VIII. had staked his all on the new Church Settlement, and the chief enemies of Church and State were the heretics who denied the Royal Supremacy. The English must accept one Church in one national State. The acknowledgment of papal authority was therefore heresy to the former and treason to the latter. More was unable to follow this development of the King's policy, though in the *Utopia* he had questioned the Divine institution of the Papacy. The way in which he paid the price of his refusal is one of our priceless heritages. When he first took office he nobly stipulated that he must " first look to God, and after God to the King." By the singular irony of history the persecutor of the consciences of others died himself a martyr for the rights of conscience.

For a time More broke away from the spell of the past, the spell of custom, the spell of tradition, but in the end they proved too much for him. He was unable to understand to the very last that on the one hand the new tendencies at work were identifying the policy of Henry with that of the nation, while on the other hand the Papacy was steadily becoming anti-national. The conciliar movement attested the truth of the change in one direction, while the papal policy after the Council of Trent attested it in another.

King Utopus himself, though he saw the absurdity of one man compelling another by force to accept his own belief, saw also that if it came to civil strife the best and holiest of religions would be trodden under foot by the vainest and the most superstitious. It is in vain for Dr Gairdner to plead this exception and to argue that it was *because* More was by nature so tolerant that he entertained such a strong dislike to heretics who, in acts and deeds as well as in words, were quite ready to outrage the most cherished beliefs of the community. Thomas Paine asserted that Burke bid men sorrow for the plumage of the bird when it was dying. " Furibus, homicidis hæreticisque molestus," ran the Chancellor's epitaph, but it is not the least of our misfortunes that he was troublesome to honourable men. Sir Thomas More recited the fifty-first psalm on the scaffold, but the very policy of this conscientious man drove many to use it in similar circumstances. Roland Taylor repeated it amid the flames of martyrdom, and was struck on the mouth for not saying it in Latin; just as the Roman Catholics, who would not betray Parsons the Jesuit, were ill-treated at their execution for not saying it in English. It may not be altogether without significance that the first verse of this very psalm supplied the "neck verse" of mediæval justice, and that it fell from the dying lips of one who was as much a martyr to mediævalism as to conscience.

The martyr to mediævalism felt that obedience to a royal command was by no means an easy matter. The generation of English reformers before the reign of Mary I. experienced as little difficulty in commending obedience as the French reformers felt before St Bartholomew's Day. That day marks as grave a turning-point in the thought of Continental publicists as the reign of Mary I. does among ourselves. Every book written since 1859 bears, directly or indirectly, the imprint, Charles Darwin, his mark. "Bloody" Mary's imprint is felt in all tracts bearing in any wise on the duty of obedience to the monarch, just as the imprint of the year 1572 is felt in the fugitive pamphlets of Europe. Let anyone who cares to test this point turn to the fifty-five volumes published by the Parker Society, practically containing all the important writings of the English reformers. Thomas Cranmer, the Archbishop of Canterbury (1489-1556), in company with Becon[1] and Bradford,[2] Latimer[3] and Norden,[4] assures us that kings and princes must ever be honoured and obeyed. In 1549 the rebels of Devonshire demanded, in their articles, the observance of all general councils and the decrees of our forefathers. Cranmer reminds them that: "Although the Papists have abused your ignorance in propounding such articles . . . yet you should not have suffered yourselves so much to be led by the nose and bridled by them that you should clearly forget your duty of allegiance unto your sovereign lord, saying unto him, 'This we will have'; and that saying with armour upon your backs and swords in your hands. . . . But answer me this: Be you subjects or no? If you be subjects, then I admonish you, as St Paul taught Titus, saying, 'Warn them to be subject to princes and rulers, obeying them at a word.'

[1] *Early Writings*, pp. 82, 211; *Catechism*, p. 475.
[2] *Sermons*, pp. 411, 435, 478.
[3] *Ibid.*, p. 265.
[4] *Progress of Piety*, pp. 167, 170.

But tell me again : Pertaineth this to subjection and obedience
to say, ' This we will have '? St Peter saith : ' Be subject unto
kings, as unto chief heads, and to other rulers sent by them.
For so is the will of God.' God's will is that you should be
ruled by your princes. But whether is this to be ruled by your
king, or to rule your king, to say, ' Thus we will have the realm
governed '? Your servants be by the Scripture commanded,
as they fear God, to be obedient to their masters, whether
their masters be good or evil. And can you think it meet and
lawful for you to disobey your undoubted king . . . ? " [1] Such
obedience is required, in Cranmer's opinion, by the fifth
commandment. [2]

If we turn to the teaching of Hugh Latimer (*c.* 1490-1555),
is it in any wise different from that of the Archbishop? Not in
the least. Latimer speaks plainly to his hearers. " I hear say,"
he tells them, " ye walk inordinately, ye talk unseemly, otherwise than becometh Christian subjects : ye take upon you to
judge the judgments of the judges. I will not make the King
a pope ; for the Pope will have all things that he doth taken
for an article of our faith. I will not say but that the King and
his council may err ; the parliament houses, both the high and
low, may err ; I pray daily that they may not err. It becometh
us, whatsoever they decree, to stand unto it, and receive it
obediently, as far forth as it is not manifest wicked, and directly
against the Word of God. It pertaineth unto us to think the
best, though we cannot render a cause for the doing of every
thing ; for *caritas omnia credit, omnia sperat.*" [3] He insists that
this covers the authority of officers under the princes as well
as the princes themselves. [4] For " Scripture is plain in it, and
showeth us that we ought to obey his [*i.e.* the King's] officers,
having authority from the King, as well as unto the King
himself." Soldiers on duty in Norfolk were slain in putting
down the rebels. Still, he preached in his last sermon, in
the presence of Edward VI. : " If the King command thee to
go, thou are bound to go ; and serving the King thou servest
God. If thou serve God, He will not shorten thy days to thy

[1] *Remains and Letters*, p. 164.　　[2] *Ibid.*, p. 103.
[3] *Sermons*, p. 148.　　[4] *Ibid.*, p. 373.

hurt." [1] The whole passage breathes the purest doctrine of predestination.

In his letter to Sir Edward Baynton, a favourite of Henry VIII., Latimer points out that high and low alike are bound to render obedience to the Sovereign.[2] In a sermon preached at Stamford, 9th November 1550, on the appropriate text, "Reddite ergo quæ sunt Cæsaris Cæsari, et quæ sunt Die Deo," he eloquently showed that it is the bounden duty of the subject to pay the King all that Parliament had granted by way of taxation,[3] "for it is due debt, and upon peril of thy soul thou are bound to obey it. Yea, I will say more: if the King should require of thee an unjust request, yet are thou bound to pay it, and not to resist and rebel against the King. The King, indeed, is in peril of his soul, for asking thee an unjust request; and God will in His due time reckon with him for it: but thou must obey the King, and not take upon thee to judge him. God is the King's judge, and doubtless will grievously punish him if he do anything unrighteously. Therefore pray thou for thy King, and pay him his duty, and disobey him not. And know this, that whensoever there is any unjust exaction laid upon thee, it is a plague and a punishment for thy sin, as all other plagues are; as hunger, dearth, pestilence, and such other. We marvel we are plagued as we be; and I think verily this unjust and unfaithful dealing with our princes is one great cause of our plague: look therefore every man upon his conscience."

We all have our reserves, and Latimer had his. He is careful, therefore, to maintain that though we obey the King in unjust demands, yet we are not to obey him if he commands what is contrary to the orders of God.[4] Still, he must not be resisted. In his fourth sermon on the Lord's Prayer he is explicit on this head: "Almighty God hath revealed His will as concerning magistrates, how He will have them honoured and obeyed: they [i.e. the people or the rebels] were utterly bent against it. He revealed this will in many places of the Scripture; but especially by St Peter, where he said, "Subditi estote omni

[1] *Sermons*, p. 265.
[2] *Remains*, p. 329.
[3] *Sermons*, p. 300.
[4] *Ibid.*, p. 512.

humanæ creaturæ ' : that is thus much to say in effect, ' Be ye
subject to all the common laws made by men in authority ; by
the King's majesty, and his most honourable council, or by a
common Parliament : be subject unto them, obey them,' saith
God. And here is but one exception, that is, against God. When
laws are made against God and His word, then I ought more
to obey God than man. Then I may refuse to obey with a good
conscience : yet for all that I may not rise up against the magistrates, nor make any uproar : for if I do so, I sin damnably.
I must be content to suffer whatsoever God shall lay upon me,
yet I may not obey their wicked laws to do them. Only in such
a case men may refuse to obey ; else in all the other matters
we ought to obey. What laws soever they make as concerning
outward things we ought to obey, and in no wise to rebel,
although they be never so hard, noisome and hurtful. Our duty
is to obey, and commit all matters unto God ; not doubting but
that God will punish them, when they do contrary to their
office and calling. Therefore tarry till God correct them ; we
may not take upon us to reform them, for it is no part of our
duty. If the rebels, I say, had considered this, think you they
would have preferred their own will afore God's will? For,
doing as they did, they prayed against themselves. But I think
that ignorance was a great cause of it. Truly I think if this had
been opened unto them, they would never have taken such an
enterprise in hand." [1]

It is our duty, and it should be our pleasure, to pray for kings
and all set in authority over us.[2] Nor is our loyalty merely a
lip loyalty. For we pay our dues with no grudging heart.[3] To
pray and to pay seemed to the homely Latimer but two aspects
of one and the same loyalty. Again and again he harks back
to the doctrine that kings must not be resisted. Fighting
against the King is the devil's service : fighting against the
enemies of the King is God's service.[4]

Like Latimer, Tyndale will not obey the monarch in anything against the commands of God.[5] The commands of God

---

[1] *Sermons*, p. 371. [2] *Ibid.*, p. 391.
[3] *Ibid.*, p. 307. [4] *Ibid.*, pp. 416, 496.
[5] *Doctrinal Treatises*, p. 332.

must take precedence of those of any man. For all that, his *Obedience of a Christian Man*, published in 1528, plainly inculcates the obedience of subjects to kings, princes and rulers. Like Bodin, he compares kingly authority to paternal.[1] " The judges are called gods in the Scriptures, because they are in God's room, and execute the commandments of God."[2] He proceeds to give us his exegesis of 1 Samuel xii. : " Why did not David slay Saul, seeing he was so wicked, not in persecuting David only, but in disobeying God's commandments, and in that he had slain eighty-five of God's priests wrongfully? Verily, for it was not lawful. For if he had done it, he must have sinned against God ; for God hath made the king in every realm judge over all, and over him there is no judge. He that judgeth the king judgeth God ; and he that layeth hands on the king layeth hands on God ; and he that resisteth the king resisteth God and damneth God's law and ordinance. If the subjects sin, they must be brought to the king's judgment. If the king sin, he must be reserved unto the judgment, wrath and vengeance of God. And as it is to resist the king, so is it to resist his officer, which is set, or sent, to execute the king's commandment."[3] Nor is it even lawful for a Christian subject to resist his Prince though he be a heathen man.[4]

Tyndale contemplates the monarch in general apart from his good or bad character. It is the office he is analysing, not the man who holds it. For " though he be the greatest tyrant in the world, yet he is unto thee a great benefit of God, and a thing wherefor thou oughtest to thank God highly. For it is better to have somewhat, than to be clean stript out of all together. It is better to pay the tenth than to lose all. It is better to suffer one tyrant than many, and to suffer wrong of one than of every man. Yea, and it is better to have a tyrant unto thy king than a shadow ; a passive king that doth nought of himself, but suffereth others to do with him what they will, and to lead him whither they list."[5]

---

1 *Doctrinal Treatises*, p. 174.
2 *Ibid.*, p. 175.   3 *Ibid.*, p. 177.
4 *Ibid.*, pp. 177, 194.
5 *Ibid.*, p. 179. *Cf.* p. 195.

There is no right of resistance in the philosophy of Tyndale.[1]
" Neither may the inferior person avenge himself upon the
superior, or violently resist him for whatsoever wrong it be.
If he do so, he is condemned in the deed-doing; inasmuch as
he taketh upon him that which belongeth to God only, which
saith, 'Vengeance is mine, and I will reward' (Deut. xxxii.).
And Christ saith, Matt. xxvi., ' All they that take the sword
shall perish with the sword.' Takest thou a sword to avenge
thyself? So givest thou not room unto God to avenge thee, but
robbest Him of His most high honour, in that thou wilt not
let Him be judge over thee."

Tyndale elaborately examines the argument that subjects
ever choose their ruler, and make him swear to keep their
law and to maintain their privileges and liberties, and upon
that agreement submit themselves unto him. Whose office it
is to bind, argued some, to the same belongs to loosen. By no
means, replied Tyndale, because " God, and not the common
people, chooseth the prince; though He choose him by them.
For God commandeth to choose and set up officers; and therefore is God the chief chooser and setter up of them: and so
must He be the chief putter down of them again; so that
without His special commandment they may not be put down
again. Now hath God given no commandment to put them
down again; but contrariwise, when we have anointed a king
over us at His commandment, He saith, ' Touch not mine
anointed.' . . . The authority of the king is the authority of
God; and all the subjects, compared to the king, are but subjects still, though the king be never so evil; as a thousand sons
gathered together are but sons still, and the commandment,
' Obey your fathers,' goeth over all as well as over one. Even
so goeth the commandment over all the subjects: obey your
prince and the higher power, and he that resisteth him, resisteth
God, and getteth damnation. And unto your argument, ' Cujus
est ligare, ejus est solvere,' I answer: ' He that bindeth with
absolute power, and without any higher authority, his is the
might to loose again; but he that bindeth at another's com-

<hr>

[1] *Doctrinal Treatises*, p. 175. *Cf.* pp. 196-197, two important pages. *Cf.* also
pp. 333-334; *Expositions*, pp. 64, 66.

mandment, may not loose again without the commandment of the same.'" [1]

The instruction given is strong meat, and Tyndale thought that all ought to receive it. Is there no remedy against evil princes? Such a question must often have been put to the reformers, and up to the advent of Mary I. it was not too difficult to solve it. Tyndale solves it by invoking the sovereignty of God in a fashion that would have rejoiced the heart, as well as the head, of Calvin. We must receive all things, good or bad, from God. We must humble ourselves under His mighty hand. We must submit ourselves to His nurture and chastisement. We must in particular read Hebrews xii. for our comfort. Fundamentally we come to his old conclusion that " if we resist evil rulers, seeking to set ourselves at liberty, we shall, no doubt, bring ourselves into more evil bondage, and wrap ourselves in much more misery and wretchedness. For if the heads overcome, then lay they more weight on their backs, and make their yoke sorer, and tie them shorter. If they overcome their evil rulers, then make they way for a more cruel nation, or for some tyrant of their own nation, which hath no right unto the crown. If we submit ourselves unto the chastising of God, and meekly knowledge our sins for which we are scourged, and kiss the rod, and amend our living ; then will God take the rod away, that is, He will give the rulers a better heart. Or if they continue their malice and persecute you for well-doing, and because ye put your trust in God, then will God deliver you out of their tyranny for His truth's sake." [2] In fact Tyndale, as becomes a Christian, stoutly upholds the idea that we are in the world to grow in grace, or, to use modern phraseology, to develop in character. Evil rulers, from this angle, are simply wholesome medicines for the soul. Unlike some of us moderns, he is not prepared to patronise the Gospel : he is—a far rarer quality—prepared to live it in his daily life.

The publicist to-day scarcely attempts to peruse the writings of Cranmer, Latimer and Tyndale—who begins political theory in England—but if he does peruse them, he remarks : " Why, this is pure Erastianism ! " And of course there is much truth

---

[1] *Expositions*, p. 65.   [2] *Doctrinal Treatises*, p. 196.

in such a remark. The English reformers before the accession of Mary I., just as the French reformers before 1572, were inclined to lean heavily upon the State. Why should they not? For their State—not our State—was their Church, and well they realise that this was so. We call the principle of Thomas Erastus[1] (1524-1583) the doctrine of the supremacy of the civil magistrate in matters ecclesiastical, but that certainly is not a sixteenth-century frame of mind.

The " renowned Thomas Erastus, Doctor of Medicine," gave forth to the world in 1589 the work that he had begun to compose twenty years before, *An Examination of that most grave Question, Whether Excommunication, or the Debarring from the Sacraments of Professing Christians, because of their Sins, be a Divine Ordinance, or a Human Invention?* Rejecting the wide use of excommunication practised by the Romanists, he narrowed the whole question down to this, that excommunication is simply exclusion from the participation of the sacraments because of sin committed with a view to amendment of life. It is not exclusion from the public worship of God, and neither is it deprivation of the privileges of civil life. In true mediæval manner Erastus thrusts to the one side the consideration of such persons as the ignorant, the heretic, or the apostate. He is discussing the case of the Christian. His thesis is that such a man cannot be punished for his offences by exclusion from the ordinances of God. How, then, is he to be punished? He carefully elaborates his answer, and it is : " By the civil magistrate, whose especial duty and office this is."

We have travelled far from the proposition that the King governs and reigns. Now he does not govern; he simply reigns. Erastus is travelling far from the proposition that the Church exercises excommunication for offences or for sins. His strongly maintained view is that it is the duty of the clergy to teach the people, and it is no less the duty of the magistrate to govern them. The opponents of Erastus drew four main arguments from the Old Testament founded upon the sacrifice for sin, the doctrine of legal uncleanness, the parallel between the

[1] He was a Heidelberg physician, and this seems a natural place to consider his scheme. His real name was Thomas Lüber.

Passover and the Lord's Supper, and of course expulsion from the synagogue. Minutely he analyses these arguments, and with a logical precision that is amazing he demonstrates the worthlessness of the four of them. If an individual—he is not aware of the fact that till Ezekiel's time there was not a single individual in Israel—offered a sacrifice, that was a matter for himself, and the reason is plain. He had committed an offence, and this offence required expiation. The offering of the sacrifice, however, furnished no ground of exclusion from taking his part in public worship. Some alleged that as men had to appear thrice a year before the Lord in Jerusalem, this meant that only godly men were to share in the sacrifice. Erastus contends that the requirement was that all men should attend in order to celebrate a ceremony. He employs the example of John the Baptist to buttress his case, for he emphasises the circumstance that all, the evil as well as the good, came to be baptized in the River Jordan.

For a moment Luther grasped an illuminating truth when he said: " I see something which the blessed Augustine saw not, and those that come after me will see that which I see not " —a fleeting glimpse of the comparative angle. Such a glimpse was never vouchsafed to Erastus, and he encounters grave difficulty when he seeks to meet the argument that legal uncleanness, under the Old Covenant, typified sinful uncleanness, under the New Covenant. His answer is practically to claim that analogy is never a consideration of weight. Besides, the tabernacle represented not the Church on earth but the Church in heaven, and therefore the whole objection falls to the ground. No one whose internal nature—not his external—had not been purified by the blood and the spirit of Christ could enter the heavenly temple. Nor is the argument drawn from the Passover really relevant. For the Lord's Supper is not the Passover, and is never styled so throughout the New Testament. Christ sacrificed for us is our Passover, but the Lord's Supper is nothing of the kind.

Erastus meets the plea grounded on expulsion from the synagogue. Once more he presses the point that analogies are delusive. The synagogues were under the care of the Pharisees, whose conduct, instead of meeting with approval, met with disapproval of a marked kind. No argument, he boldly enounces, can be taken from the practice of the Jewish Church for the conduct of the Christian Church. Besides, we find that persons cast out of the synagogue were never cast out of the temple, so that even on narrow grounds this forms a worthless consideration. How can the judgment-seat of the Elders stand before such assaults?

When he reviews Old Covenant arguments to his satisfaction he passes on to examine those of the New Covenant. He states that he cannot find that Our Lord or His Apostles either taught or practised excommunication. At the same time he does find that so notorious a traitor as Judas attended the first celebration of Holy Communion, and that permission to attend it was given to the Corinthian Christians who had behaved shockingly at the very celebration. From the general argument he travels on to the particular one, the three passages, Matthew xviii. 15-20; 1 Corinthians v.; and 1 Timothy i. 20. The first, " Tell it to the Church," simply means, " Tell it to the magistrate of thy own people, or religion, before bringing thy co-religionists into a heathen court." The delivering to Satan, mentioned in the two later passages, was, in his judgment, some miraculous infliction, and was not excommunication. What is to be the fate of sinners? Is there to be no public admonition on the part of the Church? To the latter question he as unhesitatingly returns an affirmative as he returns a negative to the former. Rebuke the sinner by all means in the presence of all, but rebuke and excommunication differ by worlds. In truth, the Erastian theory is fundamentally a question of the terms on which Christians ought or ought not to be admitted to the sacraments. It is not, as commonly supposed, any view as to the relation of Church or State. Erastus was considering only a State in which one religion—the true one of course—and one religion only was tolerated. There is not, in his opinion, any competition between the authority of the civil magistrate and the Bible. " For, as in managing secular affairs, the magistrate may not transgress the bounds of equity, justice and honour laid down in the laws of the State; so, much less, in disposing of and arranging religious matters and those which relate to the worship of God, is it permitted him to depart, in any particular, from what God has prescribed in His Word. This Word he should follow as his rule in all things, without departing from it at any time in the smallest particular."[1] So this terrible Heidelberg doctor maintains the Headship of Christ, teaching that He is our Supreme Chief, to whom all other authority yields. He does not, however, maintain the doctrine that there is some other authority to which we should submit in preference to that of the Lord Jesus. All men, ministers and magistrates alike, are subject to Him who is King of kings and Lord of lords. At the same time there cannot be two supreme magistracies in the State, just as there cannot be two supreme legislatures.

In one of his most illuminating essays,[2] F. W. Maitland described a man who would have appreciated Erastianism as the Rev. Professor Dr Sir Thomas Smith, Kt., Dean of Carlisle, Provost of Eton, Ambassador to the Court of France and Secretary of State to Queen Elizabeth. Smith published in 1583 and 1584 his *De Republica Anglorum*,[3] his acute discourse on the commonwealth of his native country. Though he does not employ the term sovereignty, he spends his strength in Book I. on justice and law with an incidental analysis of " the ruling and sovereign part " of the commonwealth. This ruling part may be one man, the few, or the many. Monarchical, aristocratic and democratic states differ from one another much like men of " cholericke, sanguine, phlegmatique and melancholique " temperaments. In chapters seven and eight he considers kingship in the abstract and in chapter nine in the concrete—in England in fact. His conclusion is that " at the last the realme of Englande grew into one Monarchie." The comparative point of view just emerges in his survey of the progress from patriarchal kingship in the small community, through an intermediate aristocratic constitution, to the democratic government adapted to the

---

[1] *Confirm.*, lib. iii., c. 1.

[2] *English Law and the Renaissance.*

[3] I use Mr Alston's competent edition.

community that has progressed from the heterogeneous to the homogeneous.

In Book II. he analyses the authority of Parliament, and he does so with uncommon power. Himself a Principal Secretary of State, he passes such an official by just as he passes the Privy Council and Convocation. Three long chapters investigate the Prince and the Parliament, and we learn that the former " giveth all the chiefe and highest offices or magistracies of the realme, be it of judgement or dignitie, temporall or spirituall." Smith, in spite of such a passage, possessed nothing like so firm a grip on the doctrine of sovereignty as Bodin. Though the Prince is all he describes him to be, nevertheless he sets out with the announcement that " the most high and absolute power of the realme of Englande consisteth in Parliament." Which is his real view? Which view is correct? After such a sentence on the power of Parliament, Smith sets immediately down that " For as in warre where the king himselfe in person, the nobilitie, the rest of the gentilitie, and the yeomanrie are, is the force and power of Englande : so in peace and consultation where the prince is to give life, and the last and highest commaundement, the Baronie . . . the knightes . . . the bishoppes . . . bee present to advertise, consult and show what is good and necessarie for the common wealth. . . . That is the Princes and whole realmes deede." Where is power in the last resort? It is either with the King at the head of his army or it is with the King when he is present in Parliament.

The notion of unity dominated the Middle Ages, and Smith does not shake himself quite free from its influence. He assumes that power is with the King with his army or with the King with his Parliament. But what if these two high authorities differ? Such a point of view does not cross his thought, and when we realise that till the defeat of the Spanish Armada in 1588 and, above all, in 1596, our fathers always had in the background of their mind the fear of Spain, we can grasp the idea that the Sovereign and his army or his Parliament were obliged to be at one among themselves; for otherwise they ceased to exist. Mediæval as he is in some respects, he is becoming modern in others, for in his *De Republica*

Anglorum we do not meet with references to such familiar conceptions as the law of nature, the contract theory of government, the law of God and the Divine right of kings. Like Sir John Fortescue, Sir Thomas Smith manifests a fervent patriotism. Just as the former eulogises the industry and the incorruptibility of the judges, so the latter eulogises the absence of both torture and bondmen. Both believe in the future of England, her laws and institutions. Our legislation is more " favourable and good " to us, in Fortescue's opinion, than that of France. Similarly Smith thinks that no one had discovered any better methods of shortening lawsuits than those of England.

The world of Sir Thomas Smith is a new world : the world of George Buchanan (1506-1582) is a very old one indeed. The scourger of monks, Buchanan was the intimate friend of Guillaume Budé and Vinet, and probably knew Rabelais himself, and indeed an essayist of distinction has bestowed upon Buchanan the title of the Scots Rabelais.[1] Guy Patin declared that Virgil wrote no better verses than Buchanan, and that it took fifteen centuries to create another Virgil. Joseph Scaliger composed an epigram of equal extravagance :

> " Namque ad supremum perducta Poetica culmen
> In te stat, nec quo progrediatur habet.
> Imperii fuerat Romani Scotia limes :
> Romani eloquii Scotia finis erit."

Humanist to the core, Buchanan read his classics not only for pleasure but for profit in the conduct of ordinary life. Nor is it singular that among his favourite heroes were Brutus and Timoleon. M. Tarde has taught us all how the laws of imitation apply to institutions ; they apply every whit as strongly to individuals. So Buchanan and many another humanist experienced. A man who lived in Scotland in the days of Queen Mary could hardly help occasionally wondering if the labours of men in classical times were not worthy of respect from men who lived in his own times. From respect to imitation

---

[1] C. Whibley, *Essays in Biography*, p. 90.

is no long step to take, and not a few took it. The deeds of
a Brutus, a Jacques Clément or a Ravaillac proved a potent
cause of the deeds of a Hamilton, a Felton and a Charlotte
Corday. Nor was Buchanan without relations with Hotman
and other Calvinist writers.

Composed in 1568, Buchanan's *De Jure Regni apud Scotos*
did not appear till 1579. It owes much to the thought of
Duplessis-Mornay, and its conclusions agree with those of
the *Vindiciæ contra Tyrannos*. On the other hand Buchanan's
book is as philosophic in texture as Mornay's is theological.
Its object was the plain one of offering an *apologia* for the
faction of the Earl of Moray in 1567, as Milton's[1] *Defence
of the People of England* was to offer an *apologia* for Cromwell
and the Regicides in 1649. Scotland and England stood
arrayed in the dock of public opinion, and it was the business
of the advocates, Buchanan and Milton respectively, to secure
a verdict of not guilty for their clients. The dethronement of
Mary in 1567 was in accordance with the teachings of John
Calvin and John Knox. That more was wanted than this
George Buchanan felt, and it was this that inspired him to
write his *De Jure Regni*. Writing to a correspondent in 1579,
he says he sends him the *De Jure Regni*, written in turbulent
times, but now given to the world after a moderate period,
when the tumult was subsiding, and men's ears had grown
accustomed to opinions of the kind it contained.[2] In his dedication to King James he also says it was written when Scots
affairs were in a state of unsettlement, and that his object was
to put before his readers the origin and limits of the Royal
Prerogative in Scotland. The book, he continues, had served
a good purpose at the time, by silencing the clamour of those
who had protested against the existing arrangement in the
State; but as affairs had become more settled, "he had
dedicated his arms to public concord." In looking through his
papers he had lately come upon his *Dialogue*, and it occurred
to him that its publication might be of real service to James

---

[1] In his preface to *The Medal*, Dryden accuses Milton of having stolen his
thunder from Buchanan.
[2] *Epis.*, xxiv. *Cf.* Treumann, *Die Monarchomachen*, pp. 50, 52, 54, 55.

himself, in showing him in true colours what a king of Scotland should aim at being.

In form the *De Jure Regni* is an imaginary dialogue between its author and Thomas Maitland, a younger brother of Secretary Maitland. Young Maitland is represented as having recently returned from France, and, by way of introduction, Buchanan asks him how late events in Scotland are being talked of on the Continent. He learns that men speak very freely of the seditious character of the Scots, as shown in the murder of Darnley and in the dethronement of Mary. But, demands Buchanan, if they are so indignant at the murder of Darnley, why are they so full of pity for Mary? If Mary was guilty of Darnley's murder she undoubtedly deserved punishment. Those who will not admit this must belong to one of three classes—those who pander to the desire of princes, because they hope to profit by their misdeeds; those who, for their own selfish ends, approve of peace at any price; or, lastly, the ignorant multitude, who are unwilling to quit the beaten track, because they deem every novelty a crime. Blackwood also urges another motive in his *Pro Regibus Apologia*,[1] a book that powerfully assailed the whole position of Buchanan. He suggests that Buchanan meant to prepare the way for the good Regent Moray to ascend the throne of his sister Mary.

In the question of origins Buchanan betrays a slight and superficial interest. Like Beza, Hotman and Mornay, he manifests little curiosity on the nature of the act of union by which men form themselves into a body. There are shadowy references to the cave-dwellers and the Homeric picture of the Sicilians. Both the speakers in the dialogue adopt the Aristotelean assumption that man is by nature a political animal, and in this well-worn sentence the author contrives to re-arouse our interest. Utility with him provides no sufficient explanation of men coming together, for such a doctrine leads straight to the dissolution of society if each man considers simply his own career. There is an instinct, " conformable to nature," that drives man to forsake the " vagrant and solitary

---

[1] Pp. 34-35.

life." In fact, society comes directly from God : it is due to
" the law implanted in our minds by God at our birth." Men,
with conflicting careers, compose society. How is this conflict
to be composed? The answer is the Platonic one, that what
the physician is to the body, the King is to society. The King
is in truth the father, the shepherd of his people, and such
titles bestowed freely upon him argue that he exists for the
sake of the common welfare. The aim of the physician and of
the King is the same, for both endeavour to preserve health
and, when lost, to restore it. In an appendix Buchanan calls
attention to the account of the ideal ruler given by Seneca in
the *Thyestes*. In the State as in the body there is a certain
temperamentum. For the State Buchanan thinks that this
temperamentum is justice, whereas Maitland, with Aristotelean
ethics not far from his mind, suggests that it is temperance.

We glean that the origin of kingship is to be found in
natural right (*jure illo naturæ*), and indeed all the assumptions
of such right are loosely present to the thought of Buchanan,
who of course adumbrates the social contract. Kings justly
arise when the people choose them. Buchanan explains that
though the people can choose their ruler, yet they cannot
render him efficient for his office. The collective wisdom of
the ages has gathered a collection of precepts to enlighten him
in his difficult task, and these precepts form law. *Lex* is *Rex
mutus*, whereas the monarch is *Rex loquens*. Which is it to be:
Is *rex* to be *lex*? or is *lex* to be *rex*? Buchanan decides in
favour of the latter alternative. Maitland observes that if the
Sovereign is a simple servant of the law, why should anyone
seek such an unenviable position? Buchanan answers this by
the view that kings exist for justice, not for pleasure. Calvin's
French disciples assume kingship as the ideal form of government, differing only on the point whether it ought to be elective
or hereditary. Buchanan takes up a far different position. To
him it is a matter of indifference what form of government
there is, so long as there is a government. King, doge, consul
—all are alike to him. There is an anticipation of Montesquieu's
thought in the idea that the monarch may divide his functions
into legislative, executive and judicial.

The *raison d'être* of the Sovereign is justice. Because he failed to administer justice, the law, after the reasoning of St Paul, was added on account of the failings or transgressions of kings. Now the doctrine is " Rex, rex loquens ; lex, lex mutus." Fundamentally for the origin of *lex* we come back to the people, and indeed in Buchanan's scheme of thought this forms the prime consideration. If the people elect kings, they create law also. Nor is the task of creation of jurisprudence their only function. For a judge can interpret law so cunningly that it may prove to be what Mr Justice Berkeley termed it, in Hampden's case, "an old and trusty servant of the King's ; it is his instrument or means which he useth to govern his people by : I never read nor heard that *lex* was *rex* ; but it is common and most true that *rex* is *lex*."[1] Berkeley, it is obvious, had never perused *De Jure Regno*, for in its pages he would certainly have learned that *lex* is *rex*. The people, therefore, claim the power of the interpretation of law in order that it may not be wrested to their disadvantage. Maitland suggests that the King might make the laws, but, as Buchanan shows, how can he make the very laws that are to control him ? Buchanan deliberately lays down the proposition that " I would allow the people (*populus*) who have conferred the sovereignty upon him to set bounds to that sovereignty."[2] Be it noted that his *populus* is no more the plebs than Calvin's. The *populus* are the elect, not *hoi polloi*, for Buchanan, in common with the humanists, felt contempt for the last. The *universi populi judicio* is a mere mob, wholly unfitted for the task of composing statutes. That is to be delegated to the *selecti*, who should form a council for this purpose, and their labour should come to the people for final ratification (*id ad populi judicium deferretur*). Now it is perfectly possible to find by diligent search something in, say, the *De Regimine Principum* of St Thomas Aquinas that might, in the hands of a skilful dialectician, prove to be a sort of anticipation of the theory of evolution. Similarly, we might find in this suggestion of Buchanan's the referendum,

---

[1] Hallam, *History of England*, p. 311 (one-vol. ed. of 1893).

[2] " Populo qui ei imperium in se dedit, licere volo, ut ejus imperii modum ei præscribat."

but surely we all can say that it is a crude thought to think it could possibly be applied in the Scotland of 1579.

Buchanan returns discursively to the conception that the Sovereign was created for the good of the people (*non sibi sed populo creatus*). The law stands over him, and in case of wrong-doing he can be brought to account in a court of justice just the same as any other culprit. If he refuses, as Charles I. did, to appear before such a court, force, to the extent of a civil war, is legitimate. In truth, there is a mutual compact between King and people (*Mutua igitur Regi cum civibus est pactio*). The coins stamped at the coronation of the infant King James VI., in 1570, bear on the reverse a drawn dagger and the motto, "Pro me si mereor in me"—a grim version of the theory of contract. The phrase is said to have been used by Trajan when handing a sword to the prefect of the Prætorian guard. In his version of Morton's speech Buchanan expressly alludes to this story.

Buchanan has not much to say about the Kirk; nevertheless it is always in the background of his thought. Not a generation ahead Andrew Melville was to announce to King James at Falkirk in 1595 that there were "two kingdoms in Scotland, two kings and two jurisdictions." The Sovereign was "God's silly vassal." Of the relationship between the two kings the language of Melville was wholly unambiguous. "There is Christ Jesus," so James heard,[1] "the King, and His kingdom the Church, Whose subject King James VI. is, and of Whose kingdom not a king, nor a lord, nor a head, but a member. And they whom Christ has called and commanded to watch over His Church, and govern His spiritual kingdom, have sufficient power of Him and authority to do so, both together and severally; the which no Christian King nor Prince should control and discharge, but fortify and assist." Buchanan's "i's" have been dotted and his "t's" have been crossed, with the outcome that "new presbyter is but old priest writ large." The wheel had come round in full circle with a vengeance.

That the King can do no wrong is an idea far removed from the consideration of Buchanan. Obviously he may turn out to

[1] J. Melville, *Diary*, pp. 368-371.

be a tyrant. How are we to recognise him when he is such? Is a tyrant one who has seized power by force or fraud instead of by the will of the people? Is he one who has made *rex lex*? Just as Sir Thomas Smith wavers in his doctrine of sovereignty, so Buchanan wavers between the views suggested by the last two questions. Maitland pleads that in Scotland kings are hereditary, not elective. Must not the people therefore be content with whatever ruler comes to them? In reply, Buchanan urges that the Scots have always retained and exercised the right of calling evil kings to account and of punishing violence offered to good ones. At this stage we meet with rather a minute account of Scots history which our author invokes in order to justify his position. The coronation oath asks the King to swear to preserve the laws of the country, thereby limiting his authority. Did not the Scots nobility reject John Baliol because he acknowledged the suzerainty of Edward I.? The murderers of James I. were severely punished, whereas the death of James III. was left unpunished. No doubt the turbulence of the Scots nobility formed one source of the advanced theory which based all society on contract between man and man. Another source came from the comparative powerlessness of the Scots kings.

What is to be the fate of the tyrant? From a review of the reigns of Nero and Caligula, Maitland suggests that St Paul taught submission to the powers that be on the ground that they were ordained of God. He employs such texts as Romans xiii. 1-7, 1 Timothy ii. 1-2 and Titus iii. 1. In the Old Testament he falls back on 1 Samuel viii. 11. Where, asks Maitland pertinently, can you find a passage in the Bible authorising the slaughter of tyrants to go unpunished (*quid tandem e Scripturis profers cur liceat Tyrannos impune occidere?*). All Buchanan has to say is, that as the Scriptures command the extirpation of crimes and criminals in general, they also demand that of tyrants in particular. The omission of a practice from the Bible is by no means the same thing as prohibition. Of course the whole position is assumed in the social contract, but Buchanan does not always carry his principles to their legitimate conclusion. In answer to Maitland he prefers to argue that St Paul is concerned with the principle of authority, not with kingship. Clearly, we glean, this is so ; for otherwise if the Apostle had meant unconditional obedience to every kind of ruler, his words would just as readily apply to all grades of office. How, then, could we punish judges or other subordinate officials? Besides, there is a clear reason for the circumstance that the Bible contains no instance of the punishment of a king by his subjects. Was not God the founder of the Jewish kings? Were they not, consequently, accountable to Him alone? The Bible could not contain any such account as Maitland demands, for the circumstances of a theocracy like Palestine and a democracy like Scotland were absolutely dissimilar. On the subject of tyrannicide Buchanan will not commit himself.

Buchanan glances at the past history of other countries as well as that of his own, and his glance confirms him in his position that the people possess the right to punish the evildoer, even though he be a sovereign. He might name twelve or more bad kings of Scotland who were imprisoned, exiled or put to death by their subjects. Waiving the details of these twelve or more instances, he urges that the one case of James III. is quite decisive. Here the Assembly of Estates enact that James had justly suffered death, adding a clause that no one should be injured who had been concerned in the conspiracy against him. This Act of Parliament, passed in 1488, apparently converted the murderers of James III. into patriots who deserved well of their country. Maitland raises the question, May not the measure of 1488 do harm abroad as well as harm at home? Not so, thinks Buchanan, for in that case every law may be called in question. Besides, he had two more arguments in reserve. One is the old one, *lex* is *rex*, and the other is that all that had happened to the Scots monarchs was in agreement with the law of nature. The Huguenot pamphleteers thought that the right of judgment against the tyrannical ruler never lay with the individual, thereby limiting what was in any case a dangerous remedy. Buchanan utterly casts away this limitation, for he openly avows the right of any individual whatsoever to take upon himself the removal of the unjust ruler. Maitland promptly protests, and Buchanan is unable to answer his protest. " If it be declared lawful for anyone to kill a tyrant, see what a fatal door for villany you open to the wicked; what a source of danger you create for the good; what licence for evil-doing you permit; in what a universal turmoil you involve all men and affairs ! Any murderer of a good king, or at least of one not manifestly evil, could put the cloak of honourable motives over his crime." The history of Scotland in the sixteenth century and of Ireland since 1916 afford ample commentary on the wisdom of Maitland's protest.

There is a change in the *temperamentum* when we cross the Border and travel towards the serene atmosphere breathed by Richard Hooker (1553-1601). The last ten years of the sixteenth century witnessed not only the end of Elizabeth's reign, but also the publication of Hooker's *Of the Laws of Ecclesiastical Polity*, of the first works of Shakespeare, of a play of Ben Jonson, of the *Faerie Queene* of Edmund Spenser, and of the first *Essays* of Bacon.

Throughout the sixteenth century one difficulty in understanding the tracts and the answering tracts that appeared is that each side is so conscious of its own position that it is scarcely possible for it to grasp the position of any other. It was so hard for a controversialist to make out his own meaning that he could not make out the meaning of anyone else. Not the least merit of Hooker is the singular ability with which he applied himself to the understanding of the mental attitude of his opponents. " There will come a time," he held, " when three words uttered with charity and meekness shall receive a far more blessed reward than three thousand volumes written with disdainful sharpness of wit." If ever there was a Bayard of ecclesiastical controversy, it is he. When an adversary used largely sheer abuse, his answer simply was : " Your next argument consists of railing and of reasons; to your railing I say nothing; to your reasons I say what follows." If Hooker did nothing else, he left to the Church of England a tone and a temper which constitute one of the finest of his legacies. There was a craze in his day for definitions, and to this craze the Church of Rome and the Church of Calvin fell victims. Both insisted on laying down elaborate accounts of dogma. The Church of England never forgot—it is one of her chief glories—that truth is too great to be confined within a creed, and that all that a creed can do is to set forth the main articles of belief. All that is primary must be in a creed, but all that is secondary need not. Truth is great—so great that in all its amplitude it cannot be defined. So the heads of the Church of England perceived, and it was for Hooker to justify their attitude.

Hooker's *magnum opus* is great theology and it is also great literature. Take the magnificent sentence with which the first book concludes : " Wherefore that here we may briefly end : of law there can be no less acknowledged than that her seat is the bosom of God, her voice the harmony of the world; all things in heaven and earth do her homage, the very least as feeling her care, and the greatest are not exempted from her power ; both angels, and men, and creatures of what condition soever, though each in different sort of manner, yet all with uniform consent, admiring her as the mother of their peace and joy." Hooker was not an Aristotelean for nothing. To him there was a law of natural revelation, and that he found in the world all around him. It was as plain to him when he lived in Bishopsborne as it had been when he lived in Boscombe. To him there was also a law of supernatural revelation, and that he found in his Bible. Fundamentally the two revelations were one. In his judgment the Puritan ignored that law of nature which in Hooker's eyes was only another name for that majestic order he discerned in all things, human and divine, and to conform to which is the outstanding object of human endeavour. " All things," we gather from him, " do work, after a sort, according to law; all things according to law whereof some superior unto whom they are subject is the authority ; only the works and operations of God have been both for their worker and for the law whereby they are wrought. The being of God is a kind of law to his working, for that perfection which God is, giveth perfection to that He doth."

In no part of his book does Hooker exhibit his breadth of

mind more clearly than in his section in the third book in which
he discusses the nature of the Church. There is, he notes, the
Church mystical, the mystical body of Christ, which cannot
be distinguished by men. It has its clear marks, as it has its
distinctive lineaments, but the marks and the lineaments are
known to none save God. There is also the visible Church,
and it is with her that questions and systems of ecclesiastical
polity bear their part. Who are her members? According to
Hooker, all who own Christ as Lord, and embrace the faith
He published and have been baptized, are members of His
visible Church. Some of them may be wicked and some of
them may be excommunicate, and yet if they have these three
notes they belong to the Church. In an age when Puritan
congregations were eager to separate the tares from the wheat,
Hooker, like his Master, was willing to allow both to grow
together till the time of harvest. " Men remain in the visible
Church," so he declared, " till they utterly renounce the profession of Christianity," [1] Their doctrine may be unsound in
part, their life may be vicious, but they are still members of the
Church if they hold the main substance of the faith, if they
acknowledge Christ as Lord. So long as they retain their
membership there is always the possibility that they may
rise to a fuller realisation of all that it means. In an age when
separation of the elect from the non-elect was the fashion with
some of the Puritans, in an age when excommunication was
the fashion with the Church of Rome, it is refreshing to meet
with a profound thinker who hoped to extract the best that was
possible out of each man.

As there are stages in the knowledge of God, so there are
stages in the membership of His Church. " To him that hath
shall be given," so run the words of Her Head. The more
a man uses his privileges as a member the closer he comes
into contact with Christ. " Albeit not every error and fault,"
in Hooker's opinion, " yet heresies and crimes which are not
actually repented of and forsaken, exclude quite and clean
from that salvation which belongeth unto the mystical body
of Christ; yea, they also make separation from the visible and

[1] III. i. 12. *Cf.* VIII. i. 2.

sound Church of Christ; altogether from the visible Church
neither the one nor the other doth sever. As for the act of excommunication, it neither shutteth out from the mystical, nor
clean from the visible, but only from fellowship with the visible
in holy duties." It is worthy of note that this was the position
of Savonarola when he was martyred, and of Luther when he
was excommunicated. "Both heresy and many other crimes,"
concludes Hooker with Erastus, "which wholly sever from
God do sever from the Church of God in part only." Hence
"the Church of God may, therefore, contain both them which
are indeed not His, yet must be reputed His by us that know
not their inward thoughts, and them by whose apparent wickedness testifieth even in the sight of the whole world that God
abhorreth them. For this and no other purpose are meant those
parables which our Saviour Christ in the Gospel hath concerning mixture of vice with virtue, light with darkness, truth with
error, as well as openly known and seen as a cunningly cloked
mixture."

"That which therefore separateth utterly, that which
cutteth off clean from the visible Church of Christ, is plain
apostasy, direct denial, utter rejection of the whole Christian
faith as far as the same is professedly different from infidelity.
Heretics as touching these points of doctrine wherein they fail;
schismatics as touching the quarrels for which or the duties
wherein they divide themselves from their brethren; licentious
and wicked persons as touching their several offences or crimes,
have all forsaken the true Church of God, the Church which
is sound and sincere in the doctrine that they corrupt, the
Church that keepeth the bond of unity which they violate,
the Church that walketh in the laws of righteousness which
they transgress, this very true Church of Christ they have left,
howbeit not altogether left nor forsaken simply the Church
upon the main foundations whereof they continue built, notwithstanding these main breaches whereby they are rent at the
top asunder." [1]

To a man of Hooker's frame of mind there was no point
in discussing the relationship between the Church and State.

---

[1] III. i. 13; V. lxviii. 6.

" There is not," he says, " any member of the commonwealth which is not also a member of the Church." If men were born into the State, they were baptized into the Church. If they owed civil duties to the State, they owed spiritual duties to the Church. " With us," he points out, " therefore the name of a Church importeth only a society of men, first united into some public form of regiment, and secondly distinguished from other societies by the exercise of Christian religion. With them on the other side the name of the Church in this present question importeth not only a multitude of men so united and so distinguished, but also further the same divided necessarily and perpetually from the body of the commonwealth; so that even in such politic society as consisteth of none but Christians, yet the Church of Christ and the commonwealth are two corporations, independently each subsisting by itself."

" We hold, that seeing there is not any man of the Church of England but the same man is also a member of the common-wealth; nor any man a member of the commonwealth which is not also a member of the Church of England; therefore as in a figure triangular the base doth differ from the sides thereof, and yet one and the selfsame line is both a base line and also a side; a side simply, a base if it chance to be the bottom and underlie the rest; so, albeit, properties and actions of one kind do cause the name of a commonwealth, qualities and functions of another sort the name of a Church to be given unto a multi-tude, yet one and the selfsame multitude may in such sort be both, and is so with us, that no person appertaining to the one can be denied to be also of the other." [1] We are travelling considerably from the positions either of George Buchanan or of John Melville.

In essence the Church and the State are precisely the same body regarded from different angles. It follows, then, that the legislature is competent to pass laws on spiritual matters as well as on temporal matters, for to Hooker " the Parliament of England, together with the convocation annexed thereunto, is that whereupon the very essence of all government within this kingdom doth depend; it consisteth of the King, and of

---

[1] VIII. i. 2.

all that within the land are subject unto him. The Parliament is a court, not so merely temporal as if it might meddle with nothing but only leather and wool." This ideal was the ideal of Burke no less than of Hooker. Such an ideal we have left far behind us, but what a loss we have suffered during our travel! One of the last men to hold it was Arnold of Rugby.[1] For all laws passed there must be public approbation, and indeed they are not really laws unless they secure this approbation. In fact, Hooker emphasises the element of consent or agreement in a way which suggests the theories of Hobbes and Locke. Unconsciously he felt the influence of the traditional habit of thinking about government under the formula of contract, and consciously he felt the influence of the doctrine of the sovereignty of the people, a doctrine he inherited from the ecclesiastical politicians of the Middle Ages. Implicitly he holds that society bases itself upon contract, and that the people is sovereign. Through Hooker these doctrines reach Locke, who bases his political thinking upon Hooker, because the Anglican Tories accepted Hooker's authority as final.

Persecution, in the mediæval sense, is never a weapon of the Church of England. The age of persecution was, however, renewed in the sixteenth century, and there was a danger that force might be used towards men to alter beliefs they held dear. Under the hand of God the *magnum opus* of Hooker averted this danger, for he showed that instead of force there was the better method of persuasion. He understood his opponents, he understood their position, and they felt that he was much more concerned to show *why* they were wrong than to show they were wrong. There was in Hooker an instinctive faith in the power of truth, and he possessed the gift of enabling others to feel this power. He commended the employment of history and antiquity to the judgment of man. His commendation was all the more impressive because it was couched so persuasively. His merits were acknowledged in his own day. Walton tells us that a learned English Romanist—either Cardinal Allen or Dr Stapleton—read the first book to Pope Clement XII., who declared " there is no learning this man

---

[1] Stanley, *Life of Arnold*, i., pp. 198-200.

hath not searched into; nothing too hard for his understanding," desiring that it should be translated into Latin. James I. and Charles I. also admired it, and the latter recommended it to his children " as an excellent means to satisfy private scruples and settle the public peace of the Church and kingdom." Nor has the succession of our divines been one whit behind this royal admiration. It begins with Bishop Andrewes, and continues to our own day. John Donne absorbed Hooker's book though he never mentioned Hooker's name. Another dean, Jonathan Swift, specially praised the pure style of the *Ecclesiastical Polity*.

Richard Hooker and Edmund Burke are strikingly alike in their circumstance, in their thought, and in their outlook upon life. Both men were the products of circumstance, governing their conduct by the distinguishing colour, the discriminating effect time gave to the event. Just as Hooker saw in the Romanist and in the Puritan the menace to balance, harmony, organic unity, so Burke saw in the French revolutionists precisely the same danger. When a matter came before them they invariably pressed it back to principles which raised it above the dust of the temporal into the pure air of the eternal. Both invariably passed the incidents of the day into the region of great ideas. It is a mark of the philosophic to see human life, no less than nature, as a whole. Hooker and Burke then were emphatically philosophers of this rare type. They felt that they must diffuse the light of eternity over the awful tides of human circumstance. This they did with a power and with an austerity that make us their debtors for ever. Men may, like a barrister, plead for a case; thinkers plead for a cause. If ever men pleaded for a cause, it was Hooker and Burke. Their pleading not seldom wore a restrained form, but when the accidents of the day pass away this is the only form of pleading able to move posterity. " In reality," Burke wrote to his intimate friend Laurence, when his end was approaching, " you know that I am no enthusiast, but according to the powers that God has given me, a sober and reflecting man." [1] With real enthusiasm neither Burke nor Hooker had any quarrel, but there is an

---

[1] 10th February 1797.

enthusiasm which often turns to the bitterness of party passion, and with that enthusiasm they had every reason to quarrel. "Please God," Burke once said when describing his own procedure, "I will walk with caution whenever I am not able clearly to see my way before me."[1] If Burke was cautious, deliberate, sober in thought, rational in action, Hooker was equally so.

In the untying of the tangled knot of events, Hooker, no less than Burke, emphasised the need of prudence, that sober-mindedness that Aristotle glorified. Both knew " how many a weary step is to be taken before they [*i.e.* the people] can form themselves into a mass which has a truly politic personality,"[2] for they were familiar with the slow process of the discipline of nature as it operates through the centuries. Hooker feared the "red ruin and the breaking up of laws in the Church" every whit as much as Burke feared them in the State. An individual may fall in a moment: the Church and the State may similarly be bereft of the results of the ages. With the example of Russia fresh in our memories this is not so improbable as it at one time might have seemed. Undoubtedly Hooker believed that the madness of the revolutionary might destroy the treasures of countless ages. Burke and he perceived that human nature was more apt to feel grievances than to prescribe remedies, and these remedies might perchance prove poisonous to true life.

That God willed the State, that He willed also the nation of man, and that the whole course of a nation's life is " the known march of the ordinary providence of God "[3]—these articles are as fundamental in Hooker's creed as they are in Burke's. To both thinkers man's nature and the State are alike manifestations of the Divine will, harmoniously adapted each to the other. Hooker and Burke were passionately convinced that Church and State had their foundations in religious faith, and that they could not survive its disintegration. No one can understand the sixteenth century who does not grasp the fact

---

[1] Letter on the Duration of Parliaments.
[2] *Appeal from the New to the Old Whigs.*
[3] *Regicide Peace*, Letter i.

THE STATE IS THE CHURCH

Burke set forth : " In a Christian commonwealth the Church and the State are one and the same thing, being different integral parts of the same whole." [1]

REFERENCES

Bonnard, A., *Thomas Éraste*, Lausanne, 1894.

Brown, P. Hume, *George Buchanan*, Edinburgh, 1890.

Brown, P. Hume, *John Knox*, London, 1895.

Buchanan, George, *Glasgow Quatercentenary Studies*, Glasgow, 1907

Buchanan, George, *Hugh Latimer*, London, 1881.

Demaus, R., *William Tindale*, London, 1925.

Figgis, J. N., *From Gerson to Grotius*, Cambridge, 1907.

Figgis, J. N., *The Divine Right of Kings*, Cambridge, 1914.

Hunt, J., *Religious Thought in England from the Reformation*, London, 1870-1873.

Hutton, W. H., *Sir Thomas More*, London, 1895.

Lang, A., *John Knox and the Reformation*, London, 1905.

Lee, R., *The Thesis of Erastus touching Excommunication*, Edinburgh, 1844.

Mullinger, J. B., *The University of Cambridge*, Cambridge, 1873 and 1884.

Murray, R. H., " Utopian Toleration," *Edinburgh Review*, January 1914.

Murray, R. H., *Richard Hooker and his Teaching*, London, 1924.

Paget, F., *An Introduction to the Fifth Book* (of Hooker's *Ecclesiastical Polity*), Oxford, 1889.

Pearson, A. F. S., *Thomas Cartwright and Elizabethan Puritanism*, Cambridge, 1925.

Pollard, A. F., *Thomas Cranmer*, New York, 1904.

Ruble, A. de, *La Première Jeunesse de Maria Stuart*, Paris, 1891.

Seebohm, F., *The Oxford Reformers of* 1498, London, 1911.

Stephen, Sir J. F., *Horæ Sabbaticæ*, London, 1892.

Storm, G., *Maria Stuart*, München, 1896.

Sudhoff, K. C., *Olevianus und Z. Ursinus Leben und ausgewählte Schriften*, Elberfeld, 1857.

Thornton, L. S., *Richard Hooker*, London, 1924.

Treumann, R., *Die Monarchomachen Eine Darstellung der revolutionären Staatslehren des XVI. Jahrhunderts* (1573-1599), Leipzig, 1895.

Vauthier, G., *De Buchanani Vita et Scriptio*, Toulouse, 1886.

Wordsworth, C., *Ecclesiastical Biography*, London, 1853.

---

[1] Speech, 11th May 1792.

GENERAL WORKS OF REFERENCE

Bluntschli, J. K., *Geschichte der neueren Staatswissenschaften,* München and Leipzig, 1881.

Brown, I., *English Political Theory,* London, 1920.

Cunningham, W., *Historical Theology,* Edinburgh, 1864.

Cunningham, W., *The Reformers and the Theology of the Reformation,* Edinburgh, 1868.

Dunning, W. A., *Political Theories, Ancient and Mediæval,* New York, 1910.

Dunning, W. A., *Political Theories, from Luther to Montesquieu,* New York, 1905.

Figgis, J. N., *Cambridge Modern History,* vol. iii., Cambridge, 1904.

Figgis, J. N., *From Gerson to Grotius,* Cambridge, 1907.

Figgis, J. N., *The Divine Right of Kings,* Cambridge, 1914.

Franck, A., *Réformateurs et Publicistes de l'Europe : Moyen Âge-Renaissance.* Paris, 1864.

Franck, A., *Réformateurs et Publicistes : Dix-Septième Siècle,* Paris, 1881.

Gettell, R. G., *History of Political Thought,* London, 1924.

Gierke, O. von, *Johannes Althusius und die Entwicklung der naturrechtlichen Staatstheorien,* Breslau, 1913.

Gumplowicz, L., *Geschichte der Staatstheorien,* Innsbrück, 1905.

Hallam, H., *Literature of Europe,* London, 1839.

Hearnshaw, F. J. C., Ed., *The Social and Political Ideas of some Great Thinkers of the Renaissance and the Reformation,* London, 1925.

Janet, P., *Histoire de la Science Politique,* Paris, 1887.

Meinecke, F., *Die Idee der Staatsräson,* München and Berlin, 1924.

Pollock, Sir F., *History of the Science of Politics,* London, 1890.

CHRONOLOGY OF WRITINGS

1460. Ficino begins his translation of Plato.

1471-1476. Fortescue's *On the Governance of England.*

1495-1498. First printed edition of the *Politics* (the Aldine ed.).

1500. Perrault's *Insignis Pecularia.*

1513. Machiavelli composed *The Prince*, which is published in 1532.

1515. Budé's *De l'Institution du Prince*, which is published in 1521.

1516. More's *Utopia.*

1519. Seyssel's *La Grande Monarchie de France.*

1520. Luther's *To the Christian Nobility of the German Nation*, his *Babylonish Captivity* and his *Freedom of a Christian Man.*

1523. Luther's *On the Secular Power : How far Obedience is due to it.*

1527. Machiavelli's *History of Florence.*

1528. Tyndale's *Obedience of a Christian Man* and *How Christian Rulers ought to govern.*

c. 1530-c. 1533. Saint German's *Treatise concerning the Division between the Spirituality and the Temporalty.*

1532. More's *Confutation of Tyndale's Answer.*

1534. Castellion's *Traicte des Hérétiques*, and Beza's *Concerning the Duty of Punishing Heretics by the Civil Magistrate.*

1535 or 1536. Gardiner's *De Vera Obedentia.*

1536. Calvin's *Institutes of the Christian Religion.*

1539. Melanchthon's *Ethicæ Doctrinæ Elementa.*

1544. Salamonius's *De Principatu Libri Sex.*

c. 1546. La Boëtie's *Discourse sur la Servitude Volontaire.*

c. 1548. Castellion's *Traicte des Hérétiques.*

1554. Beza's *Concerning the Duty of Punishing Heretics by the Civil Magistrate.*

1556. Poynet's *Short Treatise of Political Power.*

1557. Victoria's *Relectiones.*

1558. Goodman's *How Superior Powers ought to be obeyed*; Knox's *First Blast against the Monstruous Regiment of Women*, and his *Appellation.*

1560. Hotman's *Epistre envoiée au Tigre de la France; H.* Pasquier's *Recherches de la France*, and his *Pourparler du Prince.*

1566. Bodin's *Methodus ad facilem Historiarum Cognitionem.*

1568. Bodin's *Réponse à M. de Malestroit touchant le fait des Monnaies.*

1570. Haillan's *De l'Éstat et succes des Affaires de France.*

1571. Gentillet's *Anti-Machiavel.*

1573. Hotman's *Franco-Gallia.*

1574. Beza's *De Jure Magistratum*, and the *Réveille-Matin des Français.*

1575. Calvin's *Letter on Usury*, and Louis LeRoy's *De l'Excellence du Gouvernement Royal.*

1576. La Boëtie's *Contre-un* and Haillan's *Histoire Générale de France.*

1577. Bodin's *La République.*

CHRONOLOGY OF WRITINGS

1578. Marnix Ste Aldegonde's *Réponse à un petit Livret n'aguères dublié et intitulé : Déclaration de l'Intention du Seigneur Don Jehan d'Autriche.*

1579. Duplessis-Mornay's *Vindiciæ contra Tyrannos*; Buchanan's *De Jure Regni apud Scotos*; Paruta's *Perfezione Politica*; and Lensaeus's *De Unica Religione.*

1580. Peeters's *De Christiani Principis officio.*

1581. Blackwood's *Apologia pro Regibus*, and Ayala's *De Jure et Officiis bellicis et Disciplina militari.*

1582. R. Browne's *Treatise of Reform.*

1583. Sir T. Smith's *Commonwealth of England.*

1585. Hotman's *De Jure Regni Galliæ, libri tres*, and his *De Jure Successionis Regiæ.*

1586. Latin translation of Bodin's *République.*

1588. Boucher's *De Justa Abdicatione Henrici.*

1589. Erastus's *An Examination of that most grave Question . . . Excommunication.*

1590. *De Iusta Reipublicæ Christianæ in Reges Impios* (Anonymous).

1592. Rossaeus's *De Justa rei Publicæ in Reges Impios et Hæreticis Auctoritate.*

1593. The *Satire Ménippée;* H. Molina's *De Justitia et Jure* (Part I.), Part II. appeared in 1600; and Boucher's *Sermons de la Simulée Conversion* (of Henry IV.).

1594. The first part of Hooker's *Of the Laws of Ecclesiastical Polity*, and Pithou's *Libertés de l'Église Gallicane.*

1596. Daneau's *Politices Christianæ.*

1599. Mariana's *De Rege et Regis institutione*; and James I.'s *Basilicon Doron.*

1600. Barclay's *De Regno et Regai potestate adversus Monarchomacos.*

1603. Althusius's *Politica Methodice Digesta.*

1609. Grotius's *Mare Liberum.*

1611. Bellarmine's *De potestate summi Pontifices.*

1612. Suarez's *De Legibus ac Deo Legislatore.*

1623. Campanella's *Civitas Soli.*

1625. Grotius's *De Jure Belli et Pacis.*

286

INDEX

ABEL, 224-5

Abraham, 71, 106, 138

Achilles, 32

Acton, Lord, the psychology of conscience, xix; backstairs' knowledge, 10; indignation with Creighton, 29; Machiavelli a constant influence, 34-5; St Bartholomew's Day, 170-1; survey of toleration, 244-5

Adam, 106, 225, 230

Adams, John, eulogises Calvin, 112; verdict on Ponet, 124; his *Defence of the Constitution of the Government of the United States*, 209

Adolphus, Gustavus, the limits of statesmanship, 45

Adrian VI., xvii, 47

Ægidius, 23

Agathocles, his treachery, 29-30

Agricola, John, 180

Alciat, Andrew, believes in astrology, 131

Alençon, the Duc d'. See Anjou, the Duc d'

Alençon, the Duc d', François, the friend of Coligny, 200; his death, 212

Alexander the Great, 233

Alexander the jurisconsult, 134

Alexander VI., xvi, 267; his son, Cæsar Borgia, 6; his deceptions, 33

Alfonso (X.) of Castile, his *obiter dictum*, 85

Allen, William, 278

Almain, Jacques, his *Expositio . . . super potestate summi pontifices*, 69

Alstedius, Johann Heinrich, 117; *lex naturæ*, 118

Althusius, Johannes, 117; the civil power spiritual, 57; natural law, 67; a courageous magistrate, 118; contract theory, 119; the schoolmen, 149; *Politica Methodice Digesta*, 118-9

Alva, the Duke of, his devilries, 69

Alvarez, Francis, his *History of Ethiopia*, 135

Ambiorix, 196

Ambrose, St, liberty of conscience, 2; the Church, 51; the State, 52

Ambrosiaster, the State, 52

Anabaptists, the, 152, 187; their anarchical tendencies, 51, 75, 92-3, 206, 246; attitude to the Bible, 74; frighten More, 150

Andrewes, Lancelot, admires Hooker, 279

Angelo, Michael, his *David*, 9-10; statue of Julius II., 46-7

Anjou, the Duc d', 129, 130

Anquetil du Perron, Louis Pierre, 220

Antony, King of Navarre, 189; Beza's remark, 104

Appian, 134

Aquinas, St Thomas, 100; the bad Prince, 11; government and perfection, 50; social contract, 67; the law of nature, 229; tyrannicide, 231; *De Regimine Principum*, 75, 269

Aristogeiton, 159, 234

Aristotle, 82, 139, 144, 196, 268, 274; the destruction of the City-State, 5; parallel with Machiavelli, 14-5, 17-8; Luther's attitude, 41; the moral law, 66; man a political animal, 84, 267; influence on Bodin, 132, 134, 151; slavery, 152-3; sovereignty, 164; sober-mindedness, 280; *Politics*, 14; *Ethics* and *Physics*, 40

Arnold, Thomas, his ideal of Church and State, 278

Arundel, Thomas, 249

Asa, 106, 119, 182

Asceticism, 83, 88, 125

Astrology, 131-3, 139

Athaliah, 203

Athanasius, St, liberty of conscience, 2

Athens, 12, 15, 16, 160

Augustine, St, 181, 261; the robber-State, 35; his vast influence, 41; teaches Luther, 43-4; the State, 52-3, 68, 71; the priesthood of the believer, 56; his toleration, 69; Calvin's quotations, 82; priority of the State, 125-6; the law of nature, 229; *De Civitate Dei*, 1

Augustinus, 2

Augustus, the Emperor, his treachery, 137

Aurelius, Marcus, 37, 199

Austin, John, his *obiter dictum*, 41; Bodin anticipates him, 153

BACON, Francis (Viscount St Albans), his *tres magi*, 4, 193; amateur in science, 19; accepts progress, 20; assaults the schoolmen, 222; *Novum Organum*, xx

Bagehot, Walter, his dictum on the House of Commons, 137

Baglione, Giovanni Paolo, loses his opportunity, 24; his character, 24-5

Bainham, James, 248

Baldus, 134; the first to say " *Rex est imperator in regno suo*," 153

Baliol, John, 271

Barclay, William, his *De Regno et Regalia Potestate adversus Monarchomacos*, 209

Barcochba, 206

Bareus, 117

Bartolus, 114, 134; the essence of tyranny, 205

287

INDEX

Bayard, Pierre du Terrail, 273

Bayfield, Richard, 248

Bayle, Pierre, 165, 218

Baynton, Sir Edward, a favourite of Henry VIII., 255

Bebel, Heinrich, his *Facetiæ* and *Triumphis Veneris*, 222

Becanus, Martin, his *Controversia Anglicana*, 223; the original contract, 226

Becon, Thomas, royal obedience, 253

Beda (or Bedier), Noel, denounces Erasmus, 181

Behain, Martin, a cosmographer and a navigator, 239

Bellarmine, Roberto Francesco Romolo, 123, 214, 227; *De potestate summi Pontificis*, 223

Bellugne, Pierre, an authority on Aragonese law, 134

Bembo, Pietro, 135

Bentham, Jeremy, attacks lawyers, 222

Bentley, Richard, xx

Berkeley, George, Bishop of Cloyne, his law, 20, 42

Berkeley, Sir Robert, 269

Bernard of Clairvaux, his theocratic ideal, 125

Bethmann-Hollweg, Theobald von, palliation of the invasion of Belgium, 36

Beza, Theodore, 117, 169, 172, 188, 198, 203, 267, 268; the character of Calvin, 80, 83; massacre of Vassy, 104; edition of the Vulgate, 112-3; metrical version, 113, 179-80; Calvin's disciple, 113, 173; question of obedience, 113-4; tyrannicide, 114, 122; professor, 174-5; his Poissy speech, 175-6; edition of the New Testament, 177; the shock of the Massacre, 179; lack of toleration, 182-4; his theology, 185; theory of political Calvinism, 186-8; for tyrannicide, 188, 214; the Aragonese oath, 197; Mornay repeats his points, 204; *Du Droit des Magistrats sur leurs Sujets*, 113-4, 185-8, 203, 207; *Life of Calvin*, 180; *Histoire Ecclesiastique*, 180; *Confession of the Christian Faith*, 180; *Concerning the Duty of Punishing Heretics*, 180, 182, 184; *Icones*, 184

Biel, Gabriel, God the author of natural law, 228

Bilney, Thomas, 248

Bismarck, Otto Eduard Leopold von, Prince, 207; *obiter dictum*, 7, 36; cause of his fall, 37; limits of statesmanship, 45; parallel with Luther, 77-8

Blackwood, Adam, his *Pro Regibus Apologia*, 267

Blanche, Queen, 200

Blücher, Gebhard Leberecht von, 173

Boccaccio, Giovanni, his *Decameron*, 5

Bodin, Jean, xv, 257; surveys European history, 12; denies progress, 20; attacks *The Prince*, 36, 136-7; Luther anticipates him, 55; Church and State, 82; against the rule of women, 120-1, 151; a man of affairs, 129; stability of system, 130; believes in astrology, 131; influence of Plato, 132-3; influence of Aristotle, 134; range of reading, 135-6, 141; his toleration, 138-9, 140; view of history, 141-3; the importance of climate, 144-9; political economy, 149-50; sovereignty, 150-5, 161, 164, 167, 193; the absolutism of the Prince, 156-7, 159; forms of the Commonwealth, 157-61; the just mean, 160; revolution, 163-4; *Methodus ad Facilem Historiarum Cognitionem*, 129, 130, 140, 141, 144; *Réponse à M. de Malestroit touchant le Fait des Monnaies et de l'Enchérissement de Toutes Choses*, 129, 130, 141, 149; *Six Livres de la République*, 130, 136, 141, 144, 151, 167; *Théâtre de la Nature*, 130; *Heptaplomeres*, 130, 138-9, 141; *La Demonomanie*, 131; *Amphitheatrum Naturæ*, 141

Bodmann, Karl von, 47-8

Boetië, Étienne de la, 173

Boetius, Hector, 135

Bonarsans, Charles (Scribani, Charles), encourages assassination, 226

Boniface, St, 2

Boniface VIII., 214; his Bull *Unam Sanctam*, xvii

Borgia, Alexander, 28

Borgia, Cæsar, Duke of Valentinois and Romagna (son of Pope Alexander VI.), the campaign of 1502, 6; the ideal of Machiavelli, 7-8, 29; his new State, 28; strangles Fermo, 30; his cruelty, 31-2; a failure, 137

Bossuet, Jacques Bénigne le, Bishop of Meaux, his dictum on the State, xviii

Boswell, Alexander, his dictum of Charles I.'s execution, 121

Boucher, Jean, 226; the priest in politics, 214-5; his commanding influence, 218-9; satirised, 222; rejects the Salic law, 223; *Histoire tragique de Gaveston*, 216; *De justa Abdicatione Henrici tertii*, 216-7

Bourbon, Charles of, Cardinal, styled Charles X., 220

Bourgoing, Jean François, 221

Bradford, John, royal obedience, 253

Bradford, William, 112

Brandt, Sebastian, 45; his *Ship of Fools*, xiii, 222

Brenz, Johann, 180

Briquemault, François de Beauvais, massacred, 170
Brisson, Barnabé, murdered, 221
Browne, Robert, his *Treatise of Reform*, 70-1
Browning, Robert, 240
Brunehaut, 200, 203
Brunelleschi, Filippo, his dome, 9
Brunfels, Otto, 181
Brutus, 159, 234, 265, 266
Buchanan, George, 112, 277; natural law, 66; contract theory, 122; the Scots Rabelais, 265; the influence of Mornay, 266; little interest in origins, 267; *De Jure Regni apud Scotos*, 122, 266-73; *Dialogue*, 266
Buckle, Henry Thomas, the influence of climate, 148
Budé, Guillaume, 184, 188, 265
Bullinger, Henry, Hotman's letters, 190
Bunyan, John, *The Pilgrim's Progress*, 64-5
Burke, Edmund, 252, 278; unity in human nature, 21; the State divine, 57-8; liberty in America, 77; unconcerned with origins, 153; the penal laws, 240; truth and peace, 246; Church and State, one, 247; parallel with More, 246-7; the share taken by circumstance, 249; parallel with Hooker, 279-81
Butler, Joseph, his *Analogy*, 34
Butler, Nicholas Murray, his *obiter dictum*, 26
Butler, Samuel, attacks the Puritans, 222

Cadoudal, Georges, 235
Cæsar, Julius, 28, 196, 233; the crossing of the Alps, 42; an opportunist, 78
Cain, 224-5
Caligula, 271
Calixtus III., threatened by Puccini, 11
Calvin, John, xi, xv, 116, 118, 124, 159, 171, 177, 178, 185, 186, 188, 198, 207, 213, 259, 266, 269; horizontal and vertical divisions, xii; a layman, 56; his individualism, 59; his supporters, 64; natural law, 66, 84, 93; his learning, 80, 82, 230; pitiless logic, 81; a systematiser, 83; the sovereignty of God, 85-7, 100-1, 108-9; his theology, 85-90; origin of the State, 87; Christian liberty, 88-9, 96, 103; his Discipline, 90-1; ministerial authority, 92; the question of tyranny, 93-4; the State and a moral content, 94-5, 97-8; tremendous factor in Holland, England and New England, 95; no divine right, 99; the benevolent despot, 101-2; ideal government, 102-3; no democrat, 103, 107, 125; the pact, 105-7; passive resistance, 108; vast circulation of The

Calvin—*continued*
Institutes, 110-1; edition of the Psalms, 113; verdict on Goodman, 123; widespread influence, 126-7; boundaries of countries, 146; teaches obedience, 172; Beza's friend, 173; death of Servetus, 182, against tyrannicide, 188; Hotman's devotion, 193; *Institutes of the Christian Religion*, 81, 82, 83, 89, 102, 109-12, 126
Calypso, 193
Camerarius, Joachim, 173
Campanella, Thomas, accepts progress, 20; attacks *The Prince*, 36
Canning, George, his *obiter dictum*, 3-4
Capet, Hugh, 198
Capitalism, the rise of, 61, 71
Capitolinus, Julius, 194
Capponi, Gino, his encomium, 14
Carlstadt, Andreas Bodenstein von, 44, 45, 53
Carlyle, Thomas, the effects of Rousseau's works, 75
Caron, Charondas de, believes in astrology, 131
Cartwright, Thomas, 112, 122, 123; resembles Wyclif, xv-xvi; the new individualism, xix; the Church prior to the State, 126; at Heidelberg, 179; *Second Reply*, 125; *Second Admonition to the Parliament*, 125
Cassius, 159
Castellion, Sebastian, his *Traicté de Hérétiques*, 180-1
Casticus, 196
Castrao-Palao, Alphonso, the *jus gentium*, 228
Casaubon, Isaac, xx
Cavagnes, Arnaud de, massacred, 170
Cavour, Camillo Benso, Count, his *obiter dictum*, 26; the prophecy of Machiavelli, 36; statesman of prudences and imprudences, 215
Caxton, William, the printing of the vernacular, 249
Celtes, Conrad, 135
Charles I., 270; right of censorship, xiii; seizure by Joyce, 8; his execution, 121, 122; influence of Calvin's disciples, 209-10; admires Hooker, 279
Charles IV., conversation with Coligny, 171-2
Charles V., 145, 153; his absolutism, xix; peruses *The Prince*, 35; overthrows free constitutions, 162; the rights of conscience, 245
Charles VI., 200
Charles IX., 129, 130, 200, 206; delighted with the Massacre, 171; his madness, 193

INDEX

Charles the Bold, 200

Chastel, Jean, tries to assassinate Henry IV., 226-7

Chateaubriand, François Auguste, Vicomte de, his dictum on liberty, 104

Childebert, 200

Childeric, 198

Chiron, 32

Chlodowig, 197

Chrestien, Florent, a Politique, 221

Christina of Sweden reads Machiavelli, 36

Chrysostom, St John, 176, 181

Church, the, 178; the State, 2; Luther's State-Church, Chap. II. *passim*, 86, 88, 96, 104; the attitude of the Fathers, 49-54; of Hus, 56; of Calvin, Chap. III. *passim*; of Knox, 121-2; of Goodman, 123-4; of Cartwright, 125-6; of the Jesuits, 223-36; of the English reformers, 251-60; of Buchanan, 270; of Hooker, 275-9

Cicero, 1, 53, 82, 196, 208; the State divine, 57; source of inspiration, 133; his orations, 189

Ciompi revolt in 1378, 22

Clement (I.) of Rome, the State, 50

Clement VII., 36; unshocked by Machiavelli, 35

Clement of Alexandria, the State, 51

Clément, Jacques, 266; assassinates Henry IV., 214, 235; the martyr, 220-1; the Dominican, 235

Cleomenes puts the Ephors to death, 23

Climate and its influence, 130, 144-9, 151

Clotaire, 200

Clotilde, Queen, 176, 200

Clovis, 212

Coccio. See Sabellico

Coleridge, Samuel Taylor, Burke's consistency, 77; his aphorism, 246

Colet, John, xiii; aid to his labours, xii; speech on reform, xvii; the working of the Church, xviii

Coligny, Gaspard de, 169, 179; persuades Calvin to countenance resistance, 107; massacred, 170; conversation with Charles IV., 171-2; his loyalty, 172; enforced idleness, 174

Columbus, Christopher, discovers America, xi, xvi, 4, 41-2, 44, 73, 238, 239, 241, 247-8

Commines, Philippe de, 196; attitude to Louis XI., 7; the father of modern history, 141; Bodin's view, 147

Condé, Prince of (Henry of Bourbon), Beza's counsels, 179

Condé, Prince of (Louis of Bourbon), 169, 176-7, 190, 201-2

Constantine I., the Great, the State, 51-2

Constantinople, the capture of, 42

Contarini, Vincenzo, 135

Contract, the Social, the attitude of Hooker, 67, 75, 278; of Aquinas, 67, 75; of Locke, 75; of Rousseau, 75; of Calvin, 105-6; of the Scots Covenant (1638), 107; of the Solemn League and Covenant (1643), 107; of Hotman, 114, 188-9; of the Huguenot Synod (1560), 115; of Althusius, 119; of Knox, 119-21; of Buchanan, 122, 268-73; of P. Martyr, 122-3; of Beza, 186-7; of Mornay, 203-9; of the Jesuits, 225-36

Copernicus, Nicholas, astronomical discoveries, xvi, 3-4, 42, 44, 238, 239, 241; Bodin attacks him, 130, 139, 140

Corday, Charlotte, 266

Cotton, John, 112

Council of the Lateran, xvii-xviii; of Antioch, 82; of Trent, 252

Cranmer, Thomas, xv, 259; royal obedience, 253-4

Creighton, Mandell, dictum on the Reformation, xviii; the hold of conscience, xix; Acton's indignation, 29

Cromwell, Oliver, 169, 266; an opportunist, 43, 78; his fundamentals, 155

Cromwell, Thomas, brings *The Prince* to England, 35; policy of reformation, 77

Crotus Rubianus (Johann Jäger), 45; his *Epistolæ Obscurorum Virorum*, 222

Cujas, Jacques, Bodin attacks him, 143

Curce the Zwinglian, 139

Curio, Cælius Secundus, 181

Curoni the Catholic, 139

Cusanus. See Krebs

Cyprian, 53

Cyrus, 233

DANEAU, Lambert, a natural law, 66

Daniel, 100, 110; his prophecies, 144

Dante, Alighieri, conception of hell, 4; *De Monarchia*, 1, 49

Darnley, Lord, 267

Darwin, Charles, his theory of evolution, 42; connection with Luther, 65; his influence, 253; *Origin of Species*, 241

D'Aubigné, Theodore Agrippa, a staunch Huguenot, 202

David, 53, 257

Death, the Black, its far-reaching effects, 5, 9, 18, 35, 93, 136, 247-8

De Bohier, Nicolas, 134

De Castro, Paulus, 134

De Caumont, Jacques Nonpar, massacred, 170

De Coulanges, Fustel, 200

De Cusa, Nicholas, astronomical discoveries, 3

INDEX

De Lancre, Pierre, believes in astrology, 131

De Malestroit, his *Paradoxes*, 149

Denifle, Heinrich, Luther's lack of originality, 44

Denys of Halicarnassus, 134

De Rosate, Alberic, 134

De Sainte-Croix, Prosper, his outlook, 212

De Salas, Jean, the *jus gentium*, 228

De Seyssel, Claude, 167, 223; his *La Grande Monarchie de France*, 165, 195

D'Espinac, Pierre, Archbishop of Lyons, satirised, 222

De Thou, Christopher, praises dissimulation, 200

De Thou, Jacques Auguste, appreciates Bodin, 167; a thinker, 169; disapproves of Boucher, 215

De Victoria, Francis, the *jus gentium*, 228

Diet of Augsburg, 177

Diocletian, 249

Doleman. See Parsons

Dominic, St, rescues Christianity, 18

Donne, John, admires Hooker, 279

Du Bellay, Joachim, 170

Du Bois, Pierre, his nascent nationalism, 135

Dubourg, Anne, martyrdom, 189

Du Haillan, Bernard de Girard, 167; fundamental laws, 166

Dumoulin, Charles, the great jurisconsult, 188

Duplessis-Mornay. See Mornay

Dupuy, Pierre, 223

Dürer, Albrecht, 45

Eck, Johann, 47-8

Edward I., 271

Edward II., 216

Edward VI., 254

Eginhard, 196

Ehud, 234

Eleazar, 220

Election, view of Calvin, 91-2, 105, 109; of Hotman, 114, 197; of Mornay, 114, 204; of the League, 213; of the Jesuits, 224; of Buchanan, 268-73

Eliot, George, the highest lot, 41

Elizabeth, Queen, 34, 213, 263, 273; William the Silent and the Sovereign, 116; opposition to Knox, 120; notices Mornay, 202; Mornay notices her, 207

Emmanuel the Great, his toleration, 245

Emmanuel, Victor, the prophecy of Machiavelli, 36

Emperor, the Holy Roman, 155; the successor of Cæsar, 1; mediæval comparison, 6; altered attitude, 13; no one over him, 51; the son of the Church,

Emperor—*continued*
52; his authority from God, 53; his border-line of duty, 54; his distance, 150

Empire, the Holy Roman, 102, 158, 213; its theory, 1, 49; absolute jurisdiction, 2; vanished authority, 12-3; decay, 18; undermined, 42; prevents the conception of sovereignty, 150

Eoban of Hesse (Helius Eobanus Hessus), 45

Ephors, the, 114-5; kill Ægidius, 23; view of Calvin, 111-2; of William the Silent, 116; of Alstedius, 118; of P. Martyr, 122-3; of Ponet, 124-5

Equality and liberty, 21-2; the Ciompi conception, 22; French Revolution, 49; Gregory the Great's view, 53; American Civil War, 60; Luther's view, 75; the Parable of the Talents, 86-7; Calvin's view, 103; Bodin's view, 133, 160, 163; the *jus gentium*, 228

Erasmus, Desiderius, xv, xvi, 44, 180, 184, 192; the share of satire, xiii-xiv; his edition of the New Testament, xx; his Latin Paraphrases, xx-xxi; judgment of Luther, 45; did not move the people, 47; his want of force, 80; his influence, 169; *Enchiridion Militis Christiani*, xiii; *Encomium Moriæ*, xiv, xxi, 245; *Supputatio Errorum Bedæ*, 181; "Letter to the Would-be Evangelists," 181; *Declarationes ad censuras Lutetiæ vulgatas sub nomine Facultatis Theologiæ Pariensis*, 182; *Apologia adversus articulos aliquot per monachos quosdam in Hispania exhibitos*, 182

Erastus, Thomas, his *Examination of that most grave Question, Whether Excommunication, or the Debarring from the Sacraments of Professing Christians, because of their Sins, be a Divine Ordinance, or a Human Invention?* 260-3

Estienne, Henri, 177

Estienne, Robert, 177, 184

Étaples, the Treaty of, 4

Etruscans, the, 16-7

Eudæmon-Joannes, his *Apologia pro Henrico Garneto*, 223

Ewald, Georg Heinrich August, connection with Luther, 65

Ezekiel, 261

Ezra, 107

Farel, Guillaume, forces Calvin to go to Geneva, 81; a Frenchman, 82; flies for his life, 83; *Summaire briefve declaration d'aucuns lieux fort necessaires a ung chascun chrestien pour mettre sa confiance en Dieu et ayder son prochain*, 83

Fellinus, 134

INDEX

Felton, John, 266

Fénelon, François de Salignac, de la Mothe, his *Plan de Gouvernement*, 201

Ferdinand I. permits toleration, 245

Ferdinand the Catholic (of Aragon), 4, 11, 28, 193 ; refuses the Inquisition over the Moors, 245

Fermo, Oliverotto da, secures Machiavelli's admiration, 29 ; his treachery, 30

Feudalism, 13 ; Machiavelli's attitude, 21 ; its system of liberties, 22 ; Mornay's adaptation, 204

Fichte, Johann Theoph, the State divine, 57 ; connection with Luther, 65

Field, John, 251

Filmer, Sir Robert, appreciates Bodin, 167 ; Suarez refutes him, 230

Fletcher, Andrew, the value of ballads, 179

Florence, 15 ; its constitution, 11 ; a City-State, 12

Fogliano, Giovanni, 30

Fortescue, Sir John, 265

Foxe, John, 251

France, the new rôle, 4

France, Anatole, attacks superstition, 222

Francis I., 184 ; persecutes the Huguenots, 81, 107 ; Calvin's Preface, 89-90, 110 ; connives at Lutheranism, 245

Francis, St, of Assisi, rescues Christianity, 18

Franck, Sebastian, 180

Fraternity and the French Revolution, 49

Fredegonde, 200

Frederick, Count Palatine of the Rhine, Hotman's dedication, 192

Frederick the Great, the first servant of the State, 141 ; acts first, 173 ; *Réfutation du Prince de Machiavel*, 36

Frederick the Lutheran, 139

Frederick the Wise, 45

Freeman, Edward Augustus, the unity and continuity of history, 195-6

Froude, James Anthony, 251

Fuggers, the, Luther denounces them, 73

GAIRDNER, James, xii, 252

Galen, Claudius, 146

Galilei, Galileo, 140

Gallicanism, 90

Gallius, his conspiracy, 137

Gama, Vasco da, 239, 241

Garibaldi, Giuseppe, the prophecy of Machiavelli, 36

Gaveston, Piers, the favourite of Edward II., 216

Gebhart, Emile, mediæval symbolism, 131

Gentillet, Innocent, 200 ; *Discours sur le Moyen de bein Gouverner et Maintenir en bonne Paix un Royaume, contre Nicholas Machiavelli*, 207

Geography, its growth, 3-4, 41-2, 140, 238-41

George, Duke of Saxony (Albertine), 47-8

George, David Lloyd, 19

Gibbon, Edward, attitude to religion, 21

Gideon, xiv

Gierke, Otto von, 229

Gillot, Jacques, a Politique, 221

Gneisenau, August Wilhelm Anton Neidhardt, Count of, 173

Gnostics, the, the reading of the Bible, 74

Godofred, Denys, 118

Goethe, Johann Wolfgang von, 173 ; dictum on the Reformation, 80 ; the condition of all greatness, 250

Goodman, Christopher, 122 ; *How Superior Powers ought to be obeyed of their Subjects, and wherein they may lawfully be by God's Word disobeyed and resisted*, 123-4

Gratian, the *Decretum*, 59

Gregory (I.) the Great, the State, 53-4, 68

Gregory of Tours, 196

Gregory VII., 214, 216, 227

Gregory XIII., delighted with the Massacre, 171, 220 ; pardons beforehand those who attempt to murder Queen Elizabeth, 235

Gretser, Jakob, his *Commentarius Exegeticus*, 223

Grey, Lady Jane, 120

Grindal, Edmund, Beza's letter, 179

Grotius, Hugo, 228 ; appreciates Bodin, 167 ; verdict on Bodin, 139 ; *De Jure Belli et Pacis*, 67

Gualter, Rudolph. See Walther

Guerchy, Antoine de Marafin, massacred, 170

Guicciardini, Francesco, 135 ; backstairs' knowledge, 10 ; the cyclical theory, 12 ; the end justifies the means, 23 ; unshocked by Machiavelli, 35 ; use of history, 141

Guincestre, Jean, 223 ; the priest in politics, 214 ; believes Roze, 218 ; supports the Paris *curés*, 219 ; satirised, 222

Guise, Henry, Duke of, the Massacre of Vassy, 185 ; assassinated, 188, 219

Gunpowder, its invention, 5 ; its efficacy, 8, 19

Guttenberg, Johann, makes Luther's work possible, 59

Guyard, Jean, 223

HAMILTON, Alexander, 105

Hamilton, James, 266

Hampden, John, 269

Harmodius, 159, 234

Harnack, Adolph, his *obiter dictum*, 65

INDEX

Harrington, James, Machiavelli "the only politician," 36; reads Calvin, 111; respects Mornay, 209

Harvey, William, attitude to Bacon, 19

Hedio, Caspar, 180

Hegel, Georg Wilhelm Friedrich, his *obiter dictum*, 42; the State divine, 57; Bodin anticipates him, 144; *Phænomenology*, 43

Henneberg, Barthold von, 47-8

Henry II., 96-7, 153

Henry III., 111, 236; reads *The Prince*, 35-6; the League, 212; addresses the Sorbonne, 215; Boucher's attitude, 216-7; his murder, 220

Henry IV., 169; styles himself King of France, 14; reads *The Prince*, 35-6; Beza's counsels, 179; his battles, 202, 232; heir to the throne, 212-3; the League view, 214; Paris well worth a Mass, 223; his assassination, 226-7, 235

Henry VII., 4, 193

Henry VIII., xv, xvi, 193, 255; his work, xviii-xix, 57; Calvin denounces him, 96; his practice, 162; nationalism, 248; the Church settlement, 251-2

Hercules, 138

Herder, Johann Gottfried von, influence of songs on the Reformation, 180

Herodotus, his fictions, 132

Hesiod, Bodin's appreciation, 139

Hilderic, 197

Hippocrates, 144

Hobbes, Thomas, 278; his contempt, 26; preaches deceit, 33, 37; natural right, 67; the State, 71, 164; careful about origins, 153; appreciates Bodin, 157; the *Leviathan*, 155

Hollen, Gottschalk, the worth of work, 63

Hollis, Thomas, his *Memoirs*, 201

Homer, 193; Bodin's appreciation, 139; the *Iliad*, 40

Hooker, Richard, xvi; natural law, 66; social contract, 67, 187; reads Calvin, 111; a Bayard of ecclesiastical controversy, 273; writes great literature, 274; the Church, 274-6; Church and State, 276-8; his influence, 278-9; parallel with Burke, 279-81; *Of the Laws of Ecclesiastical Polity*, 75, 273-9

Hooker, Thomas, 112; quotes Mornay, 209

Hooper, John, Bishop of Gloucester, his *Declaration of the Ten Holy Commandments of Almighty God*, 70

Hotman, Antoine, 223

Hotman, François, 116, 117, 141, 159, 169, 172, 266, 267, 268; natural law, 66; Calvin's disciple, 113; notion of liberty, 114; colleague of Beza, 175; the pact,

Hotman—*continued*
186, 189, 200; against tyrannicide, 188; joins the Huguenots, 190; writes to Bullinger, 190; a patriot, 192-4; the unity and continuity of history, 195-9; the Salic law, 199-200, 203; the *Parlements*, 199-200; Mornay repeats his points, 204; the League repeats his points, 214; the States General, 217; the decline of the Estates, 233; *Franco-Gallia*, 105, 114, 191-201, 203, 207; *Epistre envoiée au Tigre de la France*, 189; *Anti-Tribonian*, 190-1.

Humboldt, Wilhelm von, his *Ideen*, 71

Hurault, Michel, exposes the League, 221

Hus, John, 44, 184; wrong treatment, 49; the essence of the Church, 56; the priesthood of the believer, 60; his extremists, 74

Hutten, Ulrich von, 45; his *Vadiscus*, 48, 222

Huxley, Thomas Henry, his dictum on the State, 71

Hymenæus, 182

Ignatius, Bishop of Antioch, the State, 50; the priesthood of the believer, 55

Imbart de la Tour, Philippe, 90

Index Librorum Prohibitorum, xii-xiii, 249

Individualism, the rise of, xix, xxi-xxii, 12-3, 58-9, 64, 70-1, 81, 152

Innocent III., 214; nascent nationality, 48; his ideals, 95

Innocent IV., his theory of sovereignty, 49

Innocent VIII. buys his tiara, 46

Irenæus, Bishop of Lyons, the State, 50; the priesthood of the believer, 55

Isabella, 200

Isabella the Infanta, 217, 222

Isaiah, 92

Isidore of Seville, the bad ruler, 53

Ithuriel, xiv

James I. and VI., 223, 266-7, 270, 271; his Parliament, 162-3; admires Hooker, 279

James III., 271, 272

Jeremiah, 92, 224

Jeroboam, 110

Jerome, 181; the priesthood of the believer, 56

Jerome of Prague, 184

Jesuits, the, 23; the State a mere means, 94; the heretic, 174; tyrannicide, 188; Chap. VI. *passim*

Jews, the, their expulsion, 5

John, Rex Angliæ, 15

John of Salisbury advocates tyrannicide, 124

293

INDEX

Jonson, Ben, 273
Joinville, Jean, Sieur de, 196
Jörger, Dorothy, Luther's advice, 73-4
Joseph II., his work, 57; his prematureness, 77
Josiah, 106, 182
Jove, Paul, 135
Joyce, George, the seizure of Charles I., 8
Judas, 262
Judith, 220, 234
Judith, Queen, 200
Jugurtha, King of Numidia, Roman venality, xvi, 48
Julius II., 6, 24; convokes a General Council, xvii; his statue, 46; his *obiter dictum*, 47
Junius, François, his *Biblia Sacra*, 113
Jus Gentium and the law of nature, 22, 155, 197, 226, 228
Justin Martyr, the State, 51; the priesthood of the believer, 55
Justinian I., his Code, 2, 173; views on usury, 73; Hotman's indictment, 190-1; his *Institutes*, 135
Juvenal, xiv

KANT, Immanuel, his connection with Luther, 65; the moral law, 66; *magnum opus* after fifty, 82
Kelvin, Lord, denies the possibility of the aeroplane, 19; connection with Luther, 65
Kempten, revolt at, 4-5
Kepler, John, his *obiter dictum*, 240
Kleinberg, Georg, 181
Knox, John, 105, 112, 122, 169, 266; the incarnation of Puritanism, xv; natural law, 66; leadership of Christ, 89; contract theory, 119-21; *Appellation*, 119-20; *The First Blast of the Trumpet against the Monstruous Regiment of Women*, 120, 123; the *Second Blast*, 120
Krebs, Nicholas, Cardinal, an astronomer of genius, 239-40

LABITTE, Charles, 214
Lactantius, 180
Lainez, James, the sovereignty of the people, 230
Lamarck, Jean Baptiste Pierre Antoine de Monet, *magnum opus* after fifty, 82
La Noue, François de, presses Mornay, 202
La Place, Pierre de, massacred, 170
Lassalle, Ferdinand, the iron law of wages, 72
Latimer, Hugh, 259; royal obedience, 253-6; his reserves, 255-6

Laud, William, cautiously praises the *Institutes*, 111
Laurence, French, 279
Lavardin, Jean de Beaumanoir, massacred, 170
Lavoisier, Antoine Laurent, 170
League, the, 167, 201; Chap. VI. *passim*
Le Maistre, Jean, allows anyone to kill a Huguenot, 227
Lenin, Nicholas (U. L. Ulianov), 34
Leo X., xvi, xvii, 36, 54; unshocked by Machiavelli, 35; an absolute worldling, 47; his failure, 48; Calvin invokes his authority, 92; accepts Erasmus's dedication, 245
LeRoy, Louis, his teaching, 166-7
LeRoy, Pierre, a Politique, 221
Lessing, Gotthold Ephraim, 19
Lessius, Leon, the powerlessness of the Commonwealth, 225; the *jus gentium*, 228
L'Hôpital, Michel de, 141, 167, 184, 221; his toleration, 138, 243; a noble figure, 165-6; a thinker, 169; *Traité de la Réformation de la Justice*, 166; *Harangue aux Etats d'Orleans*, 166
Liberty and liberties, 15; equality, 21-2; attitude of Luther, 46, 58-63, 65, 74-5; of Proles, 63; of Hollen, 63; liberty and order, 74; liberty and security, 77; Calvin furthers freedom, 80, 103; liberty and justification, 88; liberty and licence, 92-3; ecclesiastical power and liberty, 96; liberty of conscience, 104-5; Hotman's liberty, 114; revolution, 163; the *jus gentium*, 228
Lightfoot, Joseph Barber, definite knowledge, 41
Livy, the commentary of Machiavelli, 12 (see the *Discorsi* passim); his fictions, 132
Locke, John, 105, 124, 278; Rousseau's debt, 44; social pact, 75; reads Calvin, 111; careful about origins, 153; respects Mornay, 209
Loisel, Antoine, 223
Lorraine, Charles, Archbishop of Rheims, Cardinal of, composes an inscription, 171; Hotman's attack, 189
Louis IX., 171, 200
Louis XI., 4, 7, 157, 193, 198, 234
Louis XII., 28, 157, 165; the ideal of Seyssel, 195
Louis XIV., 34, 236; his work, 57, 101; recalls the Edict of Nantes, 180; the influence of Calvin's disciples, 209-10
Louis XVI., 75
Louvel, Pierre Louis, 235
Loyola, Ignatius, 80; General of the Jesuits, 94; his suggestion to Mariana, 230

Loyseau, Charles, reads Bodin, 167
Lüber, Thomas. See Erastus
Lucan, his *Pharsalia*, 134
Lucian, xiv
Ludendorff, Erich, 34
Luther, Martin, xv, 105, 110, 159, 169, 222, 276; original sin, 13; the low level of human character, 20; agreement with Machiavelli, 40, 77; no shades of meaning, 41; his theology, 43-4, 85; not a statesman, 45; Roman exactions, 46, 87; attacks Tetzel, 47; frees the State from the control of the Church, 48; his toleration, 49; the State has a moral nature, 54, 68; the priesthood of the believer, 55, 60; substitutes secular authority, 57; individual reason, 58; attitude to business, 61, 71-3; joins divided ideals, 62; dislike of democracy, 63; his supporters, 64; his influence, 65; obedience to the secular power, 68-70; the peasants, 74-5; the Church and governing power, 76, 189; parallel with Bismarck, 77-8; his force, 80; reliance and criticism, 81; his two catechisms, 83; the free mind, 88; no machinery, 90; promotes despotism, 103; the superman, 108; vast circulation of his Bible, 112; assaults authority, 177; gives confidence to his followers, 178; importance of hymns, 179-80; sermon on the tares, 181; the comparative standpoint, 261; *To the Christian Nobility of the German Nation on the Improvement of the Christian Estate*, 45, 48-9, 54, 62, 64, 68, 72-3; *A Prelude on the Babylonish Captivity of the Church*, 45-6, 54-6, 58-9, 62, 64; *On the Freedom of a Christian Man*, 46, 58-63, 64, 77; *Exposition of the Psalms*, 56; *On the Secular Power: How far Obedience is due to it*, 68-70, 181; *Von Kauffshandlung und Wucher*, 71; *An die Pfarhernn wider den Wucher zu predigen*, 73; *Against the Murderous, Thieving Hordes of Peasants*, 74; *Exhortation to Peace*, 74.
Lycurgus, 160; his laws, 23
Lyell, Sir Charles, his *Principles of Geology*, xi

MACAULAY, Lord, 145
Macbeth, Lady, 138
Machiavelli, Nicholas, xv, 66, 85, 102, 138, 139, 192, 214; his seeming passionlessness, 5; severs the tie with theology, 6; dissection of diplomacy, 7; national militia, 8, 11, 18; the Prince's will, 9; grasp of a general position, 10; the cyclical theory, 12; Italian individuality,

Machiavelli—*continued*
13; his paganism, 14; parallel with Aristotle, 14-5, 17-8; aggrandisement of Republics, 16-7; destroyer, not creator, 17; denies progress, 19-20, 143; his fatalism, 21; believes in the *jus gentium*, 22; the end justifies the means, 23; methods of rule in a city, 24; advocates force and fraud, 25; *raison d'État*, 26, 31; his narrowness of vision, 27; his realism, 28; analysis of principalities, 29; justification of cruelty, 30; the consent of the people, 31; the duty of not keeping one's word, 32-3; attitude to the people, 34; his influence, 34-7; the State purely human, 40; little sympathy with the past, 41; Roman exactions, 46; frees the State from moral law, 48; substitutes secular authority, 57; dislike of democracy, 63; parallel with Luther, 77, 40; Church and State, 82; the State a mere means, 94; his empiricism, 136-7; use of history, 141; westward trend, 145; Mornay's reply, 202; parallel with the Jesuits, 225; parallel with Mariana, 233-4; *Discorsi*, 7, 11, 12, 15, 18, 21, 22-3, 27, 28, 29, 35; *Il Principe*, 7, 10, 11, 12, 14, 15, 21, 22, 26, 27, 28, 34, 37-8, 136, 233; *Vita di Castruccio Castricani*, 7; *L'Arte della guerra*, 8
Machon, Louis, his *apologia* for *The Prince*, 36
Mackintosh, Sir James, 170
Macrinus, his cruelty, 194
Magellan, Fernando de, his chivalry, 239-40
Maitland, Frederick William, 263
Maitland, Thomas, his dialogue with Buchanan, 267-73
Maitland, William, 267
Mandeville, Bernard, his *Fable of the Bees*, 13
Marlborough, the Duke of, 34
Mariana, Juan, natural law, 66; advocates tyrannicide, 226-7, 235-6; the state of nature, 232-3; force and fraud, 233-4; *De Rege et Regis Institutione*, 122, 223, 226-7, 230, 232-5; *History of Spain*, 230
Marnix, Ste Aldegonde, counsels William the Silent, 116
Marot, Clément, 184; translates the Psalms, 113; the Huguenot Psalter, 180
Marsiglio (Menandrino or Marsilio) of Padua, 59; membership of the State, 2; the priesthood of the believer, 1, 56; *Defensor Pacis*, 1, 2, 68-9
Martyr, Peter, teaches active resistance, 121-2; Ponet with him, 123

INDEX

Mary, Queen of Scots, 15, 200, 265; dethroned, 117, 121, 266-7; interview with Knox, 120; attacked by Goodman, 123

Mary I., 253, 259, 260

Maximilian I., 6; Roman exactions, 48

Mayenne, Charles of Lorraine, Duke of, head of the League, negotiates with Parma, 217; chastises the League, 221; satirised, 222

Mazzini, Giuseppe, the prophecy of Machiavelli, 36

Medici, Catherine de', 176, 193, 200-1, 203, 206, 218; peruses *The Prince*, 35; her statecraft, 136; appoints L'Hôpital Chancellor, 165; her teaching of the Huguenots, 209

Medici, Giuliano de', his new State, 28

Medici, Lorenzo de', his death, 4; Machiavelli's epistle, 28

Medina, Peter de, the common good, 226

Melanchthon, Philip, 74, 173, 178; teaches Luther Greek, 40; not a statesman, 45; a layman, 56; natural law, 66, 84; the principal member of the Church, 76, 89; tyrannicide, 188; *Loci communes rerum theologicarum seu hypotyposes theologicæ*, 83

Melville, Andrew, 123, 277; the two kingdoms, 270

Ménippée, the *Satire*, 221-3

Mercantilism, 71-2, 149-50

Meredith, George, "the rapture of the forward view," 142

Michelet, Jules, the new Messiah, 18; verdict on Calvin, 126; success of Hotman, 201; dictum on Vico, 242

Milton, John, 105; natural right, 67; reads Calvin, 111; *Areopagitica*, 69; *Tenure of Kings*, 118, 123; *Defence of the People of England*, 121, 266; *Defensio Prima*, 201; *Defensio Secunda*, 201, 219

Mirandola, Pico della, speech on reform, xvii

Molina, Luis, 227; his *Justicia et Jure*, 223

Montaigne, Michel de, 173; denies progress, 20; Rousseau's debt, 44; the novelty of ideas, 140; his mercantilism, 150; appreciates Bodin, 167

Montesquieu, Charles de Secondat, Baron, 63; influence of climate, 147-8; division of functions, 268; *Esprit des Lois*, 144, 167

Montfort, Basil, 181

Montpensier, the Duchess of, patronises the preachers, 219

Moors, the, their expulsion, 5

Morality, public and private, 8, 23, 33-5, 37-8, 94

Moray, Earl of, 266; the Good Regent, 267

More, Sir Thomas, 136, 152, 165; liberty and security, 77; toleration, xix, 140, 243-4, 246-7, 249-50, 252; frightened by the Anabaptists, 150; the way to justice, 241; the state of the law, 242; the new conception of society, 242-3; parallel with Burke, 246-7; unable to adapt himself, 248-9, policy of persecution, 250-1; the martyr of conscience and of mediævalism, 252-3; *Utopia*, 139, 241-8, 251-2; the *Dialogue*, 249-51; the *Confutation of Tyndale's Answer*, 250-1; *Vindicatio Henrici VIII. a calumniis Lutheri*, 251

Morley, Lord, Machiavelli a living force, 34-5

Mornay-Duplessis, Philippe de, 105, 117, 169, 172, 198, 267, 268; natural law, 66; the superman, 108; Calvin's disciple, 113; against tyrannicide, 188; the Aragonese oath, 197; embraces Calvinism, 201; replies to Machiavelli, 202; his four questions, 203; the tyrant, 205-7; his loyalty, 214; influences Buchanan, 266; *Vindiciæ contra Tyrannos*, 114, 202-9, 266; *Exhortation aux Estates*, 209

Morton, Earl of, 270

Moses, 106, 182, 206

Münzer, Thomas, his policy of revolution, 77

Murner, Thomas, xix, 45

Mutianus, Conrad (Konrad Muth), his circle, 45, 173

Napoleon, attends lectures, 33; deference towards Mohammedanism, 34; the acts of a statesman, 36; cause of his fall, 37; smashes Germany, 64; an opportunist, 78

Nationalism, nascent, xvi-xvii, xviii, 6, 48, 102, 135, 150, 190, 192, 194-5, 222, 247-8

Nature, the law of, the *jus gentium*, 22; attitude of Machiavelli, 35, 202; of Luther, 65-6; of the Reformation, 67; of Calvin, 84, 93; of Melanchthon, 84; of Beza, 113; of Alstedius, 118; of Bodin, 120-1, 155-6; of Knox, 120-1; of Ponet, 124; of Hotman, 197; of Mornay, 202; of the Jesuits, 228-36; of Hooker, 274-5

Nehemiah, 107

Nere, Giovanni dalle Bande, his *obiter dictum*, 26

Nero, 157, 194, 249, 271; an evil ruler, 52, 99; his empire a great brigandage, 102

Nerva, 37

296

INDEX

Nessus, 44

Nevers, Francis of Cleves, the Duke of, his *Traité de la Prise d'Armes*, 221

Newman, John Henry, belief in him, 44; quoted, 118

Newton, Sir Isaac, his *Principia*, 241

Nicolas V., a worldling, 46

Nightingale, Florence, her unrelenting will, 86

Nihilist murderers, 235

Noah, 106

Norden, John, royal obedience, 253

Ockham, William of, 44; his *Dialogus*, 68-9

Octave, the Mohammedan, 139

Optatus of Milevis, the State, 51-2

Origen, the State, 51; the priesthood of the believer, 55-6; Calvin's quotations, 82

Orpheus, 138

Osorius, Jerome, government and the Fall, 224

Otto of Freisingen, 196

Pact, Social. See Contract, Social

Paine, Thomas, his *obiter dictum*, 252

Papinian, 164

Paré, Ambroise, believes in Astrology, 131

Pareus (Wängler), David, the cause of the magistrate, 117-8

Parma (Parma Alessandro), Duke of (3rd), 217

Parsons, Robert, 252; his *Next Succession to the Crown of England*, 223

Paruta, Paolo, reads Bodin, 167

Pascal, Blaise, the heart's reasons, 44; assaults the Jesuits, 222

Pasquier, Etienne, 141, 223; at Hotman's lectures, 188

Passerat, Jean, a Politique, 221

Patin, Guy, appreciates Buchanan, 265

Patriotism, 99-100

Pattison, Mark, opinion of Erasmus's edition of the New Testament, xx; verdict on Calvin, 126-7

Paul, St, quoted, 56, 60, 66, 69, 85, 97, 100, 106, 110, 176, 229, 253, 262, 269, 271

Paul, Father (Sarpi Paolo), his *obiter dictum*, 14

Peasants' War, 74, 77, 246

Pellevé, Nicholas de, Archbishop of Sens and Cardinal, chants the Mass for the Massacre, 171

Pellican, Conrad, 181

Penry, John, 112

People, the, *v.* the Populace, 103, 204, 269

Pepin, 198, 200

Peter, St, quoted, 56, 69, 110, 178, 224, 226, 254-6

Petit, Jean, justifies the murder of the Duke of Orleans, 234

Peuerbach, Georg, an astronomer of genius, 239-40

Peutinger, Conrad, 45

Philetus, 182

Philip II., 34, 238; his work, xviii-xix 57; his yoke, 117; overthrows free constitutions, 162; his power, 212; supports Boucher, 217; corrupts the preachers, 221

Philip III., 230

Philip of Hesse, his discernment, 45

Philips, Thomas, 251

Philo, 134

Physiocratic ideas, 72

Piccini, Jacopo, threatens Calixtus III., 11

Pigenat, François, the priest in politics, 214; eulogises the Guises, 219

Pilles, Armand de Clermont de, massacred, 170

Pirkheimer, Wilibald, 45

Pisa, its fortresses, 24

Pistoia, its factions, 24, 32

Pithou, François, 141

Pithou, Pierre, 141; a Politique, 221

Pitt, William, cast in a mould, 83

Plague, the. See the Black Death

Plato, 20, 136, 138, 139, 141, 144, 150, 152, 158, 160, 196, 268; influence on St Augustine and Dante, 1; the moral law, 66; influence on Valla, 66; Calvin's reverence, 82, 94; influence on Bodin, 132-3, 151; sovereignity, 164; influence on More, 241-2; the *Phædo*, 40; the *Atlantis*, 142; the *Republic*, 242

Plectrude, 200

Plotinus, 134

Plutarch, 134

Poincaré, Henri, 228.

Politiques, the, xix, 129, 138, 165, 169-70. 209, 212, 221

Pollard, Alfred Frederick, xiv-xv.

Poltrot, Jean de, murdered the Duke of Guise, 114, 159, 188

Polybius, 144, 196; disapproves of the mixed State, 134

Polycarp, Bishop of Smyrna, the State, 50; no sacrificial priesthood, 55

Pompey, 162

Pomponazzi, Pietro, attacks belief in immortality, 46

Ponet, John, 122, 123; respects Mornay, 209; *Short Treatise of Political Power*, 124-5.

Pontano, Giovanni Gioviano, character of the Prince, 31; his *De Principe*, 11-2

INDEX

Pope, the, 155, 158; a Mediterranean Power, xi; struggle with the Emperor, 2; mediæval comparison, 6; altered attitude, 13; Machiavelli's hatred, 14, 21; *imperium in imperio*, 22; crowns the Emperor, 49; view of Luther, 49, 56, 58, 73; of Calvin, 89, 97; of Boucher, 216; of Tanquerel, 219; of the League, 221; of the Jesuits, 223-36

Porphyry, 134

Posidonius, the State, 68; occupation in heaven, 132-3

Possevin, Antonio, condemns Bodin, 167

Postel, Guillaume, 223; *De Orbis terrarum concordia libri quatuor*, 19-20

Prierias, Sylvester Mazzolini, reply to Luther, 55

Priesthood of the believer, 49, 55-6, 58, 69, 103-4, 105

Proclus, 134

Progress, denied by Machiavelli, 19, 29; by Bodin, 20, 140; by Montaigne, 20; by the ancients and mediævalists, 238, 241; accepted by Postel, 19; by Rabelais, 20; by Campanella, 20; by Bacon, 20

Proles, Andreas, the worth of work, 63

Prussia, its rise, 42-3

Pufendorf, Samuel, Baron, appreciates Bodin, 167

Putnam, George Haven, xiii

QUADRIVIUM, the, 4

Quesnay, François, his *obiter dictum*, 34

RABELAIS, François, accepts progress, 20; in Paris, 80; probably knew Buchanan, 265; *Pantagruel* and *Gargantua*, 222

Rainolds, William, his learning, 135

Ramus (Ramée), Pierre de la, massacred, 170

Ranke, Leopold von, 48; Bodin anticipates him, 143

Rapin, Nicholas, a Politique, 221; the test of wit, 222

Ravaillac, François, 266; assassinated Henry IV., 235

Reformation, the, 45, 153; its background, xi-xxii; Machiavelli's blindness, 5; the influence of Copernicus and Columbus, 42; the cities of Germany, 43; lack of guidance, 45; Luther's share, Chap. II. *passim*; the element of negation, 49; the connection with capitalism, 61; natural law, 67; T. Cromwell's influence, 77; restoration of freedom, 80-1; justice to the past, 144; share taken by women, 174; influence of hymns, 180; political institutions, 247; individualism and nationalism, 248

Regiomontanus (Müller Johannes), Archbishop of Regensburg, 241; an astronomer of genius, 239; a popular lecturer, 240; *Ephemerides*, 239

Rémond, Florimond de, the value of the Psalms, 113

Rémy, Nicolas, believes in astrology, 131

Renaissance, the, 153; did not touch the people, xxi; the rise of political speculation, 1; its character, 3-4; individual virtue, 9; influence on Machiavelli and Guicciardini, 12; the spirit of humanism, 13; its true spirit, 20; darker aspects, 93, 170; Hotman, 195; its tragedy, 247-9

Reuchlin, Johann (Capnio), 184

Revolution, the French, its influence, 15

Ricardo, David, evolves the economic man, 7

Richelieu, Armand Jean Duplessis, his policy of Thorough, 23; his enemies, 26; appreciates *The Prince*, 36; limits of statesmanship, 45; *la patrie*, 192

Rieux, Le Sieur de, satirised, 222

Rights, natural, the attitude of the Reformation, 67; their varying destinies, 67-8; view of Calvin, 109; slavery, 152-3; the French Revolution, 178; view of Beza, 187, 204; of Mornay, 204; of the Jesuits and Dominicans, 227-36; of Buchanan, 268

Rio, Diego del, condemns Bodin, 167

Rochefoucauld, François III., Count of, La, massacred, 170

Roman law, 74, 134, 190-1

Rome, influence on political thought, 1, 12, 16-7, 22

Romulus, care of the State, 23, 38

Ronsard, Pierre de, 170

Roper, William, 246

Rossæus. See Roze

Rousseau, Jean-Jacques, 187, 223; debt to Montaigne and Locke, 44; the sovereignty of the individual, 59; the law of nature, 67-8; Carlyle's *obiter dictum*, 75; reads Calvin, 111; Rousseau and Althusius, 119; careful about origins, 153; equality, 160; the state of nature, 232-3

Roze, Guillaume, condemns Bodin, 167; the priest in politics, 214; fiery supporter of the League, 218; widespread influence, 219; satirised, 222; defines a tyrant, 226; the origin of civil power, 231; *De Justa rei Publicæ in Reges impios et Hæreticos Auctoritate*, 231

SABELLICO, Mark Antonio Cocceius, 135

Sacheverell, Henry, 219

INDEX

Sachs, Hans, Luther the nightingale, 180

Salmeron, Alphonso, government and the Fall, 224

Salomon the Jew, 139

Samuel, 6, 95-6

Sanderson, Robert, Bishop of Lincoln, praises the *Institutes*, 111

Sandys, Edwin, letter to Gualter, 179

Santarelli, Antonio, the Pope a heretic, 224

Saul, 6, 53, 95-6, 107, 257

Savonarola, Girolamo Maria Francesco Matteo, 184, 250, 276; a weaponless prophet, 6; character of the Prince, 31; assaults the Papacy, 46; *Del Reggimento del Governo della Citta di Firenze*, 11-2

Scaliger, Joseph Juste, xx, 184; his learning, 135; Bodin's confusion, 141; epigram on Buchanan, 265

Schiller, Johann Christoph Friedrich, 173

Schleiermacher, Friedrich Daniel Ernst, the reading of the Bible, 74

Scribani, Charles. See Bonarsans

Seebohm, Frederic, 251

Seeley, Sir John Robert, history a school for statesmen, 141

Selden, John, quotes Hotman, 201

Senamy, the worshipper at all shrines, 139

Seneca, Marcus Annæus, the State, 49-50, 68; source of inspiration, 133; *De Clementia*, 82, 101-2; *Thyestes*, 268

Servetus, Miguel, 112; his death, 182

Sessa, Agostino Nifo di, plagiarises *The Prince*, 35

Severus, Alexander, his catholicity, 138

Sforza, Francesco, 28

Shaftesbury, Anthony Ashley, (3rd) Earl of, opposes enthusiasm, 222

Shakespeare, William, 273; England "that utmost corner of the West," xi

Sidgwick, Henry, on public and private morality, 37-8

Sidney, Algernon, 124; reads Calvin, 111; respects Mornay, 209; *Government*, 201

Sidney, Sir Philip, 170

Sidonius, 196

Sièyes, Count Emmanuel Joseph, Abbé, "I lived," 18

Sigismund of Heberstein, his *History of Muscovy*, 135

Simmias asks for confirmation, 178

Sinn Feiners murderers, 235

Sixtus IV., xvii

Sixtus V., 215; ponders the maxims of *The Prince*, 36; bull against magic, 131; restive under the League, 213; rejoices over Clément's deed of murder, 220

Slavery, 152-3, 241

Sleidan, Johannes, 135

Smith, Adam, his *Wealth of Nations*, 240

Smith, Sir Thomas, doctrine of sovereignty, 271; *De Republica Anglorum*, 263-5

Societas perfectas, 96, 229

Socrates, 138, 178; the moral law, 66

Solomon, 110

Soto, Dominic, his attitude to slavery, 229

Sovereignty and inequality, 21-2; supremacy of the Sovereign, 40; Innocent IV.'s views, 49; natural law ideas, 67; sovereignty of God, 85-7, 100-1, 108-9; of Bodin, 150-5; of Beza, 186; of Hotman, 195-9; of the League, 214, 221; of Boucher, 216; of the Jesuits, 223-36; of Sir T. Smith, 263-5; of Buchanan, 267-73

Spalatin, Georg (Burkardt Georg from Spelt), 45

Sparta, 12, 16

Spencer, Herbert, doctrine of evolution, 3

Spenser, Edmund, 170; *Faerie Queene*, 273

Spinoza, Benedict de (Baruch), might is right, 31; his toleration, 243

Stapleton, Richard, 278

State, the, the Church, 2; the mediæval State, 2; Machiavelli's conception, Chap. I. *passim*, 40, 48; the classical State, 12; Hobbes's view, 33; Luther's conception, Chap. II. *passim*, 86, 96; the attitude of Seneca, 49-50; of the Fathers, 50-4; of Althusius, 57; of Burke, 57-8; of Cicero, 57; of Hegel, 57; of Calvin, Chap. III. *passim*; of the Huguenots, 115; of Ponet, 124-5; of Bodin, Chap. IV. *passim*; of Beza, 185-7; of Hotman, 191-201; of Mornay, 202-9; of the Jesuits, 223-36; of the English reformers, 251-60; of Hooker, 276-9

Staupitz, Johann, against the publication of *The Christian Nobility*, 46

Stoics, the, the cyclical doctrine, 20; Luther's attitude, 41; Valla's attitude, 66; the State, 68; conception of wisdom, 132

Stow, John, 124

Strachey, Mr Lytton, 86

Strafford, Earl of, his policy of Thorough, 23

Strennius, Jacobus (Strein Johann) Hotman's letter, 191

Suarez, Cyprian, 227, 235; the State secular, 225; the general Jesuit position, 227; his theocracy, 228; democratic doctrines, 230; two opinions on tyrannicide, 231-2; tyranny, 232; the decline of the Estates, 233; *De Legibus ac Deo Legislatore*, 223, 229-32; *Treatise on Laws*, 231; *Defence of the Catholic Faith*, 231-2

INDEX

Sudbury, Simon de, 266

Suetonius, 134

Sully, Maximilian de Bethune, Duke of, advice to Henry IV., 202

Suriano, Michele, report on the Huguenots, 115

Swift, Jonathan, xiv; his realism, 32; admires Hooker, 279

TACITUS, 134, 147, 196

Taine, Hippolyte Adolphe, *obiter dictum*, 3

Talleyrand-Perigord, Charles Maurice, his *obiter dictum*, 34

Tanner, Adam, his *Defensio Ecclesiasticæ Libertatis*, 223

Tanquerel, Jean, defends papal excommunication, 219

Tarde, Gabriel, 265

Tauler, John, his influence, 42

Taylor, Roland, 252

Teligny, Charles de, massacred, 170

Terence, his *obiter dictum*, 208

Tertullian, Quintus Septimius Florens, the priesthood of the believer, 55; his *obiter dictum*, 189; his toleration, 244

Tetzel, Johann, sells indulgences, 43; Luther's attack, 47, 177

Teucer, 192

Tewkesbury, John, 248

Theiner, Augustin, 170

Themistius, 82

Theophilus of Antioch, the State, 51

Theudas, 206

Thrasybulus, 234

Thucydides, his skill, 132

Timoleon, 234, 265

Tocqueville, Alexis de, dictum on Christianity, 100

Toleration, during the Renaissance, 3; view of Luther, 49, 69-70; of Milton, 67; of Williams, 67; of St Augustine, 69; of More, 77, 242-6, 249-50, 252; of Calvin, 97-8; of Bodin, 138-9, 140; of L'Hôpital, 165-6; of Erasmus, 181-2; of Beza, 180, 182-4

Toralba, the devotee of natural religion, 139

Torquemada, Tomas de, expulsion of the Jews, 5; the Moors, 245

Trajan, 157, 270

Treitschke, Heinrich Gotthard von, 141-2; influence of climate, 148

Tremellius, Giovanni Immanuel, his *Biblia Sacra*, 113

Tritheim, Johannes, his *History of Ethiopia*, 135

Trivium, the, 4

Tunstall, Cuthbert, 249

Turgot, Anne Robert Jacques, Baron, his edict, 248

Tyler, Wat, 74

Tyndale, William, his reserves, 256-7; no right of resistance, 258-9; the beginning of English political theory, 259; *An Answer to Sir Thomas More's "Dialogue,"* 250; *Obedience of a Christian Man*, 257

Tyrannicide, 114, 122, 124, 154, 188, 226-7, 229-34, 272

Tyrant, the, attitude of Calvin, 93-4; of Mornay, 114, 119, 203, 205-7; of the Dutch, 115-7; of Zanchius, 118; of Alstedius, 118; of Althusius, 119; of Bodin, 157-9; of Beza, 186-8; of Hotman, 193-4, 197-9; of Boucher, 215-6; of Roze, 218-9; of the Jesuits, 226-36; of Buchanan, 271-3

ULYSSES, 193

Unity, its mediæval basis, 2

Urbanus Rhegius, 181

Usher, James, 130

Usury, 73, 91

VALLA, Lorenzo, xx; his "Lust," 66

Vasari, George, paints frescoes of the Massacre, 171

Vasquez, Gabriel, natural law independent of God, 228

Versoris, Pierre La Tourneur de, founds the League, 129

Vespucci, Amerigo, 239, 241

Vico, Giovanni Battista, the origin of the State, 152; Michelet's verdict, 242

Vinci, Leonardo da, his dictum on truth, 59

Vinet, Elie, 265

Virgil, first in Luther's regard, 40; Buchanan another Virgil, 265; the *Georgics*, 133, 134

Virgil, Polydore, 135

Vittori, Francesco, confident of Machiavelli, 10-1

Voltaire, François Marie Arouet de, xiv; on Montesquieu, 63; dislikes Boucher, 215; attacks superstition, 222

WALPOLE, Sir Robert, the necessary lengths, 23

Walsingham, Thomas de, 216

Walther, Bernard, a generous patron, 239-40

Walther (Gualter) Rudolph, 179; Hotman's letter, 190

Walton, Izaak, 278-9

Wellington, the Duke of, 34

Westcott, Brooke Foss, dictum on the Reformation, 80-1

INDEX

Whitehead, Arthur Whiston, 170
Whitgift, John, Archbishop of Canterbury, complains of Beza, 179
Wier, Jean, believes in astrology, 130
William II., German Emperor, 15
William III., 34
William the Silent, attitude to authority, 115-7
Williams, Roger, 112 ; natural right, 67
Wimpheling, Jakob, out of sympathy with the Reformation, 45, 47-8
Winstanley, Gerrard, and the diggers, 242
Wolmar, Melchior, affects Calvin and Beza, 173
Wordsworth, William, 240

Wyatt's Rebellion, 123-4
Wyclif, John, 74, 184, 204, 250 ; a real precursor of the Reformation, xv-xvii; narrowness of sympathy, xv-xvi ; his translation forbidden, 249

XENOPHON, his *Life of Cyrus*, 25

ZACHARY, Pope, 198
Zanchius, Jerome, 117 ; the duty of resistance, 118
Zwingli, Ulrich, natural law, 66 ; headship of Christ, 89 ; *Commentarius de vera et falsa religione*, 83